ECCLESIOLOGY

SACRA DOCTRINA SERIES

Series Editors

Chad C. Pecknold, *The Catholic University of America*

Thomas Joseph White, OP, *Pontifical University of Saint Thomas Aquinas*

ECCLESIOLOGY

Guy Mansini, OSB

The Catholic University of America Press
Washington, D.C.

Copyright © 2021
The Catholic University of America Press
All rights reserved
The paper used in this publication meets the minimum requirements of American
National Standards for Information Science—Permanence of Paper for Printed Library
Materials, ANSI Z39.48-1984.
∞

Cataloging-in-Publication Data available from the Library of Congress
ISBN 978-0-8132-3327-7

CONTENTS

Part 3. Ecclesiology Systematic

ACKNOWLEDGMENTS

This book was written in a cold and rainy season, so I have many friends to thank for its completion, for "a faithful friend is a sturdy shelter" (Sir 6:14). I thank Matthew Levering who helped me to find a job and Roger Nutt and Michael Dauphinais who gave me one. I shall be always in their debt. Thanks to Betsy Dunman and Janet Werne, and also to John and Sandy Wilson, constant supports.

I am blessed with a steadfast family: Joe and Diane Robinson, Lucille and Bob and Ryan Rehkamp, and Larry Connel. Colman Grabert, Jeff Lee, Amador Garza, and Jeremy Gries, faithful priests, are faithful friends. Reinhard Hütter teaches many things, and also hospitality to Benedictines.

Professor Lawrence Welch and Fr. Michael Johns read the manuscript and helped tighten it up. I owe them many thanks.

ABBREVIATIONS

ACW   Ancient Christian Writers

ANF   Ante-Nicene Fathers (ed. Roberts et al.)

FOTC   Fathers of the Church (The Catholic University of America Press)

SCG   *Summa Contra Gentiles* (Aquinas)

ST   *Summa Theologiae* (Aquinas)

ECCLESIOLOGY

INTRODUCTION

Ecclesiology (from *ecclesia*, Latin for "church") aims to come to a true understanding of the church. It is a part of what Catholics and other Christians call theology or sacred theology. The point of calling it sacred theology is to distinguish it from natural theology. That is the kind of theology Aristotle does in his *Metaphysics*. The presuppositions of that kind of theology are human reason and human experience, and enough experience, perhaps, to know (by reason) that what is real is not exhausted by material reality, and that reality extends beyond what is available to our senses. The presuppositions of sacred theology, on the other hand, are God's revelation and the theologian's faith in God's revealed word. As this ecclesiology is written for people for whom this book may be the first and perhaps only book of theology they read and so is introductory not just to ecclesiology but to theology in general, something will be said at the beginning of part 2 about revelation and the nature and sources of revelation and the reception of it in faith.

Ecclesiology is just one part of sacred theology, some of whose other component parts include Christology, Trinitarian theology, and sacramental theology. In all of these parts, there is a twofold aim. The first aim is to get at what is revealed about the thing in question, which comes down to asking what is reported about it in scripture, and what it is that the church traditionally hears about it in scripture, and what the church explicitly teaches about the thing in question—Christ or the Trinity, or the church, or the Eucharist, etc. This is sometimes called "dogmatic theology." For a *dogma* in Greek is a doctrine, a teaching. The accomplishment of this aim gives us real and true cognitive possession of the reality in question. In ecclesiology, it gives us that possession of the church that the church wants us to have. This is a first and evidently very important goal of theology.

There is, however, a further goal, too, which is not just access to the reality in question—Christ or the church or the Eucharist, and so on— but a comprehensive understanding of it. That is, we do not want simply to touch the reality, but, as far as this is possible when we are faced with holy things, to penetrate it, to grasp its intimate nature. For ecclesiology, this is a matter of understanding the church according to its causes. We want to know not just the elements out of which it is made and its architect (what an Aristotelian would call the material and efficient causes), but we want to know its end, what good its nature inclines it to (final cause), and we want to know the thing that is the most difficult to possess, namely, the single intelligibility, the idea of the church that makes it one thing, that gives it unity. This is the formal cause, and it is the ground of understanding why she has the other properties she does besides unity, as the Nicene Creed lists them, namely, apostolicity, catholicity, and holiness. We want, in other words, a definition of the church, a definition that delivers to the believing mind the core reality, the essence of the church. Only such an understanding will enable us to see why she has the powers she does—apostolic powers—and how her reality is displayed in the world and instantiated in her actions. If cognitive access is the product of consulting the New Testament, tradition, and the church's teaching (part 2), and if we call that dogmatic theology, then working out a formulation of the church's nature, causes, properties, and powers is "systematic theology" (part 3).

Dogmatic theology aims to produce *true* propositions about its subject matter (Christ, sacraments, Trinity), true propositions known to be true because revealed, while systematic theology aims at that *understanding* of the mystery that reason can attain when illumined by faith and of which the First Vatican Council spoke. The understanding may be partial and imperfect and will certainly be analogous, because we come to an understanding of transcendent, divine, and supernatural things only by way of comparison to things we naturally know, that is, by way of analogy. But the Council insists also that this understanding is "most fruitful."[1] The fruit that is borne by such an understanding nourishes both piety and practical effectiveness. Insofar as we understand the church more fully, we will love her and the Lord she makes present to us more ardently, and we will be able to serve her and her Lord more successfully. Prior to these very significant fruits, however, there is also the simple delight in beholding the beauty of the church, a beauty we behold the more we understand her, a beauty which reflects the beauty of Christ.

When theologians do systematic theology, the church has recommended and still does recommend that they pay attention to the wisdom of St. Thomas Aquinas.[2] This book will do that, through the medium of several modern and contemporary followers of Aquinas who have devoted themselves to understanding the church.

From what has been said about dogmatic theology, it is evident that we will depend on the church in coming to know the church. Our cognitive access to the church depends in part on the church herself, and there can seem to be some circularity in this arrangement: we do not know the church, and that is why we are reading an ecclesiology, to find out what she is; but yet we have somehow already to know her in order to know that what she says about herself is trustworthy. Our access to the church depends on the scriptures of the church, on the tradition of the church, on the magisterium or teaching office of the church, and so on the dogmas of the church about the church. This is fine if we are happy Catholics, already confident of the role of the church as the guardian of the whole of revelation, a revelation which speaks also of her. If we are happy Cath-

---

1 First Vatican Council, the Dogmatic Constitution *Dei Filius*, April 24, 1870, chap. 4, which can be found in *The Decrees of the Ecumenical Councils*, ed. Norman P. Tanner, SJ (London / Washington, D.C.: Sheed and Ward / Georgetown University Press, 1990), 2:804–11. See also Pope John Paul II, *Fides et Ratio*, Encyclical Letter, September 14, 1998, pars. 77, 93, and 97, best found in *Restoring Faith in Reason: A New Translation of the Encyclical Letter of Pope John Paul II*, ed. Laurence Paul Hemming and with commentary by James McEvoy (London: SCM Press, 2002). For the understanding of the nature of dogmatic and systematic theology operative here, see Bernard J. F. Lonergan, SJ, *Method in Theology*, 2nd ed. (New York: Herder and Herder, 1972), chaps. 5, 12, and 13.

2 See, e.g., John Paul II, *Fides et Ratio*, par. 78.

olics, then we take it for granted that the church is a divinely accredited and therefore supremely trustworthy witness about Christ, the Trinity, and the church herself.

On the other hand, it can seem that we are presupposing a foundation for our construction that has yet to be laid, or, depending where we treat the teaching authority of tradition and pope and bishop, it can seem that at some point we will have to pick up an edifice already under construction—we will have to pick up the building by its steeple in order to shove a foundation under it. Here is how a distinguished theologian of the past century puts the problem.

It is true, of course, that the Church is one of the articles of faith, which we profess when we say: "I believe in the Holy and Catholic Church"; and from this point, all the questions about the Church can be treated dogmatically. But before we can argue dogmatically, it is necessary to establish the foundation upon which the whole of dogmatic theology is built. This foundation of dogmatic theology, however, is the doctrinal authority of the Church, to which it has been divinely committed to guard and infallibly to declare the doctrine of faith and morals deposited in the fonts of revelation.[3]

"It is necessary to establish," Salaverri says, for he is supposing a view of theology that takes very seriously the duty of theologians to respond to Enlightenment attacks on the credibility of the fact of revelation, on its possibility even, and the Enlightenment and post-Enlightenment attacks on the historicity, that is, the historical trustworthiness, of the New Testament, especially the Gospels, such that Jesus' foundation of the church was made to seem dubious if not altogether incredible.

So it was that until the mid-part of the last century, it was common for treatises *de ecclesia* to be half apologetic and half dogmatic. The apologetic part appealed to philosophical reason to establish the possibility of revelation, and to historical reason to establish the fact of revelation in Jesus, who both founded the church, which church, it was then argued,

---

3 Ioachim Salaverri, SJ, *De Ecclesia Christi*, no. 6 (my translation), in *Theologia Fundamentalis: Introductio in Theologiam. De Revelatio Christiana. De Ecclesia Christi. De Sacra Scriptura*, with Michaele Nicolau, SJ, Part I of *Sacrae Theologiae Summa iuxta Constitutionem Apostolicum "Deus scientiarum Dominus"* (Madrid: Biblioteca de Autores Cristianos, 1956). There is a complete English translation of the work: *On the Church of Christ*, in *Sacrae Theologiae Summa* IB, trans. Kenneth Baker, SJ (Ramsey, N.J.: Keep the Faith, 2015).

is demonstrably identical with the Catholic church of today, and who also commended the message of revelation to her magisterial authority to guard and expound. Then and only then do we come to know the canon of inspired scripture and the dogmatic value for faith of both scripture and tradition as delivered to us by the church. Then and only then can the dogmatic treatment of the church begin in ecclesiology, which receives in faith what scripture and tradition and the magisterium say of its subject matter, the church herself.

Now, the burden of this present book is dogmatic and systematic and not apologetic. We will stand on the word of God and not natural reason. Still and all, it is good for us to know how ecclesiology was done for many years, and it is good for us to be aware of the issues that the apologetic half of ecclesiology addressed. Evidently, they are still important issues. And sooner or later, every competent theologian, and maybe we should say, every intellectually responsible Catholic, must be prepared to give an answer to those who ask a reason for our hope (1 Pt 3:15), even especially when the questions come from Enlightenment and historical critical objections, objections which are still current and, for many, powerful.

There are, then, some important apologetic issues that even today especially touch Catholic faith in the church. They will not be dealt with in the comprehensive way the old fundamental theology or apologetics did, and I give some of them a novel formulation and a fast, not to say peremptory, resolution. But it is especially worthwhile to focus them directly, and especially for those first entering into Catholic theology, which as has already been noted may well be the case for those picking up this book. They make up part 1 of this book. They are, in order: (1) the antecedent probabilities of a revelation and of a church to which revelation is confided; (2) the antecedent probability of the historicity of the Gospels and the factual historical credibility of the Gospels; and (3) the historical credibility of Jesus' foundation of the (actual) church.

ECCLESIOLOGY
APOLOGETIC

CHAPTER 1

ANTECEDENT PROBABILITIES OF REVELATION AND A CHURCH

The Idea of a Church

The idea of a "church" is the idea of a society of men and women who share a common life with God and one another. A common life proper to persons is a life of understanding the same things, knowing the same truths, prizing the same dispositions that make for successful human agency, and loving each other so as to ensure a common possession of these things. In its bare simplicity, this idea includes nothing about how such a society would be established or about its internal order, or even how it would be recognized. But just as such, the antecedent probability of such a thing, of the existence of a church, is quite high. This is to say that, antecedent to revelation, the probability of such a thing can be known by reason.

For what is it, after all, that we want? It is very much a question of "we." No human being wants to live by himself and unto himself. We want true friends: friends that are interested in the truth and want true goods for one another, goods that will bring us to completion as human beings. Among these true goods is certainly the truth itself, the important truths about human nature, human destiny, and more widely, the origin, order, and destiny of the world. Among these goods there will also be the capacity to act according to the truth, which is freedom, and the ability to install the truth of human nature into our human acts, and so acquire what Plato and Aristotle recognized as the moral virtues.

But we are interested in these truths together, in sharing them, in sharing the virtues, and more, in a mutually knowledgeable sharing of these things. This is easily illustrated. Who, for instance, wants to go sightseeing by himself? We go sightseeing together, say, to see the National Mall and the Lincoln Memorial and the Washington Monument. We are interested in the sights, of course. But we are also interested in the seeings—that is, in how the sights show up to intelligent perception. I see that you understand how the Memorial and the Monument work to define a noble space that speaks worthily of both men, of their character and of their lives, and how integral the reflecting pool is for this definition, how it unites the achievements of both men. At the same time, you know that I know that you understand this, and I know that you know that I know this thing too. This shared consciousness in friendship brings with it its own peculiar pleasure, a pleasure that friends know cannot be bought or attained in any other way and which is itself a sort of unmerited and gratuitous flower of love.

Just so, the most distinguishing feature of friendship in communion of truth and love is the regular concourse and being with one another of the friends. What is most characteristic of friends, Aristotle says, is the common life, the fact that friends live together and spend time together.[1] So we arrive at the idea of a community, a community that embraces both the spiritual or mental and the bodily aspects of human nature. We cannot really have a common mind unless we bodily occupy a common space at least at some point, for some time, nor can virtual space in the

1. *Nicomachean Ethics* VIII.5, 1157b19–20. The translation of the *Ethics* by W. D. Ross can be found in *The Basic Works of Aristotle*, ed. Richard McKeon (New York: Random House, 1947).

end totally supply for this if it has never existed. Already with this idea we approach the idea of a church.

But why must we drag God into it? Because if there is a God, how can we not want him to be dragged into the community of friends just outlined? God, if there is a God, will know all that is importantly true about human life, because he creates it, and he will be the master of all the circumstances and goods that make for a good human life, including also the conditions of community life. The common truth and common good that involves both God and man, moreover, will evidently be a truth and a good that is chiefly about God and only secondarily about men. For if God exists, he will be his own truth—that is, he will not be measured by anything or any standard outside him. On the contrary, he will be the measure of the truth of all other things, the things he creates. In relation to him, all other truths will be created participations of his truth. The same structure will hold in the order of the good. What is God's good is God himself, and cannot be anything outside him, and all other goods will be participations of his good. But the truth and good that God is, supposing he exists, will necessarily concern us. For we are knowers and lovers, and as such are made in his image. If he exists, we will naturally be in his image the way something concave and empty is the image of the convex and the full. That is, we will be set up by nature to seek the truth and the goodness he is, which will include living up to and possessing the truth we are and instantiating the good we are meant to possess in ourselves.

Now, if God is to share his own truth and his own good just as they are with us, more than what we could figure out on our own by triangulating from created goods, especially from ourselves made in his image, then he must speak to us. Friends, after all, do not become friends without a lot of shared conversation. The idea of a church is not that of a group of people looking on God from afar, as revealed in his created works. That is how Aristotle thought God entered into the circle of philosophical friends. The idea of a church is rather the idea of a people called to be with God—called to a common life with God—as befits friends, a common life that will therefore be inaugurated and established by his Word.

Aristotle did not envisage this idea of a church. He thought that friendship with God, just because of the disproportion between the divine and human natures, put it out of question.[2] Friends have to be on the same level. It is hard for the rich and the powerful to be friends with the poor and lowly. It is impossible for us really to be friends with our pets. So also, the great gap between the divine and the human precludes friendship with God. For such disproportion and inequality to be addressed so that there could be a real possibility of friendship with God, then, would require at the least that God speak to us, that he share his knowledge with us—it would require revelation. God would have to speak to us about matters difficult for us to know or even quite beyond our suspicion, but easy for him to know, for all such truths would depend on his wisdom, on his good will and pleasure.[3]

This very abstractness of the idea of a church here so barely outlined and the similar abstractness of the revelation required for it saves both these ideas from being presumptuous. They do not include anything about a mediator of the revelation such a church presupposes. And they do not presuppose that the finality of this revelation and church would lead us to the strictly supernatural end of knowing God as he knows himself and loving him in the power of his own intimate love.[4] They do not presuppose even that we know by our own lights that such an end is even possible.

The modest point being made here is this: showing that a church so envisaged is probable depends on making good the antecedent probability of revelation. But the antecedent probability of revelation is itself also very high. This can be made plain in short order.

2. *Nicomachean Ethics* VIII.7, 1159a4–5.

3. On the moral necessity for God to speak to us about things within the compass of reason to know, but only with difficulty, things about God and the natural law, see the Pope Pius XII, *Humani Generis*, Encyclical Letter, August 12, 1950, pars. 2–3; available at www.vatican.va. The relevant section can also be found in *The Christian Faith*, 7th ed., ed. Jacques Dupuis (New York: Alba House, 2001), nos. 144–45. A friendship established by such a revelation would, it seems, approach the idea of a friendship between unequals that Aristotle envisages between God and man at *Nicomachean Ethics* VIII.12 and 14.

4. St. Thomas offers an entirely rational argument for the necessity of the revelation of the moral law in his *Summa Contra Gentiles* [hereafter *SCG*], Book Three: *Providence Part II*, trans. Vernon J. Bourke (Notre Dame, Ind.: University of Notre Dame Press, 1975), chaps. 114–29. Moreover, this revealed moral law is to be fulfilled from charity, a strictly supernatural virtue, that binds together both God and men in one society—a "church." He supposes also that our natural desire to know will not be fulfilled except in the vision of God; see *Summa Contra Gentiles*, Book Three, *Part I*, trans. Vernon J. Bourke (Notre Dame, Ind.: University of Notre Dame Press, 1975), chaps. 37, 51, and 63.

The Antecedent Probability of Revelation

Let us back up a few steps. Human beings are given over to truth. We like to behold it. We like to do it; that is, we like to install it in the things we make and in our moral actions. Beholding it can be difficult; doing it can be dangerous. Still, we are, as has been finely said, "agents of truth."[5] This is easily illustrated.

There is, of course, the fact of our practical engagement in the world—in an economy, in business, in growing things, and in making machines. When we are so engaged, we are always thinking about whether some contemplated action, some means to an end, is a good means, a good way to it. We could also just as well say that we are always thinking about whether the contemplated action is a *true* way to get to our end and maybe the best (truest) way to get there. But this "poetic" engagement in agriculture, commerce, and manufacture—making (*poiesis*) a crop, making a profit, making a machine—is not perhaps the best place to notice our constant engagement with the truth. We are ordinarily too interested in the result of our making to pay attention to how we make it, with constant attention to the truth of things.

In fact, thinking of our deployment of reason in order to make things, make money, get places, get ahead will make us think that reason is good always and only for figuring out the means to get to some end. Reason will be the soul of utility but never extend beyond that. Reasoning will be exhausted in calculating and calibrating the steps we have to take to get somewhere. But as to where we are going, as to the end we want to get to, we will think that reasoning or understanding has nothing to do with that. The ends we have will be a function of freedom, of will. Reason is for how to get what we want, but what we want is settled prior to or independently of reason. This reduction of reason to a technological instrument gives us a most misleading picture of human agency, however. It is not a blind will that determines our ends. Or if it is, then we will have unfortunate lives. It is a discerning will that determines ends. What is discerned is the intelligibility of things, their internal truth and goodness. And what we discern in ourselves is our own internal truth—what it is that will make us more

5. Robert Sokolowski, *Phenomenology of the Human Person* (Cambridge: Cambridge University Press, 2008), 1.

human, more ourselves. Only then do we have some chance of choosing an end not only freely but wisely. Discernment of such ultimate and final things, however, is the premier work of mind, of intelligence, of reason. Human beings have always to do with the truth, whether of means or of ends, whether we conceal this from ourselves or not.

Sports is a good place to notice our involvement with the truth, because one facet of this involvement is so clearly and manifestly contemplative for ordinary men and women. An athlete is someone who installs order and intelligence in his or her bodily action. Bodily action that is ordered and intelligent is an excellence. It is a pleasure to behold. It is beautiful. That is why the nation largely gives itself over to the contemplation of sports weekend after weekend. What are we looking for? The deft move, the graceful lay-up, the fast break, the difficult but elegant catch, the neat tackle, the daring (courageous) charge. We are looking for intelligence in bodiliness, the truth of the body itself displayed on the field or within the court. And we give ourselves, our own bodies, over to sports because in the first place there is an enjoyment of that same elegance and intelligence in our own movement. There is enjoyment also in measuring our strength and the graceful movement of our bodies against the strength and movement of others, which is competition. With team sports, the interactions between members is complicated and constant and also highly intelligible, and there is a truth about being a team member that is also wonderful to behold, as the dispositions of courage and courtesy and their excellence are more evidently and constantly engaged. Competition itself touches the issue of truth quite directly: we want to know who is better, who is best, which is to say, who is the truer athlete, and what team plays more truly than any other.

Concern for truth is also most signally and inescapably manifest in our practical activity, our moral activity (*praxis*). There is an important difference between moral activity and sports, however. As was just noted, there is a truth, an ideal, that governs our appreciation of sports, either playing or watching. Moreover, there is a sort of built-in, given limit in the body that dictates what intelligent motion can be like, a limit we do not set. Even so, however, it is we who make the rules of the game, sport for sport. Sport for sport, it is our setup. But in moral action, we do not make the rules, but simply recognize them. Moreover, there is a sort of limitlessness to the ideal that distinguishes moral activity from athletic activity. The standard of justice is above us, and seemingly unlimited—we cannot be too just. Can you be too fast in soccer? Perhaps not; but you can become musclebound if you train wrong. The standard for athleticism is within us, in the nature and limits of our bodiliness. But the standard of justice, as well as the standards of such things as purity and chastity, or of telling the truth, is above us. We measure up to them—*up*, notice—or we do not.[6] But we do not set the standards. We do not make them. We recognize them.

Now, the entire dignity of man and his abject misery both become known to us, at one and the same time, once we take reflexive possession of the phenomenon of our moral conscience. First of all, conscience makes plain to us our capacity to recognize moral values just as such, and makes us realize that we live in a world absolutely transcendent to the limited region of animal instinct and appetite, and even of practical concern and calculation (what we are to eat, what we are to wear). We break out from the subterranean cave, and, seeing in the intelligible light, we know what is truly good in itself, the values embedded in the virtues of justice and chastity and fidelity, whose importance does not depend on us or our wants and desires or decisions but rather ennobles us in our very recognition of them.[7] With this realization, we leave the cave of positivism and scientism, and realize that there is an intelligibility, a truth, and a knowledge of this truth, beyond what the empirical sciences can know. People who have experienced their transcendence and submitted to the majesty of values are more personable than those who have not. They are more real, more of what it is to be a person. This is because there is no space for persons in a positivist universe, and the features of persons seem anomalous, and provoke endless but always unsuccessful attempts to explain consciousness and knowledge itself in terms of causes that know no reasons, in terms of neurons and networks of neurons and chemical events.[8] In such a search, we become illusions to ourselves, and we distrust

6. We might be said in sports to have to measure up to past, historical precedent, the mark set by another, previous athlete. Still, the dominant note is that we are measuring ourselves against, while in morals we are measuring up.

7. See Dietrich von Hildebrand, *Christian Ethics* (Chicago: Franciscan Herald Press, 1953), 132–41 and 172–224.

8. See Roger Scruton, *The Soul of the World* (Princeton, N.J.: Princeton University Press,

our very experience of what it is to be an agent of truth. But persons who acknowledge their transcendence ratify and appropriate the adventure that being a person is.

Second, we experience the call of conscience to respect such values as justice and truthfulness as a real call, a voice. And this intimates to us the existence of God—not only the God who can be known as first cause and last end of the universe,[9] but of a personal God, a God, that is, whose knowing and loving and whose authority are turned to us, are facing us, and address us in our everyday and inmost moral experience.[10] Conscience is the natural viceroy of God that delivers his rule to every person who wants to be a person. Conscience is not God. But it speaks with his authority, not our own. It speaks with an authority not that of the city or culture to which we belong, as Protagoras would have us think. It is an authority antecedent to that of the city.[11]

Just here, where we behold conscience as the antechamber beyond whose enclosure there must be some holy place where there dwells a divine legislator and a divine judge, we say goodbye to a metaphysical alternative of great and, it would seem, abiding significance in human history, an alternative with many forms, some sophisticated and seductive, some more simple-minded. We say goodbye to all the monisms of natural mysticism and of the Eastern religions. In these monisms, the All is One and the One is All, and we are just parts that, before enlightenment, do not recognize our already and inescapable belongingness to an antecedent harmony of love and unity of consciousness.[12] We do not have to make

---

2016), chaps. 2 and 3, or his *On Human Nature* (Princeton, N.J.: Princeton University Press, 2012), chaps. 1 and 2.

9. See Rom 1:19–20 and the First Vatican Council, *Dei Filius*, chap. 2.

10. John Henry Newman, *An Essay in Aid of a Grammar of Assent*, ed. I. T. Ker (Oxford: Clarendon Press, 1985), esp. 73–81 (105–18 in the online version at the Newman Reader, found at www.newmanreader.org; subsequent parenthetical Newman citations refer to this source). See also Newman's letter to the Duke of Norfolk in *Certain Difficulties Felt by Anglicans on Catholic Teaching Considered* (London: Longmans, Green, and Co., 1896), esp. 2:246–49 and 255–56.

11. If we want, we can redescribe the voice of conscience as the imagination of a spectator of our actions, an impartial judge. See Scruton, *The Soul of the World*, 81.

12. For Joseph Ratzinger, the Hinduism of Radhakrishnan is a good example of this view; see his careful comparison of monist mysticism and monotheism in "The Unity and Diversity of Religions: The Place of Christianity in the History of Religions," in his *Truth and Tolerance: Christian Belief and World Religions*, trans. Henry Taylor (San Francisco, Calif.: Ignatius Press, 2004), 15–44.

this harmony because it always already includes us, although we cannot know this if we sleep the sleep of ordinary life and its distractions. Consciousness is primordially unitive; it is an ocean that precedes and includes us and of which we are but drops, whose real distinction from it is ultimately illusory. Or again, consciousness is unitary and "non-dual," meaning that the distinction between the person and all that is not him is not ultimate.[13] We can realize we are parts of the one consciousness/reality, however, only if we forsake the useful but nonbasic distinctions of ordinary life and logic and take leave of Western (Greek) thought. But *also*, we can come to the simultaneously exhilarating and comforting realization that we are but parts of the One and the All only if we give up the pangs of conscience. Why must this be?

The monisms of natural mysticism, Gnosticism, the Jungians, New Age spiritualities, and (for another example) the Hinduism of Radhakrishnan are morally comforting because the distinction of good and evil disappears with the distinction of persons from the nonpersonal. We are all equally innocent and equally guilty. If the voice of *conscience* is real and is the reverberation of God in our hearts, however, this cannot be true. The acute experience of conscience has to be flattened out in a monism that includes good and evil as coequal parts (Jung). The moral experience of conscience can be final and not deceptive and irreducible only if there is a final and ineradicable reality of our *own* inalienable personal responsibility. This means we are distinct, and must be ever distinct, not only from the persons with whom we live and are morally connected and ever answerable to, but also from a person, a Person, more personable than us, and more unbreakable than our own diamond-like personal center, someone who is the standard of the personal, someone we can ignore but not really finally forget, someone whose presence we can obscure but only at the risk of whatever disaster awaits those who could have been but refused to be persons.[14]

13. For a contemporary example of this thinking, see the gnostic, "non-dualist," panpsychist, conscience-less views of Cynthia Bourgeault, *The Wisdom Jesus* (New York: Shambhala, 2008). For what is considered a sophisticated version, see C. G. Jung, *Psychology and Religion: West and East*, 2nd ed. (Princeton, N.J.: Princeton University Press, 1975).

14. For those who refuse to be persons, see the first circle of hell in *The Inferno*.

But then, we *do* refuse to be persons, and we *try* to obscure the presence of God to us (Rom 1:31–33), which brings us to a third point. No sooner do we recognize the claim of conscience, the authority of the values of such things as chastity and courage and truthfulness and justice, than we know also that though we are called to measure up, we do not in fact measure up. No sooner does our dignity as persons responding to moral values and responding to God appear to us, that at the same time, our moral failure, our moral poverty is also manifest to us.[15]

There is a story Cardinal Newman tells in his *Apologia*, a parable of original sin. Suppose we meet some boy who seems to be of good background and raised in gentle circumstances but who is now alone and seemingly cast out, as if banished from lands and inheritance. "What has happened to him?," we would ask. But we are that boy. There is as great a distance between our "promise" and our actual "condition" as there is between the thwarted promise and the miserable condition of the boy. According to Newman, this great distance argues either that we can be no product of a good God in our present morally miserable straits, or that in some way we have fallen from a better, original condition.[16] But the voice of conscience assures us we are the product of a good God and cannot be gainsaid.

This is a first thing, this conundrum of the difference between our moral promise and aspiration on the one hand and our morally compromised existence on the other. There is a second thing, too, and that is our ignorance of what will befall us at death. Do we continue past death in some wakeful form? Is there some "place" or "places" dead souls inhabit? For a third thing, there is the impossibility of knowing God's mind for us from the natural order of the world. These three things together make it antecedently probable that a good God will give us direction, which is to say that he will reveal what we need to know about the moral law, about our history and station, about our prospects and his dispositions.[17]

15. See Blaise Pascal, *Pensées*, trans. W. F. Trotter (New York: E. P. Dutton and Co., 1958), no. 397: "The greatness of man is that he knows himself to be miserable." See also nos. 365, 398, 409, and 416.

16. John Henry Newman, *Apologia pro Vita Sua* (1865) (London: Longmans, Green, and Co., 1908), 241–43.

17. That we be on the lookout for such a revelation seems to be contained in the natural law as understood by St. Thomas. See his *Summa Theologiae* I-II, q. 94, a. 2, according to which it is

What this revelation will contain is in the first place and fundamentally news about a renewal of the promise of our created personal being as responsive to moral values and oriented to a seemingly unlimited possession of the true and the good. As to such an unlimited possession, the mere fact of God's personal speech to us is a sort of guarantee that our desire for the true and the good will have everything to do with our relation to him. If the Truth speaks to us, and where we understand "speaking" itself as personal revelation and bestowal of self, and not just a conveyance of information, then we have assurance that in some way, somehow, happiness is possible for us—a possession in some form of the divine truth and the divine goodness. As yet, to be sure, nothing is resolved in this anticipation of revelation as to how and in what manner we are to share in the divine truth and goodness. Will it be a sharing formally the same as God's own possession of himself in knowledge and love, which is to say, the vision of God? This we cannot anticipate, even as to its possibility, and it is mentioned here only by way of stealing something on the other side of the actual revelation God has made.

Nor can we anticipate that sharing in God's truth and a love will be made possible by the revelation of an incarnate Son of God, an incarnate Word and Truth, who will fix our condition of sin by his own love for us, his own satisfaction on our behalf for our sins, his own merit for us of the grace that will heal our wounds. We cannot anticipate that the incarnate Son of God will share this grace by sending the Holy Spirit into our hearts, a grace that therefore also elevates us to be like him, sons of his Father.

Back to the Idea of a Church

The incarnation is antecedently inconceivable, as is the mission of the Holy Spirit. Before they happen we cannot think they will happen or

---

a precept of the natural law to seek the truth about God. The most convenient Latin edition of the *Summa* is the Marietti edition (Torino: Marietti, 1952). In English, the handiest and most accessible edition is the *Summa Theologica*, trans. English Dominican Province, 5 vols. (New York: Benziger Bros., 1948). I cite the *Summa* [hereafter *ST*] according to part (I, I-II, II-II, III), question number, and article number (for the corpus), and "ad" with number, for replies to objections. For the duty to seek God and his possible word to us, see Newman, *Grammar of Assent*, 255–56 and 260 (397 and 404).

even know their possibility. Prior to our knowledge of the incarnation and the actual shape of our redemption, however, which are things we cannot in any way foresee, we *can* foresee "church." For if revelation is antecedently probable, then one of its results, because it is a revelation to us, is a church. This is not difficult to see if we remember the political nature of man. Our hopes for the realization of happiness in this age, a happiness suited to human nature and as described by Aristotle in his *Nicomachean Ethics*, depends also on the conditions he lays out in the *Politics*. We need a society organized and articulated, whose citizens are friends one to the other, and which possesses a way to preserve what is good in its laws and knowledge over time—a kind of human tradition that depends on education.[18] With this, we have a natural analogue for a society of men who have given themselves over to hope for a more than purely natural possession of happiness, one that involves friendship with God. Do we think that God would, or even could, deal with us one by one? Ahistorically? Atemporally? Each man taken as a pure monad, unrelated to any other? He does not deal even with the angels in that way, but illumines one through another.[19] No. We must expect some society, constituted by the word of God and enduring through the ages to the end of the world. A patriarch may do for a family, as we see in the last half of the Book of Genesis. For a people, however, we want a prophet, and the organized people he speaks to. For a people, we want something like Moses.

Together with a revelation of the moral law addressing our fallen condition and which is necessary for society, we must also expect some news about human destiny, about death and salvation from death. If death is the wages of sin, then will not forgiveness of sin save us from death? How can this be imagined? Furthermore, just because human history is a history of embodied virtue and embodied vice and injustice, and so a common history, no sufficient word can declare to us our final worth without declaring the worth of all. Speaking a word of divine judgment on that history and doing justice to its embodied character therefore supposes a general resurrection of the dead. Whatever church restores grace to the

18. Aristotle, *Politics* VII.13–17 and VIII.1–7. The *Politics*, translated by Benjamin Jowett, can be found in *The Basic Works of Aristotle*.
19. Aquinas, *ST* I, q. 107, a. 2.

course of history, therefore, will meet its final end in a common judgment where all history is recapitulated in a justice meted out to bodily beings restored in their bodily nature.[20]

The argument here is not that God owes us some sort of revelation because of the natural inclination of our mind and will to infinite truth and goodness, and certainly not that he owes us the revelation of his intimate Trinitarian life and a share in his own happiness. The argument is that our *misery*, as something certainly not intended by a good God, and whose goodness is demonstrated in the created order as a whole and the moral promise of man, makes some sort of revelation antecedently probable, and therefore some form of "church" antecedently probable.[21] In fact, the probabilities are met with an unanticipable divine generosity, both as to what is promised us as our end, the vision of God and a share in Trinitarian life by both knowledge and love, and as to the way to that end, the incarnate Son of God, his passion and death and resurrection, and the actual church, which makes the grace and truth of Christ available through his Spirit. But that our misery calls down the word of God to us and therefore makes a church—the argument of this chapter is that *that* is antecedently probable. At the point of the actual fulfillment of this probability, in our actual history, we see further that, even without sin, there must have been intended a church before any Fall. For what God gives us in our misery, and which reveals a plan to give us a share in his own life, he would also have given us in the integrity of our first creation—a creation, therefore, in grace. But we do not argue for this as antecedently probable from the inclination of our mind to truth and our will to the good; we have no unclouded or uncompromised experience of such an inclination.

Of course, insofar as the word of God will declare our release from sin and the deliverance of some help for us to keep the moral law and enjoy the friendship of God, then it comes to us with "grace," too. Revelation just as such effects a change in our cognitive possession of the real, includ-

20. See Benedict XVI, *Spe Salvi*, Encyclical Letter, November 30, 2007, pars. 42–44; available at www.vatican.va.

21. See above, note 3, as to the moral necessity of revelation. See also Newman, *Grammar of Assent*, 272–75 (422–27), on the antecedent probability of revelation given God's goodness and our misery.

ing divinity. Grace, however, effects a change not just in our mind, not just in what we know, but also in our will, in our passions, in the springs of our moral action. It includes healing the wounds of sin (*gratia sanans*). Moreover, as something not antecedently anticipable, grace also and in fact raises us up so as to be able to share friendship with God in such a way that a just order is maintained between us and God (*gratia elevans*). That grace heals us and the springs of our moral action, however, might be said to be anticipated in thinking about our natural friendships. For true friends help each other become virtuous, both by example and advice. That kind of help comes from outside of us. God, of course, can help from inside of us by giving us over to the good thoughts and good desires that make virtuous action more probable.

Still and all in this anticipation of God's help, we are very far from the concrete shape of the real church. But we can say this: just because revelation and grace will be shared commonly by all those who accept the help of God, they just of themselves call for some common form of life together. The high antecedent probability of there being such a thing as a church as has been here argued for it is not always adverted to in contemporary ecclesiologies. In fact, however, its recognition instills a serene and pacific confidence in the proceedings for the rest of part 1. Had there been no sin, to be sure, we would not have needed any speculation on antecedent probabilities. The history of revelation and grace would never have been broken, and we would always have enjoyed the truth and love of God, his company in friendship. Death would not have perplexed us, for without sin, we would not have been relegated to a purely natural order where death naturally comes for the old. Whether sinless or sinful, however, and if man is truly the microcosm of the entire created order, we can say this: the church, some church, there must be as that for which all things have been created.[22]

---

22. I set aside here any discussion of the relation of the angels and men to one another in such a primordial church where the history of man was untouched by sin and the relation of human sin to angelic sin.

Coda: Modern Anthropology and the Revealed Plan of God

Reflections on the antecedent probability of revelation provoke a question when confronted with the deliverances of modern anthropology, physical and cultural, which seem to make revelation and even God very *im*probable. For cultural anthropologists, civilization in a form like unto ours—organized, stratified, with complex management of grain crops and domestic animals—is six thousand years old. According to physical anthropologists, however, anatomically modern humans have been around for two hundred thousand years, and earlier humans go back from two to six million years further.

Suppose, then, that the first human beings ("Adam and Eve") were called to friendship with God and fell from this high estate many, many thousands of years ago. The question is this: what was God doing for all those long years of human ignorance of him, where religion often did not rise to any clear conception of a transcendent and moral God, where man was ignorant of his destiny, where the knowledge of the natural law was only fitfully and incompletely acquired? The answer is not "preparing hell for those who ask such questions." The answer is subtle, but illuminating. The answer is that it takes a long time for nature unaided by grace and unenlightened by revelation to display what it can and cannot do on its own by way of discovering the natural moral law, mastering field and forest, formulating the laws of being, investigating the natures of things, and advancing answers to the religious and metaphysical questions latent in every man. How long? Just as long as the cultural and physical anthropologists tell us. For the supposition is that the anthropologists can be telling us only of fallen humanity, that is, of a humanity following a real and historical fall from grace, such as the third chapter of Genesis teaches us. The display of our natural neediness and indigence, however, and exacerbated by the unrestrained concupiscence and malice which come with the Fall, and by a darkened consciousness thrown back entirely on its own resources, is a good thing.[23] Ignorance and malice are bad things, of course. But the *display* of what we can and cannot do on our own is good for us. It is

23. For the consequences of the Fall, see Aquinas, *ST* I-II, q. 85, a. 3.

a kind of knowledge. It is good for us to know what our native, unaided capacities can do on their own, for this helps us appreciate the word of revelation and the aid of grace, and they stand out for what they are all the more readily against the foil of fallen nature.[24]

Thus can theological intelligibility be given to the fact that there is no evidence at all of any connection to or revelation from God for thousands of years. Granted this fact, it counts for nothing against the antecedent probability that Newman's parable brings to light: a good God will address us, sooner or later, in our parlous condition. And our conscience gives insistent witnesses to the existence of this good God.

24. See Aquinas, *ST* I-II, q. 106, a. 3, co., third argument.

CHAPTER 2

THE HISTORICAL TRUSTWORTHINESS OF THE NEW TESTAMENT

If there is a great antecedent probability that God will reveal himself and a way of salvation for us and so establish a church, how would we recognize it were it to occur, or were it to have already occurred? This is a historical question. There is a narrow way and a broad way at this juncture, but both are related to the topic of the previous chapter as actuality is related to probability, as a question of fact is related to questions of likelihood.

The narrow way is to look at the account of the foundation of the church in the Gospels, which means looking at their account of the founder, Jesus of Nazareth. The narrow way concentrates on the face of Jesus, seeing his love for his friends and companions, and indeed, seeing his love for all men. It concentrates on seeing him die for us and for our sins and likewise rising for us, for his resurrection is indispensable in giving us answers to the questions about sin, death, and our destiny identified in the previous chapter.

The broad way is splashed on a much wider swath of history, where there is such a thing as "history"—tribes and nations, nations intersecting with each other in commerce and war, dealing with the divine by sacrifice and atonement, and with enough wealth and leisure for their citizens to reflect on all these things within the parameters of human life, love, and death, and with the capacity to record these reflections in written narrative and law. The broad way begins with Israel's recollection of her patriarchal and Mosaic beginnings, and so throws us back to the second millennium B.C., and continues to the time of Jesus and the foundation of the church, and into the history of the church. The basic outline of the story is of hope established and hope fulfilled: Israel's hope for a Messiah who will complete the promises given to Abraham, Moses, and the prophets; hope fulfilled in Jesus of Nazareth; fulfillment missed in the failure of most Jews to recognize him, and fulfillment embraced in the recognition of the Gentiles.

I will touch on parts of the broad way in chapter 5, on the people of God; I will touch on the narrow way in this chapter. But for both ways to work, we have to know the Gospels as historically trustworthy records that tell us who Jesus claimed to be and which tell us of the confirmation of his claim. I will save his foundation of the church for the next chapter.[1]

The Antecedent Probability of Historically Trustworthy Scripture

The Catholic church claims to be the real fulfillment of the idea of "church" just evoked. If she is, she will be the custodian and expositor of the word of God, the word she claims to possess in scripture.[2] For into the custody of those called together by the public revelation of God accomplished in history through the words and deeds of God and the re-

---

1. What about the historical credibility of the Old Testament, particularly the exodus from Egypt? If Jesus unlocks the meaning of the Old Testament, and if he is a "historical" key (see below), then the lock has also to be largely historical, too. For an extended summary of the historicity of the Pentateuch and the exodus, see John Bergsma and Brant Pitre, *A Catholic Introduction to the Bible: The Old Testament* (San Francisco, Calif.: Ignatius Press, 2018), 71–89 and 188–91.

2. See the Second Vatican Council, *Dei Verbum*, nos. 7–10, where the primacy of the church and its apostolic tradition relative to scripture are nicely asserted. In *Decrees* (ed. Tanner), 2:971–81.

sponding words and deeds of men,[3] there is also given a record both of the events in which revelation was given, and its content.

The antecedent probability of such a record is as high as that of the antecedent probability of a revelation and a church. Without such a record, it is unlikely that the content of the message of revelation can be credibly maintained through a long time that spans many generations. If the revelation is addressed to all men, however, we should expect it to take considerable time to reach all men, insofar as it will be conveyed to men by other men, by ways of human conveyance. And the revelation will be addressed to all men, because God is the creator of all men, and can be expected to want all men to be saved (1 Tm 2:4). Without a revelation accomplished in history, in words and deeds of which there are in principle many witnesses, and of which deeds and events there is also a written record, revelation ceases to be public and social and becomes gnostic and private, and its content reduces to a sort of series of sayings whose provenance is obscure and whose authority is therefore dubious. Public events, of course, are more credibly recordable than private deeds; that is, the authority of their witness is more apprehensible and more evidently worthy of trust.

If the antecedent probability of a divine revelation comes together with the antecedent probability of a written record both of the event and content of revelation, we should expect both the written record and its custodian, the church, to make express claims for the historical reliability of the record. This is bound up with the fact that the revelation whose antecedent probability we are contemplating will have to come to us *as* revelation.[4] Without our ability to come to a responsible judgment as to its reality and so its claim on us, it disappears as revelation; that is to say, it disappears as a revelation that is recognizable as such. But the historical credibility of the Gospels is a necessary condition of making such a judgment, of recognizing the revelation as real. We should thus expect providence to arrange the production of the New Testament such that we can trust it as reliable. Now in fact, in claiming to be the real fulfillment of the

---

3. *Dei Verbum*, no. 2.

4. This is, of course, just the claim John Henry Newman made for Christian revelation in *An Essay on the Development of Christian Doctrine* (Notre Dame, Ind.: University of Notre Dame Press, 1989 [1888]), 79–80.

idea of a church established by the events of revelation, the actual church claims also that we can come to this knowledge historically, according to the witness of the record of the culminating events of revelation, which record is the record of the New Testament.[5]

The Historical Credibility of the Gospels

We have therefore to ask with what warrants the New Testament writings, particularly the Gospels, claim to be historically credible. The story of Jesus of Nazareth, and especially for the purposes of this apologetic part of the book, the story of his foundation of the church, have to be credible stories, credible history. This historical credibility is also an object of faith, of course: a Christian's God-given faith in Jesus as the Son of God and redeemer redounds back onto or we might say simply includes the faith he has in the witness of the New Testament, and this faith supports and makes it easier to discern the natural, human faith everyone should have in the credibility of the Gospels. We are not claiming here to do a chemically pure apologetic argument. Nonetheless, it is readily to be seen that this historical credibility has to address reason itself. Just as it is an object of faith that the existence of God is *philosophically* knowable, for otherwise faith responding to revelation would be unreasonable, so it is also an object of faith that the credibility of the New Testament is *historically* knowable (that is, knowable to reason when we are thinking historically), for otherwise and similarly, faith responding to revelation would be unreasonable.[6]

Now it is generally assumed by many people today that the warrants of the Gospels to be historically credible are pretty slim, not to say nonexistent. Slightly educated people think they know enough to suppose that, as literary works, the Gospels are late relative to living memories of Jesus of Nazareth, which is to say, they are, at the very least, separated from the events they purport to speak of by a long and historically careless course of oral traditions, full of inventions for the differing needs of disparate

5. *Dei Verbum*, nos. 18–19; see also the Pontifical Biblical Commission's *Sancta Mater Ecclesia*, April 21, 1964; available at www.vatican.va.

6. See John Paul II, *Fides et Ratio*, par. 67, on the necessity for faith of the possibility of a rational demonstration of the existence of God.

Christian communities. Anonymous works, remotely related to the life of Jesus, and bent to the authors' various theological purposes, which it is supposed may sit very loose to history, the Gospels are to be approached with suspicion. No single verse can be given historical credence as to what it reports as said or recounts as done unless it is corroborated by some other witness.

This assessment of the Gospels, a presupposition of what is called "form criticism," is false, and it therefore offers a thoroughly misleading approach to them.[7] In the first place, the nature of the Christian confession made Christians indefatigably and we might say obsessively interested in the history of Jesus. There were two reasons for this. First, they thought their salvation and their eternal destiny depended on the news Jesus actually preached, the moral instruction he truly delivered, and the factual, historical events of Jesus' life—his passion, his death, and his resurrection. Let us bracket the resurrection for a moment. The news Jesus announced pretended to be the final news from the God of creation and the covenants. The moral instruction depicted a way of life that was commensurate with this final news. And the death of Jesus, bloody and ugly and "historical" as it was, was *theologically* laden for Christians. It was the sacrifice of the last and eternal covenant. It was expiation for sin. Its sacrament, celebrated in the church from its first days (Acts 2:42), made for communion with God in Christ. They could therefore not be indifferent to its actual facticity. So, the actions of all the players surrounding that death, all their motives and interactions, all the things that give historical depth and density to the accounts we have in the Gospels, were of interest to the first Christians.[8]

A second reason for their interest in the history of Jesus was that the identity of Jesus was something known, not just by his bare claim to be

7. For an introduction to contemporary biblical criticism with attention to form criticism and Rudolph Bultmann, see John Barton, "Biblical Studies," in *The Blackwell Companion to Modern Theology*, ed. Gareth Jones (Oxford: Blackwell, 2007), 18–33. See also the thoughtful but quite critical essay of Pierre Benoît, OP, "Reflections on 'Formgeschichtliche Methode,'" in *Jesus and the Gospel*, trans. Benet Weatherhead (New York: Herder and Herder, 1973), 1:11–45, especially on the method's presupposition of the disappearance of eyewitnesses to the career of Jesus and on the "creative power" of the community it alleges (36–38). Note that this essay first appeared in French in 1946.

8. See Ben F. Meyer's argument for the expectation of the historicity of the Gospels in his *The Aims of Jesus* (London: SCM Press, 1979), chap. 3, summarized on 72.

the Messiah or Son of God, or divine Wisdom, but was something known by how his actions and the events of his life matched up with prior Old Testament prophecy and history. The first Christians were alert, and according to the nature of their faith in Jesus, had to be alert, to the details of his history that made it evident for them that it was in the line of the Old Testament, considered both as a story in which the future was prefigured, and in line with the Old Testament's promises and prophecies. The events of Jesus' life either matched—could be seen as matching—or they did not. But for the argument for his identity to be made in this way, these details—such things as his presenting himself as the eschatological and messianic herald (see Lk 4:16–24 and Is 61:1–2) or riding on the foal of an ass (Mt 21:1–6 and Zec 9:9), or such things as were done to him, as with the opening of his side on the cross (Jn 19:34–37 and Zec 12:10)— had at least to be accurately remembered. The first Christians were supremely interested in the history of Jesus, and would be uninterested in any account of the life of Jesus which was not. That is to say, they would be supremely uninterested in the Gospels such as form critics understand them. If early Christians cooperated in the project of adjusting the story of Jesus to local and immediate community concern, they would have known themselves to be guilty of obscuring saving knowledge.

In the second place, then, assessing the historical credibility of the Gospels depends on what one makes of the fidelity and purposes of the oral tradition of the stories and words of Jesus. Some role for oral tradition is acknowledged by all the critics. But was such tradition informal and uncontrolled, as the founders of form criticism supposed? Or was it more formal, more studied, where those who learned could be recognized as having truly learned by those who taught, and was it controlled by efforts at memorization?[9] Beyond such evidence as we have for oral traditions that are controlled and formal, much depends on what one supposes the tradition aimed at. Were the stories about Jesus a kind of clay that

---

9. For an introduction to the issues, see Jan Vansina, *Oral Tradition as History* (Madison: University of Wisconsin Press, 1985); see also the discussion in Birger Gerhardsson, a critic of form criticism, in *The Reliability of the Gospel Tradition* (Peabody, Mass.: Hendrickson, 2001), 9–14 on oral tradition, and 29 for criticism of Bultmann. See also Richard Bauckham, *Jesus and the Eyewitnesses: The Gospels as Eyewitness Testimony* (Grand Rapids, Mich.: Eerdmans, 2006), chaps. 10, 12, and 13, and the discussion of Mats Wahlberg, *Revelation as Testimony: A Philosophical-Theological Study* (Grand Rapids, Mich.: Eerdmans, 2014), 177–79.

could be molded to suit a variety of not always coordinated community concerns? Or were the stories important just as stories bearing on what Jesus said and did, and just because of the saving significance of the actual, factual Jesus?

In the third place, the Gospels are recognizably instances of the ancient *bioi* ("lives"), the genre that most closely approximates contemporary biography, and like contemporary biography is hospitable to and even insistent on eyewitness testimony.[10] This genre, moreover, wanted eyewitness testimony from those who participated in the very events and their aftermaths in question.[11] Now in fact, the Gospels present themselves as either written by eyewitnesses (Matthew and John), very much involved in the events, or written by those with access to eyewitness testimony (Mark and Luke), very much interested in the events.[12] John and Luke wear this concern for eyewitness testimony up front, as it were, on their title pages (Lk 1; Jn 1—"we have seen his glory"; and Jn 19:35 and 21:24).

In the fourth place, and corroborating the concern for eyewitness testimony—eyewitnesses, therefore, who would have to be named—the Gospels never circulated anonymously. They were always and from the beginning of their reception by their readers tied to the four names—Matthew, Mark, Luke, and John. There just is no evidence of their anonymous circulation.[13] Moreover, if they *had* circulated anonymously, as already intimated, they would have been useless to the very readers they were written for, who would have had no reason to keep and copy them. The historical interest of Christians demanded, so to speak, that the chain of custody of the eyewitness accounts be public, and something known. No Gospel was historically and thus *theologically* useful if it was an unknown production. Furthermore, if the Gospels had circulated anonymously and were only later dignified with authoritative credentials, we should not expect the church to assign two of them—Mark and Luke—to men who do not show up in the Gospel narratives. Last, we should expect different

10. Richard Burridge, *What Are the Gospels? A Comparison with Graeco-Roman Biography* (Cambridge: Cambridge University Press, 1992).

11. Wahlberg, *Revelation as Testimony*, 180, and his discussion of Byrskog.

12. For Mark, see Bauckham, *Jesus and the Eyewitnesses*, chaps. 7 and 9.

13. Brant Pitre, *The Case for Jesus: The Biblical and Historical Evidence for Christ* (New York: Image, 2016), chap. 2.

attributions for the same book, for which there is no evidence.[14] There are also the testimony of Papias to the authenticity of the names that accompany the Gospels and the tradition according to which Mark was the mouthpiece of Peter.[15]

The upshot of such considerations as the forgoing is that the credentials of the Gospels to be taken as reporting things fair and square are strong. This holds also for the historicity of two crucial things, Jesus' claim that he is the divine Son of God, and the confirmation of this claim that his resurrection makes.

Jesus' Claim about Himself

Jesus' claim about himself is pervasive in what is reported of his teachings and deeds in the Gospels; it is pervasive in the authority with which he does everything he does. He preaches authoritatively, peremptorily demanding faith in what he says (Mk 1:15); he teaches authoritatively, to the astonishment of the crowd (Mt 7:28–29); he interprets scripture authoritatively (Lk 4:21 and Mt 22:29); he heals and exorcizes with a word of command, which is to say, with authority (Mt 4:36; 8:15).

He makes plain the ground of his authority. He presents himself fairly directly as the messianic heir of David and the servant of the Lord in the synagogue at Nazareth when he applies Isaiah 61:1–2 to himself (Lk 4:16–21; Is 42:1). More indirectly, he discloses his identity as the Wisdom and Word of God when he tells the crowd that with him, something greater than Solomon and the prophets is present (Lk 7:35, 11:29–32). He does this again when he says that he "knows" the Father just as the Father "knows" him, the Son (Mt 11:25–27). More directly, he tells us who he is in the parable of the vineyard—no prophet or servant, but the very Son of the owner of the vineyard (Mt 21:33–43; Is 5:7). To the pious in John's Gospel, he says that Abraham rejoiced to see his day, and that "before Abraham was, I am" (Jn 8:56, 58).

This claim about himself, which Jesus made in the many ways provid-

14. For these arguments, see Martin Hengel, "The Titles of the Gospels and the Gospel of Mark," in *Studies in the Gospel of Mark*, trans. John Bowden (Philadelphia: Fortress Press, 1985), 64–84.

15. For Papias, one can begin with chap. 2 of Bauckham's *Jesus and the Eyewitnesses*.

ed for by the Old Testament, the church later summarized in the teaching of the Councils of Nicaea, Ephesus, and Chalcedon. According to this teaching, the one person acting in Jesus is the Son of God, the second Person of the Trinity, the Word of which John speaks in the first chapter of his Gospel. This one Person is truly divine, with the same divinity verified in the Father and Spirit. But because of the incarnation ("enfleshment"), because of the humanity he takes up in the womb of Mary, this one Person is also human. So Jesus is one person existing in two natures, human and divine. The natures designate the *ways* in which the Son of God exists, in a human way and a divine way; but "person" designates *what* exists. As another word for person is "hypostasis," the union of the natures is a "hypostatic union"—that is the way the Councils of Ephesus (332) and Chalcedon (451) and the Second Council of Constantinople (553) give us to speak. Just because there is only one person in Christ, you can say that Jesus created the world—as God, not as man. And you can say that the divine Word died—as human, not as divine.

Before we leave this section, it is important to realize that people believed in Jesus before his resurrection. Peter, speaking for the Twelve, confesses him to be the Son of God (Mt 16:16) and the holy one of God (Jn 6:69). This is not simply because of his miracles, as when the man born blind, now sighted, worships him (Jn 9:38), or even because, when he heals the paralytic, it is in evidence that the Son of Man, himself, has the power to forgive sins, a divine work (Mk 2:10). It is also in virtue of the great charity with which he heals people: he wants to help the man born blind and the paralytic, and the lepers and the lame. And his charity is instant, showing in his immediate compassion (Mk 1:41; 3:3, 5). His teaching, too, is a work of love, a work of charity which his joy manifests at several places: his joyful triumph when he identifies himself for his people as the Messiah in the synagogue at Nazareth, the one who can set captives free (Lk 4:18, 21); his joy when he reveals the Trinity to little ones (Lk 10:21–22). It should be remembered that Jesus was a popular man; great crowds of people followed him and wanted to be with him (e.g., Mt 8:1, 9:36). He was a man of authority who could help them by word and deed; he wanted to help them because he loved them; and he was a joyful man and glad to be with people he could help. That is a powerful combination.

It is his authority and his charity together that make him the convincing figure he is in his teaching, in his forgiving sins, in his miracles, in his dying for us. Still today, many readers of Matthew or Mark or Luke or John are convinced long before they come to the last chapters of these Gospels, to which now we turn.

The Historical Credibility of Jesus' Resurrection

The New Testament provides testimony both as to the appearances of the risen Jesus to his disciples and as to the emptiness of his tomb on the third day after his death and burial. These testimonies can be recognized in their probative character if framed by the realization that between the death of Jesus and the evangelizing activity of the apostles and disciples, announcing that the one crucified for human sins was raised to life by the power of God, something big and extraordinary had to have happened. What could it have been? There is no good explanation for why the first disciples said what they said about Jesus and his life and resurrection except that he really did claim to be the Son of God, and his claim about his person was vindicated by an event bearing on his person, namely his resurrection.

What are the alternatives to his resurrection? The appearances of the risen Jesus to the disciples were hallucinations? Hallucinations that involved more than one person at a time? Not especially plausible psychologically. That the disciples dissembled and fabricated a story so that … so that what? It is hard to supply a plausible morally convincing motive. So that they could become rich and powerful? Except that none of them did. Nor is it easy to think they could think that.

As to the reports of the empty tomb, in getting rid of them, it is easier to suppose a naturalistic explanation for them than for the appearances. Did the women get mixed up as to where the tomb was located? And the disciples share their confusion? Or did someone steal the body? Their motivation for doing so would be … what? To sow confusion in Jerusalem? To make it possible so to preach a risen Lord, so that the impostors would … become rich and powerful?

A check on hypotheses explaining either the reports of the appearances or of the empty tomb is that those who reported them subsequently died martyrs' deaths. A "martyr," of course, is a witness. If the first martyrs, who knew Jesus in the flesh and knew of his death, are false witnesses of his resurrection, and were self-consciously false witnesses, we have to have some commensurable good for which they would give such witness at the price of their blood. Of course, taking things the other way around, it is easy to find the commensurable good for which they would lay down their lives for the truth of the resurrection. Eternal life and the perfect and inexhaustible enjoyment of God's goodness and truth in a risen body like unto Christ's—that would be a commensurable good.

Another check on naturalistic hypotheses explaining both the reports of the appearances and the reports of the empty tomb is that they will necessarily be unrelated to one another. Hallucinations of a risen Christ do not explain why the tomb was reported to be empty. And mistaking the location of the tomb and supposing it empty does not explain why that would induce a false vision of a risen Jesus. In this way, as N. T. Wright has pointed out, naturalistic explanations of why the first disciples believed Christ to be raised in glory are more complicated, and to that extent less plausible, and so more unbelievable, than that they reported him raised from the dead because he was raised from the dead.[16]

Conclusion

If the above arguments have any merit, then the Gospels are restored to our appreciation as what they really are, ensembles of testimony. For many modern critics, the formation and content of the Gospels present a vast constellation of evidences, of clues, as to what Jesus said and did, and what was done to him, that call for a patient sifting of now one hypothesis and now another. We are to treat them as collections of material such as a crime scene investigator might face. He has no antecedent trust in what any alleged witness says. He looks first of all to what cannot lie—the position of the body, the entry wound, the time of death. And in this way, none of the voices that meet us in the Gospels is taken at face value—that is, at personal value, at the value we would impute both to a person and

16. N. T. Wright, *The Resurrection of the Son of God* (Minneapolis, Minn.: Fortress Press, 2003), 686–88.

to what he is telling us when he testifies to us.[17] To the contrary, when we read the Gospels we hear voices that urgently bid us to pay attention to what they say, and to trust what they say, so that we may believe Jesus is the Christ, the Son of God, and that we may have life in his name (Jn 20:31). Now, what do they say also about the foundation of the church?

17. Wahlberg, *Revelation as Testimony*, 172–82.

CHAPTER 3

JESUS' FOUNDATION
OF THE CHURCH

Confidence in the church's mediation of the truth and grace of Christ in her understanding of scripture and in her celebration of the sacraments depends first of all on confidence in the historical foundation of the church by Christ. If the acts and teachings and promises of Christ that envisage a people, a community, having his mind and moved with his power are appreciated simply in their positive character, in their givenness according to the testimony of the Gospels, then they give in their turn the lively sense that connection to the church is connection with Jesus of Nazareth both in his historical reality as reported by the Gospels and in his ascended reality now sitting at God's right hand. The people who called themselves the "church" in the first years after Christ's ascension certainly had this sense of things, and therefore a sense of themselves, precisely as something communal, as something social, as something intended by Jesus of Nazareth.

Is there an alternative to thinking that Jesus founded the church? What would the historical relation between them be? Many historians, exegetes, and theologians have thought that though the church is certainly the result of Jesus' ministry and mission, it was nonetheless not an intended result. Johannes Weiss (d. 1914) and Alfred Loisy (d. 1940) thought this. The church is therefore founded or instituted by the first disciples responding to and reacting to Christ once he is removed from them. A lot depends on this. Our confidence in having a real access to the truth and grace of Christ seems substantially to depend on whether or not we think that he founded the church, and precisely as something he intended and *empowered* to guard his teaching and offer his grace. If the church is simply the result of Christ's career, a mere reaction of men to that career, we shall have no confidence at all that we find his grace in the church or even his truth. And however one might negotiate questions about our access to Christ on the supposition that Jesus did not found the church in any strong sense, there is still more that depends on the question of foundation. If the church was really the invention of the first disciples, the question will arise as to why we may not reinvent the church for our own time and place. That is, the ordering and structure of the church will seem to be much more open to rearrangement, even radical rearrangement, on the supposition that the church is not Jesus' foundation but the disciples' construction in reaction to him. Of course, why we would bother about the church in the first place would be problematic on the view that it is a purely human construction.[1] But it is easy to see that contemporary pastoral and theological issues get bound up with the historical question of foundation.

Founding as Coterminous with Jesus' Mission

The foundation of the church is not really something *within* Christ's mission, but rather one way of naming his mission as a whole.[2] This becomes clear if we keep in mind the corporate object of Christ's preaching and action, the object of which is Israel.[3] To say that his mission is to gather Is-

---

1. Some people think we might suppose the Holy Spirit guards the church, even if Christ did not intend the church. But it is hard to have confidence in the presence of the Holy Spirit in the church unless Christ promised the Spirit. And if he promised the Spirit, then etc.

2. International Theological Commission, "The Consciousness of Christ concerning Himself and His Mission" (1985), in *International Theological Commission: Texts and Documents*, ed. Michael Sharkey (San Francisco, Calif.: Ignatius Press, 1989).

3. Meyer, *The Aims of Jesus*, chap. 7, and *The Church in Three Tenses* (New York: Doubleday, 1971).

rael for eschatological renewal and redemption (Lk 2:16–24) just is to say that his mission is to found the church.[4] That is what founding the church is, for she is nothing but the eschatological form of the pilgrim people of God. "Jesus is the eschatological shepherd, who gathers the lost sheep of the house of Israel and goes out in search of them, because he knows and loves them (Lk 15:4–7 and Mt 18:12–14)"; and Pope Benedict continues: "Through this 'gathering,' the Kingdom of God is proclaimed to all the nations."[5] A renewed Israel becomes the sign of salvation for all the nations.

Once it is realized that "founding the church" is a frame within which all the activity of Jesus can be compassed, then identifying discrete "founding" acts becomes both less urgent, apologetically, and at the same time easier. In this light, the whole Sermon on the Mount becomes a founding act; it is the provision of the eschatological people of God with an eschatological ethic.[6] It founds the church by providing the people of the church with the realization of divine blessedness within the pattern of the cross (the Beatitudes); it founds the church by radicalizing the terms of the Mosaic covenant, the Ten Commandments, on the basis of the availability of the grace of the cross. The Lord gives his people a distinctive way of prayer both as to attitude (Mt 6:5–7), even as to the very words to use (6:9–13).[7] So doing, he extends his own relation to God to his disciples. The provision of a group of men with a common and distinctive prayer, however, founds them as a religious community. It is a church-founding act. Further teaching, like the establishment of standards of community relations in the teachings on fraternal correction and the forgiveness of offences (Mt 18:15–17, 21–22), similarly add definition to the new community that is the church.

If the foundation of the church is simply coterminous with Jesus' mission, this means additionally that we cannot really have Jesus unless we have the church. This is an issue of contemporary relevance. "Christ, yes; the church, no," say those who want to tailor-make their own and individ-

4. Benedict XVI, "General Audience of March 15, 2006"; available at www.vatican.va.

5. "General Audience of March 22, 2006"; available at www.vatican.va.

6. Meyer, *Aims*, chap. 7.

7. Ratzinger, *Called to Communion: Understanding the Church Today*, trans. Adrian Walker (San Francisco, Calif.: Ignatius Press, 1996), 24; see the *Catechism of the Catholic Church*, 2nd ed. (Vatican City: Libreria Editrice Vaticana, 1997), no. 875.

ual form of Christian spirituality. A Christ apart from and separated from the church, however, did not exist historically, and, as we will see theologically in part 2, does not exist now.[8] There is to be discerned an identity of Christ and the church.[9] Within the encompassing mission of Christ to renew and restore Israel, four things in particular count as founding acts: Jesus' preaching of the nearness of the kingdom of God; the charge he gives to the apostles; his empowerment of the apostles with the Holy Spirit; and the institution of the Eucharist.

Preaching the Kingdom

If there is one thing we know Jesus did, it is that he preached the coming of, the nearness of, the kingdom of God (Mt 4:17). This is a church-founding act. The kingdom Jesus preaches evidently is inclusive of a people, and this people is anticipated in the church.[10] The church is not simply to be identified with the kingdom, therefore, but preaching it founds the church.[11] The church bears the kingdom within her to the extent she bears Christ within her. For in an important sense, the kingdom is Christ.[12] Insofar as she heralds Christ, therefore, she heralds the kingdom. But insofar as Christ heralded the kingdom, he heralded and founded the church.

When Jesus announces the nearness of the kingdom, he steps into the shoes of the herald of Isaiah 52:7:

> How beautiful upon the mountain
> are the feet of him who brings good tidings,
> who publishes peace, who brings good tidings ["gospel"] of good,
> who publishes salvation,
> who says to Sion, "Your God reigns."

---

8. See Benedict XVI, "General Audience of March 15, 2006," on the attempt to possess a Christ in a way contrary to Christ's own intentions.

9. Benedict XVI, "General Audience of November 22, 2006"; available at www.vatican.va.

10. Ratzinger, *Called to Communion*, 21–22.

11. On the relation of the kingdom and the community established by Jesus, the church, see Rudolf Schnackenburg, *God's Rule and Kingdom*, 2nd ed. (New York: Herder and Herder, 1968), chap. 17, esp. 230–32.

12. Joseph Ratzinger/Benedict XVI, *Jesus of Nazareth: From the Baptism in the Jordan to the Transfiguration*, trans. Adrian Walker (New York: Doubleday, 2007), 49.

It is clearer in Mark 1:15: "The time is fulfilled, and the kingdom of God is at hand." That is, the time for the herald to announce the kingdom is fulfilled. The herald, the one who brings the good news of the kingdom, is to start announcing it. In Isaiah 61:1, this herald is anointed with the Spirit of God, and is a messianic figure. The "good tidings" include the redemption of Israel (Is 40:1; 43:1), the new and final exodus from captivity to the land of promise (Is 40:3–5; 43:2), and the conversion of the nations, their acknowledgment of God (Is 60:3, 12), and even a new creation (Is 66:22).

The good tidings also include the advent of the kingdom of God ("Your God reigns"). How is this reign or rule of God to be characterized? Jesus' answer to the Baptist's embassy, asking whether he is the one to come, gives some signs characteristic of the kingdom. John's disciples are to say to him: "the blind receive their sight and the lame walk, lepers are cleansed and the deaf hear, and the dead are raised up, and the poor have the good news preached to them" (Mt 11:5). This conflation of Isaiah 29:18–19 (the deaf and the blind and the poor), 35:5–6 (the deaf and the blind, the dumb and the lame), and 61:1 (good tidings) is another, still indirect, claim to be the Messiah, and so to bring the kingdom. The kingdom does not come with signs and wonders (Lk 17:20). It is manifested in Jesus' healing of the sick and afflicted, undoing the burden of Adam; it is manifested in his forgiveness of sins and casting out of demons (Mk 2:5; Lk 11:20) and his table fellowship with sinners (Lk 7:13–14); it is manifested by the concern for service rather than status (Mk 10:45); it is manifested especially by Jesus' care for the poor and the outcasts and the marginalized.[13]

The bare announcement of the nearness of the kingdom does not of itself tell us how it will be perfectly established. That unfolds in Jesus' career, when we learn that to the witness of the herald of the kingdom there is to be joined the humiliation and exaltation of the Suffering Servant (Is 52:13–53:12; 50:6–9), who will in that way restore Israel (49:5–6) and bring justice to the nations (42:1, 49:6).

---

13. Richard Bauckham, *Jesus: A Very Short Introduction* (Oxford: Oxford University Press, 2011), 38; he emphasizes Jesus' concern for the poor and outcast on 40–42, 47–50, and 75–79. See also Meyer, *The Aims of Jesus*, 130–34. John Paul II picks up on this in his *Redemptoris Missio*, Encyclical Letter, December 7, 1990, par. 14; available at www.vatican.va.

In his preaching of the kingdom and in his subsequent humiliation, death, and resurrection, Jesus brings with him the very things that make God's rule present in history and for all the nations. Also, he promises to return and perfect his work at the end of the age (Mk 13:24–27). Between his first and second coming, he establishes a sort of sacrament of the kingdom, a sign and instrument of its secret presence but effective working, and that is the church.[14] Preaching the kingdom is therefore a church-founding act.

In the first place, both kingdom and church have a universal scope. The kingdom is the final ingathering of all nations, and the church has a universal mission. Second, Jesus' announcement of the kingdom is continued by the teaching of the church. Third, the signs of the incoming kingdom that Jesus gave us—healing and exorcism and the forgiveness of sins—are continued in the sacraments of the church. The kingdom is present in Jesus (Lk 17:20); he is himself the kingdom, as both its cause (efficient and meritorious) and in the exemplarity of his relationship to his Father.[15] But the head of the church is Christ, and thus the kingdom is present also in the church. It is not the church, but neither is it separate from the church; the church is both its sign and an instrument of its continuing arrival.[16] Thus *Lumen Gentium* teaches that the kingdom is the "goal" of the church (no. 9).[17] We have, after all, still to pray every day, "Thy Kingdom come." And again, "the Church, to which we are all called in Christ Jesus, and in which we acquire sanctity through the grace of God, will attain her full perfection only in the glory of heaven" (no. 48).

The Call and Charge of the Twelve

Three distinct moments of the call and charge of the apostles can be picked out: the call of the Twelve; the charge to Peter; the charge of the risen Jesus.

14. John Paul II, *Redemptoris Missio*, par. 20; Benedict XVI, "General Audience of March 15, 2006": "the Church has been made the sign and instrument of the Kingdom of God in our midst."

15. John Paul II, *Redemptoris Missio*, par. 13. The kingdom is both Christ and Christians; the church is both head and body.

16. Ibid., par. 20.

17. *Lumen Gentium* is the Second Vatican Council's Dogmatic Constitution on the Church of November 21, 1964, in *Decrees* (ed. Tanner), 2:849–900.

The Call of the Twelve

The call of the Twelve is itself part of the announcement of the kingdom: it represents the refounding and more perfect founding of the people of God, the fulfillment of the promise of an eschatological return to the original shape of Israel prophesied by Ezekiel (37:15–19; 39:23–29; 40–48).[18] The call of the Twelve is presented as a considered act with a well-defined purpose (Mk 3:13–15): Jesus prays about whom he will call (Lk 6:12); he calls whom he wills; those called are to be with him and to be sent out, even as he is with the Father always, and yet sent into the world. What Mark asserts of the Twelve relative to Jesus, John asserts of Jesus relative to his Father (Jn 7:28, 10:38, 16:32); and they are called to preach what he preached, to heal, and to reconcile (Mt 10:7–8, 13). In short, they are called to further his own mission. For the sake of analysis, one can pick out the following functions of the Twelve assigned within the time of the ministry of Jesus. First, their number makes them signify the fullness of the eschatological gathering of Israel set afoot by the Lord. Second, in the future kingdom, they are to judge the twelve tribes of Israel (Mt 19:28). Even before the passion and resurrection of Christ, third, they are to help effect the gathering of Israel by preaching the same message as that of the Lord, namely the nearness of the kingdom (see the missioning in, e.g., Mt 10:1–42; Mk 6:7–13, 30). Fourth, after the passion and resurrection of Christ, but signified prior to it, they are to bind and loose on earth in a way effective for heaven (Mt 18:18; 16:19).

The third and first functions work together: the Twelve are truly signs of a renewed Israel because they help bring about what they signify. Likewise, the second and fourth things work together. Luke 12:8 has it that only if one recognizes Jesus now, will he be recognized by the Lord in the eschaton. Only if one conforms to the earthly witness and teaching of the Twelve will he be acquitted at the judgment. The witness and preaching of the Twelve are even now authoritative and normative for heaven. The great historical plausibility of the saying in Luke 12:8 makes the establishment of the Twelve as eschatological judges also plausible. Relative to the teaching of both Christ and the apostles, eschatological fate depends on present faith.

18. See Benedict XVI, "General Audience of March 15, 2006."

The Charge to Peter

Within the commissioning of the Twelve, there is also the special commissioning of Peter. With the place of Peter, the founding of the church comes especially to light, and this is true both within the ministry of Jesus (Mt 16:18) and after the resurrection (Jn 21:15–17). Peter is given charge especially of the unity of the church both as spiritual communion and as social structure. This is conveyed not only in the saying that what he enacts on earth visibly and temporally is enacted also in heaven, spiritually and eschatologically, but in the very idea that he is a foundation-stone, or better, that his faith is the single, one, foundation-stone of what is one structure. What is built on Peter is what the Messiah was expected to build, namely, the new and eschatological temple of God. The eschatological and the institutional are therefore not to be played off against each other. The institution maintains the availability of eschatological grace for as many years as are included in that "hour" in which Christ works our salvation.[19]

The Charge of the Risen Lord

In addition, the risen Lord charges the apostles to preach and baptize (Mt 28:19), and as well to forgive sins (Jn 20:22–23). The resurrection in itself functions as a founding act in that it constitutes the Twelve as witnesses to the inauguration of the kingdom as already effected by Christ's redeeming passion, resurrection, and outpouring of the Holy Spirit. The church's subsequent sacramental practices of baptizing and forgiving sins enact the witness of the apostles to the resurrection of the one who died for the forgiveness of sins.

All these apostolic functions, established throughout the course of the Lord's mission and after his resurrection, render the ministry of the apostles "sacramental" in a quite determinate sense. On the basis of such texts as Matthew 10:40 and John 15:5, Ratzinger renders the self-understanding of the sacramental minister as follows: "Sacrament means: I give what I myself cannot give; I do something that is not my work; I am on a

---

19. See Hans Urs von Balthasar, *Theo-Drama: Theological Dramatic Theory*, vol. III: *Dramatis Personae: Persons in Christ*, trans. Graham Harrison (San Francisco, Calif.: Ignatius Press, 1992), 93–101 and 109–22.

mission and have become the bearer of that which another has committed to my charge."[20] Or we could say with scholastic precision, as teachers they are *second* causes, repeating what they have heard, and as givers of grace they are *instrumental* causes.

Above, it was noted that the Twelve have the same relation to Jesus as does Jesus to the Father, the relation of being sent. This is further specified in John, when the Lord tells the disciples that he sends them as he has been sent (Jn 17:18; 20:21). This means that, just as Jesus was sent with the power to send, so he sends them with a like power to send. Thus, these sayings in John's Gospel envisage a time for the church after the death of the last apostle (Jn 21:21). We see within the New Testament, especially but not exclusively in the pastoral epistles of St. Paul, that this time after the death of the last apostle is provided for by the appointment of successors.

The Promise and Sending of the Spirit

Jesus promises to send the Spirit in John 7:37–39. This is a promise to give the Spirit to everyone who believes in him. He promises also after the resurrection in Acts 1:8. The gift of the Spirit after the resurrection, however, is hierarchically, that is, "institutionally" structured. The promise and the gift are thus very evidently acts by which Jesus founds the church. In John 20:22, Jesus breathes on the disciples, the eleven remaining apostles, and imparts the Holy Spirit to them for the forgiveness of sins. In Acts 2:2–3, the Spirit comes with a great wind, and settles on the now full company of the Twelve in tongues of fire. Thence the apostles give the gift to others (e.g., Acts 8:17). According to St. Thomas, the breath signifies the power to sanctify, and the tongues signify the power to teach truly and faithfully.[21] This gift fulfills the promise made in Joel for an eschatological outpouring of the Spirit (2:28–29). It makes of the church herself a sort of full and perfect sacrament: she is no empty sign of holiness and sanctification, but possesses what she signifies.

---

20. Ratzinger, *Called to Communion*, 113.
21. *ST* I, q. 43, a. 7, ad 6.

The Institution of the Eucharist

Equally striking as a founding action is the institution of the Eucharist. As the church as a whole replaces the temple, as we will see in more detail in part 2, so the Last Supper replaces the action of sacrifice within the temple.[22] The Last Supper showed forth the meaning of the saving sacrifice of Christ in anticipation as the sacrifice of a new and eternal covenant by which the church lives and gives fitting worship to God, fulfilling Jeremiah 31:31. The Eucharist, instituted by the command, "Do this," continues to make present Calvary's fulfillment of all sacrifices and in this way brings to fulfillment the chief public institution of the old alliance, namely the temple, as the place of atonement.

The institution of the Eucharist on the night before his death as a rejected Messiah evidently foresees the institution of a new Israel distinct from the Israel that does not believe Jesus is the Christ. The vineyard will be given to other tenants who will give its produce to the master when he calls for it (Mt 21:33–46).[23]

Faith and History

To trust the New Testament account of Christ's foundation of the church is, of course, to trust the church's own account of her beginnings and mission. However, if the New Testament is not to be trusted *in globo* as to the facts of the founding, then neither is it to be trusted on anything else. Such things as the choice of the Twelve, the institution of the Eucharist, the missionary sendings, the position of Peter, the cleansing of the temple, and the claim to be the fulfillment of the prior Testament in both word and sacrament are so pervasive in the Gospels that, if one gets rid of them, there is small reason to trust the little that remains as having any evidentiary value on its own for the reconstruction of the first century after Christ.

Having faith and thinking that the New Testament tells us more or less straightforwardly what happened go together. Without faith, then of course we will suppose whatever happened did not happen as reported.

22. See N. T. Wright, *The Challenge of Jesus* (Downers Grove, Ill.: InterVarsity Press, 1999), 83–84 and 111–14.

23. Where "foundation" is taken to include the anticipation of division, of a community separate from a Jewish remainder, then Jesus' institution of the Eucharist, in the context of the knowledge of his rejection by the Jewish establishment, sufficiently shows such an anticipation.

For everything as reported depends on the belief of those reporting that Jesus of Nazareth rose from the dead and was alive again in his body. So, without that faith, pretty much every account of what happened, both in his life and after his death, must be thought to be tainted. If that is the case, an important piece of human history, the origin of Christianity, turns into a sort of black hole. You can fall into it. But you will not get out with a plausible *historical* account of the origin of the church. The only plausible account is the church's own account in her reading of the New Testament.

Moreover, the church *needs* an historical explanation. The best explanation is that Christ rose from the dead, as noted in chapter 2. Unless a dogmatic commitment to positivism prevents one from embracing that explanation, then it turns out that history and historical reason are more hospitable to faith than the Enlightenment was willing to grant. Just as grace presumes, heals, and elevates nature, according to the old axiom, so faith presupposes, heals, and elevates reason in its historical deployment.

Institution and Mystery

As an institution or society, the church has been appreciated in classical political categories as a "perfect society." As a society the church is in a way as visible and as palpable as the Kingdom of France or the Republic of Venice, as Robert Bellarmine put it in the sixteenth century. Moreover, as a perfect society, she has within herself everything it takes to realize her end relative, not indeed to God, but to every other such visible and palpable and "historically available" entity of the *saeculum*, and depends upon them in no way for anything that is essential to her. From this follows the political freedom of the church. It is by divine right that the church possesses her mandate to preach and sanctify, and she needs the permission of no earthly kingdom or state to prosecute her mission. Rather, no attempt of the state to subjugate or control the church can be legitimate. We will return to this important issue in the final chapter below.

Should the church as an institution and so as "instituted" or "founded" be the first thing that comes to our mind when we think of the church? Commensurate with the witness of the fathers, Henri de Lubac says it is better to speak of the birth of the church rather than of her institution or foundation, because only the former connotes the personal character of the church's reality, her character as "Mother Church."[24] He points here to an important truth when the church is appreciated in a fully theological way. But it is necessary even so to express the church as instituted and as an institution in order to make good the public availability of the grace and truth of Christ in her (*Lumen Gentium*, no. 8).[25] "Institution," moreover, connotes the abiding character of the church as a political reality, as something that occupies political space.

Although the church is more than an institution, she is at least an institution, and subsists and has subsisted with the original shape, structure, and mission given to her by her founder since the time of her founding. The "more" that she is a matter of supernatural grace and the divine indwelling and therefore a matter of mystery. The church abides as an institution but lives by grace from above. On the other hand, the channels of this grace are historically—and thus "institutionally"—continuous. She is not created episodically by a grace from above that is intermittent. The church is the lake connected to the spring, not the pond filled by the summer rain.[26]

The abiding character of the church follows from the description of the church as the new temple, built on the faith of Peter. For in the nature of things, buildings are something permanent, and the messianic temple is everlasting. Further, just as there is no body without a head, so neither can the head be without his body. If the Christ who is the head abides, therefore, so does the body. And Christ's faithfulness to his bride ensures that his bride always remains for him to be faithful to.

The body of Christ and his bride, the eternal church is at one and the same time the institutional church, the establishment of which can be found in every diocese and indeed, in every local parish. Abiding as a people, the church abides as a visible society, to be sure, but not all of her gifts and endowments are equally visible to the eyes of the flesh. The church, then, is the institution of the mystery of grace, the mystery of grace in institutional form.

---

24. Henri de Lubac, SJ, *The Motherhood of the Church*, trans. Sister Sergia Englund, OCD (San Francisco, Calif.: Ignatius Press, 1982), 16–20; see 153–68.

25. See also Pius XII, *Mystici Corporis*, Encyclical Letter, June 29, 1943, par. 64; available at www.vatican.va.

26. For this way of contrasting the Catholic and Protestant sense of things, see Yves Congar, OP, *Christ, Our Lady and the Church*, trans. Henry St. John, OP (Westminster, Md.: Newman Press, 1957), 31–35. Remember the water that flows down from the temple in Ezekiel.

PART 2

ECCLESIOLOGY
DOGMATIC

CHAPTER 4

THE WAYS OF CATHOLIC DOGMATIC THEOLOGY

Just because ecclesiology aims at a true understanding of the church, it shares the general presuppositions of theology as a whole. The goal of this second part of the book is to gather up what Catholic Christians must confess as *true* about the church. (Attempting to come to some *understanding* of these truths is for part 3.) Many of those presuppositions, as immediately focused for getting at what is true about the *church*, are summed up in the following large sentence—a big breath for expressing one big compound-complex idea. This big breath, however, will also and at the same time provide a summary anticipation of where we are headed in part 2.

Cognitive access to the reality of the church is available to us in the words of the New Testament that truly express her relation to Christ, his Spirit, and his Father, because she is founded on and founded by Christ and is his body and bride and is the temple of the Spirit and is the people of God, but only where those words of the New Testament and their Old Testament background are read within the framework of the church's tradition, especially the creed and the Church Fathers, and according to the dogmatically normative statements delivered to us by the church herself, by means of pope or council, and where all the statements of scripture, tradition, and the magisterium (popes and councils) are received as true on our part by divine and Catholic faith.[1]

The parts of this sentence can be unpacked as follows.

"Cognitive Access"

There may be such a thing as an experiential access, an affective access, a practical access to the church, but ecclesiology is part of theology, theology is sacred doctrine, and doctrine alone, in whatever form it takes (in the New Testament, in conciliar canons, patristic commentary on scripture, papal encyclicals, the catechism, sermons, etc.) gives the mind access to the church. We might be said to have "experiential access" to the church in that we are practicing Catholics, or even merely in that the church is a part of our social environment. In this second way, we might collect such data on the church as to produce a sociological study of the church or some small part of it or aspect of it. None of that would be theology. In the first way, our individual experience of the church would not give us the kind of cognitive access to the church that we want. Ecclesial reality is a part of revealed reality. Access to that reality is in the fonts of revelation, for which see below. Of course, our immediate experience of the church would be essential to understanding closely and fully what the fonts tell us about the church.

We might be said to have "affective access" to the church insofar as we love the church. Insofar as we greatly love the church, we may have a way immediately to measure what people say about the church, because love conforms the lover to the beloved.[2] And then we could measure what people say as congruent or not with our own sense of ourselves as Cath-

---

1. The understanding of many of the topics listed here insofar as they touch on the cognitive objectivity of revelation, the dependence of revelation on human language and on propositionally formulated knowledge, the location of revelation in Scripture and tradition and its capacity to be articulated in creed and dogma, is developed in what is called "fundamental theology"—fundamental because dealing with the foundations of theology. Many of these same topics, including especially the relation of the Old and New Testaments, are also dealt with in what is sometimes called a theology of revelation.

2. Aquinas, *ST* I-II, q. 28, a. 1, ad 2, and a. 2.

olics. St. Thomas calls this kind of knowledge "connatural knowledge." It is the knowledge of some object one has by being like the object, conformed to the object. This kind of knowledge is obviously dependent on faith.[3] That is to say, affective access presupposes cognitive access: knowledge of the beloved is presupposed to loving the beloved—*nihil amatum nisi praecognitum.*

We might be said to have "practical access" to the church by way of sharing in the church's worship of God and by way of our practicing the corporal and spiritual works of mercy and, in general, by observing the second of the two great commandments. Practical access of this sort presupposes affective access and obedience to the first of the two great commandments. Practical access adds to affective access in that it builds up the connatural knowledge of the church that affective access brings with it by building it into our imaginations and bodies.

The cognitive access first mediated to us in doctrine may also be embedded in art, architecture, and music. But doctrine is primary.

"The Reality of the Church"

The reality that is the object of our discourse, the thing to be understood and known, is the church, and not the history of Christian thinking about the church, or even what some New Testament writer thought about the church, or what some pope or council thought about the church. Of course, what some pope or council or New Testament writer taught about the church will, for anyone who is a Catholic, be normative and inform us how to think truly about ecclesial reality. We are interested in them just because we suppose they will tell us truly about the church.

---

3. See, e.g., Aquinas, *ST* II-II, q. 45, a. 2. See the discussion of Jacques Maritain, *The Degrees of Knowledge*, trans. Gerald B. Phelan (New York: Charles Scribner's Sons, 1959), 254–65.

"The Words of the New Testament"

First, Words

The meaning or intelligibility of any reality comes to us formally and fully in words and only in words. Experience, whether sensory experience or the borrowed experience we can have in other peoples' reports of what they see and hear, may contain the potential meaning of the things of this world. But the meaning is not actually possessed by us until we can speak it. This is true of the church, too. Cognitive access to the church comes to us first of all in the words of doctrine.

The words that deliver the meaning of the things of the world to us do so formally only once they are arranged so as to express a proposition. A proposition is a possible judgment whose actuality consists in asserting or denying some predicate of some subject. In the proposition, some reality is intended and grasped as it is in itself, independently of the knower and his act of knowing (or any other of his acts). The subject of the proposition fixes the reality we are concerned about. And the predicate illuminates it, brings some part or aspect of it to light. Nothing is known as it is in itself by a human being without the judgment that produces a proposition. Propositions are expressed in declarative sentences, and a proposition may be understood as a rule for the formation of the declarative sentences that express it.[4]

If the church is to be known by us, we *must* rely on judgment to mediate her reality and meaning to us. For although the members of the church are sensibly available to us in their bodiliness, what makes them members of the church, their faith and charity, their living relations to the Persons of the Trinity, is not touchable or seeable by us. Remember St. Paul's *fides ex auditu* (Rom 10:17): "how are they to believe in him of whom they have never heard?" (10:14). And the hearing is the hearing of *language*, the speech that retells the narrative of the Gospel, that repeats the teaching of Christ.

It is especially important to be clear about this today, when concern for one's "spirituality" has for many people come to displace their alle-

---

4. For which see Robert Sokolowski, *Presence and Absence: A Philosophical Investigation of Language and Being* (Bloomington: Indiana University Press, 1978), chap. 9.

giance to Christianity. People speak of their "experience" of God, and for residual Christians, of their "experience" of Christ. It is hard to know what they mean. But often it boils down to meaning whatever they want it to mean, so as to gratify their desire to be religiously special and independent in some way or other, and especially so as to give them permission to continue to make up their own moral rules.

But this book is for Catholics. Whatever "experience" of God and Christ and the church we may have in prayer, in sacrament, or in obedience to the commandments and in which experience we can be said to know the reality of the church, it is not an experience independent of propositionally delivered knowledge. "Religious experience" of God or Christ or the church, or "the experience of God and Christ and the church in prayer"—if this names anything real, therefore, it names a *taught* experience. That is, it is an experience *informed* by scripture, creed, spiritual direction, reading, etc., all of which teaches us to name and understand and judge what it is we experience in prayer, sacrament, community, and without which we would not be able to name and understand and judge what it is we experience in directing our mind to God. Suppose, for instance, that we receive some consolation of the Spirit in prayer. How do we know of the Spirit, except from having been taught the doctrine of the Trinity? How do we know that the Holy Spirit is especially the Consoler? What, after all, do spiritual directors mean by *discernment*? The criteria of discernment are received from scripture and tradition (e.g., the rules of St. Ignatius). "Religious experience," therefore, does not stand on its own and does not of itself declare its meaning and value apart from the meaning mediated by Christian discourse. The experience of holy realities in prayer, we may say, requires verification, and this verification is provided by its conformity to tradition and by its fruits.

Second, the New Testament

It is not just because part of the reality of the church is unseen that we rely exclusively on words to come to know it. The fundamental reality of the church is a supernatural reality. Coming to know it is therefore not like a scientist's coming to know, say, micro-entities (quarks and photons and such) by some inference from the data of our senses. The fundamental reality of the church is a supernatural reality whose being and nature depends on the disposition of divine wisdom. Therefore, in coming to know it we rely on the word of God, the word of revelation. This word is recorded in scripture.

The Old Testament provides an indispensable framework for understanding the New, for "the end of the law is Christ" (Rom 10:4): its *telos* is Christ, the *telos* of its meaning is Christ. This is to say that the literal sense of the Old is oriented to its Christological, figurative sense as to its perfection. Without the Old Testament, furthermore, Christ and his church are incomprehensible to us. The figures, institutions, narratives, meditations, praise, and worship recorded in the Old Testament are a sort of a grammar and vocabulary in which the meaning of Jesus is already adumbrated, a sort of lock to which Christ is the key.[5]

It is the New Testament, however, where the revelation of God concerning the church is completed. The New Testament is a composition of the first recipients of and witnesses to the revelation made in and by Christ. The authority of the New Testament rests on the double fact that (1) it is a composition deriving from the first historical witnesses to Christ, the first Christians, the first church, who saw and heard and touched what they spoke of; thus, its authority is "apostolic" (see *Dei Verbum*, nos. 7 and 17–20). In addition, (2) it is a composition guaranteed by reason of the Holy Spirit whom the church recognizes as guiding and assisting its composition (*Dei Verbum*, nos. 7, 11), such that God can be said to be the "principal author" of scripture.[6]

"Words That Truly Express"

It is also necessary to say something about what it means to say that a proposition is "true." We mean true by correspondence, not by coherence or because the proposition insofar as it directs action "works." A judgment, a proposition such as "the cat is on the mat," is true if the cat is on the mat; it is false if the cat is not on the mat. Thus, "true" means *adequa-*

5. For the relation of the Old to the New Testament and the Christological meaning of the Old Testament, see Benedict XVI, *Verbum Domini*, Apostolic Exhortation, September 30, 2010 (Vatican City: Libreria Editrice Vaticana, 2010), pars. 37–41.

6. On the theology of inspiration, see Denis Farkasfalvy, O. Cist., *Inspiration and Interpretation: A Theological Introduction to Sacred Scripture* (Washington, D.C.: The Catholic University of America Press, 2010), 211–21.

tio mentis ad rem—correspondence or adequation or agreement of mind and thing.

Truth as "correspondence" is the ordinary sense of "true," even if it is not the original sense of "true," which according to Martin Heidegger is that of "un-concealment," where some reality discloses its intelligibility to us. To claim that a proposition is true is in a certain way to attain to something timeless. True propositions, true judgments, are timelessly true: if the cat is on the mat now, it will be forever true that at such a time on such and such a date the cat was on the mat: the state of affairs captured by the proposition is time-relative, for cats and mats and their relation to one another are timed things. But the truth of the proposition is not similarly time-relative. If true, it is always true. Thus, if the Church Fathers truly affirmed that belonging to the church in some way is necessary for salvation, then the affirmation is true today as well. We ought not say: "It was true for them, but as for us, etc." This latter position embraces the doctrinal relativism of Catholic Modernism.[7]

On the other hand, though timelessly true, there may be a history to the discovery of propositions and to the formulation of the understandings they express. In this sense, there is indeed a "historicity of truth": the concepts of which the proposition is composed may be more or less relative to some determinate way of understanding things, a way that may be hard to think ourselves into today, a way that may not serve our own insights very well, a way, certainly, that may be incomplete. Thus, not every true proposition, notwithstanding the timelessness of truth, is a "timely" truth for us. Not to take account of the "time-transcending" or "absolute" character of truth is to be committed to some form of what is called "historicism," a species of relativism. Not to take account of the historicity of truth in the above sense invites an abstract and sometimes anachronistic reading of tradition, such as can be found in some nineteenth- and twentieth-century Neo-scholastics.[8]

7. For this rather Modernist sense of "true," true back then but not now, see Eugène Portalié, "Dogma and History," part 3 of "Autour des fondements de la foi" (1904), in *Defending the Faith: An Anti-Modernist Anthology*, ed. and trans. William H. Marshner (Washington, D.C.: The Catholic University of America Press, 2017), 121–85, esp. 152 and 165.

8. For authoritative engagements with the historicity of doctrine, see the letter of the Congregation for the Doctrine of the Faith, *Mysterium Ecclesiae*, June 24, 1973, and Paul VI, *Mysterium Fidei*, Encyclical Letter, September 3, 1965; both available at www.vatican.va.

"True" should also especially be distinguished from "expressing the complete reality." One does not have to say everything about some reality for what one does say of it to be true, and to claim that a proposition is true is not to claim *completeness*. Adequation does not mean adequate in the sense of exhaustiveness. To say that Jesus is true God and true man does not tell us everything we want to know or that can be known about Christ. To say that the cat is on the mat does not tell us everything about the cat. But for all that a proposition does not completely capture and exhaustively mediate the reality of something to us, this is not to say that, *as far as it goes*, it is not true.

When people speak of some formula or other as "aiming at the truth" or being a worthy "approximation to the truth," therefore, they may mean one of two things. They may be simply adverting to the fact that the formula or proposition in question does not express the whole of the reality of what it is about. This is an unexceptional and uncontroversial thing to say. On the other hand, they may be claiming that the formula or proposition does not have the absolute value of truth, and can, therefore, be denied with impunity. This is an altogether different claim.

"Christ, His Spirit, and His Father"

The church is a theological reality, but theological reality in itself is the Trinity. So understanding the church means understanding it in relation to the three divine Persons, what they say about it, how they are connected to it, just as the New Testament and subsequent tradition understand it.

"Founded on Christ"

Christ is the foundation stone of the church in 1 Peter 2:6 and 1 Corinthians 3:11. More particularly, for the Fathers, the church is founded on the saving mysteries of Christ, his death and resurrection, for the church is drawn from his side on the cross as the New Eve from the New Adam, in the blood and water of the sacraments of baptism and the Eucharist.

"Founded by Christ"

Christ is the foundation; also, he founds the church by discrete acts that "institute" the new community of his disciples as his disciples, as we saw in chapter 3. He appoints the Twelve apostles who signify the renewed people of God and help bring it to eschatological fullness; he institutes the meal, the Eucharist, that will make him and his sacrifice present through all the ages of the church and provide her with the bread of heaven and the medicine of immortality.

"Body of Christ"

This is probably the dominant New Testament image of the church, founded in St. Paul's own conversion experience: "Why are you persecuting me?," the Lord asks. The truth the question supposes is that Saul is persecuting Christ, and this bespeaks a certain identity of Christ and the church, as of a man and his body or a head and its body. See 1 Corinthians 12 and Romans 12.

"Bride of Christ"

While the body-image can make the distinction of Christ and the church insufficiently adequate, depending on how it is taken, the church as bride nicely restores to the church her own as it were personal identity *vis-à-vis* Christ. See Ephesians 5.

"Temple of the Holy Spirit"

The church that the Lord Jesus says he will build on Peter (Mt 16) is the eschatological temple of the eschatological and eternal covenant that Christ seals in his blood (see Jn 2; 1 Cor 3). This covenant of peace is realized by the Spirit (Ezek 34:25, 36:26–27) that God will pour out on the church in the last days (Jl 2:28; see Acts 2:17).

"People of God"

This Old Testament designation of Israel is taken over in the New Testament to name the church, the renewed people of God (1 Pt 2). It is an important designation because it bespeaks the historical course of a "people" through the time of its existence, and is closely related to the kingdom of God (also indicating a multitude in unity) that was the initial theme of the preaching of Jesus.

"The Framework of the Church's Tradition"

Scripture "contains" the truths of revelation, but we cannot think of it as a collection or list of the truths of revelation. All the words of scripture are the word of God. But it is not as though scripture were to be conceived as a list of propositionally expressed truths each one of which conveys something like an article of the Apostles' or Nicene Creed. Doubtless it is the case that some statements in scripture can indeed be taken as propositionally expressed revealed truths each conveying a saving truth. But truths are also communicated in narratives and parables and other such forms that may be said to "contain" them.

It is not the case, however, that scripture is self-interpreting. Texts do not speak; they are not persons. Readers and proclaimers and preachers of texts speak. If they speak rightly, God speaks through them. They speak rightly when they bring the right framework of interpretation to their reading and preaching. Now, tradition is the necessary and normative framework or context within which scripture will be rightly interpreted (*Dei Verbum*, no. 9). Scripture is one of the contents of tradition: it is something "handed on" (*traditum*), and it expresses the apostolic preaching "in a special way" (*Dei Verbum*, no. 8). But the Gospel is not *exclusively* expressed there, and there is more to the content of tradition than scripture. What is handed on in addition to the New Testament and the teaching function of bishops (*Dei Verbum*, no. 7) includes the life and worship of the church as a whole (*Dei Verbum*, no. 8). Christian life and worship conform the Christian to the realities spoken of in scripture, especially to Christ himself, and so enable right reading and right interpretation. Tradition grows from age to age by a more profound understanding of scripture (*Dei Verbum*, no. 8). Tradition therefore grows by the dogmatic definitions of the church (see *Dei Verbum*, no. 10).[9]

"The Creed"

The creed or the rule of faith is central to the framework that tradition provides for reading scripture: according to St. Irenaeus, the rule of faith is the correct "hypothesis" with which we approach scripture, a sort of anticipatory statement of what they teach. For Irenaeus, apart from the creed, we cannot save ourselves from Gnostic and other heretical readings of scripture. This key is "delivered" to us; that is, it is a part of tradition. So to speak, scripture does not come to us without its operating manual, the tradition of the church. The creed is in a way a summary of scripture as a whole, the church's summary, and in presiding over the interpretation of every part of scripture, the whole of scripture thus comes to ensure the correct interpretation of every part (see *Dei Verbum*, no. 12).

Some theologians want to say that scripture is "materially sufficient" for faith, meaning that it contains all revealed truth in one way or another. However, it is certainly not "formally sufficient" just by itself to instruct us in the truths of faith—it has to be provided with the right framework of interpretation (tradition), which is to say it has to be interpreted by the right reader (the church). Only then does scripture possess an effective sufficiency (*Dei Verbum*, nos. 9 and 10).[10]

As was noted, scripture is also something that is handed on, and is a part of the *traditum*. In this way, scripture is to objective tradition as is a part to a whole, and in this way, tradition is prior to scripture.[11] But *within* the whole of what is handed on, there is a priority of scripture insofar as it includes the apostolic witness of the generation within which the fullness of revelation was accomplished and thus "closed" (*Dei Verbum*, no. 4). Because scripture requires a framework of interpretation in which it can be rightly and so normatively read, tradition can be called a "norm"

---

9. Joseph Ratzinger, *God's Word: Scripture, Tradition, Office*, ed. Peter Hünermann and Thomas Söding, trans. Henry Taylor (San Francisco, Calif.: Ignatius Press, 2008), 61–62.

10. See Yves Congar, OP, *Tradition and Traditions*, trans. Michael Naseby and Thomas Rainborough (New York: Macmillan, 1966), 101–18 and 409–22.

11. *Dei Verbum* thus rightly treats tradition as a reality prior to scripture (chap. 2).

of scripture. But in another sense, insofar as it is scripture alone that is being interpreted and taken to be the word of God on which alone the church stands, scripture is "un-normed," a *norma non normata* of faith. This is captured by saying that the teaching authority of the church "is not above the word of God but stands at its service" (*Dei Verbum*, no. 10b).

Theologically, tradition is a function of the mission of the Holy Spirit (*Dei Verbum*, no. 8), the same Spirit who inspires scripture (*Dei Verbum*, no. 11). Just as "no one can *say* [and say truly in words of faith] 'Jesus is Lord' except by the Spirit [who effects the interior light of faith]" (1 Cor 12:3), so no one can read (correctly, truly, faithfully) scripture—which witnesses to Christ and whose content is Christ—except within the tradition (the life of the church, whose principle of unity is the Holy Spirit).[12]

"The Church Fathers"

The Church Fathers (people like St. Athanasius, St. Cyril of Alexandria, St. Augustine, Pope Gregory the Great) are authoritative theological voices because, especially where they are concordant, they represent the first great "hearing" of the word of God, of revelation as completed in Christ, and are as it were the first and fullest echo of the word of God in human history.[13]

"Dogmatically Normative Statements Delivered to Us by the Church by Means of Pope or Council"

The deliverance of the key to scripture, which is tradition, is ongoing, and extends through the historical exercise of the magisterium of bishop and pope down to us, whether this exercise be the extraordinary teaching of council or pope, as in a council, or the common ordinary teaching of the bishops scattered throughout the world (*Lumen Gentium*, no. 25).

The competent witness from whom we immediately receive true judgments about Jesus and the church, either reading the scriptures with her

---

12. See Congar, *Tradition and Traditions*, 264–70, 338–46, and 379–409.

13. Joseph Ratzinger, "Importance of the Fathers for the Structure of Faith," in his *Principles of Catholic Theology: Building Stone for a Fundamental Theology*, trans. Sister Mary Frances McCarthy, SND (San Francisco, Calif.: Ignatius Press, 1987), 133–52.

or taking catechism lessons or hearing a sermon or going to a theology course in a seminary, is therefore the church. Sociologically, the church is the *congregatio fidelium*; theologically, the church is one mystical person with Christ (St. Augustine) through the indwelling in us and in Christ of the same Holy Spirit.

Within the church, of course, Catholics recognize a teaching authority. But we must not restrict the witness of the church to the magisterium. One first hears about Jesus Christ from one's parents, from sisters and catechists and priests who teach young people, from priests who preach on Sundays; later, one learns from books of catechesis and theology, from magisterial documents, etc. In short, we learn from *other people* who, collectively, constitute the church and tell the next generation about Christ.

Historically, the church is the competent witness about Jesus and the church because of her historical continuity with Jesus of Nazareth through the apostolic ministry established by him. Theologically, the church is the competent witness about her own reality, not only because of her historical continuity with Christ (apostolicity), but also because of the Holy Spirit of Christ, which is as it were the "soul" of the Church, making the sociologically describable members of the church participants in a communion of faith, hope, and love, and indeed, both Christ's "body" and his "bride." The church is the *only* competent witness to her true reality, both historically and theologically.

"Faith," Divine and Supernatural

Many of the truths in question (e.g., "the Church is the body of Christ") are not available to ordinary, natural human understanding and affirmation. If we are to know them, God must tell us them (through Christ), and he must give us the interior help of grace to assent to them. The assent to the propositions is therefore the assent of faith.

The reception of truths about anything whatsoever from competent witnesses or experts is a reception of them by faith, engendering beliefs. Some of these truths could perhaps in principle have been generated by someone on the basis of his own experience, insight, and rational deliberation. But the judgments received from the church about the church are not such as (even in principle) could be generated by any merely human experience, insight, and reason. That is, they cannot be known to be true by the unaided human mind; they cannot be reasonably affirmed in the way they are intended to be on any evidence, by any reasoning, available to ordinary human intellectual operation or authority. These judgments are reasonably affirmed only on the authority of God, and with his aid. See *Dei Filius*, no. 3:

The Catholic Church teaches that this faith, which is the beginning of man's salvation, is a supernatural virtue whereby, inspired and assisted by the grace of God, we believe that the things which he has revealed are true; not because of the intrinsic truth of the things, viewed by the natural light of reason, but because of the authority of God himself who reveals them, and who can neither be deceived nor deceive.

That is why the church was above called a "witness." Her authority to teach is an authority of witnessing to what God teaches on his own authority.

The formal object of faith is God, God as speaking to us, who can neither deceive nor be deceived.[14] God himself as speaking (the formal object of faith) is attained in the act of faith, when we assent to propositions (the material object) that have his authority.[15] God speaks and is to be heard in the teachings (propositions) of scripture and in the dogmas (propositions) of the church.

Revelation also occurs in deeds, as has been noted above. But the deeds need the words that accompany them to become intelligible (*Dei Verbum*, no. 2). How, for instance, would we know the meaning of Calvary had Christ not declared it at the Last Supper?

Assenting to revealed propositions, whether they come in the teaching of prophets, of Christ, or of the apostles, and whether we behold them in the deeds that embody them and accomplish their truth, requires trust in and obedience to the God who freely enters into personal communication with us. Such trust and obedience, the gifts of God, are the horizon within which we apprehend the material objects of faith whose meaning and truth are expressed in judgments and propositions.

14. For more on the distinction of formal and material objects, one can consult Avery Dulles, SJ, *The Assurance of Things Hoped For: A Theology of Christian Faith* (New York: Oxford University Press, 1994), 187–90.

15. Ibid., 213–14.

If the intrinsic truth of the judgments of faith escapes human reason, then they can be reasonably affirmed, responsibly affirmed, only on the authority of God, whose understanding is such that their intrinsic truth does not escape it, or whose power and freedom is such as is competent to make these truths true. The truths affirmed in faith are *known* to be true: first, because God cannot deceive; thus, when he speaks, we know that what he says is so; and second, because the church, the competent witness to revelation, cannot fail to remember and to teach the truths of revelation (see Jn 14:26). Thus, we do not just *happen* to have true judgments about Christ and the church; we know them to be true. Hence, our reception of the judgments about the church will be "justified true belief," in the phrase of contemporary epistemologists, and so, in that sense, knowledge.[16]

Given the brevity of this introductory ecclesiology, the following report of what the sources tell us will also be compact. This is all the easier to do insofar as that part of the tradition dealing with the church and that has found expression in magisterial statements is relatively recent, including the two Vatican councils and the more recent popes.

16. See James F. Ross, *Introduction to the Philosophy of Religion* (London: Macmillan, 1969), chap. 2, and his "Ways of Religious Knowing," in *The Challenge of Religion: Contemporary Readings in Philosophy of Religion*, ed. F. Ferré et al. (New York: Seabury, 1982).

CHAPTER 5

THE CHURCH AS THE MESSIANIC PEOPLE OF GOD

As has been explained, theology, and so ecclesiology as one of its parts, is entirely dependent on God's revelation, of which the Bible, read within the tradition of the church, is the exclusive record.[1] The core of the Bible is a story, the record of the deeds and words by which God shows himself and his free decisions to us, a story that includes the responding deeds and answering words of the men first addressed.[2]

More particularly, the Bible is a *messianic* story, a story where the Messiah is anticipated in hope, active in history, and looked for once again in his return. Messianic hope is inaugurated in the Old Testament within the call of Israel, and it is realized in the New Testament by the church. It is focused on the person and work of one man, who meets the promises made to Abraham, Moses, and David by fulfilling the more finely articu-

---

1. For theology as depending on scripture and tradition, see *Dei Verbum*, no. 24; and for the unity of scripture and tradition, see no. 9. Scripture is the exclusive record of the revelation that meets us *as* revelation.

2. For deeds and words constituting revelation, see *Dei Verbum*, no. 2; for revelation as revelation of God himself and his free decisions, see *Dei Verbum*, nos. 2 and 6.

lated hope of the prophets, who sends the apostles to gather the nations into the new Israel, the church, and who will return on the last day to judge the living and the dead. This man, Jesus, is the Christ—the Messiah. The narrative of the Bible prepares for and leads up to Christ in the Old Testament, tells of his life, death, and resurrection in the Gospels, reports the first history of the church in the Book of Acts, records the apostolic reception and elaboration of Jesus' teaching and work in the epistles, and closes with an anticipation of his return and the consummation of all things in the heavenly liturgy of the church in the Book of Revelation.

Focused on Christ as it is, the story of revelation is therefore the story of a people, the people who look for the Messiah, the people who have found him in faith—the people of God. This people, just precisely as a messianic people, fulfills within time the communion of men with God on which there was some initial speculation in chapter 1. That is, this people is the church. The "Christ" is the "anointed one." But Jesus is anointed only so that what first graces Aaron's beard runs down onto the collar of his robes (Ps 133:2). Christ cannot be understood except in relation to a people with whom he shares his anointing. This he does by sharing the Holy Spirit with them, the Spirit which makes him the Christ. In the Spirit, the people of God enjoy that intimacy with his Father that he knows before the foundation of the world. Thus there is communion with God. The messianic principle is the person of Christ, the incarnate Son; but the messianic fulfillment is the church, the people he redeems in order that they share in his own dignity as Son, giving them the Spirit of adoption (Gal 4:4–6).

That the Bible is a messianic story is a fact. But why is it so? Why is it the story of a people anticipating one man, a story that then shows a people formed by and subsequently implementing that man's agency, and at the same time handing on the legacy of his teaching? Why does the pattern of salvation, the narrative of revelation and redemption, have this hourglass shape to it, narrowing down from the nations to Israel to the one Christ, broadening out from the Christ to the apostles to the churches and unto one, final, anticipated church embracing all nations? There are two reasons for this. The first reason is the reality of representation. Human beings do not come to the fullness of their own identity except as lending themselves to corporate traditions of intellectual discovery aimed at the true and institutional endeavors aimed at the good. This calls not only for organization, but for *representation*, where many identify with the understandings and goals of one, or, correlatively, where one articulates an intelligibility that many share, and prosecutes a desire many hope to see fulfilled.

The second reason is that there are some things that only the Son of God can do. It is the Son, and not the Father or the Spirit, who most fittingly reveals the Trinity within human history, enacting his own identity as Son (and so revealing the identity of Father and Spirit) by deed, addressing his Father in human words, and letting himself be guided in his human actions by the Spirit of love so as to bring many adopted sons to glory (Heb 2:10). The Word according to which all things are made is also the principle of their remaking when he takes flesh from Mary.[3] Further, it is only a divine Person who can redeem the whole human race by laying down his life for us and so perfectly making up within history for sins committed within history.[4] And once again, it is only the Son who fittingly shows us what a human life looks like that is wholly enlightened by divine wisdom and completely moved by charity.[5] The hourglass pattern of revelation and salvation, therefore, is not arbitrary. It is what it is according to the wisdom of God who calls back to himself those he has made in love, and who perforce realize themselves in time and with one another, corporately, by sharing the truth and agency of a mediator who is at once both God and man.[6]

Israel as the People of God

There are four chief ways in which the New Testament characterizes the church. The church is the people of God, the temple of the Holy Spirit, the bride of Christ, and the body of Christ, and they are presented in that order. But there is a sort of obviousness about beginning with the church as the people of God, for the church first meets our eyes as a collectivity, a society. In the Old Testament, moreover, it is easier to discern a messianic people than the final shape of the Messiah. As St. Augustine says: *"Obscu-*

---

3. Aquinas, *ST* III, q. 3, a. 8.
4. Ibid., q. 1, a. 2.
5. Ibid. and q. 3, a. 8.
6. For a presentation of the economy of salvation as a principally messianic pattern, see Aidan Nichols, OP, *Lovely, Like Jerusalem: The Fulfillment of the Old Testament in Christ and the Church* (San Francisco, Calif.: Ignatius Press, 2007).

rius dixerunt prophetae de Christo quam de ecclesia" (the prophets spoke more obscurely about Christ than about the church).[7]

"People of God" first designates the people of Israel of the Old Testament (e.g., Jgs 20:2). This first people of God, the first Israel, is called, acquired, covenanted, commissioned, sealed, and prototypically messianic. These six things all have counterparts, or rather completions, for the eschatological people of God, the church.

Called

The people is God's people only by his choice, by his free election, according to Exodus 19:3–6:

And Moses went up to God, and the Lord called to him out of the mountain, saying: "Thus you shall say to the house of Jacob, and tell the people of Israel: You have seen what I did to the Egyptians, and how I bore you on eagles' wings and brought you to myself. Now therefore, if you will obey my voice and keep my covenant, you shall be my own possession among all peoples; for all the earth is mine, and you shall be to be a kingdom of priests and a holy nation."

"If you will obey my voice … you shall be my own possession." The Lord chooses; the people respond to this choice. Further, the Lord adduces his right to make Israel his people, "for all the earth is mine"; he is the creator, and he reminds them of the proof of this power: "You have seen what I did to the Egyptians."

An exceptionally clear statement of the election of God which makes clear that God chooses from among many possibilities is found in Deuteronomy 7:6–8:

The Lord your God has chosen you to be a people for his own possession, out of all the peoples that are on the face of the earth. It was not because you were more in number than any other people that the Lord set his love upon you and chose you, for you were the fewest of all the peoples; but it is because the Lord loves you, and is keeping the oath which he swore to your fathers, that the Lord has brought you out with a mighty hand, and redeemed you from the house of bondage, from the hand of Pharaoh, king of Egypt.[8]

7. Quoted in A. G. Hebert, *The Throne of David: A Study of the Fulfillment of the Old Testament in Jesus Christ and His Church* (New York: Morehouse-Gorham Co., 1941), 137n2.
8. See also Dt 14:2.

The election is for no special feature or merit of the people, but purely from love, from God's faithfulness to the patriarchs (see Gn 12:3) and so to himself.

From another point of view, Israel is not even one nation among others available to the Lord's choice before he chooses. Rather, God's dealings with Israel make her a nation. That is what is confessed at the offering of the first fruits according to Deuteronomy 26:5–9:

And you shall make response before the Lord your God, "a wandering Aramean was my father; and he went down into Egypt and sojourned there, few in number; and there he became a nation, great, mighty, and populous. And the Egyptians treated us harshly, and afflicted us, and laid upon us hard bondage. Then we cried to the Lord the God of our fathers, and the Lord heard our voice, and saw our affliction, our toil, and our oppression; and the Lord brought us out of Egypt with a mighty hand and an outstretched arm, with great terror, with signs and wonders; And he brought us into this place and gave us this land, a land flowing with milk and honey."[9]

Israel is at first no nation but rather an enslaved band of wanderers with no history or land, no possession of either time or place. God's work of redemption gives her a history and inserts her into the political landscape. God's gift of land puts Israel quite literally on the map (see Dt 6:18, 23).

Acquired

We have already anticipated this aspect of the people of God in the citations from Exodus and Deuteronomy. The people becomes God's people by God's acquisition of them, by the historical work that makes them a nation and makes them his nation: the exodus, the conquest of Canaan. In this way, the first of God's promises to Abraham is fulfilled, and Abraham is made a nation (Gn 12:2).

Why does God choose, acquire, and make covenant only with Israel? Is it not arbitrary of God to pick one nation, or make of some one clan his own nation? Does this not constitute an injustice? No, for as we shall shortly see, the vocation of Israel does not concern herself alone. Her role in history is to be a light for the nations (Is 60:3); she is an instrument unto God's revelation of himself to all. But the election of Israel is

9. See also Dt 6:20–22.

an important aspect of this manifestation of God: we do not see God's gratuitous choice of all of us unless we first see his choice only of some of us. Only in this way can the *gratuity* of God's call of all become apparent *historically*.

Covenanted

The relation established by God's election and acquisition of Israel is ratified in a covenant in which Israel assents to this election, acknowledges the acquisition, and engages herself to be God's people, a kingdom of priests and a holy nation. The covenant is announced as something promised in Exodus 6:5–8. Here, God remembers his covenant with Abraham; he promises a future covenant with the people; the formula of the future covenant is pronounced: "I will take you for my people, and I will be your God" (Ex 6:7), and this is the first time we hear of God's "people," "my people," in scripture.

The covenant that makes Israel God's people and a kingdom of priests is not enacted until Exodus 19.[10] After God lays down the Ten Commandments and the legislation regulating the common life of the people and their worship of God (Ex 20:1–23:19), and after undertaking to defend them and to give them the land of Canaan and so maintain them as his distinct possession, the ritual that establishes the covenant tells us exactly what is going on in Exodus 24:3–8:

Moses came and told the people all the words of the Lord and all the ordinances; and all the people answered with one voice, and said, "All the words which the Lord has spoken we will do." And Moses wrote all the words of the Lord. And he rose early in the morning, and built an altar at the foot of the mountain, and twelve pillars, according to the twelve tribes of Israel. And he sent young men of the people of Israel, who offered burnt offerings and sacrificed peace offerings of oxen to the Lord. And Moses took half of the blood [from the offerings] and put it in basins, and half of the blood he threw against the altar. Then he took the book of the covenant, and read it in the hearing of the people; and they said, "all that the Lord has spoken we will do, and we will be obedient." And Moses took the blood and threw it upon the people, and said, "Behold the blood of the covenant which the Lord has made with you in accordance with all these words."

10. This promises a restoration of Adamic status: Israel, "my first born son" (Ex 4:22) regains the priestly and kingly dignity of Edenic splendor before the Fall, for which see the next chapter.

The people agree to the terms of the covenant. The covenant itself, however, requires blood. Blood signifies life (Lv 17:11, the Red Cross), and common blood—half on the altar of God and half on the people—means common life: Israel shares in the life of God. Between throwing the blood on the altar and throwing it on the people, there is the reading of the book: common life with God requires a moral life according to the Ten Commandments, a just life with one another as specified previous to making the covenant in chapters 21 through the first part of 23, and it requires the worship of God as specified in chapter 23. Covenanted life with God comes to expression in both the social order and in the worship of God, living with the people in peace, and being with God in prayer and sacrifice. It is a covenant of *blood*, of life, but it is a reasoned covenant, a covenant of *words*; it is a covenant for rational animals. The covenant ritual is sealed in the common meal between God and the elders on the top of Mount Sinai as befits kinsmen (Ex 24:9–11).

The people are already recognizably a "people" in the first chapters of Exodus, as the collectivity of the descendants of Jacob. But it is the covenant at Sinai that formally establishes them as God's own people.[11]

Commissioned

The commission that the covenant relationship brings with it can be more fully analyzed.

Keeping the law

We have seen that the covenant engages Israel to live morally, to live in a community of life according to just ordinances, and to worship God. In Deuteronomy, Moses speaks insistently and urgently: "You shall diligently keep the commandments of the Lord your God, and his testimonies and his statutes, which he has commanded you, and you shall do what is right and good in the sight of the Lord" (Dt 6:17–18). Israel is to live truthfully before God and with one another.

When Israel keeps the Law, which is to say centrally and most importantly, when men keep the Ten Commandments, they realize themselves

11. Israel's status as the covenanted people of God is widely celebrated in the Psalms, for instance, Pss 50, 111, etc.

as what they are to be, because the commandments are statements of the natural law, which is the law by which nature is perfected. The habits and attitudes instilled by the commandments—chastity by the sixth commandment, truthfulness by the eighth commandment, piety by the fourth commandment, and so on—these things are virtues. That is, they are the habits that bring man's rational animality into actuality. The commands to respect and worship God have also a natural component about them: it is a part of justice to worship God.[12]

Showing God to the nations

Israel's task, however, is not only self-regarding. It has an external direction, too. According to Exodus, the result of keeping the law will be that Israel will be a kingdom of priests and a holy nation (19:6)—a sort of manifestation to the other nations of the power and holiness of God. Deuteronomy is explicit that the keeping of the law in good and just order makes Israel a people set apart and therefore *noticeable*. So Moses tells the people at Deuteronomy 6:5–8:

Behold, I have taught you statutes and ordinances, as the Lord my God commanded me, that you should do them in the land which you are entering to take possession of it. Keep them and do them; for that will be your wisdom and your understanding in the sight of the peoples, who, when they hear all these statutes will say, "Surely this great nation is a wise and understanding people." For what great nation is there that has a god so near to it as the Lord our God is to us, whenever we call upon him? And what great nation is there, that has statutes and ordinances so righteous as all this law which I set before you this day?

The distinctiveness and righteousness of Israel not only identifies her among the nations, however, but also displays the God who gives the law and himself keeps the covenant. "And if you swear, 'As the Lord lives,' in truth, in justice, and in uprightness, then nations shall bless themselves in him, and in him shall they glory" (Jer 4:2). The vocation of Israel is not just internal, but external, too. This mission to declare the name of God is discharged also within the very history of Israel: her sufferings and exile and return make of her a witness to the nations, a witness to He Who Is (Is 43:10).

12. See Aquinas on the Ten Commandments and the natural law in *ST* I-II, q. 100, aa. 1–2, and q. 94, a. 3.

Fulfilling the promise to Abraham

The fulfillment of the promise to Abraham, that all the nations will be blessed in him (Gn 12:3), is also in play. If Israel is to proclaim the deeds of the Lord to the nations and make his name known, there is a sort of unlimited scope to her vocation. So, at the dedication of the temple in Jerusalem, Solomon prays in 1 Kings 8:41–43:

When a foreigner, who is not of thy people Israel, comes from a far country for thy name's sake (for they shall hear of thy great name, and thy mighty hand, and of thy outstretched arm), when he comes and prays toward this house, hear thou in heaven thy dwelling place, and do according to all for which the foreigner calls to thee; in order that all the peoples of the earth may know thy name and fear thee, as do thy people Israel, and that they may know that this house which I have built is called by thy name.[13]

There is, then, an international dimension to Israel's covenanted vocation; all men and nations should come to know the Lord and be saved.

Exile heightened Israel's sense that her mission was universal. Not only will Israel be gathered again, according to Zechariah, the Lord dwelling in the midst of his people (Zec 2:10) but also "many nations shall join themselves to the Lord in that day, and shall be my people" (2:11), and equally will the Lord dwell in their midst, too (2:11). The exile sharpened the sense that the God of Abraham and Lord of Moses was the only God, the God for all nations, and this provoked more pointed expressions of her universal mission (as in Ps 86:8–10 and 102:21–22; also Is 45:14; 46:6; 56:3–7). But in the face of the historical postponement and failure of the expected universal acknowledgment of God, more eschatological versions of it were produced. Fulfillment is projected into a future hard to imagine or foresee in Isaiah (60:1–22; 66:18–23) and Zechariah (14:9, 16–19).[14]

Israel's failure

In important ways, Israel fails to carry out her commission. Moreover, this failure characterizes her history from the first days of the Sinai covenant, and indeed, causes the covenant to be modified. The apostasy of

---

13. See also 2 Chr 7:32–33; Pss 22:27–28, 67:1–3, 105:1; Is 2:2–3; and Zeph 2:11, 39–40.
14. See also Ezek 37:24–28.

the people in Exodus 32, where they worship the golden calf while Moses is on the mountain, makes it liable to blood penalty, to death, something also signified by the sharing of blood in Exodus 24. Moses invokes the memory of Abraham (32:13–14) and the promise once made to him, and further catastrophe is avoided. But it is no longer the case that Israel will be a "royal priesthood" (19:6), and so reassume the dignity of Adam. Rather, the priesthood is now limited to the Levites, who are consecrated by the zeal with which they slew the apostates (32:29), and there is added the burdensome legislation of Leviticus. Later, after the apostasy at Baal-Peor, the priesthood will be adjusted again and given to Phinehas and his descendants (Nm 25:10–13).

On Israel's sense of her having not fulfilled her vocation, and it being something to wait for in the messianic age, Gabriel Hebert says: "The Israel which actually existed was impotent to carry out the Mission to the Gentiles, which was nevertheless God's purpose for it. There was then a double truth about Israel which the Holy Ghost must express: God's Purpose for Israel, and the fact that this high calling lay beyond man's power to fulfil; Israel's high insight into the truth of God, and her inability to hold firmly to that truth."[15] And indeed, the Book of Daniel projects the final fulfillment of the promises to Israel into some place after the history of this world. Beyond the kingdoms of the Babylonians, the Medes, the Persians, and the Greeks, represented by the four beasts of Daniel 7, there is a final kingdom mentioned in 7:13–14:

I saw in the night visions, and behold, with the clouds of heaven there came one like a son of man, and he came to the Ancient of Days and was presented before him. And to him was given dominion and glory and kingdom, that all peoples, nations, and languages should serve him; his dominion is an everlasting dominion, which shall not pass away, and his kingdom one that shall not be destroyed.

The Son of Man receives dominion and glory and kingdom, however, on behalf of the "saints," the eschatological people of Israel, interiorly renewed and justified, for Daniel is told: "the saints of the Most High shall receive the kingdom, and possess the kingdom for ever and ever'" (7:18). Are we within history or quite beyond any ordinary history?

15. Hebert, *Throne*, 95.

Sealed

The called, acquired, covenanted, and commissioned people is also sealed in the flesh. God speaks to Abraham in Genesis 17:10–11: "This is my covenant, which you shall keep, between me and you and your descendants after you: every male among you shall be circumcised. You shall be circumcised in the flesh of your foreskin, and it shall be a sign of the covenant between me and you." There were other exterior signs that distinguished the people of God from other peoples, such as dietary laws (Lv 11 and Dt 13:3–20) and the command not to weave wool and linen together (Dt 22:11). But circumcision was the most important. Circumcision remained the sign of the covenant when Moses led the children of Abraham out of Egypt: no uncircumcised male could eat the Passover lamb (Ex 12:48–49). Circumcision remained the distinctive sign of the people of God (Jos 5:2–7), hence the scandal of removing the marks of circumcision under the rule of the tyrant Antiochus Epiphanes (1 Mc 1:15–16).

Circumcision was a sign of the righteousness of faith that makes one right before God, but it did not confer grace of itself, the grace still to be won by Christ's passion.[16] Because it was but a sign of being right before God, a sign of sharing Abraham's faith that God would make him a great nation and a blessing for all the nations, it made sense also to speak of another, interior circumcision, a "circumcision of the heart," which means docility before God and a love answering his own love. Moses speaks of this circumcision in Deuteronomy 10:15–16: "The Lord set his heart in love upon your fathers and chose their descendants after them, you above all peoples, as at this day. Circumcise therefore the foreskin of your heart, and be no longer stubborn."[17] Moses then enjoins the people to love the sojourner as does God, who gives justice to widows and orphans (18–19) and to cleave to God (20). In this passage, the people themselves will circumcise their hearts. But because this circumcision is the grace of living as friends of God, Moses says later that it is God who circumcises hearts at Deuteronomy 30:6: "And the Lord your God will circumcise your heart and the heart of your offspring, so that you will love the Lord your God with all your heart and with all your soul, that you may live."

16. Aquinas, *ST* III, q. 70, a. 4; see Rom 4:11.
17. See also Dt 10:18–21; Jer 4:4 and 9:26.

The Old Law could not of itself instill the interior regeneration of grace, charity, and the virtues required to love the Lord throughout the works of one's days. Such a regeneration of the whole people, therefore, remains in some way an object of hope, as in Jeremiah's prophecy of a new covenant in 31:31–34:

Behold, the days are coming, says the Lord, when I will make a new covenant with the house of Israel and the house of Judah, not like the covenant which I made with their fathers when I took them by the hand to bring them out of the land of Egypt, my covenant which they broke, though I was their husband, says the Lord. But this is the covenant which I will make with the house of Israel after those days, says the Lord: I will put my law within them, and I will write it upon their hearts; and I will be their God, and they shall be my people. And no longer shall each man teach his neighbor and each his brother … for they shall all know me.

The same hope is expressed by Ezekiel as a hope for a new heart. God says at 36:25–27:

I will sprinkle clean water upon you, and you shall be clean from all your uncleannesses, and from all your idols I will cleanse you. A new heart will I give you, and a new spirit I will put within you; and I will take out of your flesh the heart of stone and give you a heart of flesh. And I will put my spirit within you, and cause you to walk in my statutes and be careful to observe my ordinances.[18]

Just as circumcision was type of a better and stronger sacrament, a type of baptism, so the people as a whole was a sign of an interiorly renewed people, the church. So also, just as Israel portended the universal inclusiveness of the people of God, it is the church that God uses more effectively to realize this universality.

Messianic

What makes the Old Testament people of God messianic? There are anointed priests and prophets within it (e.g., Aaron in Ex 29:9; Elisha in 1 Kgs 19:16). Also, there are anointed kings, Saul and David after him (1 Sm 10:1; 16:13). But royal messianism, a messianism subsequently bound up with the people's hope for *itself*, begins with David and Nathan's proph-

---

18. See also Ezek 34:25, 37:26; Is 54:9–10, 59:21; and Hebert, *Throne*, 58–64.

ecy to David in answer to David's desire to build a house for God in 2 Samuel 7:3–14:

Go and tell my servant David: 'Thus says the Lord: Would you build me a house to dwell in? I have not dwelt in a house since the day I brought up the people of Israel from Egypt to this day, but I have been moving about in a tent for my dwelling. In all places where I have moved with all the people of Israel, did I speak a word with any of the judges of Israel, whom I commanded to shepherd my people Israel, saying, "Why have you not built me a house of cedar?"' Now therefore thus you shall say to my servant David, "Thus says the Lord of hosts, I took you from the pasture, from following the sheep, that you should be prince over my people Israel; and I have been with you wherever you went, and have cut off all your enemies from before you; and I will make for you a great name, like the name of the great ones of the earth. And I will appoint a place for my people Israel, and will plant them, that they may dwell in their own place, and be disturbed no more ... Moreover the Lord declares to you that the Lord will make you a house. When your days are fulfilled and you lie down with your fathers, I will raise up your offspring after you, who shall come forth from your body, and I will establish his kingdom. He shall build a house for my name, and I will establish the throne of his kingdom for ever. I will be his father, and he shall be my son.... And your house and your kingdom shall be made sure for ever before me; your throne shall be established forever."

A house for God's name is good, and God will not withhold this pledge of his fidelity to his people, realized in Solomon's temple. But more important is the pledge of the covenant, so named in 23:5, that Israel shall abide in her place, and that David's lineage will also abide (see also Ps 88:3–4; 132), and that God would be as a father to Solomon and, presumably, his further heirs (Ps 2:7). What is also important is the promise that God will make of David a "great name," great like the "great ones—kings—of the earth" (Ps 2:9), for this is the fulfillment of the second promise to Abraham (Gn 12:2). That Abraham became a nation (Gn 12:2) was fulfilled in the exodus and conquest. But now, there is a kingdom, and indeed, an empire, including Israel's near neighbors, Edom and Moab and Ammon.[19] With this covenant with David, note, the fortunes of the people and of David's heir are one and the same; the fortunes of the people and the anointed, the Messiah, stand or fall together.

19. Bergsma and Pitre, *The Old Testament*, 365.

What confidence this gives the people can be gathered from the oracles of Isaiah at the time of the Syro-Ephraimite war and the imposing threat of Assyria when Ahaz was king. So in Isaiah 9:6–7 we read:

For to us a child is born, to us a son is given; and the government will be upon his shoulder, and his name will be called "Wonderful Counselor, Mighty God, Everlasting Father, Prince of Peace." Of the increase of his government and of peace there will no end, upon the throne of David, and over his kingdom, to establish it, and to uphold it with justice and with righteousness from this time forth and for evermore. The zeal of the Lord of hosts will do this.

And again in chapter 11, there is "a shoot from the stump of Jesse" (11:1), upon whom the Spirit of the Lord rests (11:2), who judges in rightness and justice (11:3–5). But in this oracle, there is anticipated a future more difficult to imagine than simply victory over Israel's enemies: "The wolf shall dwell with the lamb, and the leopard shall lie down with the kid, and the calf and the lion and the fatling together, and a little child shall lead them" (11:6). This is the restoration of Edenic peace.[20] And "they shall not hurt or destroy in all my holy mountain; for the earth shall be full of the knowledge of the Lord as the waters cover the sea" (11:9). Hope for this restoration will be expressed also later in Isaiah (65:17–25; 66:6–24; see also Ezek 34:25–30; 36:34–35).

Davidic messianism survives the conquest of the northern kingdom, and Jeremiah predicts the gathering of scattered Israel (23:3) under the house of David: "Behold, the days are coming, says the Lord, when I will raise up for David a righteous Branch, and he shall reign as king and deal wisely … In his days Judah will be saved, and Israel will dwell securely'" (23:5–6; see also 30:4–8).

Davidic messianism survives the exile of Judah, too, and finds expression in the teeth of trial and the temptation to despair. Ezekiel foretells the reunion of Judah and Israel. Moreover, "I will set up over them one shepherd, my servant David, and he shall feed them: he shall feed them and be their shepherd" (34:23; see 37:24–25). And it keeps pace with the confusing situation of post-exilic Judea in Zechariah: "'Behold the man whose name is the Branch [of David]: for he shall grow up in his place,

20. Ibid., 730.

and he shall build the temple of the Lord'" (6:12).[21] Isaiah 61:1–4 also gives expression to it.

In all these places, we are dealing not just with one figure, the Messiah, but with a messianic people, and even, a messianic people stamped by the figure of Isaiah's Suffering Servant (42:1–4; 49:6).[22] Moreover, this messianism is closely associated with the fact that the call of Israel is the sign of a universal call to all the nations (Is 55:3–5; 61:5–7; see 11:10–11 and Ezek 37:24).[23] In both ways, the messianic people of the Old Testament is prototypical of the messianic people of the New. Just because Israel could not execute a universal mission, and just because although she signified a holy people but did not have it within her always to realize a holy and regenerate people, she stands as a sign and a promise of what is to come, the church.

Church

The first preaching of the first Christians identifies Jesus not as the Word through whom all things were made, as John does as the beginning of his Gospel, but as the one by whom God fulfills his messianic promises to the people of Israel.[24] The first preaching recorded in the Acts of the Apostles fairly dwells on what the Messiah does for his messianic people, and in the terms of the words and promises of the Old Testament.[25] In raising Jesus, God fulfills the promises made to the fathers of the Jews (Acts 13:32–33). For Jesus is God's Son (Acts 13:32–33; Ps 2:7) and the heir of David, the "man after God's heart" (Acts 13:22–23; 1 Sm 13:14). He is the Christ, the anointed (Acts 4:26 and Ps 2:2; Acts 10:38 and Is 61:1), and God's servant (Acts 3:13, 26; 13:47; Is 53). Through Jesus, God sent the message of salvation (Acts 13:26; Ps 107:20), the tidings of peace between God and men (Acts 10:36; Is 52:7). In this way, the nations are blessed in Abraham's seed (Acts 3:25).[26] So the first Christians, the church, are the light for the nations that old Israel was promised to become (Acts 13:47; Is 45:6), for

---

21. See also Hg 2:20–23, with reference to Zerubbabel.

22. See Hebert, *Throne*, 67–70.

23. For the inclusion of all the nations see also Is 60:1–3; Zeph 3:8–9; Zech 14:9, 16.

24. John identifies him in that way, too, of course: "He came to his own home, and his own people received him not" (Jn 1:11).

25. For the rest of this paragraph, see Hebert, *Throne*, 128–29.

26. Note that for Paul (Rom 8:32), Christ's death answers to the binding of Isaac in Gn 22:18.

salvation is now extended to the Gentiles (Acts 10:34; Dt 10:17) and the messianic Spirit is poured out not just on Jesus who thus becomes Christ, but on all flesh (Acts 2:17–21; Jl 2:28–32).

The church of the New Testament is self-consciously the eschatological "people of God" that old Israel foreshadowed but did not then instantiate.[27] So 1 Peter 2:9–10 has it: "But you are a chosen race, a royal priesthood, a holy nation, God's own people, that you may declare the wonderful deeds of him who called you out of darkness into his marvelous light. Once you were no people but now you are God's people [*laos theou*]; once you had not received mercy but now you have received mercy." Christians are here characterized in the same terms as the people of Israel at Sinai, as a holy nation and a kingdom of priests and God's own possession (Ex 19:5–6). They are to declare his deeds, as in Isaiah 43:21 (LXX). They are called into the light shining on Israel of which Isaiah speaks (60:3). The words of Hosea 2:23 are likewise appropriated to the church. The covenant formulary, "they shall be my people and I will be their God" (Jer 24:7), repeated in some form in various texts (Jer 30:23; 31:1; 33; Ezek 11:20; 14:11; 36:28; 37:23, 27; Hos 2:23; and Zec 8:8; 13:9), is now fulfilled in the church, not just according to 1 Peter but also according to 2 Corinthians 6:16, Hebrews 4:9, 8:10, and Revelation 21:3.

There is a distinctive choice of words in the New Testament to express this state of affairs. In the Septuagint, the people of Israel were the *laos tou Theou* (people of God) and the other nations *ethne*. In the New Testament, it is the church that is the *laos tou Theou*. The church understands herself as the successor to Israel. St. Paul is explicit about this succession in Romans 9:24–26, applying there, as does 1 Peter, the words of Hosea.[28] This does not say everything about the status of the first people of God in the time of the church, but it captures something essential: Israel was *for* the church, a preparation and sketch of things to come in the messianic age, and the church perfects and fulfills what Israel was. The Gospel of Matthew, especially, makes of the church the true Israel of God.[29] Clement of Alexandria captures this thought in calling the church the "new"

---

27. For the church as the people of God in the New Testament, see Rudolf Schnackenburg, *The Church in the New Testament* (New York: Herder and Herder, 1965), 149–57.

28. Ibid., 150–52.

29. Ibid., 71.

people of God.[30] If we reprise the six aspects under which we considered the old Israel, the newness of the new will be manifest. But it will make sense to do this in reverse order.

A Messianic People

The Old Testament people of God was a messianic people, but more in hope than in reality: it was on the lookout for the Messiah that would make it messianic in act. In the New Testament, however, the people of God is really and truly a messianic people, because it shares the anointing that makes Jesus the Christ, the Messiah. Jesus is manifested as the Christ at his baptism in the Jordan, when the Holy Spirit descends upon him in the form of a dove, and the voice from heaven affirms his Sonship (Mt 3:13–17).

Why does the beloved Son of the Father need to be anointed with the Holy Spirit? Within the Trinity, the second Person of the Trinity, the eternal Son, is with his Father the principle of the procession of the Spirit.[31] For this reason, he has the authority to promise the Spirit (Acts 1:5), and he really sends the Spirit to his disciples (Jn 16:7). Nonetheless, in his humanity, Jesus needs the Holy Spirit.[32] This is because his humanity is the instrument of his agency, of his teaching, of his surrendering of himself to his passion and death. Just so, it needs to be conformed to God by grace and the gifts of the Spirit. Only then can he in his humanity be led by the Spirit (Mt 4:1), even as we need to be led by the Spirit to conform ourselves to Christ and to carry out that share of his mission he gives us to perform.

But, and this is what is new in the New Testament, in the age of the Messiah, he shares his own anointing with us. That is the promise recorded by John: "'He who believes in me, as the scripture has said, "Out of his

---

30. Clement of Alexandria, *The Instructor* (*Paedagogus*), Book I, c. 5, in The Ante-Nicene Fathers [hereafter "ANF"] 2, ed. Alexander Roberts and James Donaldson (New York: Charles Scribner's Sons, 1905), 214: "the new people are called young, having learned the new blessings; and we have the exuberance of life in youth's morning prime which knows no old age ... for they must necessarily be new who have become partakers of the new Word." Just because the church is the *new* people, the question arises as to its relation to the still abiding "old" people of God; see Schnackenburg, *Church*, 154–55.

31. Aquinas, *ST* I, q. 36, aa. 2–4.

32. Aquinas, *ST* III, q. 34, a. 1, ad 3.

heart shall flow rivers of living water."' Now this he said about the Spirit" (7:38–39). The rivers of the Spirit flow from his open heart (from his pierced side—Jn 19:34), and that distribution of the Spirit makes us his people. So, the prophecy of Joel is fulfilled: "'I will pour out my spirit on all flesh'" (2:28). What is poured out on the head runs down on to the collar of his robes (Ps 133:2). This is the event of Pentecost, when the same Spirit that makes Jesus the Christ is poured out on those who believe in him. This means that the messianic people of the New Testament share in the offices of Christ—kingly, prophetic, and priestly—which are detailed below.

Sealed

Evidently, the new people of God are sealed with the baptism that Jesus hallowed in submitting to John's baptism (Mt 3:15).[33] Indeed, Jesus himself baptizes when the church baptizes (see Jn 1:33). In the New Testament, baptism replaces circumcision as the sign of the people of God. Just because baptism is baptism into the death of Christ (Rom 6) whereby Christ merited for us the grace of justification (Rom 8:1–4), this first sacrament of faith and Christian life cleanses consciences from sin (1 Pt 3:21; Heb 10:22), makes one righteous with the righteousness of Christ (see 1 Cor 1:30), gives grace and the infused theological virtues of faith, hope, and charity, and enables that interior spiritual and moral renewal of which circumcision was the sign but could not of itself effect.[34]

Commissioned

Just because they are anointed with the same Spirit with which Jesus was anointed, the people of God share in his mission. And 1 Peter 2:9 mentions all three offices: "you are a royal priesthood"—that is, you are a kingdom of priests, both kings and priests—"that you may declare the wonderful deeds of him who called you out of darkness into his wonderful light"—therefore prophets, as well.[35]

---

33. See Aquinas, *ST* III, q. 39, a. 1.

34. On regeneration hoped for and fulfilled, see Hebert, *Throne*, 58–64, for the Old Testament, and 171 for the New.

35. See the Second Vatican Council's *Lumen Gentium*, chap. 2, for these offices as exercised by the people of God.

Kingly keeping of the New Law

A king who makes the law is above it, and his children are therefore free of it (Mt 17:25–26). Just so, "for freedom Christ has set us free," and we no longer submit to the "yoke of slavery" (Gal 5:1), to the many judicial and ceremonial precepts of the Old Law, especially those added after Israel's apostasy with the golden calf and Baal of Peor. According to St. Thomas, Aidan Nichols writes, the Mosaic Law "defines the duties of the Israelite not just as any man but, more than that, as a *member of the people of the coming Messiah*."[36] We see that now in the New Testament. The ceremonial laws of the Old are revealed as figures of New Testament sacraments and moral laws.[37] And the judicial laws of the Old Testament, through the people they form, are also figures, and fulfilled by Christ and the church,[38] wherein the New Law is principally the grace of the Holy Spirit poured into our hearts.[39] The moral law itself we therefore keep with an interior desire to keep it, with a kingly perception of its justice and goodness. If there are new precepts, they are the precepts of charity, loving God above all things and our neighbor as ourselves and for his sake (Mt 22:37–39; see 1 Jn 2:7–8).[40] We are not only not to kill, then, but we are to refrain from the exterior acts of harming others from the right interior disposition.[41]

Thus, the common law of the new people of God is an interior law, not written on tablets of stone, but on hearts (2 Cor 3:3, 7). St. Thomas argues for this on the grounds, first, that what is most powerful in a thing is its principal part, and grace is more powerful than any written word. But also, that grace is the law of the new covenant fulfills the prophecy of Jeremiah (31:33), and answers to St. Paul's saying that we glory not in works but in the law of faith (Rom 3:27), an interior reality, and that the law of the Spirit frees us from the law of sin and death. He evokes here (but does not cite) the teaching of 2 Corinthians that while the Old Law was written on tablets, the New Law is written on hearts (3:3, 7).

36. Nichols, *Lovely, Like Jerusalem*, 268.
37. Aquinas, *ST* I-II, q. 101, a. 2; q. 102, aa. 2 and 5; q. 103, a. 3.
38. Ibid., q. 104, a. 2, and q. 107, aa. 2–3.
39. Ibid., q. 105, aa. 1 and 2.
40. Aquinas, *ST* II-II, q. 44, aa. 2–3.
41. Aquinas, *ST* I-II, q. 107, a. 2, co.; a. 4, co.; see also q. 104, a. 10, co. and ad 3.

Principally, therefore, the New Law is an interior law,[42] but secondarily though still essentially, it is something exterior. It is exterior insofar as visible sacraments give grace, and insofar as we use grace unto visible good works, audibly profess our faith publicly,[43] and keep the written moral precepts.[44] The many internal acts that the New Law of Christ comprises he teaches us in the Sermon on the Mount.[45]

The prophetic declaration of God's deeds

Just as Israel was to make God's name known to the nations by its celebration of the historical deeds by which he acquired her and by keeping the law, so the church is to declare to the nations her own acquisition by Christ in his passion and death and resurrection, and so make known the name of the Trinitarian God. The Messiah, just because he is the Word made flesh, can make known the God of Israel as Father (Jn 1:18), himself, Jesus, as Son (1:14), and his glory as the Spirit of Truth (1:14; 17:1). Jesus prayed, "Father, glorify thy name," and was answered, "I have glorified it, and I will glorify it again" (Jn 12:28). This glorification occurs in the hour of his passion. He Who Is (Ex 3:14) is then shown to be Father, Son, and Spirit, the one name in which we are baptized (Mt 28:19). For Paul, God fulfills his promise to Abraham that in him all the nations shall be blessed insofar as the Gentiles share the faith of Abraham and believe they are forgiven by the death of Christ and justified by his resurrection (Rom 4:23–25). Just in this way, Christ fulfills the law of Moses (Rom 8:1–4), and, as David's heir (1:3), extends messianic blessings to all the nations. As he summarizes his gospel at Romans 15:8–9: "For I tell you that Christ became a servant to the circumcised to show God's truthfulness, in order to confirm the promises given to the patriarchs, and in order that the Gentiles might glorify God for is mercy," and then at 15:10 he quotes Deuteronomy 32:43: "Rejoice, O Gentiles, with his people." Because Jesus' mission was the magnification of God's name, it is the mission of his messianic people. For understood largely enough, there is nothing of the church's mission that falls

42. Ibid., q. 106, a. 1.
43. Ibid., q. 108, a. 1.
44. Ibid., q. 108, a. 2.
45. Ibid., q. 108, a. 3. See Anscar Vonier, "The Heart of the People of God," in *The People of God* (London: Burns, Oates and Washbourne, 1937), on the interior grace of the New Testament people of God.

outside of the mission of making God's name known, as the way to do so is not only by preaching but by deeds (Jn 13:35). In this way and through the church, the world which proceeds from the Trinity makes a proximate return in praise of and thanksgiving to Father, Son, and Spirit, when Jesus draws all men to himself (Jn 12:32).[46]

It is worth noting in this regard, however, that the peoples and nations the church receives into herself are received without loss of their unique cultural identities. These may need reform, but they are not immaterial to the richness of the humanity all of which is to be saved and elevated by the mission of the church. The church means to be no agent of cultural imperialism and is very clear about this whenever she speaks of her missionary task.[47]

A people covenanted unto priestly service and sacrifice

The sacrifice of the new covenant of the new messianic people was celebrated sacramentally at the Last Supper and consummated in Christ's flesh on Calvary. This is important for understanding how the church is the "people." The people of God must have some analogical relation not only to the Old Testament people of God, but to any "people" whatever, if this declaration in human language of revelation is to be received by those who speak a human language formed first to speak of human things. And we have adverted to the common law and common history that make the people of God a people, for every people has a law and history. But just as a people shares a common blood, so also does the people of God. Just as it was the blood of the covenant sacrifice commonly sprinkled on all the people that signed them and sealed them as the people of God (Ex 24:3–8), then in the New Testament, so it is the blood of Christ, shared in the sacrament, that makes this people what it is by joining them to Christ and therefore to one another (1 Cor 11:17–12:31). The church, then, is the eschatological people of God, constituted by a covenant that is the new covenant in the blood of Christ (Lk 22:20), an eternal cov-

46. For the prophetic mission of the people of God in the new age, see *Lumen Gentium*, nos. 12 and 35.

47. See the decree on the missionary activity of the church of the Second Vatican Council, *Ad Gentes*, December 7, 1965, no. 22 in *Decrees* (ed. Tanner), 2:1000–1042, and Pope Francis, *Evangelii Gaudium*, Apostolic Exhortation, November 24, 2013, pars. 115–18; available at www.vatican.va.

enant according to Hebrews 13:20, a covenant fulfilling the promise of Jeremiah 31:31 and 32:38–40, which foretells an everlasting covenant (see Ezek 36:25–27; 34:25; 37:26; also Is 54:9–10; 59:21). The common blood of the new people is not the blood of an ancestor, of Abraham, shared by bodily descent, but the blood of Christ, shared in the sacrament.

The entire people is *priestly*. When the Eucharist is celebrated, it is the entire people assembled who offer the sacrifice through the hands of the priest.[48] This is the primary sacramental realization of their priesthood. It is realized also in the spiritual sacrifices, the living sacrifices of our bodies in daily Christian life that we bring to the Mass (1 Pt 2:5; Rom 12:1).[49]

Acquired

Just as God "acquired" Israel as his people by the deeds of her liberation from Egypt (Ex 19:4–5), which acquisition was ratified at Sinai, so he acquires the church through the work of Christ. The New Testament, however, speaks of Christ's acquisition of the church especially in the language that is used in Deutero-Isaiah (40–55), the language of "ransom" and "redemption"—*lutron* and *lutrôsis*, from the verb *loutrousthai*. For instance, 43:1–7:

But now thus says the Lord, he who created you, O Jacob, he who formed you, O Israel: "Fear not, for I have *redeemed* [*elutrôsamên*] you; I have called you by name, you are mine. When you pass through the waters I will be with you; and through the rivers, they shall not overwhelm you; when you walk through fire you shall not be burned, and the flame shall not consume you. For I am the Lord your God, the Holy One of Israel, your Saviour. I give Egypt as your ransom [*lutron*], Ethiopia and Seba in exchange for you. For you are precious in my eyes, and honored, and I love you, I give men in return for you, peoples in exchange for your life. Fear not, for I am with you; I will bring your offspring from the east, and from the west I will gather you; I will say to the north, Give up, and to the south, Do not withhold; bring my sons from afar and by daughters from the end of the earth, every one who is called by my name, whom I created for my glory, whom I formed and made."[50]

48. See Pius XII, *Mediator Dei*, Encyclical Letter, November 20, 1947, pars. 85–93; available at www.vatican.va.

49. For the priestly office of the people of God, see also *Lumen Gentium*, nos. 10 and 34.

50. God is the "redeemer" in Is 41:14; 43:14; 44:6, 24; 47:4; 48:17; 49:7, 26; 54:5, 8; 59:20; 60:16. For cognates, see 43:1; 44:22, 23; 48:20; 51:10; 52:3; 52:9; 62:12; 63:9.

The nations are the "price" God gives for Israel, his rearrangement of history unto his own design for the good of Israel. In 45:14, the nations seem rather to be given to Israel, included in the grace in which Israel lives. The price, then, is to be described as God's mighty historical acts, behind which is his love and fidelity, his oath (45:23).

The New Testament uses this same language for the eschatological acquisition of the people of God, the church. Christ "gave himself for us to redeem us from all iniquity and to purify for himself a people of his own," St. Paul says (Ti 2:14). He here means that the promise of an eschatologically purified people of God made in Ezekiel 37:23 is fulfilled: "they shall be my people, and I will be their God," and what Ezekiel elsewhere calls the "covenant of peace" is established (34:25). Again, "You were ransomed from the futile ways inherited from your fathers not with perishable things such as silver or gold, but with the precious blood of Christ, like that of a lamb" (1 Pt 1:18–19).[51] And it is on the lips of Christ himself: "For the Son of man also came not to be served but to serve, and to give his life as a ransom for many" (Mk 10:45).

There is also the language of the marketplace, "to purchase" (*agorazein*). "You were bought with a price" (1 Cor 6:20). "You were bought with a price; do not become slaves of men" (1 Cor 7:23). "For thou [the Lamb] wast slain and by thy blood didst ransom men for God ... and hast made them a kingdom and priests to our God" (Rv 5:9).[52] There is no special Old Testament background here. But in both ways, with both word groups, what is conveyed is that Christ acquires us for God. The language of simply setting us free (*eleutheria*) is avoided, just because there is no connotation of acquisition. God sets us free by Christ's work just in order to make us his own people, matching and surpassing the mighty deeds of which Isaiah speaks.[53]

Called

So much is the church the "called," that that is the origin of her name in the New Testament. "Church" renders for us the Latin *ecclesia*, which translit-

---

51. See also Rom 3:24; Col 1:14; Eph 1:7; Heb 9:12, 15.

52. Also Gal 3:13, 4:5; 2 Pt 2:1; Rv 14:3.

53. See Stanislaus Lyonnet and Leopold Sabourin, *Sin, Redemption, and Sacrifice: A Biblical and Patristic Study* (Rome: Biblical Institute Press, 1970), esp. 98–115.

erates the Greek *ekklêsia* (from *ekkalein*—to call forth). As R. Schnacken-burg writes, "for early Christian thought the 'Church of God' (*ê ecclêsia tou theou*) is nothing else but the people of God, so that Church and people of God are identical."[54] *Ekklêsia* renders the Hebrew *qahal*, "convocation." A *qahal* is any public gathering or assembly of people. Concordantly, it sometimes names a religious assembly of the Jewish people for the purpose of worship (Joel 2:14) or for holy war (Jgs 20:2) or covenant renewal (Ezra 10:9, 12; Neh 8:2). In such a religious context, it is translated by *ekklêsia* in the Septuagint. In the New Testament, *ekklêsia* names Christian assemblies or communities, while a Jewish assembly is a "synagogue" (*sunagôgê*).

Qahal is an important word in Deuteronomy. It names the assembly at Mount Horeb gathered to make covenant with the Lord (9:10; 18:16). It names the people as a whole, and as a holy people which no unholy person may enter (23:2, 3, 8). It names the people at the time of Moses's discourse itself (31:30). It functions to name the assembly at the dedication of the temple in 1 Kings (8:14, 22, 55). It names the whole congregation of the exiles assembled to hear the law read out by Ezra (Neh 8:17; see Ezra 10:8). The church exists in a sort of privileged way, then, when it is gathered for the work of hearing the law, or offering sacrifice as at Horeb for the renewal of the covenant or at Jerusalem for dedicating the temple. It exists in a sort of privileged way when it assembles to praise God and thank him for his gifts.

In the Book of Chronicles, there is an especially important connection between the *qahal*, the liturgical assembly, and the "kingdom of the Lord." It does not use the phrase "kingdom of God," but teaches that the "kingdom of the Lord" has been placed in "the hand of the sons of David" (2 Chr 143:8; see also 1 Chr 28:5, where this kingdom is given to Solomon). This kingdom is especially realized in the liturgical assembly for the Chronicler (see especially for the dedication of the temple, 2 Chr 29:23, 28, 31, 32; 30:2, 4, 13, 17, 23). When Jesus preaches the advent of the kingdom of God, therefore, he is indeed establishing the church, the *ekklêsia*, the assembly of the Lord where God will be truly worshiped. That the church is not the kingdom is evident if we reflect that the eschaton has not come in its definitive and perfect form, as was pointed out in chapter 3.

54. Schnackenburg, *Church*, 153.

God is not yet "everything to everyone" (1 Cor 15:28), and for that matter, neither have the dead been raised, nor have we put on imperishability (1 Cor 15:52), nor has the New Jerusalem "come down out of heaven from God" (Rv 21:2). Still, preaching the *kingdom* is establishing the church.

Ekklêsia occurs twenty-three times in Acts, sixty-two times in the Pauline literature, twenty times in Revelation, and another five times in the Catholic epistles. *Ekklêsia* connotes the members of the church as "called," called by God through Christ in the Holy Spirit. In neither Acts nor Paul is the one church the sum of local *ekklêsiai*.[55] When Paul speaks of "the church of God which is at Corinth" (2 Cor 1:1), he can be taken to mean, not a separate and independent Corinthian church, but rather the one church *present* at Corinth.[56] *Ekklêsia* also appears three times in Matthew. Matthew 16:18 and 18:17 give us to believe that *ekklêsia* is the name of the church from the lips of the Lord Jesus, and this would explain its abundant use in the New Testament and its exclusively Christian meaning.

Evidently, in discharging her messianic role at the end of the age, the people of God have a universal mission, the same mission for which Israel awaited an eschatological empowerment to carry out, an empowerment realized in the church. That empowerment comes with messianic anointing, and is expressly given to the church in the great commission (Mt 28:20), and at the beginning of its discharge of it in the Acts of the Apostles. The universal mission of the church means that the church is "catholic"—*kata holon*, "according to the whole." *Lumen Gentium* says that the catholicity of the people of God answers to the original unity of the race as made by God and so cannot be bound to any one nation or race. Rather, the church furthers the temporal welfare of the nations, and profits as a whole from the gifts and goods of each part (no. 13).

When we treat the church as the people of God, and note the link of the church considered so to its catholicity, we touch on one of the four properties of the church as in the creed. For Thomists, we touch on what we might call the material cause of the church: the human beings, and in principle and the design of God, all human beings who compose or ought

55. Jerome Hamer, OP, *The Church Is a Communion* (New York: Sheed and Ward, 1964), 37–38.

56. Ibid., 39.

to compose the church.[57] Because all are called to belong to the church, as we have noted many times in this chapter in dealing first with Israel and then the church herself, two questions arise. First, in that not every Christian is a Catholic, there is the question of the relation of non-Catholic Christians to the Catholic church. This question touches on the unity of the church and will be addressed in chapter 11. Second, there is the question of the relation of other religions to the church. This will be addressed in chapter 14, which more directly answers to this chapter on the people of God.

Dogmatic Summary and Synthesis

(1) The church is the people of God, a people first constituted in the Old Testament by God's covenant with Abraham and by the covenant mediated by Moses at Sinai, central to which on Israel's part is the observance of the Ten Commandments and the worship of God and making God's name known to the nations.

(2) The church is the messianic people of God, foreshadowed in God's covenant with David, promised by the prophets, realized in Jesus, the Christ (Messiah), and constituted by the final covenant that he enacts at the Last Supper.

(3) The church is more perfectly a people than the people of God in the Old Testament, because the blood of the final covenant is the blood of no animal but the blood of Christ, and so the one blood that unites her as a people is not the blood of a common ancestor but the blood of Christ, who is not a mere man, but the God-man.

(4) The church as the realized messianic people of God in Christ lives by the same Spirit that makes Jesus the Christ, the Spirit who enables her to fulfill the Ten Commandments from charity and worship God in the truth of Christ.

(5) Just as the sign of the covenant in the Old Testament was circumcision, the sign of the new and everlasting covenant in Christ is baptism, which brings with it what it signifies, namely the forgiveness of sins and

57. Charles Journet, *The Church of the Word Incarnate*, vol. 1: *The Apostolic Hierarchy*, trans. A. H. C. Downes (New York: Sheed and Ward, 1955), 531. See also Reginald Garrigou-Lagrange, OP, *De Revelatione per Ecclesiam Catholicam Proposita* (Rome: Ferrari, 1950), 2:198–202.

the grace to love God above all things in charity and to keep the commandments.

(6) The mission of the church is to include all peoples and nations within the one people of God, without loss of the genuine goods of culture that make peoples and nations distinct and unsubstitutable in their realization of a common humanity, and therefore the church is catholic.

CHAPTER 6

THE CHURCH AS TEMPLE OF THE HOLY SPIRIT

The mystery of the temple, as Yves Congar has it, is the mystery of the presence of God to his people.[1] God is present to all created things whatsoever insofar as every creature is a likeness of the divine goodness.[2] The presence of persons to one another, however, is a presence in knowledge and love.[3] We are present to God in accordance with how much he knows us and loves us. So, we are perfectly present to him, for he knows us perfectly and loves us perfectly. We cannot be more present to him than we are. God is present to us, correlatively, insofar as we know and love him. But this is a matter of kinds and degrees. God is naturally present to us insofar as we know him as the creator of the world from the things that have been made (Rom 1:19) and insofar as we love him as the final end to which all things incline by their natures, including us. God is supernaturally present to us in this life insofar as we know him by faith in

1. Yves Congar, OP, *The Mystery of the Temple, Or, The Manner of God's Presence to His Creatures from Genesis to the Apocalypse*, trans. Reginald F. Trevett (Westminster, Md.: Newman Press, 1962 [1958]).

2. Aquinas, *Scriptum Super Libros Sententiarum*, ed. P. Mandonnet (Paris: Lethielleux, 1929–47), Liber I, d. 37, q. 1, a. 2.

3. Aquinas, *ST* I, q. 8, a. 3.

the revelation he makes of himself as Father, Son, and Spirit, and insofar as we love him by charity, which makes us friends of God.[4] When God is present to us as known by faith and as loved by charity, then he is said to dwell within us, St. Thomas says, such that we are temples of God.[5] Now, that God dwells in a temple, and dwells in us as in a temple, is an idea with a vast biblical background. But let us stick to this more abstract way of proceeding for a moment or two.

Without creation, of course, there is no such thing as a temple, because there is nothing except God for God to be present to. A temple means the presence of God to what is not God. More exactly, a temple means the presence of God to created persons, which is to say, as St. Thomas intimated above, a presence in knowledge and love. For the angels, they themselves and just in themselves are temples, insofar as God is present to them in their knowledge and love of him. They comprise a sort of heavenly temple, and scripture reflects this when it speaks of a divine council as in Isaiah 6 or Psalm 82. For St. Thomas, human beings are temples in the same way. But things are more complicated for us. They are more complicated because the first objects of our knowledge are material things, sensed things. Because of our embodied nature, furthermore, the first persons that are present to us, human persons, are first physically present to us. We are present to one another originally by occupying the same place at the same time. There are two consequences of this for God's presence to us.

First, God will make use of the material order to signify and effect his presence to us. As we are present to one another most originally at home, in a house, he too will be present to us in a house of his own—a temple. The immaterial God will, somehow, make himself materially present to us. Second, just as our presence to one another is stretched out in time, so it will be with God's presence to us. It will have a history. The eternal God will, somehow, make himself temporally present to us. This presence, material as it must be, will have a history that is intrinsic to it, that conditions its reality as a presence. Thus, God's temple will have a history, and it will be reviewed shortly.

A second consideration is also useful before we turn to the Bible. The

---

4. See Jn 15:15 and *ST* II-II, q. 23, a. 1.
5. Aquinas, *ST* I, q. 43, a. 3.

historical character of whatever temple God gives us means that the supernatural knowledge and love of God is also historical. It is just another way of saying that. The supernatural knowledge and love of God, like the natural, therefore admits of degrees, in accordance with how we grow in wisdom and increase in charity. Unfortunately, the supernatural knowledge and love of God also admits of being extinguished, in that the act of faith and the love of charity depend on our freedom, which is not irrevocably fixed on one final end as long as we are living bodily in time. Such an extinction happened at the beginning of human history. Moreover, this extinction of the supernatural knowledge and love of God, his supernatural presence to us, also had an impact on our *natural* knowledge and love of him.

When we turn to the Bible, we see that it insists from the outset that we were originally to be friends of God: Adam and Eve used to walk with God in the Garden (Gn 3:8–9), and there is nothing more characteristic of friends than that they spend time together and enjoy each other's company.[6] And God gave gifts to his friends: immortality (Gn 3:17 and 3:22), an easy knowledge of God enjoyed by seeing him in created things,[7] and "integrity"—a sort of immunity from lust, cowardice, and laziness.[8] These more than natural gifts were fitting for those who were friends of God. They enhanced this friendship in the order both of man's knowledge and his love of God. The gifts Adam and Eve enjoyed, however, were contingent on the preservation of innocence, that is to say, on continuing friendship with God, and were fitting only for those who never preferred self to God. Nor could Adam and Eve pass on to their descendants what they no longer possessed.

Moreover, the loss of their original innocence had an impact on the natural knowledge of God available to their descendants, heirs of original sin. It made it more arduous for us to come to know God, for now we can know him only from the things that have been made and not in them as Adam and Eve did. This is the difference between arguing from effects

---

6. Aristotle, *Nicomachean Ethics* IX.12. See Aquinas, *ST* I, q. 95, a. 1.

7. Aquinas, *ST* I, q. 94, a. 1. See Gn 2:19–20: Adam's immediate and non-experimental ability to give creatures their right names implies a special knowledge of the creator.

8. Aquinas, *ST* I, q. 95, a. 2. See Gn 3:25 for the subordination of our bodily appetites and passions to reason: Adam and Eve were naked, but unashamed in each other's company.

to an unseen cause and seeing the cause in the effect.[9] The Fall made our knowledge of God more precarious and uncertain, more easily tainted by error. And this, in turn, together with our fear of and sometimes terror before death, and the difficulty of making all our appetites and passions obedient to reason, makes it impossible for us to love God above all things even with our natural powers.[10] We find ourselves, in other words, in just the parlous condition Newman depicts in his parable of the ignorance and misery induced by original sin and that was recalled in chapter 1.

The difficulty of coming to a true knowledge of God because of the disorder of our passions and desires is stated by St. Paul very directly (Rom 1:21–32), and he relies on the previous teaching of the Book of Wisdom on this issue (Wis 13). The Old Testament also presents it very effectively in the history of the patriarchs. When Abraham is set by God to wander in the land of Canaan and down to Egypt, he meets a Pharaoh who seems to know God and is certainly very God-fearing (Gn 12:17–20). Later, in Gerar, he meets Abimelech, who is also God-fearing and knows God (20:3–7). The Philistines of Gerar remain God-fearing into the time of Isaac, too (26:28–29). But with Jacob, we discover that Laban, who seems to know God, keeps "household gods" (31:30, 34). Where did *they* come from? When Joseph is sold into Egypt, Pharaoh and his household seem once again to acknowledge God (41:38–39). By the time of Moses, however, there is a new king in Egypt who knows neither Joseph nor Joseph's God (Ex 1:8); Moses's God is not simply "God" on Pharaoh's lips but "your God" (8:25; see Wis 11:15). And after the exodus, Israel finds herself among the many nations with their many gods—Moloch and Baal and Astarte. How did this happen? Man forgot God. And in the first books of the Bible, there is a forgetfulness even about *how* human beings became more and more oblivious of God. The Book of Wisdom, to be sure, will have some speculations about this subsequently (12:23–15:17).

To sum up: from Genesis to the beginning of Exodus, man moves from friendship with God, walking with him in the Garden, to utter forgetfulness of him. We forgot also that we are brothers and sisters to one another, as human malice and violence subsequent to sin attest (Gn 6:5, 11). Within

9. Aquinas, *ST* I, q. 94, a. 1, ad 3.
10. See ibid., q. 109, a. 3.

this trajectory from Genesis to Exodus, however, the divine plan for a restoration of man is already afoot with the call of Abraham (Gn 12:1), as was seen in the previous chapter. Now for the temple.

The Original Temple and the Final Temple

Temples are enclosed spaces where gods are said to dwell and where men may meet them and worship them. Does a temple withdraw some space from ordinary and profane use, and dedicate it to the assured and easy realization of a sacred presence for religious purpose? Or does a temple withdraw most space from the unpredictable and dangerous presence of the divine so as to liberate it for man's use, so to control the perilous presence of the gods within the confines of a sacred grove or a sacred building? A temple does both things: it organizes space. It makes the divine regularly accessible, and it frees up both time and space for the economic and political affairs of men.[11]

Temples are also places where a priest is to be found. A priest mediates the encounter of men with the divine within a temple. The mediation is paradigmatically by sacrifice offered through the hands of the priest. This paradigmatic mediation should not obscure the importance of priestly instruction (see Lv 10:11; Dt 33:10; Jer 18:18). These remarks are generally good for the many religions. They are good for the Old and New Testaments, too, but in a way determined by revelation.

An important step in learning about the nature of the tents and temples of the Old Testament is by contrasting them with the original venue of God's presence to man, the Garden of Eden. Gardens are neither buildings nor the untended wild; they are neither cottage nor forest, but something in between.[12] A garden has natural things in it, but is planted. It is a mix of the natural and the agency of an extrinsic intelligence. For humanly planned and planted gardens, a garden is a space where nature and man's intelligence overlap. It is not just for man's food, but is a pleasant place to walk in. The Garden of Eden, however, is planned and plant-

11. Mircea Eliade, *The Sacred and the Profane: The Nature of Religion*, trans. Willard Trask (New York: Harcourt, Brace and World, 1959), 22–24.

12. Roger Scruton, *Beauty: A Very Short Introduction* (Oxford: Oxford University Press, 2022), 67–68.

ed by God (Gn 2:8); he creates the plants on the third day (Gn 1:12–13), but he arranges certain of them for man's easy use and comfort at Eden (2:16).[13] In Genesis, the Garden is a space where the human and the divine overlap and can meet. This is by God's plan and arrangement. It is the first temple, one not made by human hands.

Eden is the original temple: the organization of space is a divine and consecrating work.[14] In the first place, the division of the land reflects the division of Solomon's temple: to the Holy of Holies there corresponds Eden proper, the mountain of God's dwelling (Ezek 28:13, 15–16); to the Holy Place there corresponds the Garden where Adam and Eve dwelt; and to the outer court of the temple there corresponds the land and the sea outside the garden.[15] Second, as the world that contains Eden and the Garden was made according to seven words of God ("God said": Gn 1:3, 6, 9, 14, 20, 24, 26),[16] so the tabernacle of Exodus and its appurtenances are established in seven stages ("And the Lord said": Ex 25:1; 30:11, 17, 22, 34; 31:1, 12) and the temple in seven years (1 Kgs 6:38).[17] Third, God "rests" in his temple (Ps 132:7–8, 13–14; 1 Chr 28:2) and rules from it (Ps 146:10) and blesses from it (Ps 134:3); just so does he also rest on the seventh day, after the six days of creation, in the cosmos that contains Eden (Gn 2:2, 3:8; Ex 20:11).[18] He rules from it, for it is the place of his viceroy, Adam (Gn 1:28). Fourth, Adam is set to "work [till] and keep" the garden (Gn 2:15), with the same verbs with which priests are set to worship and serve in the temple.[19] In the original temple of Eden and the cosmos, there are no mediators, for all would be immediately related to the God who walks with them. Fifth, Adam is set to "rule," as mentioned, and authoritatively to name things rightly, and so declare the wonderful

13. After the Fall and God's curse of the soil, Cain tills the ground, but he is in a field, not a garden (Gn 3:17–19; 4:2). Cain's murder of Abel brings a further curse; having swallowed Abel's blood, the ground will "no longer yield to you its strength" (4:11–12).

14. Eliade, *The Sacred and the Profane*, 30–31.

15. G. K. Beale, *The Temple and the Church's Mission: A Biblical Theology of the Dwelling Place of God* (Downers Grove, Ill.: InterVarsity Press, 2004), 32–36 and 74–75. Jean Daniélou, SJ, *The Presence of God*, trans. Walter Roberts (Baltimore, Md.: Helicon, 1959), 19.

16. Gn 1:11, 22, and 28 concern rather the *fruitfulness* of the earth, the air and sea, and man.

17. Beale, *The Temple*, 61.

18. Ibid., 61–62. See Also Jon Levenson, "The Temple and the World," *Journal of Religion* 64 (1984): 275–98, at 288.

19. Beale, *The Temple*, 66–67.

works of God (Gn 2:19–20; 1 Pt 2:9). He is then the archetypal priest, king, and prophet.[20] That he is priest, king, and prophet is the covenant boon God gives to him, with the proviso that he shall not eat of tree of the knowledge of good and evil (2:17). And where covenants are made, we expect sanctuaries to be established, as at Sinai and Zion, with the Mosaic and Davidic covenants (Ex 25–31, 35–40; 2 Sm 7). Sixth, the decoration of the temple recalls the Garden (1 Kgs 6:29; 7:18, 20, 22), and its inmost sanctuary was guarded by cherubim, even as was the portal of the Garden after Adam and Eve were expelled (1 Kgs 6:23–29; Gn 3:2).[21]

Now if Eden is the place of original friendship with God, recovering that friendship is the story of getting back to the Garden, to the original temple where man walked with God. Of course, it cannot be got back to perfectly in this life; rather, it remains something only remembered with the help of revelation, and then, finally, projected into an eschatological fulfillment of time in heaven. The story subsequent to the Fall is nevertheless the story of finding a place where the human and the divine overlap.[22]

Just as Eden is a temple, so the latter temple of Solomon keeps the original cosmic connections of Eden. Jon Levenson concisely sums them up by saying that the temple remains, like Eden, both central and primordial.[23] It is the center of the world for Ezekiel (5:5; 38:12; 48).[24] It is primordial, with the river Gihon arising from it as in Eden.[25] It is the epitome of the world, full of God's glory as the world is the fullness of God's glory (Is 6).[26] Like Eden, it is the *axis mundi*, where there is access to heaven and the underworld of watery chaos is controlled.[27]

If we take the Garden that God arranges for meeting and walking

20. Bergsma and Pitre, *The Old Testament*, 103.

21. For the temple and Mount Zion as Eden in both scripture and the rabbis, see Jon D. Levenson, *Sinai and Zion: An Entry into the Jewish Bible* (San Francisco, Calif.: Harper and Row, 1987), 128–37. See also Beale, *The Temple*, 70–72.

22. Congar, *Mystery of the Temple*, 245, for whom the biblical itinerary goes from temple to temple, paradise to heaven.

23. Levenson, "The Temple and the World," 282. See Eliade, *The Sacred and the Profane*, 36–42.

24. Levenson, "The Temple and the World," 284.

25. Levenson, *Sinai and Zion*, 134–35.

26. Levenson, "The Temple and the World," 289. For Josephus, Levenson reports, the temple is "the world in *nuce*, and the world is the temple *in extenso*" (285).

27. Levenson, *Sinai and Zion*, 122–27.

with men to be the cosmos itself, then the story from Genesis to Revelation is evidently a story from a first-created temple to a recreated temple coming down from heaven.[28] In the first temple, all created things spoke easily and intelligibly of God to man, and so made man always to be with God. The Fall ends that, and the world becomes opaque to man, no longer showing him God, because his mind has been darkened. It is not so much that the world has changed, but man has changed. At the end of the Book of Revelation, however, there is a new creation, a new heaven and a new earth (21:1), a new temple.[29] The new creation is the New Jerusalem coming down from heaven, which is itself God's dwelling with men, a temple. The New Jerusalem is "the dwelling of God" according to 21:2, and again, "he will dwell with them" (21:3). Thus, John sees no temple in the city, for the city is the temple (21:22). But also, "its temple is the Lord God the Almighty and the Lamb" (21:22). There is, therefore, a sort of mutual inherence: God dwells with men, and men dwell in God; to be in the city is to be in the temple where God dwells; God is in the city of the saints, and also, to be in the temple is to be in God.

The new creation once again is a place that speaks of God and just is his presence to man. The original state of man has been restored. How has this happened? It is enough to read the names on the twelve foundation stones of the city, which are the names of the apostles of the Lamb (21:14). It is by the work of the Lamb, slain and risen, that the cosmos has been restored to its original beauty. And indeed, there is no temple in the city, for the Lord God and the Lamb are the temple (21:22). But between the two cosmic temples, in which God is all in all, there are the discrete temples, built of stones literal or human, that stand out against a landscape in which, because of sin, not everything speaks of God or mirrors his majesty.

Between the Edenic temple of God and the apocalyptic temple of

28. See Jean Daniélou, *The Presence of God*, 9: "the earthly Paradise is nature in a state of grace. The House of God is the whole Cosmos." As distinct from the surrounding creation, Eden itself as the dwelling of God is a sort of concentration of the cosmos, an expression of what the whole cosmos, which we cannot see, in fact is. For Eden as the cosmic mountain, see Levenson, *Sinai and Zion*, 128–31, and for the temple as both, 132–37. For the symbolic identity of cosmos and Solomon's temple, see Congar, *Mystery of the Temple*, 94–99, and for Eden, 245, the starting point of a biblical itinerary than ends in heaven. For Levenson, "The Temple and the World," 295, the Hebrew Bible, from Gn to 2 Chr 35:23, "goes from creation (temple) to temple in twenty-four books."

29. Beale, *The Temple*, 365–67.

God—each of which is a cosmos in which there does not need to be a distinct temple, a holy place set off by metes and bounds from profane places, as all things and the whole speak of God and declare his presence—there are distinct temples, separate places. First, there is the temple of old Jerusalem, Solomon's temple and after that, the second temple of Ezra and Nehemiah after the exile, rebuilt by Herod—temples of stone. Second, there is the temple of the church, a temple built not of stones but of men (1 Pt 2:5), but still, a place set apart from the world as long as the end has not come. Between the temples of stone and the temple of the church, however, there is the body of Christ, a temple destroyed in death but built again in three days (Jn 2:19).

Now, part of the Messiah's task of renewing Israel included also and centrally his building of a final temple, and that is certainly the chief way our Lord identified himself as Messiah in the Gospels (Mt 16:18). This chapter therefore naturally follows the previous one. What is key to understanding the biblical teaching is one again the correspondence of the Testaments, the anticipation of the New in the Old, the fulfillment of the Old by the New.[30]

God's Presence to the Patriarchs and the Patriarchs' Presence to God

In the time of the patriarchs, God makes himself present episodically, in making covenant (Gn 15:1, 17:1, 22:1), in the visitations he makes to Abraham and Isaac and Jacob, renewing his promises or giving instructions (12:1, 13:14, 18:1, 21:1, 26:24, 35:1). But also, the patriarchs make themselves present to God. They do this by sacrifice, which was the principal form of Israelite worship. Later, the temple of Solomon or the post-exilic temples of Ezra and Herod were the exclusive places of sacrifice. This tells us something important about how to understand the temple.

Abraham, of course, has no temple in which to offer sacrifice to the Lord. Rather, the whole of the Promised Land is the place of concourse between God and Abraham and his descendants. Abraham acts

---

30. Without sin, we might be said to be parts of a temple but not members of a body, Christ's body, as the motive of the incarnation, is redemption. That is, "temple" is more original, encompassing, than "body."

on the promise of land by offering sacrifice throughout its breadth: from Shechem in the north (Gn 12:7) to Hebron in the south (13:8) and at Ai in between (12:8, 13:4). The whole of the land is, as it were, already in Abraham's possession and serves as a place of sacrifice—as a temple.

For what do these first sacrifices mean? They recognize God as the giver of good gifts in sharing these gifts with him, in a communal meal.[31] Sacrifice is in this way a manifestation of the reality and nature of God. Just so, insofar as the conception of God's reality and nature differs, so will the meaning of sacrifice differ. Where God or the gods are thought of simply as agents more powerful than men, sacrifice can be experienced as a mutual exchange of gifts.[32] Where God is acknowledged as the creator of all things, the creator of man and the one who sustains man's agency, sacrifice is more profound as an act of acknowledgment although no longer an instrument of human influence on the divine. It is less powerful as a rite just precisely in recognizing the infinite power of God. But then, paradoxically, sacrifice recovers a power beyond that of any pagan ritual insofar as it bespeaks true communion with God in knowledge and love, the best communion with him.

We should expect, however, that the lineaments and meaning of sacrifice—according to how it is ordained by the natural law as a just acknowledgment of the transcendence and generosity of the creator—will be more difficult to discern in a fallen world.[33] The mercy of God provides for this in the word of revelation. Thus, the Old Testament is very clear about the asymmetrical relations that sacrifice presupposes and declares,

---

31. William Robertson Smith, *The Religion of the Semites* (New York: Meridian Books, 1956 [1889]), 226–27. For Louis Bouyer, sacrifice declares the same asymmetric relation between the divine and man that Smith recognizes, and does this originally, according to Bouyer, in a sacrificial meal; see *Rite and Man: Natural Sacredness and Christian Liturgy*, trans. M. Joseph Costelloe, SJ (Notre Dame, Ind.: University of Notre Dame Press, 1963), 85: "To recognize the sacredness of a meal as being the highest form of human activity is to recognize man's total dependence, for his creation and his continued existence, upon a God who is at the same time apprehended as the one who possesses the fullness of life." But Bouyer does not contrast pagan and Jewish sacrifice so much as presume that the fullness of sacrifice, in some way continuous with pagan sacrifice, is located in the sphere of revelation. For a review of modern and contemporary theories of sacrifice, see the first chapter of Dennis King Keenan, *The Question of Sacrifice* (Bloomington: Indiana University Press, 2005), and John Milbank, "Stories of Sacrifice: From Wellhausen to Girard," *Theory, Culture, & Society* 12 (1995): 15–46.

32. Henri Hubert and Marcel Mauss, *Sacrifice: Its Nature and Function*, trans. W. D. Hall (London: Cohen and West, 1964 [1898]), 10–11, 13, 97–98, and 100.

33. For sacrifice and the natural law, see Aquinas, *ST* II-II, q. 85, aa. 1–2.

and this is manifest in the fact that the sacrifices of the Old Law are instituted not by man but by God. The sacrifice for sin, too, is God's gift to Israel. The blood of atonement and the ritual of atonement are also gifts of God, a way provided by him for Israel to mend broken relations (Lv 10:17, 17:11).

There is as well a narrative declaration of the true nature of sacrifice, and so also of the nature of the true God, to be found in the Akedah, the sacrifice of Isaac in Genesis 22.[34] Isaac is God's gift to Abraham and Sarah in two ways, for he is not only created but is the child of God's promise to Abraham to make him great. When Abraham sets out to sacrifice Isaac, it is most evident that he is returning gifts given to him, to which, of himself, he has no claim, despite his love and his hope for Isaac. That God prevents Abraham from slaying the child means that the death of the sacrificial victim, just as such, is meaningless. What is meaningful is the obedience of Abraham. So, later, it is the obedience and humility of Christ that are the interior truth of his surrendering himself to death (Phil 2:8). The sacrifice of Isaac will provide the theology of sacrifice elsewhere in the Old Testament with a sort of normative pattern of how to understand what sacrifice means. It is the acknowledgment of the transcendence and generosity of the God than which nothing greater or better can be conceived. It is the acknowledgment at the same time that this God has come close to us in a communion of knowledge and love although for nothing we can give him. This understanding of sacrifice is preserved in Christian tradition. In sacrifice, St. Irenaeus says, "we offer to Him what belongs to Him."[35]

Now, the meaning of sacrifice, moreover, is also the meaning of the temple, which meaning—and which temple—is adumbrated in the dream of Abraham's grandson, Jacob's dream at Bethel in Genesis 28:11–17:

And Jacob came to a certain place, and stayed there that night, because the sun had set. Taking one of the stones of the place, he put it under his head and lay down in that place to sleep. And he dreamed that there was a ladder set up on the earth, and the top of it reached to heaven; and behold, the angels of God were

---

34. Jean-Luc Marion, "Sketch of a Phenomenological Concept of Sacrifice," in his *The Reason of the Gift*, trans. Stephen E. Lewis (Charlottesville: University of Virginia Press, 2011), 74–75, and 83 for his criticism of Hubert and Mauss.

35. St. Irenaeus, *Against Heresies*, in ANF 1, Book IV, chap. 18, nos. 1–2 and 4–5.

ascending and descending on it! And behold, the Lord stood above it and said, "I am the Lord, the God of Abraham your father and the God of Isaac; the land on which you lie I will give to you and to your descendants. Behold I am with you and will keep you wherever you go, and will bring you back to this land; for I will not leave you until I have done that of which I have spoken to you." Then Jacob awoke from his sleep and said, "Surely the Lord is in this place; and I did not know it." And he was afraid and said, "How awesome is this place! This is none other than the house of God, and this is the gate of heaven."

Then he pours oil on the stone, his pillow, and calls the name of the place Bethel, "the house of God" (28:18–19). He next promises that, if God leads him back to his father's "house" (28:21), he will make the stone "God's house" (28:22).

This is a remarkable passage for thinking about the temple for many reasons. First, Jacob consecrates the stone, the place that is already by divine initiative the place of concourse between heaven and earth. Our consecrations and blessings are secondary to and depend on the more original consecration of God. Second, despite the definite location of this place of concourse between heaven and earth, God promises to be with Jacob wherever he goes; the Lord has special places, a house, a temple, but that does not impede his mobility, his being with whomever he loves and has promised to sustain. Third, there is a play on "house," the same play to be made in Nathan's oracle to David in 1 Samuel 7: the "house" of Jacob, his family and its prosperity, is joined to the "house" of God. The same will go for David. Fourth, the house of God is a two-lane highway: things go up, sacrifice and praise and petition; and things come down, answers and instruction for life. Fifth, the going up and the coming down is the charge of the angels, who show us that Bethel, and the house of God on earth, is a sort of extension of the heavenly court of God; Bethel is "the gate of heaven." Sixth, there is, most important, an extension of God's presence to Jacob, who becomes "Israel" (32:28), and Jacob acknowledges this in astonishment: "How awesome is this place." Thus God's true presence can be realized for those who believe in a real place that is truly God's, a place open to his heavenly presence; the God who is everywhere can have a special "where." Just as sacrifice is an acknowledgment of gift and grace, the temple also is a gift and will be the place of grace. Seventh, while the story may be originally a justification of the northern sanctuary at Bethel, within the whole Bible it points forward not just to the temple of Jerusalem, but to the Christ as also a temple, a house of God where there is again a double concourse with heaven, according to John 1:51, where the Lord tells Nathanael that he will see "the heavens opened, and the angels of God ascending and descending upon the Son of man."[36]

God's Presence to Israel: The Tent and the Temple

The song of Moses after crossing the Red Sea looks to the establishment of God's house on his "own mountain," the place he has chosen for his "abode" and "sanctuary" (Ex 15:17), in language that appears only here and in Solomon's prayer of dedication for the temple (1 Kgs 8:13).[37] In between, especially for the journey through the wilderness, there was the tabernacle (Ex 33:7–11), which was an outline in cloth and leather of the temple of stone, and whose plan God gives Moses in Exodus 26. The tabernacle and the temple housed the Ark of the Covenant (Ex 25), holding the tablets of the law, covered with the footstool of God, the "mercy seat" (Ex 25:17). The portable tabernacle and the equally portable Ark were instrumental to solving a key anxiety Moses gives voice to in Exodus 33, after the apostasy of the people while Moses was on the mountain (Ex 32:1–6), as to whether the Lord will be with Moses and the people once they depart from Sinai.[38] So, in 33:15–16, Moses says to the Lord:

"If thy presence will not go with me, do not carry us up from here. For how shall it be known that I have found favor in thy sight, I and thy people? Is it not in thy going with us, so that we are distinct, I and thy people, from all other people that are upon the face of the earth?" And the Lord said to Moses. "This very thing that you have spoken I will do; for you have found favor in my sight."

At the same time, this request is combined with another, that Moses might see the glory of God (Ex 33:18). Moses cannot see God's face lest he die (33:20), but the Lord consents to show Moses the back side of his glory (33:19–23). In showing his glory, the Lord reveals very pointedly that He Who Is (Ex 3:14) is unalterably the God of mercy. "I will make

---

36. For discussion of Bethel, see Beale, *The Temple*, 100–104.

37. Congar, *Mystery of the Temple*, 8.

38. On the historicity of the tabernacle see Thomas Joseph White, OP, *Exodus*, Brazos Theological Commentary on the Bible (Ada, Mich.: Brazos Press, 2016), 224–28.

all my goodness pass before you, and will proclaim before you my name 'The Lord'; and I will be gracious to whom I will be gracious, and will show mercy on whom I will show mercy" (33:19). God's glory is his mercy. And again: "The Lord, the Lord, a God merciful and gracious, slow to anger, and abounding in steadfast love and faithfulness, keeping steadfast love for thousands, forgiving iniquity and transgression and sin, but who will by no means clear the guilty" (34:6–7). Now, it is that God and thus the glory of his mercy whose presence the tabernacle and the temple will house.[39] They are a sort of standing record of this greater revelation of the intimate heart of God.

What becomes of the tabernacle once the people settle in Canaan after crossing the Jordan? Except for what it most importantly contained, the Ark of the Covenant, the throne or rather footstool of God, it disappears. David brings the Ark up to Jerusalem, and there in the city of David he proposes to build a house for God. We saw in the previous chapter what became of David's proposal: God will rather make a house for David, an assured lineage. This presence of God to David and his descendants is therefore closely bound up with the temple that Solomon subsequently fashions in 1 Kings 6.[40] Solomon's temple becomes a sign of the enduring presence of both the Davidic line and the presence of God.

As to the presence of God, it is not crudely asserted; rather, though heaven itself cannot contain God, his "name" shall be in the temple (1 Kgs 8:27, 29). What we would call the transcendence of God is respected.[41] That it is the name that is present does not signify a pure absence of God—it is not "only" a name. Quite the contrary, it is the name by which he may be invoked, the name by which he enters into communion with his people, that dwells in the temple.[42] Even so, at his commissioning as a prophet, Isaiah is fairly transported from the temple into the heavenly court—they are not entirely distinct, and the same awe is evoked that

39. Ibid., 279–80 and 282: "There is a certain sense in which, by being merciful on the face of sin, God is revealed even more profoundly in his immutable transcendent goodness as He Who Is for all eternity, in indiminishable, incomprehensible existence" (280).

40. Levenson, *Sinai and Zion*, 98: "Nathan's oracle weaves the existence of the dynasty and of the temple together."

41. Ibid., 125: God's presence in the temple is "not gross and tangible, but subtle and delicate."

42. Joseph Ratzinger/Benedict XVI, *Jesus of Nazareth: Holy Week*, trans. Adrian Walker (San Francisco, Calif.: Ignatius Press, 2011), 91.

Jacob knew at Bethel.[43] Those who pray in the temple will be heard in heaven (8:32, 34, 36, 39, 46). And this is good for Israelite and foreigner alike—the temple functions to discharge the universal mission of the people (8:43). Even if carried away captive out of the land of promise, the people will be heard if they turn toward the land, the city, and the house (8:48).[44]

Eden and the cosmos, the tent and the temple, are the manifestation of God's glory to men, where tent and temple recall and condense Eden and the cosmos. Thus, as Thomas Joseph White says, "the tabernacle recapitulates creation and symbolizes why God created in the first place: that he might dwell with man."[45] Present in the temple, which is a sort of concentrated symbol of the world, God is present to all creation. Thus the contradiction between the ubiquity of God and his local presence is solved symbolically.[46]

The temple is the scene of the characteristic ritual response to God's presence and covenant kindness, which is sacrifice. According to Chronicles, moreover, the temple is a reminder of the true nature of sacrifice, sacrifice as the regiving, the giving back to God, of what is first his gift to us. The temple is a reminder of this in two ways. First, because of David's prayer at the offerings of gold and silver, bronze and iron and precious stones, offerings for Solomon's building of the temple. David prays: "But who am I, and what is my people, that we should be able thus to offer willingly? For all things come from thee, and of thy own have we given thee" (1 Chr 29:14). "All things come from thee"—that is, from what you have first given us do we now regive to you. Thus, the very temple itself is a gift given *back* to God, and all the more will any sacrificial action within the temple precincts be a manifestation of what first has been Israel's reception of gifts from God. The temple, the sacrifice within it, are then

43. Levenson, *Sinai and Zion*, 123.
44. Ibid., 125.
45. White, *Exodus*, 229.
46. Levenson, *Sinai and Zion*, 138–41. The temple recalls Eden but is not Eden in every respect. This is indicated by the fact that the priesthood is not the universal priesthood of Adam, nor even the royal priesthood possessed by the nation at the making of the Sinai covenant (Ex 19:6), where Israel would be a priestly nation relative to the nonpriestly nations who would find their blessing in Israel, just according to the promise to Abraham.

true sacrifices, manifesting the truth of God and his relation to Israel as both creator and covenant benefactor.

There is also a second reminder of the nature of true sacrifice in Chronicles. Solomon builds the temple on Mount Moriah, "where the Lord had appeared to David ... on the threshing floor of Ornan the Jebusite" (2 Chr 3:1). This was the place where David offered sacrifice to atone for ordering the census of the people (1 Chr 21:18–27). But Mt. Moriah was the place where Abraham undertook to sacrifice Isaac. Thus was the daily temple sacrifice in the latter theology of the temple a sort of sacrament of the founding act of the people in the covenant faithfulness, obedience, and true sacrifice of Abraham.[47] The temple was a great witness to the whole sweep of the history of the nation, from Abraham to the restoration after the exile. Jesus and the New Testament continue and redirect this history; they do not inaugurate it.

That the temple and its worship were more symbols of the covenant response of Israel to God than its reality is clear from the subsequent history of Solomon's temple. First of all, the temple itself, the very pledge of covenant obedience, was encrusted with altars to foreign gods in all their multiplicity and depravity. The text of 2 Kings 23 provides a tour of the temple given over to apostasy and infidelity. Second, the temple could just of itself be an occasion for presumption, as Jeremiah's sermon charges (Jer 7:1–15). Because of this presumption, Jeremiah prophesies, the Lord will do to the temple what he did to Shiloh, which is to say destroy it (7:12–14).

The glory of the Lord departs from the temple in Ezekiel's vision (Ezek 10:4, 15–19; 11:22–23). The temple is profaned and destroyed, as the Lord forewarned (24:19–22). But just as deportation from Judah and the end of the kingdom did not efface messianic promise, but moved it into a new key, so also there was a further penetration of what the old temple was a sign of, what a new "temple" could be according to the oracles of restoration (chapters 33–48) after the fall of Jerusalem and the destruction of Solomon's temple.

In chapter 33, the Lord details what Ezekiel's role as "watchman for the house of Israel" consists in. To save himself, he must warn the wicked

---

47. Jon Levenson, *The Death and Resurrection of the Beloved Son: The Transformation of Child Sacrifice in Judaism and Christianity* (New Haven, Conn.: Yale University Press, 1993), 180–84.

when the word of the Lord comes to him (33:8–9). Whoever lives will live according to his righteousness, and the unjust shall die according to his fault (33:11–20). The presupposition of the justice of this the Lord's judgment is supplied in chapter 36, with the promise of a new heart, a heart of flesh, whereby the law can be kept willingly and unto the Lord's good pleasure (36:26). This interior renewal matches an exterior renewal, for there will be a reunion of the northern and southern kingdoms, Israel and Judah (37:19), under a Davidic king (37:24), where the one kingdom is bound to the Lord in a "covenant of peace," an everlasting covenant (37:26). In this way, all the nations will know the name of the Lord (37:28). Within a renewed kingdom and a renewed covenant, renewed hearts are matched with a renewed temple. The dimensions and splendor of this temple are detailed over two chapters (40–42), the description of which culminates with the return of the glory of God (chapter 43).[48] "Son of man, this is the place of my throne and the place of the soles of my feet, where I will dwell in the midst of the people of Israel for ever. And the house of Israel shall no more defile my holy name, neither they, nor their kings, by their harlotry [with other gods]" (43:7). God will be in the midst of the people forever.[49] And if we remember Ezekiel 11:16, a word of consolation spoken to the first exiles before the fall of Jerusalem, where the Lord declares "yet I have been a sanctuary to them" in the land of their deportation, then we can assert a sort of mutual indwelling: the Lord dwells in the midst of his people, and the people dwell in the Lord, who is a sanctuary for them wherever they are.

There is here, then, a sort of perfect projection of what the temple signifies, and what it shall signify in some yet to be realized age. Further, it is an age where Eden is replanted, for the Lord says: "the land that was desolate shall be tilled ... and they will say, 'This land that was desolate has become like the garden of Eden'" (Ezek 37:34–35). This promise is repeated more graphically in chapter 47, where the river of life flows from the new temple, even as a river that becomes the four great rivers flows out of Eden (Gn 2:10–14). Ezekiel's river has power even to make the salt sea fresh (Ezek 47:8)—it repairs the damages of sin and infidelity. That

48. Beale, *The Temple*, 110–12.
49. For the holy people as the Holy of Holies at Qumran and in Philo, see Beale, *The Temple*, 78 and 103–4.

the land shall be like that of Eden is again promised about the same time in Isaiah 51:3. The temple of the returned exiles, the temple of Ezra and Nehemiah, however, do not fulfill this prediction.

Jesus as the Messianic Temple

All three synoptic Gospels record Jesus' claim that he, the Son of Man, is lord of the sabbath (Mt 12:8; Mk 2:28; Lk 6:5). This he does after permitting his disciples to pick grain thereon (Mt 12:1–5) and before healing the man with the withered hand on the sabbath (Mt 12:9–14). But in Matthew, after considering the fact that the priests on duty in the temple on the sabbath profane it, Jesus also says, "I tell you, something greater than the temple is here" (12:6). Jesus is Lord of the sabbath and greater than the temple, the ultimate and paradigmatic dispositions of space and time, where the temple is charged with the glory of the cosmos and the sabbath bespeaks the Lord's rest after the six days of building his dwelling place.[50] The only thing greater than the temple and the cosmos in which God dwells is God. The only Lord of the sabbath is the giver of the third commandment, God. Jesus inserts himself into the being of God, and makes himself one with the one God of Isaiah 45:5. This is confirmed in relation to the temple in the parable of the unjust tenants of the vineyard. Here, Jesus is Son in relation to God, greater than any prophet, and is now himself the principle of the new temple because he is its cornerstone, as it were its origin: "'The very stone which the builders rejected has become the head of the corner; this was the Lord's doing, and it is marvelous in our eyes'" (Mt 21:42, quoting Ps 118:22–23).

That Jesus claims to be greater than the temple is confirmed again when, after driving out the money changers, he cures the blind and the lame in the temple (Mt 21:14), setting aside the prescription of the law that such people shall not draw near the offerings (Lv 22:18). Of course, there can be no better place to restore man to the dignity of the original creation, whole and sound, than the temple, Eden extended into the present.

The cleansing of the temple, attested by all four Gospels, shows symbolically that Jesus is somehow above it, in charge of it. In Mark, he fulfills

---

50. See Levenson, *Sinai and Zion*, 142–45.

the temple by abrogating the present regime of worship of which it is the epitome, where he declares that God's house is "a house of prayer for all the nations" (Mk 11:17, quoting Is 56:7). He thus abolishes the distinction of places for Jews and Gentiles in the extant temple; he announces that the time of the universal call of the nations to actual membership in God's people has come. The Gentiles are to come to Jerusalem, in the sense that they come to the faith of Israel. But they come to an eschatological fulfillment of that faith, where the old temple is made redundant. This is to happen through him, in him.[51]

In Matthew's Gospel, Jesus is greater than the temple precisely insofar as one who builds a building is greater than the building, and he says to Peter that he will build his church, the eschatological temple, on Peter's faith (Mt 16:18; Heb 3:3). But in John, Jesus *is* the temple. The very *first* thing Jesus says of himself in John's Gospel indicates that he is the gate of heaven and the house of God, for he says to Nathanael that he will see "heaven opened, and the angels of God ascending and descending on the Son of man" (Jn 1:51), and so recalls Jacob at Bethel (Gn 28:12). The Baptist has already identified him as the Lamb of God who takes away the sins of the world (Jn 1:29), the one on whom the Spirit rests (1:33), even the Son of God (1:34). At Cana, Jesus changes the five jars of water into wine (2:10): the Jewish law and religious regime will pass over through him into an eschatological fulfillment (Is 25:6, 55:1; Am 9:13). Then John 2:13–22 turns to the temple:

The Passover of the Jews was at hand, and Jesus went up to Jerusalem. In the temple he found those who were selling oxen and sheep and pigeons, and the money-changers at the business. And making a whip of cords, he drove them all, with the sheep and the oxen, out of the temple; and he poured out the coins of the money-changers and overturned their tables. And he told those who sold the pigeons, "take these things away; you shall not make my Father's house a house of trade." His disciples remembered that it was written, "Zeal for thy house will consume me." The Jews then said to him, "What sign have you to show us for doing this?" Jesus answered them, "Destroy this temple, and in three days I will raise it up." The Jews then said, "It has taken forty-six years to build this temple, and

---

51. For discussion of the "cleansing" as a symbolic act of eschatological meaning and the dominical sayings associated with it, see E. P. Sanders, *Jesus and Judaism* (Philadelphia: Fortress Press, 1985), chaps. 1–2.

will you raise it up in three days?" But he spoke of the temple of his body. When therefore he was raised from the dead, his disciples remembered that he had said this; and they believed the scripture and the word which Jesus had spoken.

The sign he will give them is one with his life, death, and resurrection. It is therefore not a sign they can wholly see right now. Some comments are in order.

First, he interrupts, at least symbolically if not for any great length of time, the function of the temple, which is sacrifice. He makes a declaration that the time of this temple is over.[52] Second, his saying will be used at his trial to convict him (Mt 26:61; Mk 14:57): but that means that the very testimony that convicts him at the trial, a distorted version of his saying, is used by the wisdom of God to redeem the world (see 1 Cor 2:7–10). The very saying about his being the new temple is used, through the divine permission of his death, a death brought about by false testimony as to what he said of the temple, to make him the new temple.[53] It is in this way that God's wisdom uses the death of Jesus, an evil that he only indirectly wills in sustaining the world, an evil brought about by sin he in no way wills but only permits, to undo sin altogether, and make us free of it.[54]

Third, that the new temple is the temple of his body is confirmed by Mark 14:53–58, where we have a temple "not made with human hands," a temple that is himself, therefore, made by God.[55] Fourth, verse 17 quotes Psalm 69:9, "Zeal for thy house will consume me."[56] What does it mean that the disciples "believed the scripture," this verse of the psalm? They believed that it refers to Jesus. That is to say, they believed that he is the fulfillment of the scriptures. This is a constant doctrine in the fourth Gos-

---

52. Brant Pitre, "Jesus, the New Temple, and the New Priesthood," *Letter & Spirit* 4 (2008): 49–86.

53. Daniélou is alive to this irony; see *The Presence of God*, 43.

54. For the distinction between what God directly wills, indirectly wills, and permits, see Aquinas, *ST* I, q. 19, a. 9; see also Bernard Lonergan, SJ, *De verbo incarnato* (Rome: Gregorian University, 1961), Thesis 15, Praenotamen 1.

55. On this, see also Dn 2:44–45, where a stone "cut out by no human hand" (2:34) breaks the image representing the Babylonian, Median, Persian, and Greek kingdoms: the stone is the Messiah, and the Messiah is the head of the corner of the eschatological temple (Mt 21:42) and is the kingdom of God (Dn 2:44); see Pitre, *The Case for Jesus*, 59–61.

56. This psalm later figures in Jn 19:29: "They gave me poison for food, and for my thirst they gave me vinegar to drink."

pel: the scriptures speak of him (5:39); Abraham rejoiced to see his day (8:56); Isaiah saw his glory (12:41). Just so, even here he fulfills all those scriptures that speak of a temple by indicating his status as the final temple—so also in Mark 11:17, which tells us that the fulfillment of Isaiah 56:7, a temple for all the nations, is nigh.

Fifth, this Psalm verse also reveals the interior attitude of Jesus; his motive for cleansing the temple, his motive for suffering death at the hands of sinners, and his motive for conspiring with his Father to become the new temple. The zeal that consumes him bespeaks an all-encompassing interest and passion, an interest that leaves out nothing of his life and energies. Zeal, however, is an effect of love.[57] That is, it is an effect of the Lord's charity. And this charity is first of all for his Father's house—for his Father. Second, it is charity for us, a love for us even while we were in our sins (Rom 5:8), a love to make himself the place of access to God—the "temple."

Sixth, what does it mean that the disciples, after the resurrection, "believed the word which Jesus had spoken"? They did not need to believe it insofar as it is about the resurrection. They believed it insofar as Jesus declares that his risen body really is the new temple—that is what they believe after the resurrection. His body is not the new temple until it is raised. It is the body given over to death and raised in the Spirit that is the temple. It is only that body that connects us with God, on which the angels of God ascend and descend. It is only that body that connects us, insofar as we receive it in the sacrament and imitate that very paschal movement in our own bodies.

There is one more important passage bearing on Jesus as the new temple, in John 7:37–39:

On the last day of the feast [of tabernacles], the great day, Jesus stood up and proclaimed, "If any one thirst, let him come to me and drink." He who believes in me, as the scripture has said, 'Out of his heart shall flow rivers of living water.'" Now this he said about the Spirit, which those who believe in him were to receive; for as yet the Spirit had not been given, because Jesus was not yet glorified.

When Jesus' glorification begins on the cross, the living waters flow from his heart (Jn 19:34), and when his glorification proceeds to his resurrec-

---

57. Aquinas, *ST* I-II, q. 28, a. 4.

tion, he breathes forth the Spirit into his apostles for the forgiveness of sins (Jn 20:22). The waters that come forth from the heart of Jesus remind us of the "Rock" that gave water to the Israelites in the desert (1 Cor 10:4; Nm 20:7–11), as well as Ezekiel's temple, whence a life-giving river flows (47:1–12), like unto Eden.[58] Christ (the "anointed") includes the church in his own messianic reality by extending the Spirit to the apostles.

Before we pass to the church as temple, it is worth noting that the New Testament's assertion that Christ is temple and priest, offering and sacrifice was well understood by the Church Fathers. As Fulgentius of Ruspe has it:

> For, in the sacrifices of carnal victims which the Holy Trinity itself, who is the one God of the New and the Old Testament, commanded be offered by our ancestors, was signified the most gracious gift of that sacrifice by which God the only Son according to the flesh would mercifully offer himself up for us. For, he, according to the teaching of the Apostle, "handed himself over for us as a sacrificial offering to God for a fragrant aroma" (Eph 5:2). He, true God and true priest, who for us entered once in the Holy Place, not with the blood of bulls and goats, but with his own blood. He signified that other priest who each year used to enter the Holy of Holies with blood. Therefore, this is the one who in himself alone provided everything he knew to be necessary for the effecting of our redemption, for he was both priest and sacrifice, both God and temple; the priest, through whom we are reconciled; the sacrifice, by means of which we are reconciled; the temple, in which we are reconciled; God to whom we are reconciled. By himself he is the priest, sacrifice, and temple, because God according to the form of a servant is all these things; not, however, God alone, because he together with the Father and the Holy Spirit is God according to the form of God.[59]

God's Presence in the Church, His Temple

When the veil of the temple is torn at Jesus' crucifixion (Mt 27:51; Mk 15:38), the temple of stone is finished, and we pass to the temple of flesh, the church. The rock on which Jesus promises to build his church, to build the eschatological temple, in Matthew 16:18 is immediately identifiable

58. For other such reminders of paradise see Zech 13:1, 14:8; Jer 31:12; Joel 3:18.

59. "To Peter on Faith," in *Fulgentius: Selected Works,* trans. Robert B. Eno, SS, Fathers of the Church [hereafter FOTC] 95 (Washington, D.C.: The Catholic University of America Press, 1997), 74.

as Peter in his exercise of Christological faith. This is the faith revealed to Peter by Jesus' Father (16:17), according to which Jesus is not only the Christ but the Son of God (16:16). But its meaning is unpacked according to our recognition of the rock as the rock on which the temple was understood to rest, the rock at the center of the world, the rock at the juncture of heaven and earth and under the earth—the hell whose chaotic waters were stopped and held in check by the temple of God's presence.[60] This issue will be revisited shortly. First, there is a required brief inventory of the New Testament's identification of the church as the messianic temple.

According to St. Paul

Paul seems to take it for granted that the church is God's building, and simply presupposes that the Corinthians understand this. It follows rather directly from the revelation that Christians are so united to Christ that to persecute them is to persecute him (Acts 9:4) and the apprehension that Christ's glorified body is the new place of access to God (1 Cor 1:30; 3:17–18).[61] In any case, Paul warns the Corinthians against factionalism. No one belongs to Apollos or Paul (3:4). They are servants, ministers of the Christ to whom all belong in the church. They work exteriorly, "but God gives the growth" (3:7). Then he says (3:9–17):

For we are God's fellow workers; you are God's field, God's building. According to the grace of God give to me, like a skilled master builder I laid a foundation, and another man is building upon it. Let each man take care how he builds upon it. For no other foundation can any one lay than that which is laid, which is Jesus Christ. Now if any one builds on the foundation with gold, silver, precious stones, wood, hay, straw—each man's work will become manifest; for the Day will disclose it, because it will be revealed with fire, and the fire will test what sort of work each one has done. If the work which any man has built on the foundation survives, he will receive a reward. If any man's work is burned up, he will suffer loss, though he himself will be saved, but only as through fire. Do you not know that you [plural, *umeis*] are God's temple and that God's Spirit dwells in

---

60. See for the meaning of the temple's location Levenson, *Sinai and Zion*, 183–84, and for the rock of Peter's faith upon which the eschatological temple is to be built, see Meyer, *The Aims of Jesus*, 193–95.

61. The logical order of these things is not necessarily the order of their apprehension, of course.

you [plural]? If any one destroys God's temple, God will destroy him. For God's temple is holy, and that temple you are.

The one foundation Paul insists on in 1 Corinthians works with his rebuke of factionalism: the church's one foundation means that the church built on Christ is only one; moreover, there is but one Spirit who dwells in this temple. If the foundation is Christ, and if Paul and Apollos are the builders, are the Corinthians purely passive stones or lumber? They are not. The rebuke Paul is making is addressed to them. How they take the work of Apollos or Paul, in wisdom or foolishness (3:18), builds up or tears down the church, and will be judged on the last day.

The many Christians are the one temple also in 2 Corinthians 6:16, where Paul warns the Corinthians to abstain from relations with unbelievers; the temple of God has no idols in it, and the church inherits the requirement of purity of faith and morals laid on Israel of old (6:16–18). What is common to both passages, thus, is a concern for purity of faith, as there is only *one* foundation of the church, Christ (1 Cor 3:11), as well as a concern for cooperation with grace, for there is no fellowship of "light with darkness" (2 Cor 6:14). This issue of maintaining right faith will come up again shortly.

When Paul deals with Corinthian antinomianism, with those who think there is no law against fornication, Paul invokes a higher standard: "Do you not know that your bodies are members of Christ? Shall I therefore take the members of Christ and make them members of a prostitute?" (1 Cor 6:15). Sexual commerce is ordered exclusively to the marital union of persons. Further, "Do you not know that your body is a temple of the Holy Spirit within you, which you have from God?" (6:19). That God dwelled *among* his people and in their *midst*, that the Old Testament says often. But that he dwells in each Israelite, in each Jew—that is not so clearly said. In the New Testament, each Christian is personally and by divine principle singularly and individually united to God, without prejudice to the collective, social dimension of this belonging to God. This understanding of the Holy Spirit's relation to the church is important for St. Thomas, and explicitly embraced by Pius XII in *Mystici Corporis*.[62]

This indwelling of the Holy Spirit in each Christian, moreover, is

---

62. See Aquinas, *In III Sent.*, d. 13, q. 2, a. 2, sol. 2 and ad 1. Hamer, *The Church Is a Communion*,

common to the New Testament. It is implied by 1 Peter. And in the Acts of the Apostles, the Holy Spirit is poured out on each believer at Pentecost: "there appeared to them tongues as of fire, distributed and resting on each one of them" (2:3; see also 8:17, 10:44–45, 19:6).

There is, then, a double affirmation to make relative to thinking of the church as the temple of the Holy Spirit, and it will be important in thinking about the teaching and agency of the church as such, a topic to be addressed in chapters 10 and 13, below. First, the Holy Spirit dwells in the church as a whole: all the baptized make a temple, and within that entirety, there dwells the one Spirit. Second, each Christian is himself a temple. The Spirit dwells in each Christian separately, and in the whole, as a whole. This makes the unity of the church something both mysterious and potent. It is mysterious because the identity in species of the gifts of charity and the other theological virtues is not the only thing that makes the church one. This specific identity of the virtues indeed makes the church's unity more than an ordinary moral unity, wherein many people think the same things and want the same ends. For this moral unity of the church is founded on supernatural gifts. Even more, however, the unity of the church is constituted by the one single numerically same Spirit who dwells in each Christian, and of whom it must be said that he dwells in the whole as a whole. This is a unity not otherwise known to us and has no natural analogue.

Also, this unity of the Spirit makes the church potent. First, it subsumes the agency of each into the agency of the whole: the thing that makes each one singularly a Christian, the one Spirit, is the very thing that makes the church as a whole a whole. And this means that the church herself possesses an agency not like that of some natural collectivity, some state or some corporation, where there can be no more than a legal, that is to say, fictive unity. No, there is a unity of the church such that we can, without metaphor, speak of her, in the singular, teaching and doing, teaching the faith and making the sacraments.

This unity of the church in the Spirit lets us speak of the church as in some way a person. She is not a person like we are. She is not a person like one of the Persons of the Trinity. Still, she has a unity than which no more

185, remarks: "The indwelling of the Holy Spirit gives the Church its supernatural social nature, in its numerical unity." See Pius XII, *Mystici Corporis*, par. 57.

appropriate word can be found than "personal." This idea will return dog-matically in chapters 7–8, and systematically in chapter 10.

The basic idea of the church's unity, owing to the one Spirit, finds expression also in the Letter to the Ephesians. Here, Paul is concerned especially to note the equality within the church of both Jew and Gentile. The "dividing wall of hostility" between them has been broken down (2:14), for the Old Law "of commandments and ordinances" has been abolished (2:15). The dividing wall that separated Gentiles from Jews in the Jerusalem temple has been abolished, and now all have the same access to the holy place. Or, as St. Paul puts it, by abolishing the Law, Christ creates "in himself one new man in place of the two, so making peace" (2:15). The church as temple, and the church as the body of Christ, whose head is Christ, both making one man, are close in Paul's mind and he runs them together especially in Ephesians, so that the building is said to *grow* (2:21; 4:16), and the body is said to be *built* up (4:12, 16). And indeed, although Christ is the cornerstone of the building (2:20), he is an active cornerstone, in that in him "the whole structure is joined together" (2:21). Now, the church is built up just insofar as individual Christians are placed on the "foundation of the apostles and prophets," whose cornerstone is Christ (2:20). So each Christian is a piece of the one, *whole* church in whom the Spirit dwells (2:22). And yet *each* individual Christian is sealed with the one, same Spirit (1:13, 4:30).

According to St. Peter

The text of 1 Peter does not repeat explicitly this Pauline structure of the church according to which the Spirit dwells in the whole and in each part—each Christian—composing the whole. It is implied, however, in that each stone building the temple is a living stone, living with divine life. And 1 Peter 2:4–8 adds something not explicit in Matthew, 1 Corinthians, or Ephesians:

Come to him, to that living stone, rejected by men but in God's sight chosen and precious; and like living stones be yourselves built into a spiritual house, to be a holy priesthood, to offer spiritual sacrifices acceptable to God through Jesus Christ. For it stands in scripture: "Behold, I am laying in Zion a stone, a corner-stone chosen and precious, and he who believes in him will not be put to shame." To you therefore who believe, he is precious, but for those who do not believe,

"The very stone which the builders rejected has become the head of the corner," and "A stone that will make men stumble, a rock that will make them fall"; for they stumble because they disobey the word, as they were destined to do.

This text recalls the parable of the wicked tenants of the vineyard in its invocation of Psalm 118:22, "the stone which the builders rejected." It strengthens the sense that in Christ the Old Testament is being fulfilled, and precisely in the community that believes that in him, according to Isaiah 28:16, God is "laying in Zion a stone, a cornerstone." As in Ephesians and 1 Corinthians, Christians are built into the messianic temple, and here called "living stones." At the same time that they are a spiritual house—a temple—they are also the holy priesthood (see 1 Pt 2:9) giving service in that house, offering "spiritual sacrifices acceptable to God through Jesus Christ." This tells us, as the other New Testament temple texts do not, what transpires in the messianic temple, how Christians discharge their worship within it.

The spiritual sacrifices are acceptable to God only because this people that offers them has been redeemed by the blood of Christ, "a lamb without blemish or spot" (1 Pt 1:19), now raised from the dead, so that their "faith and hope are in God" (1:21). The sacrifices of the holy priesthood common to all Christians are offered through Christ, which is to say, through and in his sacrifice. Christians have no other, "because Christ also suffered for you, leaving you an example, that you should follow in his steps" (2:21).

What, then, are the spiritual sacrifices Christians offer in the Lord's temple that they are? They are holiness of life (1 Pt 1:14–16; 2:11–12; 4:3–4), mutual love (1:22; 4:8), patient endurance of suffering unjustly inflicted (2:19–20; 3:14; 4:13–14, 16, 19; 5:10), family concord and mutual respect within the family (3:1–7), not returning evil for evil (3:9), mutual service (4:10–11), humility (5:6), and sober vigilance (5:8). They are all the Christian works that St. Paul sums up when he tells the Romans: "present your bodies as a living sacrifice, holy and acceptable to God, which is your spiritual worship" (12:1).

The Acts of the Apostles

On the day of Pentecost, the feast of the giving of the Law, the Old Law passes away because it is fulfilled and replaced by the New Law of charity (Acts 2:1–4):[63]

When the day of Pentecost had come, they were all together in one place. And suddenly a sound came from heaven like the rush of a mighty wind, and it filled all the house where they were sitting. And there appeared to them tongues as of fire, distributed and resting on each one of them. And they were all filled with the Holy Spirit and began to speak in other tongues, as the Spirit gave them utterance.

The tongues of fire and illumination become the many tongues of the various languages in which the gospel is to be preached. The wind signifies a new breath of life, the life of God instilled into each Christian.[64]

The Old Law is replaced with the interior reality of the Spirit, fulfilling Joel 2:28–32, as Peter notes (2:17–18). Moreover, if the meaning of the Old Law as a text is fulfilled by the gospel, it is the case that the place of the Old Law's celebration, the temple, is also replaced. This is not obvious, and that it is so depends on recapturing the proposed extent of the original temple, that of Eden. As we have seen, this first temple is a garden, fit for the habitation of Adam and Eve. But according to Genesis 1:28, Adam and Eve are to "fill the earth and subdue it." Those who were to fill and subdue the earth were not to exist outside the original temple, but to extend it. The microcosm would grow and more and more match the cosmos itself, and the places so included would all be part of the place where men could meet and walk with God.[65]

With the above in mind, the presence of the nations in Jerusalem on the day of Pentecost, twelve nations plus Rome, is significant (Acts 2:9–11). Gathered in the city of the old temple is a representation of the whole earth, to which the church will be extended. The church that Luke says was "*built* up" (Acts 9:31) throughout Judea and Samaria realizes the temple that never was, because of the Fall.

63. See Aquinas, *ST* I-II, q. 106, a. 1.
64. Aquinas, *ST* I, q. 43, a. 7, ad 6.
65. For the cosmic expansion of the garden sanctuary of Eden, see Beale, *The Temple*, 81–87, and for Pentecost as inaugurating a temple, 201–16.

The speech of Stephen, for which he is martyred, corroborates this line of thinking. "The Most High does not dwell in houses made with hands," he tells the Jews (Acts 7:48). He dwells in a house made by his *own* hand, when he raises Jesus from the dead (Jn 2:22; see Mk 14:58). The church which is the body of Christ is, then, also the new temple, the temple of the Holy Spirit. So, Charles Journet can say, the church "is the Holy Spirit insofar as he is manifested visibly in the world."[66] And for Anscar Vonier, the church precisely in her visibility is the visible mission of the Spirit:

That body of Christians [on the day of Pentecost] was the real and permanent sign of the coming of the Spirit. To the external symbol of wind and parted tongues of fire was added the more astonishing sign of human beings thus taken out of themselves and made an object of amazement to all men. This leads to a consideration of paramount importance in the doctrine of the Spirit, namely, that the Spirit is truly said to have come because He has made use of created signs to show His advent and His presence. Now the principal created sign is that entirely transformed group of human beings, the hundred and twenty persons who had gone to the upper room with Peter and John, James and Andrew, Philip and Thomas, Bartholomew and Matthew, James of Alpheus and Simon Zelotes and Jude the brother of James, with the women and with Mary the Mother of Jesus and his brethren; they were the Church, and they were made by the Spirit the external sign of His having come forever.[67]

Apostolic Authority in the Church

Between the sacrifice of the Lord on Calvary and the spiritual sacrifices of Christians, discharged in the body, there is the sacrifice of the Eucharist. The spiritual sacrifices that Peter urges Christians to offer are offered to God sacramentally in joining them to the sacrifice of Christ present in the Eucharist. In the eschatological temple, all are priests, as in Eden and as was projected in the covenant at Sinai (Ex 19:6). But this universal share in the priesthood of Christ is exercised through a ministerial priesthood charged, like Paul, to keep order in the household of God (see 1 Cor 11:17–22). This fact alerts us to the apostolicity of the church.

66. Charles Journet, *Théologie de l'Église* (Paris: Desclée De Brouwer, 1958), 359.
67. Anscar Vonier, *The Spirit and the Bride* (London: Burns, Oates and Washbourne, 1935), 26–27.

The warrant for this connection is in the references that these temple texts make to the apostles. It is Paul, the apostle to the Gentiles, who lays the foundation that is Christ (1 Cor 3). It is the apostles and prophets who are the foundation of the temple in the Letter to the Ephesians, joined together by Christ, the cornerstone. In the Book of Revelation, the apostles are the foundation of the New Jerusalem, which images their function in the church on earth. Most clearly, it is the Lord who charges Peter with binding and loosing when he declares he will build his church on his faith in Matthew 16. With this last text, we see that apostolic authority is not something with which the messianic people of God is later fitted out; it is rather constitutive of the people, constitutive of the church, as a foundation is constitutive of a building. This authority is a permanent part of the church, just like foundations are permanent parts of buildings. It is therefore something given to those who come after the apostles, those whom they ordain as their successors.

This authority is in the first place the authority of apostolic witness, of declaring the truth of the gospel, and then subsequently of maintaining the church on its true foundation, Christ and his truth, throughout the succeeding ages. It is a matter of guarding the deposit (2 Tm 1:13–14). That is, it is an authority given to Peter and to all the Twelve to maintain the church in the truth of the gospel. And just as the sacraments of the New Law are more powerful than those of the Old, giving what they signify—sharing in the death and resurrection of Christ in baptism (Rom 6), eating his true body in the Eucharist (1 Cor 11:29), finding forgiveness at the word of absolution (Jn 20:23)—so the gospel word, the word of Christ, is a more stable word than any purely human word, and can be infallibly declared by those credited with guarding it (Mt 24:35).

Because Christ concludes the revelation of God to man, summing it up and perfecting it, a word has been introduced into history that cannot pass away (Mt 24:35), and which calls for a custodian—"Guard the deposit" (2 Tm 1:14). There was no unerring magisterial authority in Israel, for the deposit of revelation was not complete, and there was therefore nothing to be guarded in its integrity. But now it is complete (1 Tm 6:20; Rv 22:18–19), and so there is an abiding authority that guards it: "and on this rock I will build my church." Nor can the chaos of hell prevail against it, because Peter can discern the chaff of error from the wheat of revealed doctrine.

Second, in addition to being an authority of witness, a magisterial authority, apostolic authority is an authority for sanctification, a sacramental authority. For the sacraments were entrusted to the apostles, too—baptism (Mt 28:19) and penance (Jn 20:22–23). Most especially, it is to the apostles that the Lord commends the authority to make his sacrifice, the sacrifice of the cross, present in the temple of the church when at the Last Supper he told them to "do this," to do the very thing he was doing (Lk 22:19). As he anticipated the cross at the Supper, they would, by the authority he gave them, effectively remember it in the time of the church (see also 1 Cor 11). The Christians Peter addresses therefore offer their spiritual sacrifices, better sacrifices than those of the Old Law because united to the best, that is, perfect sacrifice of Christ in the Eucharist.

If with St. Augustine sacrifice is the visible sacrament of an invisible sacrifice,[68] there is no interior sacrifice surpassing the charity of Christ with which he offers himself, and there is no more suitable expression of this than his surrendering of himself to death. Just in this way, he manifests the gifts first given him as the gifts they are in returning them to God: he returns the created humanity first received from God at his incarnation; and by means of this return of his humanity to God, he also returns himself to the self whence he proceeded, to his Father. As he says in John's Gospel in prayer: "But now I am coming to thee" (Jn 17:11), returning to the Person whence he came, and this by way of sacrifice: "and for their sake, I consecrate myself" (17:19). He does this for our sake, that we may have his joy fulfilled in ourselves (17:11) and may ourselves be consecrated in truth (18:10). The one who is given by God to the world now gives himself back to God, and with those he has made his own, having enabled their gift of themselves to God. Just because of the nature of the sacrifice of Christ, moreover, because of who it is who offers it, as one who enters the heavenly sanctuary whence he was sent (see Heb 9:12), it is a sacrifice that can be realized again and again. In sanctifying himself, Jesus also sanctifies the apostles (Jn 17:17–19). When Jesus sanctifies them in the truth, he gives them the wherewithal to "do" what they are commanded to do at the Supper (Lk 22:19; 1 Cor 11:24–25).[69] And just be-

68. St. Augustine, *The City of God*, trans. Marcus Dods (New York: The Modern Library, 1950), X.5.

69. Joseph Ratzinger/Benedict XVI, *Jesus of Nazareth: Holy Week*, 90.

cause Christ's sacrifice is meant to be available for the church always and everywhere, he gives the apostles priestly authority so that we may enter into the joy of the Lord and consecrate ourselves even as did those whom Peter addressed in his first letter.

Those who succeed to some share of the apostolic ministry, moreover, will have a special responsibility in realizing the unity of the agency of the church, adverted to above. That is, they will have a special responsibility for realizing the personality of the church, a point taken up in chapter 10. Therefore, just as Christians should associate baptism with thinking of the church as the people of God, because baptism is the entry into the people, the sign of it like the sign of circumcision, and just as Christians should associate the Eucharist with thinking of the church as the body of Christ, as will be apparent in chapter 8, so should believers associate the sacrament of holy orders with thinking of the church as the messianic temple.

Last, just as the universality of the church corresponds with thinking of the church as the people of God, so thinking of the church as the temple of the Holy Spirit links up with the apostolic character of the church. Catholicity indicates the stuff or matter of the church, the men and women who make a people. The apostles and their successors are instruments of Christ in their teaching and sanctifying work, subordinate agents of making the church—of constructing the temple.

Coda: Church Buildings

While God reveals himself and so dwells in human minds, there is also a physical correlate of this habitation, as was said in the introduction to this chapter. Where God is known in the original friendship he extended to Adam and Eve, he dwelt in the cosmos and its distillation in Eden. Where he is known as the God of the covenant promise by wandering patriarchs, he visits them episodically where sacrifice is offered, and he is present in accepting the sacrifices of the natural law. Where he is known as He Who Is to an entire people, he makes his name to dwell in the temple of Zion, by reference to which all the peoples may entreat the Lord and in which his own people offer him sacrifice that acknowledges his gifts. Finally, where he is known as Father and Son and Spirit, he dwells in the temple of the visible church scattered throughout the whole world.

This last dwelling until the cosmic dwelling is restored at the end of the age is not, however, without a physical correlate in stone or steel or cedar. Christians build many churches, many church buildings, and it is useful in conclusion to compare them with the temple of Solomon. Solomon's temple was the only temple, the sole place of worship by sacrifice. This bespoke both the unity of the people of God and its history. The uniqueness of the temple as a place of sacrifice was a hedge, not always successful, against idolatry. But Christian churches are many, as many as there are congregations in which the members can see themselves as a whole, as a single assembly, which makes the mission of the Spirit visible to the eyes of all. Each church building individually therefore seems less important than the one temple. But all in their multiplicity testify to a Spirit who has been poured out on all the nations, and so indicate the finality of the economy of grace introduced by Christ.

There is a second important contrast. In a Catholic church, the tabernacle is a holy place more holy than the Holy of Holies of the temple. The Ark of the Covenant contained the tablets of the Ten Commandments. But the tabernacle contains the sacrament of the Word made flesh. Just as the fullness of the Godhead dwells more really in the humanity of Christ than in the temple, so also does it dwell with commensurate perfection in the many Catholic churches where the sacrament is reserved in the tabernacle.

Catholic churches of old therefore regularly recalled much of the theology of this chapter in their arrangement and decoration. The disposition of space matched that of the distinction of temple court, Holy Place, and Holy of Holies. The orientation of the church building lined it up with the axes of the world and made it a reminder of creation. And the decoration, often in elaborate and ebullient detail, recounted the journey of the people of God from the temple of Eden to the temple that will come down out of heaven with the last judgment.

Dogmatic Sum and Synthesis

(1) Christ is the fulfillment of the "house"—dynasty—promised to David, because he is an eternal king, and is likewise the fulfillment of the house David wanted to build for God, Solomon's temple, in that he is the

place where man can meet God, and in that to meet him is to meet the Son of David who is the Son of God.

(2) The church, too, as it is built by Christ and because he breathes the Spirit into it, is rightly called the temple of the Holy Spirit, where the eschatological word of God—the gospel—can be heard and where the sacrifice of Christ is sacramentally made present to which are joined the sacrifices of the common priesthood of all the baptized.

(3) Just because the church foreshadows and anticipates the eschatological house of God, she is also the fulfillment in time of the original cosmic temple.

(4) Because to make the church function as that place where the truth of Christ is heard and where the sacrifice of Christ is celebrated is the charge of the successors of the apostles, which is a dominical commission, the church is apostolic.

CHAPTER 7

THE CHURCH AS BRIDE

The church is not only the people of God and the temple of the Holy Spirit but also the bride of Christ. When we say "people," we advert to the most public, noticeable fact of the church, namely that she is a sociological reality, a collection of men and women made one by some shared history and common personal decision. But the people is messianic, too, that is, anointed with the same Spirit that makes Jesus the Christ. Each of the persons assembled in the church, and in some way, the church as a whole, is thus a dwelling place for God, that is to say, a temple of the Holy Spirit.[1]

The church as both people and temple connotes a structured whole. The people is not a mob, but an organized whole, with different persons fulfilling different roles, and where the offices of bishop and priest are especially important as mediating the very Spirit that makes the people messianic. The church as temple also and just as immediately connotes a kind of articulated whole: buildings are composed of different parts; the living stones cannot all have the same position in the house of God, and

---

1. All three Persons dwell in each Christian, of course; see Aquinas, *ST* I, q. 43, a. 4, ad 2 and a. 5, co. The Holy Spirit is given preeminence, however, as the gift of grace that makes the indwelling of all possible is likened to the "Gift" that the Spirit is, and who as proceeding love is also the exemplary cause of charity. See ibid., a. 5, ad 1 and ad 2.

within this temple, once again, there are priests and ministers whose service of God is the service of the people of God.

Because the Spirit dwells in the church as a whole, and as one thing, there is a sort of unity of the church that, while presupposing the moral unity of Christian persons, goes beyond it. This was pointed out in the previous chapter. The moral unity of the church, where all know the same things by faith and love the same things by charity, is itself something supernatural. But more than this moral unanimity, the church as a whole can be said to teach, to act, to do: in some way, just because of the indwelling of the Spirit, she possesses a unified agency, and is spoken of as if she is just one agent. In this chapter, we see the face of this more-than-moral unity, of this as it were personality of the church—it is the face of a bride.[2]

We belong to a "people" and share its history and hope in its more than historical prospects, and a "temple" is something we reverence as a harbinger of heaven. But when we figure the church as bride, and then subsequently as mother, we can love her. The organizational articulations fade into the background, and the church appears in her mysterious reality as the desired consort of the incarnate Word, his own beloved for whom he died and who was washed in his blood (Eph 5). That the church is bride, and becomes one flesh with Christ, moreover, is presupposed for her being the body of Christ. But that is for the next chapter. So we have the following order: the church is a people; because she is a messianic (anointed) people, she is the temple of the Spirit; because she is the temple of the Spirit, Christians give themselves to Christ in the nuptial banquet of the Eucharist, and in this way, she has a more than moral unity and can be figured as bride; and because she is bride, she is one flesh with Christ, and is his body.[3]

It is a remarkable fact that scripture opens and closes with a marriage. The climax of both creation accounts is a wedding. In the first, there is introduced onto the finished and orderly stage of the world man, the image of God, but immediately differentiated as "male and female," with the command to be fruitful and multiply, and in this way imitate the God of

2. It is the face of a bride as animated by the one Spirit given to each member; see Vonier, *Spirit and the Bride*, 126, 146–47, and 165.

3. For some of the relations in this paragraph, see Ratzinger, *Called to Communion*, 39.

life (Gn 1:8). In the second, the garden is no sooner watered and planted than the first order of business after the creation of the man is to find "a helper fit for him," bone of his bone and flesh of his flesh (Gn 2:18, 23). It is in this way that the man and woman realize the fullness of the image of God in which they were created, in giving themselves to one another in love.[4] And scripture concludes with the New Jerusalem, the bride of the Lamb, coming down from heaven (Rv 21:2, 9–10). In the meantime, waiting for the new heaven and the new earth (21:1) and the Lord's return, the Spirit and the bride say, "Come, Lord Jesus!" (22:17, 20). But in the great meantime, between Genesis and Revelation, there are many brides, many marriages, and many women, all an inextricable part both of how revelation is accomplished, and how salvation is effected. There is, then, an Old Testament preparation and prefiguration of the church as bride, a New Testament fulfillment of this preparation, and a summing up in Mary. Hence the principal parts of this chapter: Old Testament harlots and brides; the New Testament bride of Christ; the Church Fathers and the New Eve; and the Marian church.

Old Testament

The Lord God who first meets us in the pages of Genesis has no consort, which means that sexuality is something wholly created; earthly marriage is not a sign of or reenactment of a divine coupling. Human sexuality does not imitate or draw its power from a prior divine nuptial relation. This is not to say that life itself does not bespeak divine reality. The God of the Old Testament is the God of life: he creates life, he is the living God, he loves life, he is himself lively and active. But although the divine Persons love one another, and although the Son proceeds from the Father and the Spirit from the Father and the Son, the sexual transmission of life has no divine counterpart. This has two consequences, one in the order of revelation, and one in the order of grace. In the order of grace, sexual relations, though not in themselves divine, can be consecrated: marital life can be the vehicle not only of the transmission of human life, but also a sacra-

4. John Paul II, *The Theology of the Body: Human Love in the Divine Plan* (Boston: Pauline Books and Media, 1997), 45–48. See also the Second Vatican Council's *Gaudium et Spes*, no. 24: man "can fully discover his true self only in a sincere giving of himself."

ment of divine life. In the order of revelation, sexual relations, more than being a remote shadow of the Trinitarian exchange of love, can also be turned to declare the depth and properly personal nature of the relation of God to *his people*. In both ways, marriage and sexual relations are released from the order of natural necessity. Though they remain rooted in the necessities of the animal nature of man, they are set free to express the freedom first of God's election and second of Israel's and later the church's response to the divine initiative.

We cannot comprehensively explore the wealth of Old Testament material, but the broad outline is clear enough. In the Old Testament, we pass from many individual women who play a role in the establishment of Israel, to figures of an unfaithful Israel, and last to Jerusalem-Zion, the eschatological bride of the Lord.

St. Paul sees in Hagar and Sarah types of the synagogue and the church. Hagar "corresponds to the present Jerusalem," who is in slavery to the law; "but the Jerusalem above is free, and she is our mother" (Gal 4:25–26). Types not only indicate but prepare for the future. It is a mistake to see in Sarah and Rebecca and Rachel nothing but bare signs of a future church to which they contribute nothing.[5] The history they enact, together with Hagar and Leah, Tamar and Ruth, establishes the pattern of revelation, and by their cooperation with God they contribute to its dynamism, a dynamism not perfected, of course, except in Christ. The point, however, is that they are not empty signs of what is to come, but contribute to its coming.

They contribute to its coming, moreover, precisely as women. Their maternity is entirely essential to embedding the design of salvation in history. What is said of Mary must be said of all the great and valiant women of the Old Testament, because they find their perfection in her, and that is that the Lord is more dependent on woman than he is on man for the incarnation. John the Baptist says that God can raise up children to Abraham from the very stones (Mt 3:9). True enough. But God rather wishes to raise up children to Abraham from the wombs, sometimes originally barren, of those he blesses with children.

---

5. The Fathers see in Rachel and Leah what Paul saw in Sarah and Leah: e.g., Justin, *Dialogue with Trypho*, chap. 134 (in ANF 1) and Irenaeus, *Against Heresies* IV.21 (in ANF 1).

Furthermore, the receptivity of the womb bespeaks the receptivity of the mind to the word of God, the seed of faith. The matriarchs are models of faith, too, and this is formal to their contribution to the establishment of salvation in sign and reality. Sarah laughs at the promise of a child in her old age (Gn 18:11–15). But also, she believes. Rebecca connives with Jacob so that he might receive the blessing of Isaac (Gn 27:1–29); also, she conspires with God to make Jacob the heir of the promise.

When we pass from the matriarchs to the prophets, there is an important shift, a double shift. First, the prophets make the marriage bond a symbol of the bond between the people and God. The "consort" of the Lord is not a heavenly goddess, but the people of the promise that first was made to Abraham and whose first fulfillment was the birth of Isaac. Second, the focus is no longer on the cooperation of human freedom with God to establish the pattern of salvation, but on the resistance of human freedom to God.

In the prophecy of Hosea, the covenant between Israel and the Lord passes from a contract between nations, a suzerainty covenant, to a marriage covenant: "I will betroth you to me in faithfulness and you shall know the Lord" (Hos 2:20).[6] The personal relations of husband and wife are now pressed into the service of revelation. They serve also to heighten the pathos of Israel's unfaithfulness: she is unfaithful, not simply as a nation seeking a better deal from another lord, but as a wife is unfaithful to her husband. So Hosea takes a wife of harlotry (1:2) who bears for him Not Pitied and Not My People (1:6, 9), and the Lord promises punishment for the unfaithfulness of Israel (2:1–13). The intimacy of family relations is a new key in which to express the mercy of God: "When Israel was a child, I loved him and out of Egypt I called my son," but "the more I called them, the more they went from me" (11:1–2). The great paradox, that God's offer of love potentiates the sins of men, calls forth a greater mercy: "How can I give you up, O Ephraim! How can I hand you over, O Israel! … my compassion grows warm and tender" (11:8). This theme is picked up in Jeremiah (3:1–5; 31:32), but it is Ezekiel who gives it its greatest literary development in the story of Jerusalem (chap. 16) and the stories of Oholah and Oholibah (chap. 23).

6. Levenson, *Sinai and Zion*, 77–79.

The meaning of such language for the description of the covenant relation between God and Israel and Judah is not completely apparent prior to the New Testament. But this much can be said: the troubled relations between Israel and the Lord raises the question of whether and under what conditions such relations could be untroubled. There is no full answer to this in the Old Testament. There is, however, a projection of an eschatological answer in the prophets, where daughter Zion is figured as a redeemed and perfectly faithful covenant partner to God, a worthy bride of the all-holy God.

The "daughter of Zion" is promised peace and protection, restoration and prosperity, both before (Zeph 3:14–20) and after (Zech 2:10; see 2:1–13) exile. But it is the last part of Isaiah especially that celebrates the marriage between Zion-Jerusalem and the Lord (Is 62:1–5):[7]

> For Zion's sake I will not keep silent,
> and for Jerusalem's sake I will not rest,
> until her vindication goes forth as brightness,
> and her salvation as a burning torch.
> The nations shall see your vindication …
> You shall be a crown of beauty in the hand of the Lord,
> and a royal diadem in the hand of your God.
> You shall no more be termed Forsaken,
> and your land shall no more be termed Desolate;
> but you shall be called My delight is in her,
> and your land Married;
> for the Lord delights in you,
> and your land shall be married.
> For as a young man marries a virgin,
> so shall your sons marry you,
> and as the bridegroom rejoices over the bride,
> so shall your God rejoice over you.

This restoration was still to be accomplished in Isaiah's time, and even much thereafter. Indeed, its time is the time of a new heaven and a new earth (Is 66:22).

---

7. This is not unanticipated in earlier potions of Isaiah, for instance, 1:21–26; see also 49:14–18, 50:1–4, and 54:1–8.

New Testament

Jesus' extraordinary originality and freedom *vis-à-vis* the Old Testament appear signally in his identification of the figures of the Messiah and the Suffering Servant. His identification of these figures with himself grounds the extraordinary originality and freedom and authority with which he relates to the law, the temple, the sabbath, and the regnant religious authorities. It cracks open for us his own consciousness of his mission and how he will complete it. But this identification is not the whole ground of his authority.

The Messiah, the Suffering Servant, and the prophet like unto Moses—the "Second Moses" (Dt 18:18)—these are all in the first place quite *human* figures. Even the heavenly Son of Man of the Book of Daniel, who sort of straddles the celestial-terrestrial divide, is still and for all that the Son of *Man*. But when we come to the bridegroom, when Jesus identifies himself as the bridegroom, things shift. When we say "bridegroom," of course, we imagine a human figure. But *the* bridegroom of the Old Testament, figured by the prophet Hosea, spoken of at length in the great parables of Ezekiel, whose wedding feast is described in Isaiah—*that* bridegroom is the Lord God, the creator, and so originally as first presented to us, no human being at all. So when Jesus identifies himself as the bridegroom, in whose presence it makes no sense to fast (Mk 2:18–20), in whose presence fasting would conflict with the joy of the nuptials being celebrated and would derogate from a recognition of his bounty and generosity—when he identifies himself as the bridegroom, he does something much more directly shocking than claiming messianic status, for it is very flatly and plainly a claim to belong to divinity.

This identification also changes how we should think of the bridal character of the people of God. As was noted at the beginning of this chapter, divinity transcends sexual determinations. But when the Word becomes flesh, three things happen in the ability of human language to register the realities of revelation in sexually determined language. In the first place, the Word came among us as a man, and therefore as the *Son* of God, the Son of a God who is "Father." Trinitarian reality is disclosed and named in a gendered register.[8] In the second place, as a man, he brings

8. For why the masculine gender more suitably connotes a transcendent God, see, e.g., Elizabeth Achtemeier, "Exchanging God for 'No Gods': A Discussion of Female Language for God,"

the nuptial symbolism of the Old Testament from figure to reality and restores the way that nuptial relations were from the beginning to realize the divine image in two made one flesh. He does this as the New Adam relative to the New Eve, the church. He really is the bridegroom of the new covenant relation. He raises up no children carnally, but by the gift of the Spirit he makes many to share his sonship, able to call out in no figure but in truth "Abba, Father" (Gal 4:5–7). In the third place, must not the passing from figure to reality in the position of the groom imply something similar for the church in the position of the bride? Yes, but it is hard to state. The church as bride possesses more unity, and therefore something more like personal agency, in this, the last age.[9]

It should not be supposed, therefore, that to style the church as bride and Christ as bridegroom is a purely metaphorical deployment of language. It is rather a question of participation. Christ participates in the reality of being a groom, and the church in the reality of being a bride. But we should rather say: grooms now participate in the reality of Christ the bridegroom and brides in the reality of the church, and especially when the natural participation is bumped up into a supernatural sharing in the gifts that make for supernatural nuptiality.

Christ's identification of himself as the bridegroom links together the whole drama of salvation from Genesis forward. The one flesh of Adam and Eve becomes a sacrament of the one flesh of Christ and the church, and the Jerusalem who is our mother is the Jerusalem who is the bride of the Lamb, coming down from heaven in the promise of the last pages of the New Testament.

The nuptial character of the relation of Christ to the church is especially developed in John and Paul. In John's Gospel, the Baptist is the friend of the bridegroom, who leads the bride to the wedding (Jn 3:29). That is, John leads the disciples to Christ (1:35–37). This wedding is folded into the wedding celebrated at Cana in Galilee, however, where the wine fails and Jesus supplies an abundance befitting the messianic age

---

in *Speaking the Christian God: The Holy Trinity and the Challenge of Feminism*, edited by Alvin F. Kimel, Jr. (Grand Rapids, Mich.: Eerdmans, 1992), 1–16.

9. For the passage from figure to reality with the incarnation, see Louis Ligier, SJ, "The Question of Admitting Women to the Ministerial Priesthood," 7–8; available at https://www.ewtn.com/library/Theology/ORDWOMEN.htm.

(Am 9:13; Jl 3:18).[10] Now, it was the part of the bridegroom at a Jewish wedding to supply the wine, and Jesus steps into this part, giving a sign of who he is.[11] Because of this first sign, the disciples "believed in him" (Jn 2:11). That is, they believe him to be the Lamb of God (1:29), the one who will baptize with the Holy Spirit (1:33), the Messiah (1:41). The disciples of Christ, those who believe, are now the bride of the Lamb.

Like John the Baptist, St. Paul, too, presents himself as the friend of the bridegroom. "I feel a divine jealousy for you," he says to the Corinthians, "for I betrothed you to Christ to present you as a pure bride to her one husband" (2 Cor 11:2). The purity of the bride has to do here with the faithfulness with which the Corinthians are devoted to Christ (11:3), how well they keep to the gospel as it was delivered to them by Paul (11:4). In Romans, the death of Christ entails also that the Roman Christians have died to the law (7:4) so that they may belong to the risen Christ. There is a fuller explanation in Ephesians: "Husbands, love your wives, as Christ loved the church and gave himself up for her, that he might sanctify her, having cleansed her by the washing of water with the word, that he might present the church to himself in splendor, without spot or wrinkle or any such thing, that she might be holy and without blemish" (Eph 5:25–27). By giving himself up, by his passion and death, he sanctifies us, the church, and this cleansing is imparted to us in baptism, "the washing of water with the word." The holiness of the church—and this is a necessary part of saying that the church is the bride of Christ—is the holiness she receives from Christ. Further, the "mystery" by which a man is joined to his wife to become one flesh "refers to Christ and the church" (5:31–32).

Just as apostolicity is associated with the church as temple, and catholicity with the church as the people of God, so holiness becomes the church as the bride of Christ. This will be explored more systematically in part 3. Also, just as baptism is a mark of the people of God, and the sacrament of holy orders belongs to the maintenance of apostolicity in the church, so the sacrament of marriage especially bespeaks the church as bride. From this we can deduce not only the holiness of the church, but her uniqueness and fruitfulness as well: there is one dove, one bride (Song

10. Brant Pitre, *Jesus the Bridegroom: The Greatest Love Story Ever Told* (New York: Image, 2014), 42–43.
11. Ibid., 43–45.

6:9), and she bears many children to God. The holiness of the church in this age is, as it were, the final cause of all else in the church.

In the previous chapter, it was noted that just as the church as a whole is the temple of the Spirit, so is each Christian individually. Is the same true of the church as bride, such that each Christian can rightly be styled as a bride of Christ? This is not explicitly stated in Ephesians, and many exegetes resist saying it. It is, however, very evidently implied by saying that the church becomes bride by the baptismal bath. If you are part of the bride, and she is cleansed and made bride by baptism, and if you are baptized, how can you not be bridal? This is also implied by 1 Corinthians where St. Paul reproves the use of prostitutes and likens the Christian's unity with the Lord as a unity of one flesh: "But he who is united to the Lord becomes one spirit with him" (1 Cor 6:17).[12]

From the Side of Christ

When St. Paul expresses the unity of Christ and the church in terms of being "one flesh," he is of course quoting the Book of Genesis: "Therefore a man leaves his father and his mother and cleaves to his wife, and they become one flesh" (2:24), realizing the image of God in which they were created in mutual self-gift. Because this "mystery" of the union of Adam and Eve "refers to Christ and the church" (Eph 5:32), Adam is revealed as a type of Christ. This is also evident from 1 Corinthians 15. But here, Adam is a type of Christ precisely as husband of Eve, "the mother of all the living" (Gn 2:20), and Eve a type of the church.

The priority of Christ to the church in the Letter to the Ephesians (5:24, 26) can therefore also be expressed in terms of the creation of Eve, drawn from Adam's side in his sleep. It was a "deep sleep" (Gn 2:21), but the deepest sleep is death. Hence the construction of the Church Fathers. When John Chrysostom (d. 407) explains the power of Christ's blood to his catechumens, he touches first on the blood of the paschal Lamb, sprinkled on the door (Ex 12:7), at the sight of which the destroying angel turns away (12:13). Then he reports how blood and water flowed from the side of Christ, pierced by the soldier's lance. The water is a type of bap-

12. See ibid., 139–44.

tism, and recalls for John the water flowing from the temple. So, he says, the soldier "opened Christ's side and dug through the rampart of the holy temple, but I am the one who has found the treasure." The water flows from the temple (Ezek 37), as the rivers from Eden (Gn 2:10–14). Thus we are brought to the Garden, and John writes:

"There came out from His side water and blood" [Jn 19:34]. Beloved, do not pass this mystery by without a thought. For I have still another mystical explanation to give. I said that there was a symbol of baptism and the mysteries [the Eucharist] in that blood and water. It is from both of these that the church is sprung "through the bath of regeneration and renewal by the Holy Spirit" [Ti 3:5], through baptism and the mysteries. But the symbols of baptism and the mysteries come from the side of Christ. It is from his side, therefore, that Christ formed his church, just as he formed Eve from the side of Adam.

And so Moses, too, in his account of the first man, has Adam say: "Bone of my bone and flesh of my flesh" [Gn 2:23], hinting to us of the Master's side. Just as at that time God took the rib of Adam and formed a woman, so Christ gave us blood and water from his side and formed the church. Just as then he took the rib from Adam when he was in a deep sleep, so now he gave us blood and water after his death, first the water and then the blood. But what was then a deep slumber is now a death, so that you may know that this death is henceforth sleep.

Have you seen how Christ unites to himself his bride? Have you seen with what food he nurtures us all? It is by the same food that we have been formed and are fed. Just as a woman nurtures her offspring with her own blood and milk, so also Christ continuously nurtures with his own blood those whom he has begotten.[13]

St. John Chrysostom gets a lot of work done, theological work, with this typology.[14] First, there is the absolute priority of Christ to the church, in its being and its growth. Second, there is the nature of Christian sacraments, according to which they really are what they signify, so that the cup of blessing really is the blood of Christ. Third, this last point is not simply asserted but is established by the typology: just as Eve is made

---

13. St. John Chrysostom, *Baptismal Instructions*, trans. Paul W. Harkins, Ancient Christian Writers [hereafter ACW] 31 (Westminster, Md.: Newman Press, 1963), Third Instruction, 13–19, slightly altered. This reading is used for the Liturgy of Hours for Good Friday in the Roman church.

14. As do a host of the Fathers, from Tertullian forward. See Jean Daniélou, SJ, *From Shadows to Reality: Studies in the Biblical Typology of the Fathers*, trans. Dom Wulstan Hibberd (Westminster, Md.: Newman Press, 1960), 48–56.

from the flesh and bone of Adam, so the church is made from an equally real flesh and blood of Christ. Fourth, there is given us also the through-and-through sacramental nature of the church: she comes into being by the sacrament of baptism; she attains her growth from the nourishment of the Eucharist. Fifth, there is asserted the unity, more than moral, of Christ and the church—a "mystery," indeed.

A Marian Church

From St. Paul's teaching that Adam is a type of Christ (Rom 5:12–19 and 1 Cor 15:20–22) it follows not only that Eve is a type of the church (Eph 5:31–32), but also that she is a type of Mary. When on the tree of the cross the Lord Jesus undoes the disobedience of Adam who ate of the Garden tree, he commends Mary to John with the words "Woman, behold, your son" (Jn 19:26), calling her by the first name Adam gives Eve (Gn 2:23). He says also to John, "Behold, your mother" (Jn 19:27), and so Mary is the mother of Christians, something obvious also from Revelation 12:17.

When first Mary appears in Luke's Gospel, she is already a figure of the church. She is the new Ark of the Covenant, bearing the child through the hill country of Judea to the house of Zachary and Elizabeth (Lk 1:39; 2 Sm 2:6). She is herself bodily the house of God; thus the Spirit overshadows her (1:35) just as the cloud covered and filled the tabernacle and later the temple.[15]

Thus the church is a Marian church, something celebrated already in the second century.[16] Abstractly stated, the fundamental reality of the connection between them is that both cooperate with Christ in the work of salvation such that it really depends on them, while their cooperative agency of course depends on Christ's principal agency. The symbolic communication of this truth is complex, but can be developed in five steps. First, because she is a virgin, Mary is the mother of God. Next, because she is the mother of Christ, the head of the church, she is also (though in a different way) the mother of his members. Thus, third, she is mother of the whole Christ, head and members, and so mother of the

15. Daniélou, *The Presence of God*, 21.
16. St. Irenaeus, *Against Heresies* III.22.

church.[17] Fourth, Mary's virginal motherhood of Christ is emblematic of the church's virginal motherhood of Christians. Mary's virginal motherhood is, as it were, communicated to her daughter, the church, and so the church, too, is virgin and mother. Fifth and last, Mary's holiness is reflected in the holiness of the church.

Because She Is Virgin, Mary Is the Mother of God

It is precisely because of her donation of herself to God, of her entire reality, body and soul, mind and strength, that she fittingly receives the Word of God. She is, as the angel says, "full of grace" (Lk 1:28)[18] and therefore the perfect hearer of the Word. Just because her virginity is a perfect spiritual donation to the omnipotent God for him to do with as he will, she conceives bodily by the Holy Spirit with no need of any human agent. The virginity of Mary is therefore not a negative thing, but a positive thing. It means that she finishes her personality wholly and exclusively first by her relation to God, to his Son, and to their Spirit, and then subsequently, but in virtue of this first and most basic relationship, in relation to us.[19]

The power of Mary's virginal self-donation has Old Testament foreshadowings. Virginity and barrenness have in common that there is no issue. The barren condition of Sarah, Rebecca, Rachel, Manoah's wife (Jgs 13), and Hanna (1 Sm), which they overcame by faith, which is to say they overcame by a receptivity to the wisdom and providence of God, is a sign of Mary's virginity, her own complete donation of herself to the Lord. This completeness of Mary's self-bestowal unto God is captured in the patristic saying that what Mary conceived in her womb, she first conceived in her mind by faith.[20]

17. Paul VI, closing speech to the Third Session of the Second Vatican Council, November 21, 1964.

18. That is, she is graced in every possible respect, to the fullest extent possible.

19. See John Paul II's the first, fifth, and sixth catecheses on virginity for the sake of the kingdom in his *The Theology of the Body: Love in the Divine Plan* (Boston: Pauline Books and Media, 1997), 267–70 and 273–78.

20. St. Augustine, *Holy Virginity*, trans. John McQuade, SM, in *Saint Augustine: Treatises on Various Subjects*, ed. Roy J. Deferrari, FOTC 27 (Washington, D.C.: The Catholic University of America Press, 1955), 146.

The Mother of Christ the Head Is the Mother of His Members

Should we not first say a word about what in our experience comes between virginal innocence and maternal fecundity, the spousal relation? No. The great Matthias Scheeben notwithstanding, there is no Gospel or patristic warrant for speaking of Mary as the bride of Christ.[21] Adam is to Christ as Eve is to Mary (Irenaeus). But this does not mean Mary is related to Christ as Eve is related to Adam.[22] The bride of Christ is the church.

The maternal relation of Mary to Christ, moreover, sufficiently establishes her maternal relation to Christians. This is because her maternal relation to Christ does not stop at Bethlehem and Nazareth, but extends to Jerusalem. Her mothering of her Son extends to fostering and nurturing him in his mission, and especially in her sharing his sufferings at the foot of his cross. She does first what St. Paul does later, explaining to the Colossians that he rejoices in his sufferings for their sake, for "in my flesh I complete what is lacking in Christ's afflictions for the sake of his body, that is, the church" (Col 1:24). So also Mary does this in virtue of the grace and strength first given her by Christ.[23] But she really does actively share in his work, for the Lord is not jealous of his agency, but freely includes others in his work.

Mary's share in Christ's sufferings is immediately fruitful. For when the Lord saw his mother and the disciple he loved from the cross, "he said to his mother, 'Woman, behold, your son!' Then he said to the disciple, 'Behold, your mother'" (Jn 19:26–27). And so it was: "the disciple took her to his own home" (19:27). Thus she becomes the mother of every Christian, and every Christian her child.[24]

---

21. Cyril Vollert, *A Theology of Mary* (New York: Herder and Herder, 1965), 78–79 and 130–34.

22. Ibid., 134.

23. St. Augustine, *Holy Virginity*, chap. 6 (149): Mary "is evidently the mother of us His members because she has co-operated by charity that the faithful, who are members of that Head, might be born in the Church." Augustine explains in this chapter that while Mary is the mother of Christ in the body, Christ bears Mary spiritually. In her holy members, the church is wholly the mother of Christ and wholly the virgin of Christ in spirit; in consecrated virgins, the church is the virgin of Christ in body, and in married women, mother—but not the mother of Christ.

24. See the John Paul II, *Redemptoris Mater*, Encyclical Letter, March 25, 1987, par. 23; available at www.vatican.va.

Mother of the Whole Christ and Thus Mother of the Church

If Mary is mother of Christ, the head, and mother of his members, his body, then she is mother of the church, as Paul VI taught at the conclusion of the Vatican Council. Beyond John 19, there is also John 2. When the disciples believe in Jesus at Cana (2:11) and so become the church, his bride, this is at the provocation of Mary, who moves the Lord to make the miracle, changing water to wine at the wedding. She becomes the mother of the church. Further, while Mary's presence at the Lord's birth cannot be forgotten, she is present also at the birth of the church, at Pentecost (Acts 1:14). Her motherhood of the church is thereby manifested and shown to be continued in the motherhood of the church.[25]

Mary's Virginal Motherhood Bespeaks the Church,
Christ's Bride, as Virgin and Mother

When told that his mother and brothers awaited him, Jesus said "My mother and my brothers are those who hear the word of God and do it" (Lk 8:21). Those who hear the word of God, as his mother did perfectly, are his mother and family. Should we then say that the church is *his* mother? That does not sound right. To be sure, everything that has been said in this section leads us to conclude that, in some way, Mary is the church and the church is Mary.[26] Yet the church is bride even though Mary, who is not the bride of Christ, is the church, and the church, who is the bride, is Mary. This is how Blessed Isaac of Stella (d. ca. 1169) put it: "What is said in the inspired Scriptures universally of the virgin mother, the Church, is understood in a singular way of the Virgin Mary, and what is said particularly of the virgin mother Mary is rightly understood in a general way of the virgin mother, the Church. And when either is spoken of, what is said goes for both together, practically without difference."[27]

This is a sort of rule for Catholic speech about the church and Mary,

---

25. Ibid., par. 24.

26. As Cyril Vollert says, "All the Marian dogmas ... converge towards a theological and prayerful contemplation of Mary as the archetype of the Church," *The New Catholic Encyclopedia*, 2nd ed. (Farmington Hills, Mich.: Thomas Gale, 2002), 9:258a. He concludes this after canvassing the maternity, virginity, holiness, and co-redemptive mission of both Mary and the church.

27. Sermon 51, the First Sermon for the Assumption; in Isaac de l'Étoile, *Sermons III,* Sources Chrétiennes 339 (Paris: Cerf, 1987), 205.

like the communication of idioms for speech about Christ, and the Rule of Athanasius for speech about the Persons of the Trinity. The communication of idioms has to do with one hypostasis or person sharing the attributes of Christ's two natures, human and divine. According to this rule, we can truly say that the Son of God died (although not in his divinity) and that Jesus is all-powerful (though not in his humanity). The Rule of Athanasius has to do with the three hypostases or Persons of the Trinity sharing the identically same nature without difference or distinction. According to this second rule, if the Father is truly divine, so is the Son and the Spirit. Or again, if the Spirit is perfect goodness, so is the Father and the Son—and so on for all the divine attributes. The *communicatio maternitatis* between Mary and the church has to do with sharing in the virtues and gifts that make for a good mother.[28] It is a relation in the order both of representation and causality. In the order of representation, Mary is a figure of the church, and the church displays at large an *ethos* that is Marian. As Benedict XVI puts it, "Mary's motherhood becomes theologically significant as the ultimate personal concretization of the Church."[29]

But also, the church's maternity really depends on Mary's, because the church lives by the virtues and gifts merited by Mary's Son, merited by the passion in which she also shared. She shares her maternity with the church so that the church can bring forth Christians as she has brought forth Christ. But she does not share her maternity with the church in bringing forth Christ. When we say that the church brings forth Christ, we mean that she brings forth Christians, or Christ in Christians.

So we can say the same things of both Mary and the church, as Blessed Isaac says, "practically" but not completely "without difference." What is common to them, according to Yves Congar, is that both bespeak human cooperation in the work of salvation, where the initiative belongs to God in Christ.[30] Mary cooperates in bringing forth the head, and the church cooperates in bringing forth the members.

Together, they bear the whole Christ. Because the church is one mys-

28. The maternity of the church relative to Christians is noted already in the second century.
29. Joseph Ratzinger, "Thoughts on the Place of Marian Doctrine and Piety in Faith and Theology as a Whole," in *Mary: The Church at the Source*, with Hans Urs von Balthasar, trans. Adrian Walker (San Francisco, Calif.: Ignatius Press, 2005), 30.
30. Congar, *Christ, Our Lady and the Church*, 16.

tical person with Christ (the topic of the next chapter), Mary is mother of the church, the mother of the *totus Christus*. We do not say this of the church, however. The church is not mother of the whole Christ; the church is our mother, but not the mother of Christ the head. Similarly, there really is a relation of dependence of Christians on Mary. Christians really depend on Mary, because they really depend on Christ, and because the fullness of her grace is a fullness for all other Christians, too.[31] However, Christ is not dependent on the church, but rather the reverse. And the forming of Christ in the Christian is especially the work of the clergy, who figure Christ. The church is the spouse of Christ, not his mother. Mary is the mother of Christ, not his spouse.[32]

To sum up: because Mary is the mother of Christ, she is mother of the church; and because she is mother of Christ and the church, the church is mother, too. Even so, Mary remains within the church as a member, and is a daughter of Zion. As Benedict XVI says: "Mariology goes beyond the framework of ecclesiology and at the same time is correlative to it."[33]

The virginity of Mary bespeaks the virgin church, too. It is a matter of spiritual faithfulness for both. The virginal church is the church that is faithful to the gospel, keeping and guarding the deposit of faith. Just as Mary first conceives the Word by faith, so the church is virginal precisely in the purity and integrity of her faith. St. Augustine: "How is it that you do not belong to the Virgin's birth, if you are members of Christ? Mary gave birth to our Head; the Church gave birth to you. Indeed, the

31. See Aquinas, "In salutationem angelicam expositio," in *Opuscula Theologica II: De re spirituali*, ed. M. Calcaterra (Rome: Marietti, 1954), no. 1118. If Mary's "fiat" was both free and moved by grace, and so meritorious, then her maternity relative to the members of Christ is also certainly a divine maternity, i.e., a bringing forth of supernatural life in Christians. See, for discussion, W. J. Cole, *New Catholic Encyclopedia*, 2nd ed., 9:264a–b.

32. "Spouse of Christ" is attested from the eighth century in the East according to Michael O'Carroll, *Theotokos: A Theological Encyclopedia of the Virgin Mary* (Wilmington, Del.: Michael Glazier, 1982), 333b. For a good discussion of the various grounds upon which to say of Mary that she is the "Bride of God," "Bride of the Father," "Bride of Christ, of the Word," see Veronika Trenner, "Braut," in *Marienlexicon*, ed. Remigius Bäumer and Leo Scheffczyk (St. Ottilien: EOS Verlag, 1988), 1:561b–571b. She reports that contemporary usage favors "Daughter of the Father," "Mother of the Son," and "Bride of the Spirit." I think it must always be slightly dangerous to speak of Mary as at once mother and bride of Christ, but especially today when imaginations are less thoroughly cultivated and refined.

33. Ratzinger, "Marian Doctrine," 29.

Church also is both virgin and mother, mother because of her womb of charity, virgin because of the integrity of her faith and piety."[34]

Holy Mary, Holy Church

The holiness of the church is exemplarily shown to us in Mary, in the mother of the head who is the first member of the body. It is a holiness merited by her Son, anticipated in her own immaculate conception. This holiness of Mary is not unimportant for how we think about the reception of the truth and grace of Christ in the church. It is a reception than which no greater can be conceived. Untainted by any trace of sinfulness, the revelation of Christ is perfectly conceived in the Mary, who pondered it in her heart (Lk 2:51). Untainted by any trace of sinfulness, her reception of the grace of Christ is full, and her wonder and praise and thanksgiving perfect. The nuptial relation of Christ to the church is projected eschatologically in the parable of the wedding feast (Mt 22:1–14). But Mary's possession of the goods of Christ now is a pledge to us now of the fullness our possession in the next age.

Dogmatic Sum and Synthesis

(1) The church is the bride of Christ, which is to say holy, because she is redeemed by Christ and washed by him in the laver of baptism and enlivened interiorly by the grace of the Holy Spirit.

(2) Because of her relation to Christ as her spouse, and because Christ is really and not metaphorically a man, there is introduced a concreteness into the relationship not wholly realized in the figurative relation of Israel to the Lord.

(3) As the bride of Christ, the church is signified as possessing as it were a personal unity, which goes beyond but is inclusive of the moral unity of a corporation or social group, which depends on agreeing on the end of the group and the means to reach the end. This unity subsists in the whole church in that the one Holy Spirit dwells in each Christian,

---

34. Augustine, Sermon 192.2, quoted in Luigi Gambero, *Mary and the Fathers of the Church: The Blessed Virgin Mary in Patristic Thought*, trans. Thomas Buffer (San Francisco, Calif.: Ignatius Press, 1991), 223.

but is especially directed and exercised by the successors of Peter and the apostles, as was said in the previous chapter.

(4) Because the church is the bride of Christ, she is mother relative to Christians.

(5) Mary is the mother of Christ, the head of the church, and so also of those he unites to him as his members, which is to say the grace of Christians depends also on her; therefore she is a figure also of the church, the mother of Christians, who brings them forth by the ministry of word and sacrament.

CHAPTER 8

THE CHURCH AS THE BODY OF CHRIST

The principal New Testament deliverance on the church is that she is the body of Christ. Before turning to the texts of 1 Corinthians, Romans, Colossians, and Ephesians, however, let us begin at the beginning. And the beginning is the conversion of Paul on the road to Damascus. Paul's conversion includes, or just is, God's revelation of his Son to Paul (Gal 1:16), the communication to Paul of what he calls his "gospel" (Gal 2:2). For the sake of analysis, we can say it has six components. First, Jesus is God's Son, for it is precisely Jesus as *risen* who appears to Paul on the road, confirming the extraordinary claims he had made as to his personal identity. Second, just because he is God's Son, Jesus is in his death and resurrection a resource beyond the law for producing what the law promised but of itself could not grant: forgiveness of sins, justification, reconciliation with God in the Spirit (Gal 2:2; 3:2, 5, 8, 11; Rom 3:21–22). Third, because there is now a resource for what the law promised on the other side of and independently of the law, it can be a resource also for those who are apart from the law, for the Gentiles. Thus, Paul is sent to them to preach Christ, the risen Lord (Acts 9:15; 22:21; 26:17, 23; Gal 1:16). He is sent not to make them Jews, but to make them Christians (Gal 2:14–16). Fourth, our access to justification beyond the law is by faith and baptism (Acts 9:6, 18; Gal 3:26–27), baptism into the death of Christ (Rom 6:1–6). Fifth, faith and baptism join one to Christ so closely that we can be said to "put on Christ" (Gal 3:27), and therefore, to persecute Christians is to persecute Christ himself (Acts 9:5; 22:8; 26:15).

Sixth and last, baptism makes all the baptized "one" in Christ (Gal 3:28). One what? Within the same context of explaining his gospel of which he is a minister to the Ephesians (Eph 3:7) and which gospel he is to preach to the Gentiles (3:8), Gentile Ephesians are said by faith and baptism (4:5) to be made members of the same "body" as are baptized Jews (4:5). But this same body is the "one body" of Christ (4:4).

Who is Christ that the church can be his "body"? He is the one who sends the Spirit to make other "anointed ones," other "christs." Within the Trinity, moreover, the Spirit unites Father and Son. And the Spirit accomplishes the same unifying work when sent into Christians and the incarnate Son. The same Spirit by which Christ's *natural* body is glorified (Rom 8:11) makes of us members of his *mystical* body.

1 Corinthians and Romans

That the church is the body of Christ is therefore central to the entire Pauline construal of the gospel. This teaching shows up in its most developed form in Colossians and Ephesians, where Christ is the head of the church, his body. But it is first prominent in 1 Corinthians. Paul explains to the Corinthians that there are varieties of gifts, services, and workings in the community (*charismata, diakonia, energêmata*), but that it is the same Spirit who is being manifested in the gifts (1 Cor 12:4, 7), the same Lord who is thereby served and confessed (12:3, 5), and the same God who inspires all these works (12:6), all given for the common good of the community (12:7). So there are utterances of wisdom, knowledge, and faith, healings and workings of miracles, the gifts of prophecy and tongues (12:8–10). Then we have this: "For just as the body is one and has many members, and all the members of the body, though many, are one body, so it is with Christ. For by one Spirit we were all baptized into one body—Jews or Greeks, slaves or free—and all were made to drink of one Spirit" (12:12–13).

Paul then works the analogy with the human body and its parts (12:14–26): hand and ear, eye and feet, all contribute to the good of the whole (12:19) and to the good of each part (12:25–26). Then it is back to the church: "Now you are the body of Christ and individually members of it. And God has appointed in the church first apostles, second prophets, third teachers, then workers of miracles, then healers, helpers, administrators, speakers in various kinds of tongues" (12:27–28). It is important to note that it is the whole body, head included, as indicated by mentioning the eyes and ears, that is the one body of Christ. In this text, Christ is manifested through the whole, and not by any single part, and he is not associated with any single part of the body, as will be the case in Colossians and Ephesians, where he is the "head."

It may be that the analogy with the human body of 1 Corinthians 12:14–26 is picked up from the Stoic comparison of the human body to the social whole, the body politic, where all the parts serve the good of the whole and of one another.[1] But we should think more originally about how the body presents itself to us, and how the Bible thinks of the body, in order to sound the depths of Paul's thought.

The body presents itself to us in a double-barreled way. The body is both the person and the instrument of the person. "Don't touch me," we may say, when someone bumps us or grabs our arm. The body is the person, and the person is his body. But also: "Use your hand" (to stir the water or smooth the cloth and so on). Bodily parts are instruments of the person. With death, there is something of the person left over from the body, now a corpse; namely, the immaterial soul. It is soul and body united, however, that makes the human person.[2] And the body as a whole is that through which the person is present in the world, present so as to connect with other persons, present so as to be able to rearrange the things of the world. Both of these senses of the body are entirely biblical.[3] They are not a matter of revelation so much simply as of bringing to expression our immediate experience of the body. They are both given in

1. Heinrich Schlier reports this possibility in "The Pauline Body Concept," trans. Lawrence E. Brandt, in *The Church: Readings in Ecclesiology*, ed. Albert LaPierre, Bernard Verkamp, Edward Wetterer, and John Zettler, 44–58 (New York: P. J. Kenedy and Sons, 1963).

2. Aquinas, *ST* I, q. 75, a. 4.

3. Xavier Léon-Dufour, *Dictionary of the New Testament*, trans. Terrence Prendergast (San Francisco, Calif.: Harper and Row, 1980), at "body," 117: "The body designated the person in his or

Paul's experience of the church as the body of Christ: "Why do you persecute me?" the Lord asks (Acts 9:4)—touch my body, touch me. But also, the many parts of the body serve the body unto the good of the parts and the whole: that is the teaching of 1 Corinthians 12:14–26, and the RSV English translation does not hesitate to use the word "organ," which is to say "instrument," to name a member of the body (*melos*).

Some of the operations of the members of the body, therefore, are self-serving, as it were: they maintain the one body of Christ, and the end of their operations is the good of each member and of the whole church they compose. But other operations are more outwardly directed, say, the work of an apostle (1 Cor 12:28) or evangelist (Eph 4:11). What the body does is make the person whose body it is present and active in the world and in history: it is the principle of personal agency in the world, and so, what the members do is what Christ does (we need not suppose exactly in the same sense in every case). What the members do as true members of Christ, however, can be more precisely expressed by saying that they all work so as to constitute a communion of love, the love of Christ and the love of one another in Christ. But this communion has a mission without which it cannot be itself, which mission is to include within it all of humanity through the work of evangelization and to represent all of humanity before God.

Just as the natural body is the instrument of forming the natural communions of family and city, the body of Christ is the instrument of forming the supernatural community of the church.[4] And this is to say that the union of the member of the church with Christ is more than the moral union of the members of a social whole with one another. By moral unity is meant the kind of unity that two or more people have because they understand the same truths that make for human solidarity and love the same goods that foster and result from such solidarity. The unity of the body of Christ is moral, to be sure. But it is also a unity in the Spirit of Christ, and it is produced by the sacraments that unite us to Christ, and so to the risen and glorified body of Christ, glorified precisely in the Spirit

---

her external and visible aspect," and "the body was that through which man entered into relationships with his brethren and with the universe; it constituted his ability for self-expression."

4. For the body as instrument of communion, see Joseph Ratzinger, *Eschatology: Death and Eternal Life*, trans. Michael Waldstein (Washington, D.C.: The Catholic University of America Press, 1988), 81–82.

in which it was raised (Rom 8:11). So 1 Corinthians 12:13: "By one Spirit we were all baptized into the one body ... and all were made to drink [Eucharistically] of one Spirit."

This unity with the risen Christ, his body, has showed up already in 1 Corinthians 10:16–17: "The cup of blessing which we bless, is it not a participation [or communion—*koinonia*] in the blood of Christ? The bread which we break, is it not a participation in the body of Christ? Because there is one bread, we who are many are one body, for we all partake of the one bread." We share in the one body of Christ at the Eucharist, taking part of the one Loaf and we *become* "one body," so that we *are* the "one body."[5]

The Old Testament types of the Supper and baptism have already been evoked in 1 Corinthians 10. Manna, the "spiritual [*pneumatikos*] food" (10:3) is a type of the bread, and is linked with the "spiritual drink" (10:4) provided from Christ, the "Rock" that followed the people in the desert, after their baptism "into Moses in the cloud and in the sea" (10:2). Sacramental type in the Old Testament has passed over to sacramental reality in the New. Note that, whether it is a question of types or anti-type (the sacrament), they insert one into a person, Moses or Christ. The reality of the connection to Christ, however, is to be emphasized. So Pierre Benoît:

Paul began with this conviction that salvation was brought about by the union of the body of the Christian with the dead and risen body of Christ, a union which is realized in the rite of baptism, and after that in the rite of the Eucharist, in the light of faith. Starting from this, the current metaphor of the social body, a unity yet multiple, appeared useful to illustrate the unity of Christians with one another which resulted from their common union with the same body of Christ.[6]

What the metaphor expresses is the union of Christians not only with Christ, but with one another and for one another's good.[7] It is the underlying theological reality of connection to Christ, however, that is basic. It is a reality that is supposed to govern our moral conduct, especially our moral bodily conduct, and Paul evokes it in reproving concourse with prostitutes (1 Cor 6:15). For the one risen and glorified body of Christ

5. Pierre Benoît, "Body, Head and *Pleroma* in the Epistles of the Captivity," in *Jesus and the Gospel*, 2:51–92, at 60.
6. Ibid., 57.
7. Ibid., 61. See 1 Cor 12:25–26.

"gathers to itself all those who are united to it, by their very bodies, in the rite of baptism, and become its 'members.'"[8]

That baptism is into the death of Christ so that we might be raised into the newness of life in which we walk (Rom 6:3–4) is very important for thinking through what it means to say that the church is the body of Christ. Christ acquires this body only through the death of the body he took from Mary, his mother. He abandons that very thing that, by nature, makes us present in the world of men and human relations, the body that enables communion, just in order that through the resurrection of that same body in the Spirit, we may be joined to it by the same Spirit and the charity he pours forth into our hearts (Rom 5:5).[9] The natural communion of family or city now passes over to a stronger communion in Christ. As the soul of a man is to his body, so the Spirit is to the body of Christ. And as natural love is to natural communions, so the charity of Christ is to the body of Christ. On this basis, Romans 12 returns to the church as "body of Christ" and exhorts Christians to mutual respect and ecclesial humility so that no one may "think of himself more highly than he ought to" (12:3).

If we take Romans 6 seriously, therefore, our own entrance into the church must in some way retrace the path of Christ through the isolation and loneliness that are the effects of sin unto the fullness of shared life in Christ through the Spirit. We do this sacramentally, *via* baptism. We do it also morally, by making up in our bodies "what is lacking" to the suffering of Christ "for the sake of his body, that is, the church" (Col 1:24) and by presenting ourselves, which is to say, our bodies, "as a living sacrifice, holy and acceptable to God, which is our spiritual worship" (Rom 12:1).[10]

Colossians and Ephesians

When we pass to Colossians and Ephesians, we find an importantly different understanding of the church as the body of Christ.[11] Of course, there is much that is the same. We are united to the once dead, now risen

---

8. Benoît, "Body, Head and *Pleroma*," 58.

9. See Ratzinger, *Eschatology*, 92–102, on the death and resurrection of Christ.

10. Of course, this introduces what Paul says of the church as the body of Christ in Romans.

11. In addition to Benoît, see also André Feuillet, "L'Eglise plérôme du Christ d'après Ephés., I, 23," *Nouvelle Revue Théologique* 78 (1956): 449–72 and 593–610, and Ignace de La Potterie, "Le Christ, Plérôme de l'Église, Ep 1:22–23," *Biblica* 58 (1977): 500–524.

body of Christ through baptism (Col 1:11–12), and are now reconciled to God with our sins forgiven (Col 1:13). But also, we are connected to Christ in the church precisely insofar as he can be considered the head of the church, his body (Col 1:19).

How does Christ's headship get introduced into the application of the idea of the body to the church? One is "head" in relation to another insofar as one has authority over the other.[12] So, in Colossians and addressing the concern of the Colossians as to the relation of Christ to thrones and dominions—heavenly, cosmic powers—Paul says Christ is their head, "the head of all rule and authority" (Col 2:10). For though Christ is certainly a man, "the whole fullness of deity dwells bodily" in him (2:9), and this puts him, even as a man, over all worldly and even over all superworldly but created power. Just because of and through his passion and death and his becoming the first-born of the dead (1:18), all things are reconciled in him, "whether on earth or in heaven" (1:20), and there is therefore "peace by the blood of his cross" (1:20; see 3:15). Just so, the powers and principalities are "disarmed" (2:15), and the Colossians need no longer serve or worship them (2:16–18, 20–23).

Once Christ's headship is introduced to locate his position *vis-à-vis* the cosmic powers and principalities, it is then available also to locate his position relative to the church. Here, however, Christ is no longer merely the authoritative director of the body, as in a human individual the head directs the other members of the body, especially by sight and decision. In addition, and as Greek medicine of the time understood the role of the head in an individual man, Christ is imagined as the vital principle of the church, the seat of its growth and development.[13] This is not far from common sense either: the mouth, through which the whole body takes nourishment, is in the head. So the Colossians are to hold fast to their head, "from whom the whole body, nourished and knit together through its joints and ligaments, grows with a growth that is from God" (Col 2:19).[14]

This dependence of the body on Christ is expressed in Ephesians in a

---

12. Benoît, "Body, Head and *Pleroma*," 72.

13. Ibid., 71–74. For Aquinas, the grace distributed to the church, to each member of the body, is a share in his own habitual grace; see *ST* III, q. 8, a. 5.

14. Where Benoît sees the contact of the sacraments and the sharing of the Spirit ("Body, Head and *Pleroma*," 75).

way that harks back to 1 Corinthians. The ascended Christ gives gifts of ministry, exercised by apostles, prophets, and evangelists, by pastors and teachers, "for building up the body of Christ" (Eph 4:1–12). Christ acts for the good of the whole through those he empowers to act by his gifts. The work of the minister is in some way the work of Christ. His agency remains in the world through the body of the church. But this body of Christ is once again united by more than a moral unity, for it entails that each Christian grows up "to mature manhood, to the measure of the stature of the fullness of Christ" (Eph 4:13). And this is a matter of more than natural gifts; it is more than a natural imitation of Christ with natural knowledge and love. This conformation to Christ, more than moral, can be expressed in the same vitalist language found in Colossians: "Speaking the truth in love, we are to grow up in every way into him who is the head, into Christ, from whom the whole body, joined and knit together by every joint with which it is supplied, when each part is working properly, makes bodily growth and upbuilds itself in love" (Eph 4:15–16). This love is God's love, the love that "has been poured into our hearts through the Holy Spirit which has been given to us" (Rom 5:5).

There is also a new way in which the dependence of the body, the church, on Christ her head comes to expression in Ephesians. The distinction of head and body makes the church stand out more personally *vis-à-vis* Christ, just as a bride relative to her husband. So, the common way of relating husband to wife, as authoritative "head" of his spouse, serves also to express the relation of Christ to the church: "Wives, be subject to your husbands, as to the Lord. For the husband is the head of the wife as Christ is the head of the church, his body, and is himself its Savior. As the church is subject to Christ, so let wives be subject in everything to their husbands" (Eph 5:22–24). And this suggests further ways to express the union of the church to Christ, ways that cover the same ground as the vitalist language found in both Colossians and Ephesians. First, there is the labor of Christ in making the church worthy of this union: "Husbands, love your wives, as Christ loved the church and gave himself up for her, that he might sanctify her, having cleansed her by the washing of water with the word, that he might present the church to himself in splendor, without spot or wrinkle or any such thing, that she might be holy and without blemish" (Eph 5:25–27). And then, second, there is consummation in love: "'For this reason a man shall leave his father and mother and be joined to his wife, and the two shall become one flesh.' This mystery is a profound one, and I am saying that it refers to Christ and the church" (Eph 5:31–32). The relation of Christ to the church, of husband to wife, engage both the bodily and the personal registers of knowledge and love.

Jean-Hervé Nicolas notes two differences between 1 Corinthians and Romans, on the one hand, and Colossians and Ephesians, on the other, in speaking of the church as Christ's body.[15] Just because Christ is no member of the body in 1 Corinthians and Romans but transcends the whole, he seems less closely united to it than in Ephesians and Colossians. Also, if Christ is now invisible, then the body of which he is head in Colossians and Ephesians is also likewise invisible. The church as the body of Christ is thus more obviously an object of faith. Doubtless, that the church is Christ's body in 1 Corinthians and Romans is also an object of faith. Still, to the extent that the social aspect of the church is being evoked against the background of the Stoic characterization of the state as a body, there is brought forward the empirical reality of the church, in which it is obvious, even to one without faith, that it is an organization in which people undertake different roles. This question of the visibility of the church is important in a comprehensive systematic understanding of the church.

The "Fullness"

Above, it was emphasized that by baptism and the Eucharist, Christians are united to the risen and life-giving body of Christ. It is life-giving with the life of God, to be sure, and this is expressed in Colossians also with the language of "fullness." The *plêrôma* is first of all a Stoic term for the divine principle which both fills all things and is filled by all things.[16] The idea is taken up in the Books of Wisdom and Sirach to describe the relation of the transcendent God to the created world, his immanence and omnipresence (Sir 16:29; Wis 1:7), and the word is used in a cosmic sense in the Septuagint.[17]

---

15. Jean-Hervé Nicolas, OP, *Synthèse dogmatique: de la Trinité à la Trinité*, 4th ed. (Paris: Beauchesne, 2011 [1985]), 652.

16. Benoît, "Body, Head and *Pleroma*," 82–83.

17. Ibid., 83–84.

In Colossians, the fullness is the "fullness of divinity," the fullness that just is divinity.[18] This is important for the security of those in Christ, still threatened by the "powers and principalities" (Col 2:15; see also Eph 6:12). "For in him [Christ] the whole fullness of deity dwells bodily, and you have come to fullness of life in him, who is the head of all rule and authority" (Col 2:9–10). Once they are connected to the divinity by being connected sacramentally to the risen Christ, Christians also find themselves in a cosmos that, because of the work of Christ, is reconciled to God. Christ's work reconciles all things, and not just sinners, to God (1:19–20). Moreover, because of the incarnation, the divinity that is in all things is now in the man Christ, and the members of Christ's body are united to it. And from the head, the body is now "nourished and knit together through its joints and ligaments" (2:19). In the prevalent translation of Ephesians 1:23, the fullness takes on an ecclesial sense: "And he [God] has put all things under his feet and has made him the head over all things for the church, which is his body, the fullness of him who fills all in all" (Eph 1:22–23).

So in Colossians, the fullness is the divinity, and in Ephesians, it is the church. This is awkward and improbable. But if the participle translated actively, above, as "who fills" is translated passively, and "fullness" is understood appositively, referring to Christ, then it is not Christ who is filled—also problematic—but the church that is filled with the fullness of Christ.[19] Then we would read for 1:23: "The church is the body of Christ and is filled with Christ who completely fills everything" (Contemporary English Version) or "And the church is his body; it is made full and complete by Christ, who fills all things everywhere with himself" (New Living Translation). This way is supported by Ephesians 4:11–16, where because of Christ's gifts (4:11) we are to grow up into the measure of his "fullness" (4:13), nourished and growing from the divine gifts Christ gives the church (4:15–16). It is supported also by Ephesians 3:19, where the "fullness" is the fullness of God. And it lets us understand "fullness" in the way that the Gospel of John does (1:14, 16).

18. In ibid., 82–86, it means both God and the cosmos he fills in Colossians.
19. For this way of taking things, see de La Potterie, "Le Christ, Plérôme de l'Église."

Old Testament Background

It may seem that there is no Old Testament background to speaking of the church as the body of Christ. All the talk of God's bodiliness in the Old Testament—his mighty arm, his eyes—is metaphorical, and though he may be "clothed" with majesty and glory, nothing is related to him as his body. It would seem that we have to wait for the New Testament, for the Word made flesh and for a very literal sense in which God, the Son of God, is embodied, before bodiliness can be impressed for the purpose of speaking of the relation of human beings to God.

There is, however, an Old Testament thought-form that serves as background to the idea of the church as the body of Christ, and that is the idea of corporate personality. A "corporate person" is some collective, a clan or town or nation, whose identity is originally and principally established by patriarch or chief or king, and which collective extends that identity in space and time. Or the other way around, a "corporate person" is a patriarch or chief or king whose personal identity and reality is realized and writ large in others and can be recognized in family or tribe or nation.[20] Such an identity of nation and founding person occurs in the call of Abraham. God says to Abraham: "I will make of you a great nation ... and by you all the families of the earth shall bless themselves" (Gn 13:2–3). The promise is not that God will make Abraham the *ancestor* of a great nation, but rather, the great nation *is* Abraham, and it is *Abraham* who is the future blessing for all the nations, long after the husband of Sarah is in his tomb.

One of the signs that the idea of corporate personality is operative is an alternating plural and singular number in speaking of a collectivity in relation to its identity-making head. Such fluidity of reference, singular and plural, can be found in Deuteronomy 12:1: "And Moses called the whole of Israel and spoke to them [plural]: "Ye [plural] have all seen what the Lord has done before your eyes in Egypt, to Pharaoh and all his servants and his whole land, the great marvels which your [singular] eyes have seen, each great sign and wonder." This could be a slip, or a sign of re-

---

20. H. Wheeler Robinson, *Corporate Personality in Ancient Israel* (Philadelphia: Fortress Press, 1973).

dactional work maybe. But perhaps it communicates some apprehension of the personal unity of certain groups foreign to the modern age. J. de Fraine notes that in the psalms, the singular "I" can mean not just the I of an individual, or the identity of a group personified, or its corporate and shared personality, but all three together.[21]

Is such a thought-form merely a remnant of myth, where ancestor and heir are apprehended as making a physical reality transcending space and time? It is hard to say. There is, after all, a partial physical identity between ancestor and heir, and there can be a moral identity, too. Is there any reality to speaking of the "spirit" of a people beyond the moral unity engendered by a common language and history? We do not have to decide such questions, as it seems obvious that this thought form is used to communicate properly theological truths.

For beyond a thought-form with which to think about the identity of historical persons and the groups they found or beget, it is a thought-form that is used prophetically, too. There is a noteworthy employment of corporate personality in Daniel 7:13–27, *apropos* of the Son of Man, who is both an individual and a collective, the collectivity of the saints. What is given to the Son of Man, an individual, in verse 14 is given to saints in verse 18. Like the four beasts that precede the Son of Man in Daniel's vision, the Son of Man stands for a political, social, religious group, and denotes a kind of personal unity inclusive of the king and his kingdom. But here it is a political, social, religious group strictly in relation to the one, true God of the covenant and the promises. The same phenomenon is also recognized in the figure of the Suffering Servant of the Lord in Second Isaiah: he is both an individual and the people. He certainly seems to be an individual in Isaiah 52:13–53:12, in that the sufferings are wounds and wounds are inflicted on an individual body (53:5), and the peculiar form of his individual appearance is invoked (53:2), from whom other individual men turn away (53:3). On the other hand, he suffers on behalf of the people and is wounded "for our transgressions" (53:4–5) and the sin of all the people is laid on him (53:6, 12). This does not of itself make the very people as a whole the servant. Still, the oracles of this part of Isaiah deal with the return of the people from exile, and it is very easy to read the

---

21. J. de Fraine, SJ, *Adam et son lignage* (Bruges: Desclée de Brouwer, 1959).

servant as the people in 42:1–4. The servant of 50:4–11 seems very like one, individual person. But then there is 49:1–6, with this at verse 3: "And he said to me, 'You are my servant, Israel, in whom I will be glorified.'" So, the servant is an individual who suffers and redeems, and at the same time a people who suffers and is redeemed.

With the above in mind, therefore, we can say that St. Paul's recognition of the church as the body of Christ, framed within the totality of scripture, is also a statement that the figures of the Son of Man and the servant of the Lord are fulfilled in Christ and the church. The idea of the church as the people of God, considered in chapter 5, evidently also owes much to this thought-form of corporate personality: the messianic people shares in the identity of the Messiah, of the Son of Man, of the Suffering Servant. This is important for recognizing the finality of the economy of salvation. While the action of God and the word of God were certainly introduced into the economy of salvation in the Old Testament, the Lord himself did not come among the Israelites as bearing their condition, and so they could not bear his identity in the way they could that of Abraham. But now there is a new realism of the divine presence in history, and the thought-form that united a people with its ancestor and founder can now unite a people with their divine and incarnate savior. For when we say "Christ" now, what do we mean? Jesus of Nazareth, yes. But also all those who share in the Spirit which makes him the anointed, the Messiah, "Christ."

The Holy Spirit just in himself and originally is a principle of unity. He unites the Father and the Son in the Trinity while never abrogating their distinction. This same Spirit then is the principle of the unity of the church: by the Spirit, Jesus is made the Christ, apt to share his anointing, and we, once anointed with the same Spirit, are joined to him. And just precisely as divine, he is a principle of unity of more power and capacity than any created principle of unity—some substantial form or soul. So when we say "Christ," we can and sometimes should mean Jesus of Nazareth, the original Christ, together with all those united to him by the gifts of grace and the Spirit of grace, the *totus Christus*, as St. Augustine has it, *una quaedam persona*.

The *totus Christus* in Augustine

For a thousand years, Augustine's appreciation of the church as the whole Christ, head and body, a development of St. Paul, was the ecclesiology of the Western church. A great part of this ecclesiology can be gathered from his commentary on the Book of Psalms. For Augustine, all of scripture concerns Christ; it prefigures him in the Old Testament and declares him openly in the New. But the psalms are prayers, and they remain the prayers of the church, folded into the responses to the first reading at Mass and serving as the backbone of the Liturgy of the Hours. Just because they are prayers, they are patient of a complex interpretation, insofar as we ask who is speaking about what to whom. Michael Fiedrowizc explains how St. Augustine read the psalms: "Augustine followed the pattern customary in early Christian exegesis, which interpreted the psalms as either a word to Christ (*vox ad Christum*), or as a word about Christ (*vox de Christo*), or as a word spoken by Christ himself (*vox Christi*), or in an ecclesiological perspective as a word about the church (*vox de ecclesia*), or finally as a word spoken by the Church (*vox ecclesiae*)."[22] Additionally, when Christ speaks, he speaks sometimes in his own voice, in distinction from the church, and sometimes on behalf of the church, and there we find the voice of the "whole Christ."[23] Fiedrowizc:

The idea surfaces that Christ can only be the true bearer of the prayer if he is understood as "the whole Christ" (*Christus totus*), as "one human being" (*unus homo*) in the unity of a Head and body. This concept of the "one human being" expresses organic unity, which closely corresponds to the Old Testament idea of corporate personality. This unity of Head and body, bride and Bridegroom, Christ and the Church, is the focal point of Augustine's personal interest in expounding the psalms.[24]

22. Michael Fiedrowicz, "General Introduction," in *Exposition of the Psalms 1–32, The Works of Saint Augustine. A Translation for the 21st Century* III/15, trans. Maria Boulding, OSB, ed. John Rotelle, OSA (Hyde Park, N.Y.: New City Press, 1990), 44–45.

23. Augustine is here following the teaching of Tyconius. Tyconius (d. ca. 400) was a catholicizing Donatist who wrote a book on how to interpret scripture. St. Augustine incorporated his rules in his own book on scripture. See the third book of *On Christian Teaching* (*De Doctrina Christiana*), trans. R. P. H. Green (Oxford: Oxford University Press, 2008).

24. Fiedrowizc, "General Introduction," 56–57.

Here is an example from Augustine's exposition of Psalm 142.[25]

Therefore the Lord himself, Jesus Christ, is both head and body. For he wanted to speak in us, who deigned to die for us; he made us his members. And so sometimes he speaks in the person of these members, and sometimes he speaks in his own person, as our head. For he has something that he declares without us; but we have nothing to say without him. The Apostle says: "So that I may fill up in my flesh what is lacking to the sufferings of Christ" [Col 1:24]. "So that I may fill up what is lacking," not to my sufferings, he says, but to those "of Christ." "In the flesh"—not the flesh of Christ, but "my flesh." Christ still suffers, he says, not in his own flesh, in which he ascended to heaven, but in my flesh, which still toils on earth. Christ, he says suffers in my flesh: "For I live, no longer I, but Christ lives in me" [Gal 2:20]. For unless Christ himself were suffering also in his members, that is in his faithful, Saul, on earth, would not be persecuting Christ, in heaven. And thus he explains this openly in a certain text: "For just as the body is one," he says, "and has many members, but all the members of the body, though many, are one body, so it is with Christ" [1 Cor 12:12]. He doesn't say, "So it is with Christ and his body," but "the many members are one body, and so it is with Christ." Christ is a whole; and because Christ is a whole, therefore the head says from heaven, "Saul, Saul, why do you persecute me?" [Acts 9:4]. Hold this fast, and keep it entirely fixed in your memory, as children of the Church's training and of the Catholic faith, that you may acknowledge Christ to be the head and the body, and the same Christ to be also the Word of God, the Only Begotten, equal to the Father, and so may see how great is the grace by which you belong to God, that he, who is one with the Father, has willed to be one with us. How is he one with the Father? "I and the Father are one" (John 10:30). How is he one with us? "He does not say, 'and to his offsprings,' as to many, but as to one, 'and to your offspring,' which is Christ" [Gal 3:16]. But someone will say: If Christ is the offspring of Abraham, why are not we? Remember that the offspring of Abraham is Christ; and by this, if we too are offspring of Abraham, therefore we too are Christ. "For just as many members are one body, so also with Christ," and "however many of you have been baptized in Christ have put on Christ" [Gal 3:27]. *Christ*—that is the offspring of Abraham. Nor can this be contradicted by the clearest words of the Apostle, "And to your offspring, which is Christ." For look at what he says to us: "But if you belong to Christ, therefore you are offspring of Abraham" [Gal 3:29]. Therefore that mystery is great: "There will be two in one flesh" [Gn 2:24]. The Apostle says: "This is a great mystery; but I speak of Christ and the Church" [Eph 5:32].

25. Augustine, *Ennarationes in Psalmos CI–CL*, ed. E. Dekkers and I. Fraipont, Corpus Christianorum Series Latina 40 (Turnhout: Brepols, 1956), 2061–62. The translation is my own.

Christ and the Church—two in one flesh. Account for the "two" by the difference of majesty. Plainly, there are two. For we are not the Word; we are not in the beginning God with God; we are not he through whom all things were made. He came unto flesh: and there both we and he are Christ. Do not, therefore, be surprised in the Psalms: for many things he says in the person of the head, many in the person of the members; and this whole, just as if it is one person, so it speaks. Don't wonder that there are two in one voice, if there are two in one flesh.

First, it seems to fair to say that the head-body schema of Colossians and Ephesians has absorbed the earlier schema of 1 Corinthians and Romans. Second, the link of Colossians 1:24, where Paul makes up in his body the sufferings of Christ, to Galatians 2:20, where Christ lives in Paul, is said to have its explanation in 1 Corinthians 12: *because* the church is the body of Christ, what one member suffers counts as the sufferings of Christ, and Christ is in Paul as a man is his body and is in his members. This is then driven home by recalling the original event of the revelation of Christ to Paul on the road in Acts 9:4 ("why are you persecuting me?"). The catena of these four texts is brilliant.[26]

Third, Augustine summarizes this teaching in a formal and solemn way, linking it up with the fundamental Christological confession of the church: "Hold this fast, and keep it entirely fixed in your memory, as children of the Church's training and of the Catholic faith." What we are to hold fast, as it were as part of the creed, is just this: "that you may acknowledge Christ to be the head and the body, and the same Christ to be also the Word of God, the Only Begotten, equal to the Father." So to speak, the incarnation finds its *telos* in the church: as he is united to God his Father in one divinity, we are united to him by charity and the Holy Spirit, as he elsewhere explains.[27] Augustine wants his hearers to see "how great is the grace by which you belong to God, that he [Christ], who is one with the Father, has willed to be one with us."

Fourth, the text of Galatians about the one offspring of Abraham, Christ, does not mean we are not his offspring—if we belong to Christ

26. For a contemporary statement of the importance of Col 1:24 for understanding our relation to Christ see John Paul II, *Salvifici Doloris*, Apostolic Letter, February 11, 1984; available at www.vatican.va.

27. See, e.g., *Sermon* 267, "On the Day of Pentecost," in *Essential Sermons*, trans. Edmund Hill, OP (Hyde Park, N.Y.: New City Press, 2007); *The Trinity*, 2nd ed., trans. Edmund Hill, OP (Hyde Park, N.Y.: New City Press, 2012), XV.17 and 26.

by belonging to his body, the church, we are the children of Abraham, and for this he repeats the phrase from 1 Corinthians 12. Fifth, the one Christ, the one body of Christ, always suggests to Augustine the one flesh of husband and wife, just as it should for careful readers of the Letter to the Ephesians. As in many other places commenting on the one body of Christ in the psalms, therefore, he ends with Ephesians 5:32.

The Church and the Eucharist

In the early fifth century in Hippo, catechumens were not instructed about the Eucharist prior to their baptism. At the Easter vigil, they were immersed into its reality before things were explained. Augustine undertook the explanation the day after, on Easter Monday: "What you see now on the altar is what you saw last night. But what it was, what it meant, of how great a thing it contained the sacrament—this you have not yet heard."[28] Then he states the mystery of Eucharistic reality plain and bold: "What you see, then, is bread and cup; that's what your eyes tell you. But what your faith wants to be instructed about is this, that the bread is the body of Christ, that the cup is the blood of Christ." Then he formulates the question that should arise for the newly baptized:

We know whence our Lord Jesus Christ took flesh; it was from the Virgin Mary. He was nursed as an infant ... he grew up ... he was hung on the cross, he died on the cross ... he rose on the third day ... he ascended into heaven ... and there he now sits at the right hand of his Father: how is the bread his body? And the cup, or what the cup holds, how is it his blood?

The body and blood of Christ belong to the history of his life and death and resurrection, and that body and blood are now in heaven at God's right hand; how can they be here, on the altar? Augustine first lays down a general sacramental principle: "These things are called sacraments for this reason, because one thing is seen in them, and another understood." What looks like bread to the eyes is understood by faith to be the body of Christ; what looks like wine is understood by faith to be the blood of Christ.

---

28. St. Augustine, *Sermon* 272. I have modified the translation found in J.-M.-R. Tillard, OP, *Flesh of the Church, Flesh of Christ: At the Source of the Ecclesiology of Communion*, trans. Madeleine Beaumont (Collegeville, Minn.: Liturgical Press, 2001), 41–42.

More than a statement of what faith understands is required, however. Augustine has undertaken to deliver an understanding of *why* faith understands what it does.

If therefore you wish to understand the body of Christ [i.e. to understand why it is that what is on the altar must be the body of Christ], hear the Apostle saying to the faithful: "But you are the body of Christ, and his members" [1 Cor 12:27]. If therefore you are the body of Christ and his members, it is the mystery you are that has been put on the Lord's table: you receive the mystery that you are. To what you are, you answer "Amen," and so answering, you assent to it. For you hear "body of Christ," and you answer "Amen." Be a member of the body of Christ so that your "Amen" be true. But why in the bread? Let us bring nothing of our own [thoughts] to this; let us listen to the same Apostle, who when he would speak of this sacrament says: "We who are many are one bread, one body" [1 Cor 10:17]. Understand, and be glad. Unity, truth, piety, charity! One bread: who is this one bread? "We many are one bread." Recollect that the bread is not made out of one grain, but from many. When you were exorcized, you were being ground into flour. When you were baptized, you were being moistened with water. When you received the fire of the Holy Spirit, you were being baked. Be what you see [on the altar], and receive what you are.... So also the Lord Christ signified that he wanted us to belong to him, and consecrated the sacrament of our peace and unity on his table.

Because the bread is one bread made from many grains, it signifies us, the many individuals of the congregation, the many members who really are the body of Christ. And because we really are this one body, the consecrated elements must also really and truly be his body, for—and this is the suppressed premise—they make us the body of Christ. The sacrament has to have what it takes to make us the body of Christ and so must be the body and blood of Christ. If the ultimate signification of the sacrament is realized in us, so that we are what is signified, and what is signified is the communion of charity that is the church, the body of Christ, then the sacrament must have what it takes to do that: what it takes to do that is Christ; therefore, the sanctified elements are the body and blood of the Lord.

The bread and wine are thus a double sacrament as to signification: the one bread from the many grains signifies us, whose peace and unity is that of the body of Christ; also, they signify the body and blood of the Lord in the sacrament of the altar. The bread and wine are but a single sacrament in the order of reality, however, making present the body and blood of the Lord. That true body and blood have the further effect of making us to be the ecclesial body of Christ. That is to say, the Lord's agency then effects what the bread and wine *also* signify, the communion of peace and unity that is the church. But it is just because the visible bread and wine signifies us, the church, that, once consecrated, we know they must be the true body and blood of the Lord whose end is the unity and peace of the church in charity.

In 1 Corinthians 10, Paul argues that the Eucharist makes the church: the sacrament of the body and blood of the Lord makes the ecclesial body of the Lord. "The cup of blessing which we bless, is it not a participation [or communion—*koinonia*] in the blood of Christ? The bread which we break, is it not a participation in the body of Christ? Because there is one bread, we who are many are one body, for we all partake of the one bread" (1 Cor 10:16–17). But Augustine argues the other way around: because baptized and communicating Christians are the body of Christ, therefore the bread is his body, and the cup contains his blood. Paul argues from the real presence to the church as the one body of Christ; Augustine argues from the church as the one body of Christ to the real presence.

Augustine's argument is surprising and perhaps difficult to understand because we moderns are more ready to countenance the possibility that sacramental signs may be just signs, signs empty of what they signify. We are more ready to see no real difference between the sacraments of the Old Law and the sacraments of the New. They both become Protestant *nuda signa*. But just as Augustine was confident that the humanity of Christ gives what it signifies, the Word of God, and that the Word of God must give the reality of God, so he was confident of the fullness of the sacraments instituted by the incarnate Word—these sacraments share the efficacy of the flesh whose visibility they extend to us even after the ascension.

We are therefore not far here from the question of the nature of the church in the sixteenth century. Can the church *herself* be an empty sign? But if we answer the question about the Eucharist and the other sacraments the way Augustine and the fathers (and Aquinas) did, then it is hard to doubt that, as St. Irenaeus said, where the Spirit is, there is the church, and where the church is, *there is the Spirit*—and the body of Christ, and Christ. This will be taken up in chapter 10.

If the church makes the Eucharist, then the Eucharist makes the church. The church makes the Eucharistic body, the true body and blood of the Lord under sacramental forms of bread and wine, yes; but then this true body and blood make the ecclesial body of Christ, that body of his touched by the power of his risen body, which extends its *pneuma,* which is the Holy Spirit, unto the members of Christ for their salvation. The *pneumatikos* bread (see 1 Cor 10:3) makes a *pneumatikos* church, the ecclesial body of Christ.

The church makes the Eucharist, and the Eucharist makes the church. This has played a central role in the last century's understanding of the church.[29] It has also found signal magisterial expression, the most important of which is to be found in St. John Paul II's last encyclical, *Ecclesia de Eucharistia.*[30] The opening words declare: "The Church draws her life from the Eucharist. This truth does not simply express a daily experience of faith, but recapitulates the heart of the mystery of the Church" (par. 1). And he explains by saying that the church is born of the paschal mystery, and the Eucharist is the sacrament of the paschal mystery (par. 3). The first chapter of the encyclical repeats this teaching: the "central event of salvation becomes really present in the Eucharist," for there "'the work of our redemption is carried out'" (par. 11, citing *Lumen Gentium,* no. 3). And the chapter reminds us that the Eucharist is a sacrifice in the "strict sense" (par. 13) and of the real presence of Christ under the forms of bread and wine (par. 15).

The encyclical gets down to its central purpose in the second chapter, "The Eucharist Builds the Church." "A causal influence of the Eucharist is present at the Church's very origin" (par. 21). The Eucharist effects incorporation into Christ (par. 22); it "confirms the Church in her unity as the body of Christ" (par. 23), and conduces to "fraternal unity" (par. 24), which is to say that the Eucharist establishes the church in her constitutive reality as a communion of charity. It establishes the church in

---

29. See Henri de Lubac, SJ, *The Splendor of the Church,* trans. Michael Mason (San Francisco, Calif.: Ignatius Press, 1999), chap. 4.

30. John Paul II, *Ecclesia de Eucharistia,* Encyclical Letter, April 17, 2003; available at www .vatican.va.

what she was instituted to be, the reality of the church (on earth) beyond which there is nothing further to hope for. The sacrament of the body of Christ makes the church the body of Christ. Christ, through his sacramental body, makes his ecclesial body.

The encyclical's third chapter treats of the apostolicity of the Eucharist and of the church, that is, it explains how, if "the Eucharist builds the Church," it is also true that "the Church makes the Eucharist" (par. 26). Both Eucharist and church are apostolic in three senses: they are both built on the foundation the apostles first laid down for the church after the Lord's ascension; the church lives by the faith of the apostles, and the Eucharist is today celebrated according to that same faith (no. 27); last, the church is ruled and sanctified by the successors of the apostles, the bishops, and the Eucharist is brought about by priests ordained by these successors (no. 28). Only the priest, acting in the person of Christ, sacramentally and so really links the Mass to the sacrifice of the cross and the Lord's Supper (no. 29). The fourth chapter of the encyclical treats of the Eucharist and ecclesial communion, and reiterates the necessity of visibly sharing the faith of the visible church to receive Communion (par. 38); so to speak, the characteristics of the church—here, visibility—cannot but be characteristics of the Eucharistic celebration. Just so, the holiness of the church has to be reflected in the fact that those who receive communion are in the state of grace (pars. 36–37).

Magisterial Soundings

That the church is the body of Christ is the principal (but of course not only) deliverance of the New Testament on the church; it is also the principal though not exclusive teaching of the modern magisterium in Pius XII's *Mystici Corporis* and the Second Vatican Council's *Lumen Gentium*. The Council privileges the understanding of the church as the body of Christ, in that it gives it pride of place, the last place, in its summary of New Testament teaching.

Mystici Corporis, for its part, is careful to explain why the church is called the *mystical* body of Christ. There are three senses of "body." "In a natural body," Pius says, "the principle of unity unites the parts in such a manner that each lacks its own individual subsistence" (par. 61). In a natural body, the hand or the eye do not exist on their own. But the members of the body of Christ do exist on their own; they are all substances, "natural bodies" in the sense of the encyclical. There is also "body" in the sense of a moral body or a corporation. "In the moral body the principle of union is nothing else than the common end, and the common cooperation of all under the authority of society for the attainment of that end" (par. 62).

Although there is a common end of the church and common cooperation for that end, the church is united more closely than in such a corporation. It is not only that there are supernatural gifts of grace and faith and charity that unite the members of the church in a common collaboration, there is also this, which justifies the appellation "mystical": "In the Mystical Body of which We are speaking, this collaboration is supplemented by another internal principle, which exists effectively in the whole and in each of its parts, and whose excellence is such that of itself it is vastly superior to whatever bonds of union may be found in a physical or moral body" (par. 62). This internal principle is the Holy Spirit (par. 57). This teaching will be important to us later, when the sacramentality and agency of the church are discussed in chapter 10.

Both *Mystici Corporis*, and with greater authority, *Lumen Gentium*, assert the unity of the church: the visible organization is not one thing and the interior communion of grace and charity another. No, the church is one and only one thing (*Mystici Corporis*, pars. 64–65), and *Lumen Gentium* says plainly that "the society furnished with hierarchical agencies and the Mystical Body of Christ are not to be considered as two realities" (no. 8). There is not a "visible assembly" on the one hand, and a "spiritual community" on the other (no. 8). Both texts, therefore, reassert the Catholic response to Reformation ecclesiology of the sixteenth century: the church of grace and holiness is one church with the visible society of those who profess the Christian faith and use her sacraments.

Last, we must mention that for both texts the mystical body of Christ, the church as established and endowed by Christ while he was among us on this earth, is the Catholic church and no other (*Mystici Corporis*, par. 13; *Lumen Gentium*, no. 8). *Lumen Gentium*, however, does this with greater attention to the saving reality of separated churches and ecclesial communions. It recognizes that many elements of gospel truth and sanctification exist outside the visible confines of the Catholic church, but maintains that the church established by Christ "subsists" in the Catholic church, and nowhere else. Christian reality and truth there may be outside the Catholic church, and the Council readily acknowledges this. But in its perfection as established by Christ, which is to say with all the instruments of truth and salvation (and prescinding from the question as to how well Catholic Christians use these instruments), Christ's church is found uniquely, and therefore exclusively, in the Catholic church. This issue will return in chapter 11, on the unity of the church. For evidently, as the bride bespeaks holiness, the temple apostolicity, and the people catholicity, the body bespeaks especially the unity of the church.

Dogmatic Sum and Synthesis

(1) The church is the one and unique body of Christ, and Christ is the head of the church, who nourishes it and gives it growth in grace and extent.

(2) The church makes the sacramental body of Christ in the Eucharist, and the Eucharist makes Christians members of the ecclesial body of Christ.

(3) As the body of Christ, the church extends and is an instrument of his agency in the world; she both produces an invisible communion of grace and charity and truth and is herself visible in just the way that bodies make persons visible.

PART 3

ECCLESIOLOGY SYSTEMATIC

CHAPTER 9

A NOTE ON THE HISTORY OF WESTERN ECCLESIOLOGY

The church became an object of her own dogmatic reflection much later than did, say, the Trinity, or the Person and natures of Christ, or grace.[1] This does not mean there was not a thorough patristic meditation on the church, as witnessed preeminently by St. Augustine (354–430). His *Ennarationes in Psalmos* are a sustained consideration of the *totus Christus*, the church as the whole Christ composed of head and members, nor does he fail to relate the church as body to the church as bride of Christ and as temple of the Holy Spirit. But in general, the patristic appreciation of the church was more sapiential and contemplative in nature than ordered to dogmatic delimitation. Even so it could and did aspire to such precision, as in the following solemn charge of St. Augustine to his congregation we saw in the previous chapter:

1. For the history of ecclesiology in the West, see Yves Congar, OP, *L'Église de saint Augustin à l'époque moderne* (Paris: Cerf, 1970). See also the introduction to Johann Auer, *The Church: The Universal Sacrament of Salvation*, trans. Michael Waldstein (Washington, D.C.: The Catholic University of America Press, 1993 [1983]).

Hold this fast, and keep it entirely fixed in your memory, as children of the Church's training and of the Catholic faith, that you may acknowledge Christ to be the Head and the Body, and the same Christ to be also the Word of God, the Only Begotten, equal to the Father, and so may see how great is the grace by which you belong to God, that he, who is one with the Father, has willed to be one with us.[2]

It is noteworthy that the ecclesiological formula is embedded here in a fuller Christological and Trinitarian context. The Augustinian meditation on the whole Christ is continued by such figures as St. Bernard of Clairvaux (d. 1153) and Blessed Guerric of Igny (d. 1157).

St. Robert Bellarmine (d. 1621) accounts for the late emergence of dogmatic ecclesiology by noting that only with the Reformation did there arise heretics whose heresy bore precisely on the nature and authority and structure of the church; hence, only following the Reformation does the church come to be an object of theology. This is not quite true, if one thinks of John Wycliffe (d. 1384) and Jan Hus (d. 1415) in the fourteenth and fifteenth centuries. For Wycliffe, the church is the invisible church of the predestined and not a public institution, and the papacy has no foundation in scripture. Still, it might be said that the response these latter elicited was more political than theological in nature; in the fifteenth century it was still possible for the church, or for Christendom, to deal with heretics with fire and sword. We could also think that ancient Donatism was a heresy bearing on the nature of the church; on the other hand, it might be said that the difference between the Donatists and the church bore more immediately on the nature of the sacraments than on the nature of the church.

There is a good deal of truth, then, in Bellarmine's remark. When thinking of the history of ecclesiology, it is useful to remember that there is no tract "de ecclesia" in the *Summa Theologiae* of St. Thomas (d. 1274). This may be a surprising omission to us, and its meaning is not altogether obvious. His appreciation of the church is rather to be looked for in what he says about the help angels provide to angels and men, and the help men provide to men, in attaining the beatitude to which both are called within

2. From *Ennarationes in Psalmos CI–CL*, exposition of Psalm 142, no. 3 of my translation (40:2061–62).

the one providential design wherein both are divinized by the Holy Spirit and both conformed to the eternal Son.[3] His ecclesiology can as well be looked for in what he says about the realization of the one divine design after sin by the grace of the incarnate Word as the head of the church.[4] That the heavenly church is the end to which all intellectual and rational creatures are called, and that Christians are graced pilgrims on the way to their homeland, is rather the encompassing framework of all Christian realities. That there is no "treatise" devoted to the church means that its juridical and sacramental mediation of revelation and grace has not yet been problematized, not that its reality is being overlooked. We might say that it is impossible to imagine that the church could ever be forgetful of herself, because she is part of the mystery of Christ.

Summing up the patristic and medieval centuries, we could say that the first great period of "ecclesiology" in the West lasts from St. Augustine down to the Reformation. Augustine's meditation on the church, his appreciation of it in the biblical categories of the body and bride of Christ, are the common possession of every age and all subsequent Christians, learned and unlearned.

Just after St. Thomas, however, certain things start to move the church toward a more explicit self-reflection and self-definition. Questions arise that bear very precisely on the church's mediation of revelation and grace. And it is the church considered as mediator of divine truth and saving grace that is the heart of what we ordinarily mean by "ecclesiology."

In the first place, in the late thirteenth century, there begins a serious and increasingly thorough theological consideration of the teaching authority of the pope. This is set in motion insofar as one faction or the other is either aided or hindered in its project by papal influence. Those indebted to papal favor (a group of Franciscans, originally) tend to argue

3. See François Daguet, OP, *Théologie du dessein divine chez Thomas d'Aquin: Finis omnium Ecclesia* (Paris: Vrin, 2003), chap. 3.
4. *ST* III, q. 8. For article-length introductions to Aquinas's theology of the church, see Yves M.-J. Congar, OP, "The Idea of the Church in St. Thomas Aquinas," 97–117, in his *The Mystery of the Church*, trans. A. V. Littledale (Baltimore, Md.: Helicon Press, 1960), who thinks that the absence of a treatise on the church in the *Summa* is deliberate; Avery Dulles, SJ, "The Church According to Thomas Aquinas," 149–69, in his *A Church to Believe In: Discipleship and the Dynamics of Freedom* (New York: Crossroads, 1982); and Herwi Rikhof, "Thomas on the Church," 199–223, in *Aquinas on Doctrine: A Critical Introduction*, ed. Thomas G. Weinandy, Daniel A. Keating, and John P. Yocum (New York: T and T Clark International, 2004).

for a maximal view of the papal authority; those hindered resist such a view. Second, there is the call for reflection set in motion by the conflict between church and state in the early fourteenth century (Pope Boniface VIII and Philip the Fair of France). Third, but not to be separated from the first, there is conciliarism, according to which the authority of a general council is above that of the pope, and which gained increasing prominence after the Western Schism (1378–1417), in which there were two and in the end three claimants to the papal throne. Fourth, there is John Wycliffe and Jan Hus. Finally, there is the Reformation itself.

It was in the context of the second factor that James of Viterbo (d. 1308) wrote what is recognized as the first treatise on the church, according to which, while the temporal power is naturally established in the political nature of man, it is perfected by and so subordinate to the spiritual power of the church. It was in the context of the third that the first great ecclesiology, the *Summa de Ecclesia* of Cardinal John of Torquemada, OP (d. 1463), was produced, which included a ringing defense of papal supremacy. For John, the church can be nominally defined as "the assembly or whole company of faithful who have been called together in the worship, in the profession of faith, and in the sacraments of the one true God." According to the Aristotelian causes, the real definition of the church falls out as follows. The material cause is "the people itself made up of the faithful"; the formal cause is "the very unity of the true light of Christian faith, in which the whole company of the faithful is held"; the principal efficient cause is "Christ himself, the planter and founder of the Church"; the instrumental efficient cause consists of "the sacraments, which draw their power from the passion of Christ"; and the final cause is "in the present life, the sanctity of souls, and in the end, the reception of future glory."[5]

The Reformation entertained the idea that the true church is not the public institution but an invisible church of grace. The Catholic response was given an able and long-lasting form by Bellarmine, and he may be said to have begun a second great period of Catholic ecclesiology, an ecclesiology ordered to an emphasis on the visibility of the church and on the

5. These definitions are from Torquemada's comments on the work of Augustine of Rome in 1435 and can be found in J. D. Mansi, *Sacrorum Conciliorum Nova et Amplissima Collectio* (Graz: Akademische Druck- und Verlagsanstalt, 1960–61), XXX, 1011–12.

authority of the church, on the hierarchical character of the church. It is ecclesiology in what we might call an apologetic, or fundamental theological, mold. His definition of the church is suited to these emphases and this purpose and is notably indebted to Torquemada's: "To our way of thinking, the Church is only one, not two and this one true Church is the community of men gathered by their profession of the same Christian faith, and their communion in the same sacraments, under the government of legitimate pastors, especially of the one Vicar of Christ on earth, the Roman Pontiff."[6]

It cannot be said, however, that Bellarmine's response to the Reformation laid to rest the vexed question about how the visible and invisible elements of the one church are to be related, and the attendant and equally vexing question about membership. While Bellarmine denied that the "soul" of the church could be separated from its "body," that the communion of grace could be separated from the visible institution, he had no principled way to explain this.[7]

Did not the Council of Trent (1545–63) respond to the Reformation view of the church? Catholic theology had not yet matured sufficiently to enable the Council to do this. The explicit questions about visibility and membership are not answered definitively. On the other hand, some foundations are laid with regard to the appreciation of the church as the sure and necessary mediator of the grace of Christ in her sacraments, and as the sure and trustworthy mediator of the truth of Christ in her received tradition and contemporary preaching.

Looking far ahead of Trent, it can be said that much of the ecclesiological reflection of the last century, before and after the Second Vatican Council, was unable to free itself from the confusion with which Bellarmine had left the questions of the visibility of the church and membership in the church. That is to say, no matter how much one affirmed against Protestantism that the church is not two separable communities, visible and invisible, but one only reality, both interiorly holy and always visible, it proved difficult to account for the salvation of non-Catholics and

6. From the *De Controversiis* II, lib. 3, *De ecclesia militante*, cap. 2, as cited in Benoît-Dominique de La Soujeole, OP, *Introduction to the Mystery of the Church*, trans. Michael J. Miller (Washington, D.C.: The Catholic University of America Press, 2014), 362.

7. See de La Soujeole, OP, *Introduction to the Mystery of the Church*, chap. 7.

non-Christians in such a way that the implication of separability was not realized. In this light, the work of Yves M.-J. Congar, Charles Cardinal Journet, and Benoît-Dominique de La Soujeole, OP, should be mentioned especially as pointing the way forward.

The second great age of ecclesiology, the age in which ecclesiology realizes itself as a distinct theological treatise and becomes explicitly dogmatic, is therefore from the time from the Reformation to the nineteenth century, during which Bellarmine's treatment of the church continues to be influential, as does that of Francisco Suarez, SJ (d. 1617). St. Augustine's appreciation of the church continues to exert its influence, of course, but questions about membership, authority, and the relations of church and state, of pope and council, come increasingly to the fore. In the period of the Enlightenment, these questions came to be treated in an ever-more juridical, one might say untheological, way such that the church could be considered more and more exclusively as a society like any other, except that the founder of this society was divine. By the end of this period, the church is reduced in some quarters pretty much to being a "perfect society," that is, a society in possession of the means to reach its proper goals (which in some sense it is), and where the goal of this society is especially and seemingly exclusively the moral education of man (which is a wholly inadequate apprehension of her mission). See for instance the Enlightenment ecclesiology of Ignaz H. von Wessenberg (d. 1860).

In the nineteenth century, ecclesiology began to break out of its structurally anti-Protestant and apologetic mold, a mold hardened, moreover, by Enlightenment rationalism. This was the work of the Tübingen School, especially Johann Adam Möhler (d. 1838), the father of modern ecclesiology. In part, he accomplished this by a recovery of the patristic tradition. His first monograph, *Einheit in die Kirche* (1825), was indebted to Romanticism and F. Schleiermacher, and laid itself open to opposing the institutional and visible aspects of the church to the interior realities of grace and truth, although Möhler himself did not take things so. Later, he produced a more traditional ecclesiology in his *Symbolik* (1832). In this last work, the church is described as the "ongoing Incarnation of Christ," and so Möhler returns quite firmly to a properly theological appreciation of the church. We can say that Möhler made ecclesiology a part of systematics, in the way the theology of the Trinity or the theology of the incarnation or the sacraments are. The church is appreciated not only as a teacher of the mysteries, but as herself a mystery. As to the content of this appreciation, it is an apprehension of the church especially in relation to Christ, an appreciation of the church as the body of Christ.

Möhler's work passed to the Roman School through Giovanni Perrone, SJ (d. 1874) and to other distinguished members of the Roman School—Carlo Passaglia, SJ (d. 1887), Clemens Schrader (d. 1875), and J. B. Franzelin, SJ (d. 1876). Matthias Scheeben (d. 1888) studied under Passaglia and Perrone. There is therefore a direct line from Möhler, through the Roman School of the nineteenth century, to Sebastian Tromp, SJ, and Pius XII's *Mystici Corporis*.[8]

In addition to Tromp (d. 1975), "the century of the church"—the twentieth century—was animated by such noted ecclesiologists as Emile Mersch (d. 1940), Charles Cardinal Journet (d. 1975), and Yves Congar, OP (d. 1995). Such men made the ecclesiological achievement of the Second Vatican Council possible. The twentieth century has also seen the impact of important Russian Orthodox thinkers on Western ecclesiology, such men as Nicholas Afanasiev (d. 1966) and Alexander Schmemann (d. 1983).

After the Council, we can count three waves of ecclesiological reflection. In the first, the church considered as the people of God was much in the forefront. Second, again following the explicit teaching of the Council but also picking up the work of Karl Rahner, SJ (d. 1984), Edward Schillebeeckx, OP (d. 2009), Otto Semmelroth, SJ (d. 1979), and others, the church was appreciated as a sacramental reality, a communion of divine life mediated and manifested through visible and corporeal things, including the communal life of the church itself. Third, following a by no means merely implicit but still less advertised theme in the work of the Council, the church was understood as a communion, not only of grace and truth possessed by individuals, but as a great and universal communion of local ecclesial communions. The work of J. M. R. Tillard, OP (d. 2000), is noteworthy in this regard.

8. De Lubac, *The Splendor of the Church*, 93–94.

In the last century and into the present, in America, the late Avery Cardinal Dulles, SJ (d. 2008), made many distinguished contributions to the understanding of the church. And most recently, the ecclesiological contribution of Joseph Ratzinger, later Pope Benedict XVI, has become increasingly appreciated.[9]

9. See Maximillian Heinrich Heim and Joseph Ratzinger, *Life in the Church and Living Theology: Fundamentals of Ecclesiology with Reference to Lumen Gentium* (San Francisco, Calif.: Ignatius Press, 2007).

CHAPTER 10

SACRAMENT OF COMMUNION

As we have seen, the principal New Testament approaches to the church do not let us speak of her except as in immediate relation with the Trinitarian Persons: body or bride of *Christ*; temple of the *Holy Spirit*; people of God the *Father*.[1] In these ways, the church cannot but connote divine reality.[2] We cannot think of the church in its major New Testament images without thinking of God, and in that sense, the church is a sign of God. Also, the church makes God *present*. This is most evident with the church taken as the body of Christ, for as noted above, the human body makes present the person whose body it is, and is the instrument of the actions of the person—here, of Christ. Considered in this way, the church makes those who belong to it, who are members of the body, one with

---

1. See K. Rahner, "*Theos* in New Testament," trans. Cornelius Ernst, in *Theological Investigations* (London: Darton, Longman, and Todd, 1963), 1:79–148. But we should probably not agree with Rahner that *theos* stands for God the Father in the Old Testament; see Nicolas, *Synthèse Dogmatique*, no. 28. Journet, *Théologie de l'Église*, 399, calls the definitions that relate the church to a divine Person "major definitions."

2. As does the word *church* itself if we take it as originally meaning the "the Lord's house," from *kyriakon*; and as does *ecclesia, église,* or *inglesia*, from *ekklesia*, if we take it as meaning those "called" by God, those who constitute the assembly of Israel gathered for worship (*qahal*).

Christ and so one with the triune God. In doing this, the church makes those who belong to it one with one another, too. And then we are back to "people" and "body of *many* members" and "temple of *many* stones."

The Second Vatican Council summed up these relations by speaking of the church as a "sacrament." "The Church in Christ is like a sacrament or as a sign and instrument both of a very closely knit union with God and of the unity of the whole human grace" (*Lumen Gentium*, no. 1). The church is an instrument of union with God and of human community insofar as her evangelizing and preaching and catechizing publish the word of God, and make a people of one mind by its reception in faith, and insofar as her sacraments unite this same people in charity. The people so united are then a visible, public sign of this union with God, with a distinct and public social reality. But the church is not a sign extrinsic to what she is a sign of nor is she an instrument detachable from what she effects; she just *is* the holy communion she signifies and helps bring about.[3] She is the sacrament of holy communion, a sacrament that makes that communion present, both announcing it to the mind and effecting it in reality.[4]

It is important not to confuse the logic of saying, on the one hand, that the church is the body of Christ, temple of the Spirit, and people of God, and on the other hand, saying that the church is a sign and instrument of a communion of persons, putting us in communion with the Persons of the Trinity. Body, bride, temple, and people can make us think of the Persons of the Trinity, and in that sense function as signs of them. But they do not make the Persons of the Trinity, nor are they "instruments" unto effecting divine reality in itself. Rather, the divine Persons are the principal agents of salvation, and use the *church* instrumentally to effect holy communion of persons with themselves. They use the church to make the church.

This instrumental character of the church is rather connoted in the New Testament descriptions of the church than expressly signified (which is why it can be a bone of contention between Catholics and Protestants).

---

3. See the evocation of the communion of the church at Mt 18:15–22; Jn 10:1–5; 1 Cor 6:1–6; Rv 21:2–3, 9–26.

4. This is in fact a profoundly Thomist view of the church: the church is the instrument Christ uses to make her herself, what she is, his own mystical body. See Congar, "The Idea of the Church in St. Thomas," 110 and 113.

It is closest to the surface in saying the church is the body of Christ, because bodies are that by which the person or the head acts. A people can be thought of as that by which the king or ruler is both made known and acts (unto the preservation of the people itself). In the temple image, Christ is figured as foundation (1 Pt 2:4, 6; 1 Cor 3:10–11) and architect (Mt 16; 1 Pt 2:5—"be yourselves built"), but the people, too, are active, "joining" themselves to Christ by their own action (1 Pt 2:4). The temple itself, however, does not do anything in the image except provide a common space for both God and his people, a common space where the sacrifice of Christ can be realized and evoke the sacrifice of praise. Of itself, it reminds us of the worship of the church, but does not dwell on it. Finally, with the bride, she is rather the passive recipient of sanctification in Ephesians 5, though we may say her motherhood is brought to mind there, as well. On the other hand, all the images declare a visible church, a church that can be a sign. And all except bride declare the unity of some multitude—of members or individuals or stones. "Bride" declares the unity of the church with Christ.

The images add to one another, of course, and are even expressly identified in the New Testament: body and bride in Ephesians 5:23, "for the husband is head of the wife as Christ is the head of the church, his body"; temple and body in John 2:21, where the Lord's prediction, "Destroy this temple, and in three days I will raise it up," is explained in that "he spoke of the temple of his body"; and temple and people in 1 Peter 2:5 and 9: "like living stones be yourselves built into a spiritual house, to be a holy priesthood," and "you are a chosen race, a royal priesthood, a holy nation, God's own people." The body is the bride is the temple is the people. Compared to that, there is a certain abstractness in saying "sign and instrument" as the Council does in *Lumen Gentium*. On the other hand, "sign and instrument" expresses what some of the images are not as well suited to express as the others, and "sign and instrument" gathers up what all of the images contribute to a comprehensive understanding of the church.

The advantages for understanding the church, summing up her reality by saying she is the sacrament of communion with God, are very large, and that is the road that will be taken in this third part of the book.[5]

5. The Council rather insists on the sacramentality of the church, as it comes up ten times in the texts: *Lumen Gentium*, nos. 1 (see above, in the text), 9 (the church is "the visible sacrament of this saving unity" of those who believe in Christ, and its instrumental redemptive role is

Since the Council, it is common to dwell on the sacramental nature, and on the communal nature, of the church.[6] But there are better and worse, more adequate and less satisfactory ways of taking these terms and relating them to one another. The work of Benoît-Dominique de La Soujeole is especially worth attending to. Before we get to that juncture, however, the New Testament roots of both these words should be explored.

Sacramentum/mystêrion in the New Testament

The Latin *sacramentum* translates the Greek *mystêrion*, which can be either "sacrament" or "mystery" in English. And that is the first word the Council uses when it speaks of the church, in the title of the first chapter of *Lumen Gentium* ("The Mystery of the Church"). It will repay us to look at three key passages where *mystêrion* surfaces in the New Testament, and we will see how apt a word that is to describe the church.

Mark 4:10–12

In the parable of the sower, the sower's seed falls on the path, on rocky ground, among thorns, and on good ground (4:3–9). Just before its explanation, where Jesus identifies the seed as the word of the gospel that he preaches and details its various fortunes (4:14–20), there is this: "And when he was alone, those who were about him with the Twelve asked him concerning the parables. And he said to them 'To you has been given the secret of the kingdom of God, but for those outside everything is in parables; so that they may indeed see but not perceive, and may indeed hear but not understand; lest they should turn again and be forgiven'"

---

mentioned in the same paragraph), 48 (the church is "the universal sacrament of salvation"), and 59 (the church is "the mystery [*sacramentum*] of the salvation of the human race"); *Sacrosanctum Concilium*, nos. 5 ("'the wondrous sacrament of the whole Church' [quoting the Roman Missal] is drawn from the side of Christ on the cross") and 26 (quoting St. Cyprian, the church is the "'sacrament of unity'"); *Gaudium et Spes*, nos. 42 (quoting *Lumen Gentium*, no. 1) and 45 (quoting *Lumen Gentium*, no. 48); *Ad Gentes*, nos. 1 (quoting *Lumen Gentium*, no. 48) and 5 (the church is "the sacrament of salvation," and its universality is clear from the context). *Sacrosanctum Concilium* is the Council's Constitution on the Sacred Liturgy. All these texts can be found in *Decrees* (ed. Tanner), vol. 2.

6. For the first and magisterially, see *Ecclesia de Eucharistia* of John Paul II; for the second, see the Final Report of the Extraordinary Synod of 1985; available at https://www.ewtn.com/library/CURIA/SYNFINAL.htm.

(4:10–12). The "secret of the kingdom of God" is the *"mystêrion* of the kingdom of God."

That there is some secret about the kingdom of God Jesus preaches is in line with the usage of *mystêrion* in the Septuagint. There, in the plural—"mysteries"—it designates the details of the future kingdoms of the Medes and the Persians and the Greeks and finally of God's kingdom. These details are communicated in a dream to Nebuchadnezzar, and Daniel deciphers the vision by the revelation of God (Dn 2:28–30, 47). The knowledge of these future kingdoms and their history has to be revealed, because their coming to be and passing away are all under the providence of God and depend on his free decision (2:20–23; also 4:32). Much more must the establishment of God's own kingdom be revealed (2:44–45; also 4:3, 34–35).

What then is the secret of Mark 4:11? Does "mystery of the kingdom" mean the mystery that the kingdom is, or an insight into the kingdom of God, some hidden, but now revealed aspect of it?[7] Initially, it is an insight into the kingdom, some aspect of it, hidden in the mind of God, and this seems to be in line with Daniel's usage. Because Jesus knows enough to know that the kingdom of heaven is at hand, and because he is the Son of Man to whom the kingdom is given in Daniel 7:9, he has insight into its nature and deployment. The insight is that, despite the seeming failure of the word of God, it will nonetheless bring forth a mighty harvest. The sower of the word, however, is Jesus himself. The insight, then, is that, despite the seeming failure of Jesus' whole mission, it will yet prove successful. Taking Jesus' mission in its totality, the insight is that despite Jesus' death, there will be the blessing of the resurrection, and what the resurrection brings which it, which is the great harvest of those who believe in Christ, which is to say, the church. For the Son of Man to whom the kingdom is given in Daniel (7:14) will deliver it in turn to the saints (7:22). That is, the saints are the kingdom.

The history of the word of Jesus, which is to say his history, is therefore not always triumphant (Mk 4:15–20), in the sense that everyone who hears the word believes. And it is not immediately triumphant (4:26–29). Those who do believe must be patient. But in the end, the word of Jesus is

7. Werner Kelber, *The Kingdom in Mark* (Philadelphia: Fortress, 1974), 32.

like the word of God in Isaiah 55: "it shall not return ... empty," but will accomplish what God intends (55:10–11). And in this way, the parable is nothing except a coded version of Jesus' mission as a whole, where his messianic status is revealed only in suffering (15:39—"Truly this man"), and only after suffering is it shown forth in power and glory, just as the predictions of the passion have it (8:31, etc.). In fact, it is not in spite of failure, failure sealed by death, that there will be a great harvest, but rather because of it. This is plain in John: "Unless a grain of wheat falls into the ground and dies, it remains a single grain. But if it dies, it bears much fruit" (12:24).

So, it is the structure of the story of the sower that conveys the mystery of the kingdom: first failure, then success; first suffering, then glory, where the suffering and the failure bring about the glory and the success, such that they are already hidden there in their principle. This is key: divine and saving power is in fact present in Jesus' seemingly unsuccessful mission and in his passion and death. But only those who have faith and are the good soil that receives the word know that. Jesus *reveals* the mystery in word, speaking his insight into the mystery of God; he anticipates in word what the mystery itself *does* in reality.

The identity of the mystery of the kingdom with Jesus is communicated in another way. Jesus tells the disciples, "to you has been given the mystery of the kingdom." But the only thing already given them before his explanation is Jesus himself, their master and lord. In this way, he himself must be the mystery of the kingdom, and neither he nor the kingdom are divided against themselves (3:21–24). Moreover, what the disciples suffer for Jesus' sake is suffered for the sake of the gospel of the kingdom (10:29), which is to say, for the sake of the kingdom itself, which the disciples enter and inherit just according to their suffering (10:23, 30).[8]

To sum up, (1) the mystery is first something hidden, a mystery of God's providence and known only to him, but (2) the truth of the mystery is first of all delivered in Jesus' words, something to be embraced by faith. It is delivered in a hidden way in the parable. It is delivered in a clear way to the disciples. The truth that is present in the parable to the confu-

---

8. Günther Bornkamm, "MUSTERION," *Theological Dictionary of the New Testament*, ed. Gerhard Kittel (Grand Rapids, Mich.: Eerdmans, 1965), 4:819: "The *mystérion tês basileias tou theou* which is revealed to the disciples is thus Jesus Himself as Messiah."

sion of those whose heart is hard (Is 6:9–10) is made manifest to the disciples. The mystery (3) becomes visible in Jesus' work and passion and death and is made really present there, although this is not obvious except to the eyes of faith. To those eyes, (4) the visible work of Jesus really works the invisible grace of God's salvation, which in turn (5) becomes visible in the great harvest of the church. The "mystery" is therefore all-encompassing: it includes Jesus himself, who is the principle of God's saving power in the world, and it includes those who believe in him, in whom the transcendent power of God is working. In this way, (6) it has a participative structure to it: what Christ possesses originally and fully is shared out to us who are part of his harvest. In short, what is manifest and visible in word and deed is an instrument of salvation.

1 Corinthians 2:7

There is substantial continuity between the Markan and Pauline usage of *mystêrion*. Here is 1 Corinthians 2:7–10:

> But we impart a secret and hidden wisdom of God [*laloumen theou sophian en mystêriô*—"we speak the wisdom of God in mystery"], which God decreed before the ages for our glorification. None of the rulers of this age understood this; for if they had, they would not have crucified the Lord of glory. But, as it is written, "What no eye has seen, nor ear heard, nor the heart of man conceived, what God has prepared for those who love him," God has revealed to us through the Spirit. For the Spirit searches even the depth of God.

The mystery is a function of the wisdom of God. It is first of all a work of the divine mind (as in Daniel), an intelligibility, an ordering. For this reason alone it is not apparent, and we must have the Spirit of God to know it (2:10). This mystery is nothing less than the content of Paul's gospel; it is the wisdom of God that is foolishness to men (1:23), and is "Christ crucified." Christ crucified makes the mystery now visible. Proceeding from God's wisdom, the mystery proceeds from his will, too: it is something freely "decreed" by God (2:7) and unto our good, our glorification (2:7), something prepared for those who love him (2:9). The visible work of Christ thus has an invisible effect: grace and future glorification.

Now, the wisdom of God is so deep (2:10) that it can encompass what is opposed to it, the actions of those who crucified the Lord of glory (2:8).

The design of the wisdom of God, decreed from before the ages, includes and encompasses the action of those who killed Christ, and makes of Christ's death something that can undo sin and the effects of sin, even unto our glorification, our being raised up with Christ to a status we could not have foreseen or conceived before the work and resurrection of Christ.[9] In this way, the rulers of this age, the cosmic powers and principalities of which we hear more in Colossians and Ephesians, are despoiled and deprived of their power and authority.

In short, the mystery is both the truth of Paul's gospel and the reality of the working of Christ's cross. (1) It was hidden in the mind of God. But (2) it becomes manifest in Christ. Of course, the suffering and death of Christ do not look like the wisdom of God. But underneath this visible aspect, what seems to be foolishness, there is concealed the wisdom of God, and (3) there is made present and effective his power to make us both wise and strong (1:23–31). The mystery has the value of a sign, therefore, and we can understand something of what it communicates. Furthermore, it is also effective as an instrument of God's power to save. Its scope is universal relative to all who are being saved, all whom God calls to be saved (see 1 Tm 2:4), as broad and encompassing as the wisdom and freedom of God. (4) It has a participative structure, too: for what exists first and preeminently in Christ, who is God's wisdom and power (1 Cor 1:24), is shared out to those who are in him and who thereby become wise and strong. In short, the mystery is both sign and instrument of salvation.

Colossians 1:24–28

I complete what is lacking in Christ's afflictions for the sake of his body, that is, the Church, of which I became a minister according to the divine office which was given to me for you, to make the word of God fully known, the mystery [*to mystêrion*] hidden for ages and generations, but now made manifest to his servants. To them God chose to make known how great among the Gentiles are the riches of the glory of this mystery [*tês doxes tou mystêriou*], which is Christ in you, the hope of glory. Him we proclaim, warning every man and teaching every man in all wisdom that we may present every man mature in Christ.

9. See Bernard Lonergan on the three steps of the law of the cross, *De verbo incarnato* (Rome: Gregorian University, 1961), Thesis 17: from the evil of sin to the evil of punishment; from the evil of punishment to its transformation into voluntary satisfaction; and from the meritorious good of this satisfaction to the blessing of God in glory.

The mystery is first something that can be stated; it is, as it were, a message, a "word of God" (Col 1:25–26). Also, it is a reality. For as to the content of this word of God, what it refers to, it is now something shown, manifest to the saints (1:27). The mystery just is Christ—"Him we proclaim"—and he is the content of the word of God, the gospel (1:28). It is the truth about Christ and Christ himself. But it has everything to do with the saints, for more fully, the mystery is "Christ in you" (1:27), which is to say, the salvation Christ brings, mediated to those who are saved by his invisible dwelling within them. The mystery, therefore, includes the church, and this is perhaps more explicit here than in 1 Corinthians or Mark. This gospel, this mystery, is universal in scope, and in principle encompasses all the Gentiles. Once again, the mystery, the working out of Christ's work for the salvation of the saints, is associated with wisdom (1:28). And its disclosure and realization is a matter of the divine will and freedom (1:27).

Moreover, Paul conceives of himself as somehow in his own sufferings contributing not only to the proclamation of the mystery, but to its realization: "I complete what is lacking in Christ's afflictions for the sake of his body, that is, the Church" (1:24), of which he is a minister. Only so is the word of God "fully known" (1:25). His ministerial office includes suffering, and shares in actualizing and fulfilling the mystery of Christ, helping to make Christ be in Christians, helping to make the church. The participatory character of the mystery is thus more fully stated here: the mystery is first and originally Christ; second, he shares himself with Christians by being in them, something not now apparent, but unto their future glory; and third, he uses Christians—here, Paul—to make the church fully real.

The mystery, then, (1) is something first hidden in the mind of God. (2) It is something that comes to manifestation in Paul's word, announcing and proclaiming it. Also, (3) it comes to manifestation and is visible in his suffering. What comes to manifestation is also a reality, the extension of Christ to Christians, dwelling within them. That is, (4) what comes to manifestation and is realized in the affliction of Christ is the transcendent reality of Christ as the salvation of God. Last, (5) that in which it comes to manifestation, in the suffering of Christ and in Paul's suffering, is instrumentally effective in bringing it to realization.

In these New Testament passages, the mystery/sacrament is something that makes God's plan of salvation visible. It is a manifestation or sign of it in both the word of preaching and in the life of Christ and his disciples. Also, the mystery/sacrament realizes what it signifies, so that we share in salvation. The principal agent who realizes salvation in us is, first and obviously, God, and second Christ. But also, there is an active instrumental sharing in the power of realizing this salvation, which Paul makes plain, a sharing of power in his words and suffering.

Koinônia/Communion in the New Testament

The notion of a sacrament or a mystery, as the Council uses it, is therefore deeply embedded in the New Testament. What of communion? The Council, as we have seen, says that the church is the sacrament "of unity with God and the union of the whole human race" (*Lumen Gentium*, no. 1), and it says again that the church is the "universal sacrament of salvation" (*Lumen Gentium*, no. 48). Because salvation consists in being united to God by grace and charity, and insofar as being so joined unites one to all other men already or called to be in grace, then the two phrases express the same thing. Both express catholicity (*whole* race, *universal* sacrament). The Council's first formula, however, has the advantage that it brings the visible, social, collective, community nature of the church to immediate expression. The second formula, on the other hand, brings to the fore that the unity in question is a sharing in grace and charity. We have already joined them by saying that the church is the sacrament of communion, of holy communion with God. The church is the sacrament, the sign and instrument, of holy communion of men with God.

The language of communion, just as that of sacrament or *mystêrion*, is a thoroughly New Testament language.[10] *Koinônia* can be translated variously: sharing, participation, fellowship, communion, society. It can indicate (1) sharing in an active sense, sharing out or giving a share in something, (2) sharing in in a passive sense, being given a share, receiving or taking a share, and last (3) the community of those who have something in common, constituted by their all having partaken of and possessing something given them.[11]

10. Used eighteen times in the New Testament, thirteen of which are Pauline.
11. Friedrich Hauck, "Koinos," *Theological Dictionary of the New Testament*, ed. Gerhard Kittel (Grand Rapids, Mich.: Eerdmans, 1965), 3:789–809, esp. 804–9.

So, in the first sense, Christians give a share of their goods by contributing to the collection that Paul solicits for the Jerusalem church (Rom 15:26 and 2 Cor 9:13). The churches at Rome and Corinth express their union with the church at Jerusalem, a unity established by their reception of what God has given them in Christ.

Second, *koinônia* indicates taking a share, especially, receiving a share in something given us by God or Christ. This sense is therefore quite important. See 1 Corinthians 1:9: "God is faithful, by whom you were called into the fellowship [*koinônia*] of his Son." Here, the Corinthians take a share in something Christ gives them, or share in Christ himself.[12] This sharing in Christ is established sacramentally. "The cup of blessing which we bless, is it not a participation [*koinônia*] in the blood of Christ? The bread which we break, is it not a participation [*koinônia*] in the body of Christ?" (10:16). As the next verse points out, this sharing in Christ makes of the Christians one body. This sharing in Christ is also produced by the Holy Spirit.

See also Philippians 2:1: "So if there is any encouragement in Christ, any incentive of love, any participation in the Spirit [*koinônia Pneumatos*], any affection and sympathy, complete my joy by being of the same mind." Being of the same mind, however, is having the mind of Christ (Phil 2:5).[13] This is taking a share because being given a share in in his sufferings (Phil 2:6–8; Rom 8:17), being crucified with him (Rom 6:6), being glorified with him (Rom 8:17), reigning with him (Phil 2:12), and so on, even where *koinônia* is not itself used.[14]

Sharing in Christ and sharing in the Holy Spirit give John leave to say that we have fellowship with the Father (1 Jn 1:3, 6), the third sense of *koinônia*, and this brings the language of fellowship to a kind of closure, logically and theologically: fellowship or community with those who are sent, Son and Spirit, gives fellowship with him who sends, the Father.[15] Finally, there is the "absolute" or unqualified use of *koinônia*, as in Acts 2:42, where it names the apostolic community: "And they held steadfast-

12. George Panikulam, *Koinônia in the New Testament: A Dynamic Expression of Christian Life* (Rome: Biblical Institute Press, 1979), 13–15.

13. Ibid., 73–74, and see 2 Cor 13:14.

14. Hauck, "Koinos," 806, as it is for sharing in his sufferings at Phil 3:10; Panikulam, *Koinônia*, 91–107.

15. Panikulam, *Koinônia*, 134–35.

ly to the apostles' teaching and fellowship [*koinônia*], to the breaking of bread and to the prayers."

Sacramentality of Christ, Church, Ministers, and Rites

When we say that the church is the sacrament of holy communion, two great systematic insights become available to us, one bearing on sacramentality, and the other on communion. To say that the church is a sacrament evidently links her intelligibility to that of the seven rites of the church that are more commonly called sacraments. In saying that the church is "as it were" a sacrament "in Christ," the Council evidently implies that her sacramentality depends on Christ, which is as much as to say that her sacramentality depends on the sacramentality of Christ and that the church's sacramentality is to be understood from the sacramentality of Christ. This argues for inserting the theology of the church just exactly between Christology and the theology of the sacramental rites—as it were, after question 59 of the *Tertia Pars* of the *Summa Theologiae*, the last question on Christ, and before question 60, the first question on the sacraments in general.[16] Just as important, it suggests that the notion of sacrament can be analogically applied to Christ, the church, and the sacraments.

The Sacramentality of Christ's Humanity

First, in what way can Christ be thought of as a sacrament? Evidently it will be in virtue of his humanity, for there must be something visible about a sacrament, something that makes it suited to communicating its truth and reality to human beings who first know the world through their senses. Concordantly with the Council speaking of the church as a sacrament, his humanity will be a sign and *instrument* of grace, that is, productive of grace, an instrumental efficient cause of grace, where we surmise that the principal cause is God, his own divinity, and where an efficient cause is a principle of transformation or change in the other as other. Thus, a carpenter is an efficient cause, modifying, changing, and rearrang-

16. Benoît-Dominique de La Soujeole, OP, "The Economy of Salvation: Entitative Sacramentality and Operative Sacramentality," *The Thomist* 75 (2010): 537–53, at 540.

ing the shape of the lumber from which he makes a chair. And his tools, his saw and lathe, are effective instruments of the modifications he makes.

This is the ordinary way to understand the causality of the sacraments; it is easier to read the Council of Trent on sacramental causality that way than in any other.[17] And it is the way St. Thomas understood sacramental causality, too.[18] Therefore, the question becomes, is the humanity of Christ, understood insofar as it is displayed throughout his life in his teaching and action and reaction to others, not only a sign of God's gracious will and intention for humanity, but also a principle that effects grace? For the mature Thomas, the answer is yes.[19] The humanity of Christ is a proper instrument conjoined to the Word,[20] and does instrumentally what the divinity does as principal cause. And of course, the humanity of Christ is the sign of his divinity, too, manifesting it in his preaching and miracles and the common life he spends with men.[21] In this way, the humanity of Christ answers to the idea of a sacrament employed by the Council: a sign and instrument of a supernatural reality, the divine Person of Christ, rendering it present in time and to our minds, and enabling it to act so as to effect a share of supernatural reality in us. The passion of Christ causes grace not only morally, but also as does an instrumental efficient cause.[22] The humanity of Christ is nicely called a "conjoined instrument," as it exists in virtue of its hypostatic union with the Word.

But how can the church herself as such be an instrument of grace? That she is a sign of grace presents no problem. But that she be an instru-

17. See Trent, Session VII, decree on the sacraments, canon 6, where the sacraments "contain" and "confer" grace. The decree can be found in *Decrees* (ed. Tanner), 2:671–81. The *Catechism of the Catholic Church* glosses Trent and says that the sacraments are "efficacious" of grace at no. 1127, and that the "power" of Christ and his Spirit act in and through the sacraments at no. 1128.

18. There is a shift from commentary on the *Sentences* to the *Summa*. See Bernhard Blankenhorn, OP, "The Instrumental Causality of the Sacraments: Thomas Aquinas and Louis-Marie Chauvet," *Nova et Vetera* (English edition) 4 (2006): 255–93.

19. This is not so for the early St. Thomas, for which see de La Soujeole, "The Economy of Salvation," 544. For the early Thomas of *De veritate*, q. 29, a. 5, the humanity of Christ participates in his divinity, and cannot be a principle of a properly divine act. It seems rather to be dispositive unto grace, like the causality of the sacraments, for which see *De veritate*, q. 27, aa. 4–7, esp. a. 4, ad 9.

20. Aquinas, *SCG* IV.41. See Theophil Tschipke, *L'humanité du Christ comme instrument de salut de la divinité*, trans. Philibert Secrétan, Studia Friburgensia 94 (Fribourg: Academic Press Fribourg, 2003).

21. Aquinas, *ST* III, q. 40, a. 1, ad 1.

22. Ibid., qq. 48 and 49; also q. 8, a. 5, and q. 13, a. 2.

ment demands a certain unity that is hard to verify in the collectivity of a people, an assembly. This becomes more evident if we compare this with the other things that we can call sacraments.

Sacramental Rites

The sacramental rites of the church are in the genus of signs for St. Thomas, and sacraments for him include such things as Old Testament sacrifices and circumcision as well as baptism and matrimony and ordination and the Mass in New Testament times.[23] Old Testament sacraments looked forward to Christ and prefigured him. They prefigured the very actions by which, through the instrument of his humanity, he would merit and effect the grace of the New Law. For instance, all the sacrifices of the Old Law prefigured the sacrifice of Christ, and the paschal Lamb prefigured his passion.[24] But for that very reason, looking forward to a cause of grace not yet established, they could not themselves be instrumental causes of grace. That is no longer true of Christian baptism and confirmation and the other sacraments. They can be instrumental efficient media of the grace of Christ now won and already to be given to those with faith. The unity of the sacramental rite, of course, is the unity of an action. It is the unity of an action of Christ working through the action of the minister.

Ministers

For there is also the immediate agent of sacramental action, the minister of the church. According to St. Thomas, in the supreme sacrament of the New Law, the Eucharist, ministers act in the person of Christ and so are certainly signs of Christ and his grace.[25] In addition, they are themselves instrumental causes of grace. For Aristotle and St. Thomas, ministers—servants—are just conscious and rational instruments.[26] Just as the sacraments of the New Law are instituted by Christ, so does he make men apt ministers by ordination, by the sacramental character that ordi-

---

23. Benoît-Dominique de La Soujeole, OP, "The Importance of the Definition of the Sacraments as Signs," 123–35, in *Ressourcement Thomism: Sacred Doctrine, the Sacraments, and the Moral Life*, ed. Reinhard Hütter and Matthew Levering (Washington, D.C.: The Catholic University of America Press, 2010).

24. Aquinas, *ST* III, q. 73, a. 6.

25. Ibid., q. 78, a. 1; q. 82, aa. 1 and 5.

26. Ibid., q. 64, a. 1.

nation imparts, which fits them, as it were, to the hand of Christ.[27] So, the definition of a sacrament is verified also in bishops and priests; they are signs and instruments of the grace of Christ, who uses them to give gifts to men.[28] Just as the unity of the sacraments themselves is apparent, in that it is the unity of a complete ritual action in time, the unity of the ministers is apparent, too. Bishops and priests, for all their status as instruments, evidently maintain the unity of individual human persons.

The humanity of Christ is not itself a person, of course, not itself an agent. It is rather a way of being an agent, and is used by one of the Trinitarian agents or persons, the second Person of the Trinity. The mystery of the incarnation is great; still, there is no mystery about the fact that the exercise of the sacramentality of Christ is that of only one agent, the Son of God, the Logos of whom St. John speaks in the first chapter of his Gospel.

Sacramentality of the Church

But now how can the church be an instrument of grace? She possesses the unity neither of a rite (sacrament) nor of a person (a minister) nor of a single nature (the humanity of Christ). She is rather many persons. Is it enough that she be a juridical person, of either civil or canon law? No. Such persons are fictions. That is to say, their existence is in the realm of things made by the human mind. If we all agree to treat General Motors as a person, and speak, for shorthand, of General Motors doing this, deciding that, marketing cars, making money, fine. But underneath the web of legal and economic relations that are summarized by speaking of "General Motors," there are really only just human beings, human persons, deciding alone or in concert to do certain things.

The church must be more than a juridical person, however, to do what she does as a sacrament of salvation, a sacrament of communion. We speak of the church, as of General Motors, deciding things, doing things. When she decides what scripture means, moreover, we mean that something more is going on that that a pope or council of bishops is deciding this merely as men. Merely as men, they do not have the wherewithal to

27. Ibid., q. 63, a. 2, a. 3, co., and ad 2.
28. John Paul II, *Pastores Dabo Vobis*, Apostolic Exhortation, March 15, 1992, pars. 15–16; available at www.vatican.va.

do that in their simple personal reality. In the order of grace, furthermore, the church has the wherewithal not only to declare a sacramental celebration legally in order ("licit") but also to declare a sacramental celebration null and void ("invalid") and to set the conditions for true sacramental celebrations. When the church does this, who is doing it? Certainly there is some pope or bishop or priest involved. Are they acting in a way no different than the chairman of General Motors does when we say that GM does something? If we say they are not, then the church becomes a purely human and therefore intolerable block to the saving commerce every Christian wants with Christ in the sacraments.

To conceive of the church as a sacrament, therefore, in her wholeness, we must also find a way to express her unity, a unity that is more than a fiction, a unity that is more than a construction of the juridical order. It must furthermore be a unity that is more than the unity of the moral order.[29] By moral unity we mean, as has already been said in chapter 8, the unity of a group of people who think the same things are true, and who value the same things. Thus the Society for the Prevention of Cruelty to Animals has a moral unity consisting of what people understand about animals and how they value them. This is a natural moral unity. We can certainly speak of a supernatural moral unity for the church: her members think the same things true in reciting the creed; they love the same things, God and neighbor, with the supernatural love of charity. Is this supernatural moral unity enough to understand the church in her wholeness, not only as a sign of holy communion, but as an instrument of holy communion? It is not.

If we grant that the church in her wholeness acts through the ministers through whom Christ acts in the sacraments, priests, and bishops, it still remains to conceive how the church can be one agent, after the way that Christ is one agent. Failing to do this, there seems to be no good reason why this, that, or the other priest or hierarch cannot determine on his own the conditions of valid sacramental celebration or the binding sense of the New Testament. Failing to do this, in other words, there is no properly theological reason to prevent the church from disintegrating

29. De La Soujeole, "The Economy of Salvation," 548–50. If the humanity of Christ is a "conjoined instrument of the Word," and if sacraments are "separated" instruments, de La Soujeole will have it that the church is an "adjunct" instrument of Christ.

into the thousand communions and sects of Protestantism, for there is no ecclesial reality as such, as a whole and that possesses real agency, that stands against it.

For these reasons, theologians take to speaking of the church as possessing the unity of a *mystical* person. This is a "person" or "personality" that is more than a juridical person, and more than a moral person, either natural or even supernatural.[30] The church is a mystical person in virtue of the indwelling of the one and same unique Spirit in all Christians. Grace and charity and the gifts of the Holy Spirit, while they are specifically the same, are individually distinct existing in one and another Christian. But the Holy Spirit is not divided; he is the same individual person in each Christian, and at the same time in the whole as a whole.[31] This was adverted to when we considered the church as the temple of the Holy Spirit and again as the bride and the body of Christ. The Holy Spirit dwells in each Christian, and each Christian is a temple of the Spirit. But also, all Christians are stones of one temple, and in that one temple, the church, there is dwelling the Holy Spirit. So, there is the same divine Person in each Christian person, and the this same Person presides over the whole and makes of the whole an agent or quasi-agent. In this way there is fulfilled that part of the definition of a sacrament we need—agency—if the ecclesiology is really to fit in a systematic progression from Christ to the church, to the ministers of the sacraments, to the sacraments.[32] This does not mean that the Holy Spirit does the same thing in each member, for beyond the specific identity in each of grace and charity and the gifts, he inspires many distinct and different gifts, charismatic (1 Cor 12:4–11)

---

30. De La Soujeole, OP, *Introduction to the Mystery of the Church*, chap. 12. See also Nicolas's very fine discussion in *Synthèse Dogmatique*, nos. 656–60. For Nicholas, the personality of the church subsists in all the members according to their conformation to Christ (nos. 657 and 659), which conformation by grace and charity is the work of the Spirit (no. 658) and also bridal (no. 660), and it exercises its agency through those who can act in her name (no. 659). See also Ignace Zhang Zhan Wu, *Qui est l'Église? Quaestio disputata sur la personnalité de l'Église à la lumière de quelques auteurs du vengtième siècle* (Rome: Pontificia Università Lateranense, 2003), which focuses on Charles Journet, Jacques Maritain, Heribert Mühlen, and Hans Urs von Balthasar.

31. Pius XII, *Mystici Corporis*, par. 57: the Holy Spirit "is present and assists them in proportion to their various duties and offices, and the greater or less degree of spiritual health which they enjoy. It is He who, through His heavenly grace, is the principle of every supernatural act in all parts of the Body."

32. This is the overall argument of de La Soujeole in "The Economy of Salvation."

and hierarchical (12:28–31), in the members. Charity and the gifts, more-over, can be distinct by degree.

Relative to the church's guarding the deposit of faith, the Spirit instills the charism of truth in the bishops, making them true judges of matters of faith and morals. In a different but no less real and necessary way, the Spirit provokes the *sensus fidei* in the faithful in their recognition and reception of magisterial teaching.[33] In the sacraments, too, there is the presence of the Holy Spirit, making the sacrifice of the Mass the church's sacrifice (in the epiclesis, the invocation of the Spirit at Mass), for instance, and ensuring that the offering of grace to the people through the working of the ministers is a real and fruitful offering. Last, there is a common discipline of the church, too, a discipline especially relative to the sacraments, determined by the same bishops who guard the deposit of faith.[34]

Evidently, the church subsists in her members. But she possesses a kind of more than moral unity that we encountered many times in part 2. The Holy Spirit is the immediate personal cause of this more than moral unity of the church, as was seen in chapter 6. Moreover, this more-than-moral unity enables the church to act, as a whole, as an agent. This will be important in the next chapter, too. Configuring each Christian in which the church subsists to Christ as the Spirit does, this agency has the mind of Christ, and this follows from chapters 5 and 8. Insofar as the church has to be receptive to the mind of Christ in faith, however, she has the face of Mary, as was explored in chapter 7.

Sacrament of Communion: Communion as Sign and Instrument of Common Charity

Historical Introduction

The Reformation's theology of the church was haunted by sin, by the idea of an institutional church completely empty of what she signified, the

---

33. Teaching the faith and the acceptance of this teaching are matters especially of the gifts of the Holy Spirit—knowledge and wisdom and understanding. Anscar Vonier is especially alive to the work of the Holy Spirit through the gifts making the church one in mind and action; see *Spirit and the Bride*, 147, 163–71, 184–96, and 223–24.

34. Ibid., 223–24. This would be a matter presumably of the gifts of counsel, piety, and fortitude.

grace and truth of Christ. Precisely where the church was most audible, in the contemporary teaching of her prelates and priests, the church seemed given over to a scholastic doctrine that obscured the simplicity of the gospel and the gratuity of grace and salvation. Precisely where the church was most visible, in those same prelates and priests, the church seemed given over to the establishment of a plutocracy whose rewards were pleasure and power. Yet Christ's cross could not be for nothing, and his grace could not be rendered wholly impotent. Does it work its way only invisibly in the world, like the secret leaven in the mass of dough? Perhaps, then, the church was two, and not one. The true church of those who by faith received the grace of Christ was one thing. The visible church, mired in sin, was something wholly different.

In his *On the Papacy in Rome* of 1520, Martin Luther distinguishes two ways of speaking of the church. In the first way, the way scripture speaks, the church is the spiritual assembly of souls, the community of faith and charity.[35] The essence of the church is no bodily communion, and there is no necessity to be in league with Rome to belong to it. For there is, to be sure, a second way of speaking of the church, as a "physical, external Christendom," which is, as it were, the body of a man relative to his soul, a bodily assembly relative to the communion of souls in faith.[36] This church is a human work, not Christ's, although, to be sure, there is some overlap. A similar distinction is proposed by John Calvin, a distinction between the church in the presence of God—the saints—and known only to God, and the visible assembly of those who profess to worship God and are baptized, within which there are a large number of false Christians and hypocrites.[37]

Orthodox Catholic response to such proposals were constant, from the time of Hus and Wycliffe and on through Luther and Calvin: there is one church, one church founded by Christ that is both public and visible and one church that at the same time is the body of Christ and the temple

35. Martin Luther, *On the Papacy*, trans. Eric W. and Ruth C. Gritsch, in *Luther's Works*, ed. Eric Gritsch (Philadelphia: Fortress Press, 1970), 39:65–69.

36. Ibid., 69–70.

37. John Calvin, *Institutes of the Christian Religion*, 7th ed., trans. John Allen (Philadelphia: Presbyterian Board of Christian Education, 1936), vol. 2, Book IV, chap. 1, no. 7. Calvin, too, expects some overlap of the invisible and the visible, for the public preaching of the word and the visible celebration of the sacraments we must expect to be fruitful (Book IV, chapter 1, no. 9).

of the Spirit, the household of those united in faith and charity. Robert Bellarmine picked up the terms of the issue from Luther and Calvin, and distinguished an ecclesial body from an ecclesial soul.[38] The body of the church is all those who profess the creed, use the sacraments, and obey the pope. The soul of the church is all those who possess the interior graces of faith and hope and charity. Ecclesial soul and body make one church, just as the body and soul of an individual man make one human being.[39]

But just insofar as soul and body have here been identified with collectivities of men, it seems possible, at least in principle, for the disparately described collectivities to be separate one from the other. Bellarmine *asserted* the unity of the church. But his description of the soul and the body led inevitably to the difficult question of how we can be sure they are never in fact separated. It can seem even to lead to Protestant positions. If it is possible for all those who belong to the body to fall into sin, then the visible church gives no assurance that it is the church in any real sense or that it is necessary for salvation. Salvation must be rather a matter of faith and the protestation of faith than of being touched by the visible sacraments, that, like the visible church, are empty of grace and love and whose status as infallibly conferring grace from the very objectivity of the rite itself (*ex opere operato*) must be an invention of the medieval church.

St. Thomas did not face the problem raised by the Reformers and by Bellarmine. The old way to talk was not to speak with nouns, but to speak with adverbs. There is no *group* of men that is the soul, no *group* of men that is the body of the church. Rather, each and every member of the church, as baptized, belongs *corporeally* to the church; and every member of the church imbued with grace belongs *spiritually* to the church.[40] Body and soul are nouns, of course. Corporeally and spiritually are adverbs. Of the same man it might be true, at one time, that he belongs only spiritually, and subsequently spiritually and corporeally to the

---

38. See de La Soujeole, *Introduction to the Mystery of the Church*, chap. 7. See also Charles Morerod, OP, *The Church and the Human Quest for Truth* (Washington, D.C.: The Catholic University of America Press, 2008), chap. 6.

39. Robert Bellarmine, *De controversiis chritianae fidei adversus hujus temporis haereticos* II, Liber 3, *De Ecclesia militante*, caput 3.

40. Aquinas, *ST* II-II, q. 1, a. 9, ad 3, distinguishes belonging *numero et merito*—i.e., as a publicly countable member and as spiritually united to the church; III, q. 69, a. 5, ad 1, distinguishes belonging *mentaliter* and *corporaliter*.

church, and still later only corporeally. There is only one church to belong to, however, although one can belong to it in two distinct ways, where corporeal belonging, *via* the sacraments and the profession of faith, is of course ordered to spiritual belonging.

At the level of dogma, yes, the church insists there is one and only one church, with both visible and invisible elements, spiritual and supernatural and also earthly and bodily aspects. This assertion of unity, we noted, is to be found in such texts as *Mystici Corporis*, nos. 64–65, and *Lumen Gentium*, no. 8. But given the sinfulness of the members of the church, how are we so to understand the unity of the church such that she *cannot* become an empty sign?[41] What is needed is a systematic response that explains why the one church, visible and invisible, cannot be separated into a purely visible church and an exclusively invisible communion of grace.

The well-catechized Catholic will guess that the solution has something to do with the sacraments themselves, from the fact that they do, as the medievals say, confer grace *ex opere operato*. For this is nothing more than a sort of shorthand for the church's faith that the sacraments really do extend the Lord's hand to the Christian who receives them in faith. Just as his finger opened the ears of the deaf man, so the sacraments extend his saving touch, now for the soul, to those who receive them, else he would not have commanded the apostles to baptize (Mt 28:19) nor promised them the Holy Spirit for the forgiveness of sins (Jn 20:22–23) and so on. And this was the faith of the Church Fathers, as well. For St. Augustine, when the priest baptizes, Christ baptizes.[42] This way of putting things, moreover, is well calculated to bring out the efficacy of the sacraments. We see the priest pour the water and say the words. We do not need faith for that. We believe that Christ baptizes when the priest does. And if Christ does, he does not do so to place some further invisible but empty sign. He baptizes to do something, to effect something, just as he touched the eyes of the man born blind with clay to make him see (Jn 9:6–7).

---

41. See, e.g., Walter Kasper, "The Church as a Universal Sacrament of Salvation," 111–28, in his *Theology and Church* (New York: Crossroad, 1989), 122, which recognizes the possibility of the separation of sign and signified.

42. Augustine, *Tractates on the Gospel of John*, in Nicene and Post-Nicene Fathers (First Series) 7, ed. Philip Schaff (Grand Rapids, Mich.: Eerdmans, 1986), tract 5, no. 18.

Furthermore, we might well suspect that the sacrament most useful in thinking about the structure of the church's sacramentality will be the Eucharist. For while the church makes the Eucharist, as was noted in chapter 6, the Eucharist makes the church. The structure of the Eucharist may illumine the structure of the church.

Three Moments of the Eucharist

In his *De Corpore et Sanguine Domini* (1063–68), Lanfranc of Canterbury argued against Berengarius of Tours to maintain that bread and wine become the true body and blood of the Lord at the Mass. After the consecration, what looks like bread and wine is a sign, a *sacramentum*, of the true body and blood of the Lord. The true body and blood, present on the altar, however, are themselves signs of the passion of the Lord; they are things (*res*) but also signs (*sacramenta*). And when we eat the body and drink from the cup, there are two feedings, one corporeal and one spiritual, for "then eternal life, which Christ himself is, is yearned for with spiritual desire," and "the recollection of his commandments is savored in the mind as sweeter than honey and the honeycomb," and "fraternal charity, the sign of which this sacrament enacts, is loved on account of the love of Christ" (c. 15). Charity is the thing for which the sacrament exists: it is not ordered to something else as an instrument or sign. So, in the next century, theologians distinguished three things in the Eucharist. Here is how the *Summa Sententiarum* of around 1141 put it. First, there is the *sacramentum tantum*:

The *sacramentum* which is not a thing are the visible species of bread and wine, as well as what is visibly celebrated there, for instance the breaking of the bread, laying it aside, or its elevation; for "a sacrament is a sign of something holy" [Augustine, *City of God* X.5].... Since the Church, too, is very often called the body of Christ in Sacred Scripture, so we read there that the bread and wine are sacraments of this body, the Church, since just as one bread is made from many grains and as juice from many clusters of grapes flows together into wine, so from many members the Church, which is the body of Christ, is made one [1 Cor 10:16].[43]

---

43. *Summa Sententiarum Septem Tractatibus Distincta, Tractatus Sextus*, cap. 3, in Patrologia Latina 176 (ed. J.-P. Migne), 140a–c (Paris, 1844–55). The *Summa* has sometimes been attributed to Hugh of St. Victor.

The bread and wine do not just signal the church, however. The sacrament really builds up the church. That is to say, there is also the *res* of the Eucharist, the end or aim for which Mass is celebrated and Communion received, "namely the unity of head and members" in charity. The species of bread and wine, made from many grains and many grapes, recall the multitude of members from which the one body of the church is made, even as Augustine taught, and the sacrament makes this unity happen. For this there must be something between the *sacramentum tantum* and the *res tantum*, however, a third thing which is both sign and reality, *res et sacramentum*, and this is the very body and blood of Christ. The true body and blood are realities compared to the sign value of the bread and wine, but they are also themselves signs relative to the unity and charity of the head and members of the church which indeed they effect in the members.

Three Moments of Ecclesial Communion

Just as the sacrament that signifies and makes the church has three moments, so also does the church possess an ecclesial *sacramentum tantum*, a *res tantum*, and a *res et sacramentum*.[44] The *res* is easy to identify. It is the communion of friends with and in Christ, the communion of charity. Whatever else there is in the church, that is the end, what everything else is for, and which is already an anticipation and share in eschatological reality. The *sacramentum tantum* is also easy to identify. It is everything about the church that meets the eye and is available to believer and nonbeliever alike: the social reality of the church, the social communion of the church, which is to be found in the church taken as a visible and public institution with laws, lands, and goods, with officers who govern and ordinary members with rights and duties, with meetings and common works of education and benevolence.

But what makes it be the case that the socially visible body of the church, which is as empirically available as any other institution to all men and apprehended as an institution and work of Christ for those with faith, is in fact a communion of grace and charity? It is the ecclesial *res et sacramentum*, the church considered in a third way, the church

44. De La Soujeole, *Introduction to the Mystery of the Church*, 442–49.

considered as a communion of the apostolic ministry, wherein the teaching of the gospel is infallibly maintained and wherein the grace of Christ is indefectibly and effectively offered, which is also at the same time the communion of those who receive such ministry.[45] The ministry of those who preach is enabled by those gifts of the Holy Spirit that are augmented by the grace of orders, wisdom and understanding, knowledge and counsel,[46] just as their ministry of sanctifying is enabled by the character of orders, which conforms them to Christ the priest and empowers them to place Christ's priestly acts.[47] They are fitted to offer participation in the truth and grace of Christ. On the other hand, those who are baptized and confirmed and who receive this teaching by faith subsequently manifest the *sensus fidei* of the whole church, and those who are sanctified have henceforth a common possession of the means of grace whose only impediments to their fruitful reception are subjective ones, the impediments of infidelity and grave, unrepented sin of individual sinners. It is a question here of a communion, and not of individuals taken one by one, and it is this that maintains the certainty that, wherever we find the social communion of the church we may also be assured of finding the communion of grace and faith. It is the church considered in this third way that de La Soujeole calls the "diaconal communion," a happy turn of phrase in that the active role played by the ministers of word and sacrament in this communion is indicated as wholly ordered to the service of those ministered to, to the service of the church.

It has to be noted at the outset that it is the diaconal *communion* of

45. See the discussion also in de La Soujeole's earlier *Le sacrement de la communion: Essai d'ecclésiologie fondamentale* (Paris: Cerf, 1998), 264–67. See also Jean-Guy Pagé, *Qui est l'Église?*, vol. 1: *Le mystère et la sacrement du salut* (Montréal: Bellarmin, 1977), 254: the ecclesial *res et sacramentum* "is the conjunction in Christ of the hierarchical or ministerial principle with the communitarian or charismatic principle" (my translation), and Nicolas, *Synthèse dogmatique*, no. 624, for whom the *res et sacramentum* is the faithful considered according to the real bonds established among them by the sacraments, the profession of faith, and obedience to church authority. For all three the *res et sacramentum* of the church is the communion of the church taken as effectively ordered to the realization of grace.

46. Aquinas, *ST* I-II, q. 68, a. 5, ad 1; I-II, q. 111, a. 4, ad 4; II-II, q. 45, a. 5, co. and ad 2; II-II, q. 177, a. 2. A longstanding view of the way St. Thomas understands the gifts is that they operate rarely and episodically. This view has been challenged. See John M. Meinert, *The Love of God Poured Out: Grace and the Gifts of the Holy Spirit in St. Thomas Aquinas* (Steubenville, Ohio: Emmaus Academic Press, 2018), 33, 64–70, and 114–27.

47. Aquinas, *ST* III, q. 63, a. 2, a. 3, co. and ad 2. Character is the *res et sacramentum* of the sacrament of holy orders.

those who minister and are ministered to that makes it be the case that the truth of the gospel is infallibly taught and unerringly recognized by the faithful, and that makes it be the case that the grace of the New Law is indefectibly available for those who are being saved. Bishops and priests singly and individually sometimes fail to preach true to the gospel; bishops and priests sometimes botch the administration of the sacraments; and for their part, the baptized sometimes present impediments to their assent to the truth or to the welcome reception of grace. But the church as a *whole* cannot fall out of the truth or fall into sin.

The three communions, that of grace and truth (the *res*), the social communion (the sign-*sacramentum*), and the diaconal communion of ministers and people (*res et sacramentum*), are the same communion of the church, which is looked at in three different ways.[48] The church is the communion of grace and charity, sacramentally signified in a socially visible communion and sacramentally realized by the church as diaconal communion. As de La Soujeole says, "the mystery of the Church is the mystery of unity between the means of salvation and the reality of salvation."[49]

Much depends here on what we think sacramental character is. It cannot be a mere relation of reason as has sometimes been proposed. The easiest way to understand it concordantly with Trent is to understand it as a power.[50] Certainly, it is a power for St. Thomas. The characters of baptism, confirmation, and orders conform the baptized, confirmed, and ordained to Christ the priest, and enable the worship of God that Christ instituted in the new covenant. They enable that worship—that is, they are the capacities, the powers—that make the Christian worship of God possible. The character of baptism lets the Christian offer the sacrifice from the hands of the priest.[51] Priestly character gives the power to change the Eucharistic elements and offer the sacrifice in the person of

---

48. Communion as offering a share, taking a share, and the community so established can be recognized in all three. But more prominently, the ecclesial *res* receives charity from Christ; the diaconal communion instrumentally gives a share of grace and truth; and the ecclesial social sign is evidently a community, a communion.

49. Benoît-Dominique de La Soujeole, OP, "The Mystery of the Church," *Nova et Vetera* (English edition) 8 (2010): 827–37, at 834.

50. The *Catechism of the Catholic Church*, no. 1581, speaks of an "enabling."

51. Pius XII, *Mediator Dei*, pars. 87–88 and 92–93.

Christ. Just because Christ's worship of the Father is that befitting the incarnate Son, just because our participation in his adoration of the Father requires us to punch above our natural weight, the sacramental characters are absolutely necessary for the truth of Christian worship and therefore also for the giving of grace and the growth in charity that Christian sacraments and worship bring.

Sacramental character can be looked at as a kind of promise. In a commercial transaction, one party may sign a contract engaging him to supply such and such a commodity at such and such a date. He may change his mind, and fail to comply. But the contract makes his compliance enforceable. He will comply, or pay a penalty. Sacramental character is a more gracious promise, for while it deputes us to Christian worship and in that sense calls for it, it is in the first place God's promise to us that we shall always be able to imitate the prayer and worship of Christ. More to the point of this chapter, as all the faithful—priests and laypeople—are empowered according to their order by sacramental character, sacramental character is God's promise to the church that the sacraments that give grace will be duly and properly and effectively celebrated, such that the church can never fall out of grace. God's promises, however, effect what they signify, and so the "contract" he makes with us is something written on our heart with the reality of a real modification and enhancement of our mind so as to make us able to worship him in spirit and in truth, in the Spirit of his own holiness and the truth of his incarnate Son.

Without such an arrangement, without the ecclesial *res et sacramentum* of what de La Soujeole calls the "diaconal communion," then one of two things will follow for the church. Either the social communion of the church will be able to be an empty sign, or the church will be so identified with the communion of grace and charity that it will become likewise invisible.[52]

The Church in Holy Week

What de La Soujeole and Nicolas have to say about the *res et sacramentum* depends for its technical expression on the idea of sacramental char-

52. Nicolas, *Synthèse dogmatique*, no. 624.

acter. But lest anyone think we are far from the simplicity of the gospel, their idea is easily illustrated in the mysteries of Holy Week, in the *history* of Holy Week. Think of this history from the point of view of the *community* of Christ, the original band of disciples, apostles, and followers of Jesus, as they make their way from the beginning of Holy Week to Easter Sunday and beyond.

First, let us begin at the *end*—the band of apostles and disciples at the end of Easter Sunday, in John's Gospel, or at the end of forty days after Easter, in Luke's Gospel: this is the holy community, whose own sins have been forgiven, the communion of grace and of the theological virtues. The descriptions of the Gospels are richly detailed. In John, the disciples are gathered together in one place, and Jesus breathes on them: he breathes the Holy Spirit into them (20:22). We know them henceforward therefore as the community of grace and charity, the communion that enjoys common life with God through the Spirit given them by Christ. In Luke, the Lord has already ascended to his Father, but the Holy Spirit likewise, as in John, comes down visibly, palpably: with the wind and the tongues of fire: this is the community living by the breath of God, the Spirit blowing on and into all, and with the flame of charity that moves them to their subsequent missionary preaching. This is the church of holiness, of common life with God in Christ through the Spirit.[53]

Second, let us take up the *beginning* of Holy Week: the same original band of disciples, apostles and followers and women and Mary. This is a sociologically identifiable band of people—the people with Jesus, the people who followed him, who were identified by their association with him. And it is a mixed band of saints and sinners. This is made known to us most signally in three ways: first, there is the betrayal of Judas, who with a kiss sells his master for thirty pieces of silver; then there is the denial of Peter, who three times disavows his Lord—"I do not know him" (Lk 22:57); and "he began to invoke a curse on himself and to swear, 'I do not know this man of whom you speak'" (Mk 14:71); last, there is the scattering of the disciples when the shepherd is struck (Mk 14:27). Mary does not forsake him, however, nor in John's Gospel does the beloved disciple—exceptions to the general rule of the fallibility of Christians. As a

53. Aquinas, *ST* I, q. 43, a. 7, ad 6.

whole, the socially identifiable band of Jesus' followers remains *de facto* a sign of the grace he has brought into the world.

Nonetheless, there is no assurance of finding a communion of divine life and the love of God in the band of disciples as we enter Holy Week. In principle (and setting aside the privileges of Mary), this whole band, this whole assembly, this whole church, standing at the beginning of Holy Week, can fall away into sin. No one who joined himself to it—why anyone would want to do so would be a great mystery—no one who joined himself to it, a collection of vacillating and inconstant and unfaithful people, would have the slightest assurance that he was entering the ark of salvation, the communion of the saved.

So, what makes the church not only *de facto* but *de jure* a communion of charity? That is to say, how do we get from the sociologically determinable reality of "disciples of Jesus" at the beginning the week, marred by sin as it is, to the theological community of charity at Easter Sunday in John, or at Pentecost in Luke? The question can hardly be formulated as a question if we follow out the story. It is the middle part of the story that answers it: the paschal mystery is the answer. It is the Lord, none other, who makes the band of sinners into a band of saints. The power of his cross does this: he satisfies for their sins, because his charity and obedience are worth more than all the sins of all the world can destroy, and just so, offering the sacrifice of himself to his Father, he merits the grace of justification, of sanctification, and of perseverance for those whom he loves.

But we want to attend to what is going on in the middle of Holy Week precisely as it affects the *community* of disciples, the visible band those associated with Jesus. And all we have to do here is count up the sacraments instituted or empowered in Holy Week, and, more to our point, how they are bequeathed to the band of disciples. The sacrifice of the cross is anticipated at the Last Supper before it is consummated on the cross. And it is anticipated just so that it can be bequeathed to the disciples: "Do this in memory of me." Notice that he is addressing a group, an assembly: the sacrament is bequeathed not to an individual, not to individuals as such, but to a community. Or, if you want, it is given into the custody of the apostles *in solidum* on behalf of the church.

After the resurrection, there is the sacrament of the resurrection and revivifying of the soul, that is to say, penance. When the Lord breathes on the disciples in John it is not only for their own sakes, but also so that, as ministers, they can pronounce the forgiveness of sins in the power of the cross and resurrection. "Receive the Holy Spirit. If you forgive the sins of any, they are forgiven" (Jn 20:22–23).

The Holy Spirit of forgiveness is also the Holy Spirit of truth, promised before the passion: "the Counselor, the Holy Spirit, whom the Father will send in my name, he will teach you all things, and bring to your remembrance all that I have said to you" (Jn 14:26; see also 16:13). So the post-Easter, post-Pentecost church is also confirmed in the truth of the gospel, the truth of Jesus: as a whole, it cannot fail faithfully to preach the gospel. And of course, it has charge to do so, given with the charge to baptize: "Go therefore and make disciples of all nations, baptizing them in the name of the Father and of the Son and of the Holy Spirit" (Mt 28:19).

The paschal mystery, the work of the Lord and of the Spirit who gives us access to the Lord, the Spirit who is rendered back to the Father so as to be poured out by Father and Son onto the church (Jn 19:30), thus establishes a community. It is a community, moreover, realized in that same band of sinners who betrayed and fled, a community that now has the wherewithal to make grace always newly offered in the sacraments of baptism and Eucharist and penance, a grace always newly announced in the preaching of the apostles.

Note that it is a community of service—serving the Lord as his ministers, serving the body of the Lord as beloved members thereof—we might say, a "diaconal communion." And it is one that is to be perpetuated: "as the Father has sent me, even so I send you" (Jn 20:21). That is, the apostles have authority to send men of equal apostolic authority, to preach and to baptize. Thus does Holy Week show us the three communions subsisting in the one communion of the church, and reports the constitution of the diaconal communion.

Conclusion

The exact nature of the church considered as the three communions just inventoried above can be reviewed by way of a conclusion. The communion of charity and grace, the ecclesial *res*, originates in Christ's acts of teaching and sanctifying: he gives us a share in his holiness and charity;

we take this share by our free assent of faith; the communion engendered is the communion of faith, hope, and charity, the communion that produces the fruit of spiritual sacrifice and the works of love.

The social communion of the church, the communion that greets the eye of believer and nonbeliever alike, is constituted by God's giving man a social nature and healing it in the order of grace. We take part in this gift by fostering the justice and practicing the charity that orders the society of the church.[54] Just as a visible society, however, the society thus established, a society of law and the specification of reciprocal rights and duties, looks like other human societies.

Last, the diaconal communion originates in the Lord's giving the apostles a share in his mind by his teaching and a share in his grace by his passion, and the apostolic charge. The church takes part by the confession of faith and valid reception of the sacraments. The communion thus established is that of those marked by the sacramental characters that are the pledge of the church's capacity for offering grace in the sacraments and enlightening minds by a teaching maintained by all so marked by Christ.[55]

---

54. De La Soujeole, *Introduction to the Mystery of the Church*, 443–44 and 474–76.
55. Ibid., 483–87.

CATHOLIC UNITY

Other Communions and Members of the Church

There is only one church, visible and invisible, to belong to. This follows fairly directly from the biblical data: Christ is no bigamist and there is only one bride of Christ; nor is he a monster, and the one head is the head of only one body. It follows also from the historical data of the church's foundation: Christ builds his church, the one, last, messianic temple, on one man, Peter, which is to say on one foundation, which supports one church (Mt 16:18). And when the Lord addresses the apostles as a whole, he addresses them as having the moral unity it takes to act in unity—"whatever you [plural] bind on earth shall be bound in heaven" (Mt 18:18). This is to say that unity follows from the diaconal communion of the church, especially from those responsible for maintaining it in truth and grace. The unity of the church follows also from the communion of grace and charity that makes the *res* of the church. The one charity that is the glue of the church is specifically one, while the one Spirit of which charity is a participation is numerically one.[1]

1. Aquinas, *ST* II-II, q. 23, a. 3, ad 3.

Although Christ founded and he and his Spirit sustain only one church, its unity is not something once and for all given without the co-operation of its members. Not for nothing did St. Paul exhort the Corinthians to avoid schism (1 Cor 1:10–17). For that matter, not for nothing did Christ pray that his disciples be one on the night before he died (Jn 17:11, 21).

The church is one, but its unity is complex, for the one church is composed of many elements, visible and invisible, as *Lumen Gentium*, no. 8, says:

Christ, the one Mediator, established and continually sustains here on earth His holy Church, the community of faith, hope and charity, as an entity with visible delineation through which He communicated truth and grace to all. But, the society structured with hierarchical organs and the Mystical Body of Christ, are not to be considered as two realities, nor are the visible assembly and the spiritual community, nor the earthly Church and the Church enriched with heavenly things; rather they form one complex reality which coalesces from a divine and a human element.

If it is possible for a person to enjoy some of these ecclesial elements without possessing all, then the unity of the church can become a difficult thing not only to realize but also to speak about adequately. This possibility, however, is expressly recognized by the Council, where, in the same paragraph, it recognizes that "many elements of sanctification and of [revealed] truth" are to be found outside the visible and social structure of the church.

While one either does or does not belong to the communion of grace, insofar as one does or does not possess the interior virtue of charity, belonging to the church considered as a social and diaconal communion is therefore more complicated. Congruently with the recognition of these many elements, visible and invisible, and while it remains that there is only one church as founded by Christ to belong to, the Council seems also to recognize that there can be degrees of belonging to it. Speaking explicitly of the "full incorporation" of Catholic Christians into the church (*Lumen Gentium*, no. 14), the Council implies that we can speak of partial incorporation or degrees of incorporation which are visibly manifested at the level of social communion. Thus, in place of the on/off switch of

Mystici Corporis, according to which one either belongs to the church or does not, *Lumen Gentium* gives us a rheostat. This admission of degrees of belonging has an application, *mutatis mutandis*, both to churches and ecclesial communions as well to individuals.

Churches and Ecclesial Communions

It is easiest to speak first of churches in perfect communion with the Catholic church, and the priority of this great church to these churches. These churches are sometimes called particular churches; this distinguishes them from the universal or "catholic" church as a part from a whole. These churches are sometimes called local churches because they exist in one place, while the universal church is in all places. These churches possess a certain fullness of ecclesial reality, because the one who presides over them is a bishop who has the fullness of orders and proper jurisdiction and belongs to the episcopal college.[2] In the West, these churches are called "dioceses," after the name for provinces of the late Roman empire, from the Greek *dioikein*—to manage or administer (from *oikos*—house).

The one universal church is called the "catholic" church. The "universal" is a "one" (*unum*) "turned to" (*versus*) or in relation to a many. The "catholic" is something "according to" (*kata*) the "whole" (*holon*). The one church is called catholic not in the New Testament, but immediately after, in the letter of Ignatius of Antioch to the Smyrnaeans.[3] According to the Acts of the Apostles, the one and whole church is a reality prior to any particular, local church: "they were all together in one place" on the day of Pentecost (Acts 2:1). The same thing is clear also from 1 Corinthians, where the body of Christ, the church, is one body (12:12), and all the apostles, prophets, teachers, and other workers (12:27–28) all belong to this one body.

In the New Testament, *ekklesia* can name the local church assembled for worship (1 Cor 11:18, 22; 14:4, 5, 12, 19, 23, 28, 35; Rom 16:5, 23; Col 4:15–16; Phlm 2), and so is suitably used to name particular churches,

---

2. See *Lumen Gentium*, no. 23.

3. Ignatius to the Smyrnaeans, no. 8, in *The Epistles of St. Clement of Rome and St. Ignatius of Antioch*, trans. James A. Kleist, SJ, ACW 1 (Westminster, Md.: Newman Bookshop, 1946).

city by city, that is to say, the group of Christians in a locality, assembled or not—the church of Corinth, the church at Antioch, in the singular (e.g., Acts 13:1; 1 Thes 1:1; 2 Thes 1:1; 1 Cor 1:2, 4:17, 6:4, 10:32; 2 Cor 1:1; Rom 16:1; Phil 4:15; Rv 2:1, 8, 12, etc.) or in the plural (1 Thes 2:14; 2 Thes 1:4; 1 Cor 7:17; 11:16; 16:1, 19; 2 Cor 8:1, 18, 19, 23, 24; 11:8, 28; 12:13; Gal 1:2, 22; Rom 16:4, 16; Rv 1:4, 11, 20). Also, it names the one, great, universal church (Gal 1:13; Eph 1:22; 5:23, 25, 27, 29, 32; Col 1:18, 24). *Ekklesia* connotes the members of the particular or universal church as "called," called by God through Christ in the Holy Spirit.

Just because it is God who calls us and inserts us into the church by baptism into the death of Christ, and just because there is one God for all who are so called, there is a certain priority to the one church so assembled out of the nations, the universal church. There is "one Lord, one faith, one baptism, one God and Father of us all, who is above all and through all and in all," Paul tells the Ephesians (4:5–6). Just so, there is "one body and one Spirit" (4:4). There is one body of Christ, so, one church, the universal church, which just because of the transcendence of the one God transcends the particular churches.

Churches Fully and Perfectly United to the Universal Church

It is misleading to think that the relation of a Catholic diocese or local church to the Catholic church is that of a part to a whole. On the purely sociological level, this is true enough: the thousands of people belonging to the diocese of New York make up just a part of the millions of people belonging to the church as a whole. At this level, the church is a collective whole, and its diocesan parts add one to another to make the whole.[4] But this is not the complete truth. The church is also a kind of distributive whole: the universal church is called a "church"; also, each diocese or particular church is a "church." Even more, the whole reality of the universal church is somehow present in the local church: "the one, holy, catholic and apostolic Church is truly present and active" in the particu-

---

4. See the decree on bishops of the Second Vatican Council, *Christus Dominus*, no. 11: a diocese is "a portion of the People of God entrusted to a bishop," and no. 6: a particular church is "part of the one Church of Christ." In *Decrees* (ed. Tanner), 2:921–39.

lar church.[5] In this light, John Paul II taught that "the universal Church cannot be conceived as the sum of the particular Churches, or as a federation of particular Churches."[6] We must speak, he said, of the "mutual interiority" of the universal and the particular churches.[7]

The reality of the mutual interiority of the particular and the universal church is expressed by saying that a local church is "in communion" with the great church and all the other local churches, and this fact is manifested (and strengthened) in the most literal way by way of Eucharistic intercommunion, and the fact that baptism in a local church is baptism in the universal church and gives the baptized the right to receive Communion in any and all the other local churches.[8] It is the principal task of the local bishop to guard this communion by keeping communion with other bishops, and especially Rome, and it is a principal task of the pope to strengthen this communion of all the local churches with Rome and with one another.[9]

How is this mutual interiority not just expressed but explained? The Congregation for the Doctrine of the Faith explains it in terms of the presence in each particular church or diocese of both the Eucharist and a member of the episcopal college, a bishop.[10] The presence of the Eucharistic celebration in a particular church ensures that the head of the body is present there, the head from which the body as a whole is nourished and guided (Eph 4:16). The Congregation notes that some take this to found a sort of independence or self-sufficiency of each particular church unto its self and on its own.[11] But it is rather the opposite that is true: the presence of the Eucharist in the particular church ensures the openness of

5. *Christus Dominus*, no. 11.

6. John Paul II, "Address to the Bishops of the United States of America," September 16, 1987, par. 3; available at www.vatican.va.

7. John Paul II, "Address to the Roman Curia," December 20, 1990, par. 9; available at www.vatican.va. These relations of the universal to the particular churches are restated in the *Letter to the Bishops of the Catholic Church on Some Aspects of the Church Understood as Communion* of the Congregation for the Doctrine of the Faith, May 28, 1992, par. 9; available at www.vatican.va.

8. For an ecclesiology whose master idea is that the church is a communion of communions, see J.-M. R. Tillard, OP, *Church of Churches: The Ecclesiology of Communion*, trans. R. C. De Peaux, O Praem (Collegeville, Minn.: Liturgical Press, 1992).

9. For the local bishop as maintaining the public unity of his own church and unity with other churches, see Ratzinger, *Called to Communion*, 94.

10. Congregation for the Doctrine of the Faith, *Letter on Communion,* nos. 11–14.

11. Ibid., no. 11.

that church to all the other local churches, to the universal church itself. No celebration of the Eucharist is the exclusive possession of one local church, but is a celebration in principle open to all other churches, to the whole, because it makes sacramentally and so really present the head of the church, the entire and sufficient treasure of the church. We could say that the presence of the Eucharist in each particular church means that that church cannot even be understood apart from its relatedness to the other churches, and calls for a sort of "hospitality" relative to those churches, sacramental, pastoral, catechetical.

The presence of a member of the episcopal college also ensures this openness of the local church. The college is, as it were, represented in the local church. What is signified by this representation is not only the unity through time of the apostolicity of the church, a diachronic unity, but also the unity that exists now, the synchronic unity of all the churches, such that no decisions touching the whole of the church can be decided apart from the whole, the whole of which the college as a whole has charge. Nor does this college exist apart from the pope, of course, whose peculiar task is the maintenance of its unity, and so the unity of the church as a whole, doctrinal and disciplinary. Moreover, the *immediacy* of his universal jurisdiction in every particular church, as taught by the First Vatican Council, is an especially signal and important way in which the universal church is interior to each particular church.[12]

Thus, at the level of the "diaconal communion," of the previous chapter, there is a presence of the supreme power of the church in the person of the bishop. This presence does not mean that the bishop can act with the freedom of the episcopal college as a whole, but his presence makes that college really if only partially present to the local church. The bishop in hierarchical communion with the other bishops and the pope makes the church he heads united to the whole and to all the other churches. This presence of the college in the particular church also makes it possible to speak of the interiority of the universal in the particular church.

There is a further explanation of this interiority, when the question of the relative priority of local to universal or of universal church to lo-

12. Ibid., no. 13; see the First Vatican Council, *Pastor Aeternus*, chap. 3, in *Decrees* (ed. Tanner), 2:811–16.

cal church is raised. This, too, was addressed by the Congregation, which gave the only answer possible, and that is that the universal church is prior, both ontologically and temporally, to the particular church.[13] It is prior in time in that Christ founds the church—*the* one single universal church—in establishing the apostolic college as a whole, for the whole, and in commending the Eucharist to this whole, for the whole church. He did not found this, that, and the other particular churches and then add them up. Thus, the universal church is prior in that the diaconal communion whence the local churches were subsequently founded by missions of evangelization was itself established in the apostolic college, with the fullness of both the authority to govern in charity, to teach the gospel infallibly, to celebrate the Eucharist, and to give grace sacramentally. The mission of the Spirit to the church also indicates this priority. There is a fullness of "church" on the day of Pentecost in Jerusalem prior to every further articulation of this church into churches, and this is signified by the presence of "devout men from every nation under heaven" (Acts 2:5). Before Athens and Corinth, before Boston and New York, there is the universal church, and this is obvious from the history of the church.

The universal church is prior ontologically to every particular church, and the Congregation explains this by recalling the teaching that the mystery of the church precedes creation in the mind of God. She is that for the sake of which the world was made. It follows from this double priority once again that no particular church can settle matters that touch the discipline and faith of the church as a whole. In these matters, the whole acts for the whole, through the episcopal college or the one who presides over it, the successor of Peter.[14]

Churches and Ecclesial Communions Imperfectly United to the Universal Church

There is a terminological note to register here, the use of "church" and "ecclesial communion." The custom of the church's magisterium at the

---

13. Congregation for the Doctrine of the Faith, *Letter on Communion*, no. 9.

14. Joseph Ratzinger discusses the issues raised by the *Letter on Communion* in "The Ecclesiology of the Constitution *Lumen Gentium*," in his *Pilgrim Fellowship of Faith: The Church as Communion* (San Francisco, Calif.: Ignatius Press, 2005), 123–52, at 133–39.

time of the Second Vatican Council and subsequently is to call no Christian body a "church" unless it celebrates the Eucharist validly (because it has a validly ordained priesthood).[15] Without the Eucharist, such a body is an "ecclesial communion," a body that does not fully measure up to the sacramental nature of the church because it does not validly celebrate the sacrament that most of all makes the church the church, the Eucharist. This is a matter of theological usage and makes a fundamental point about the Catholic church's understanding of the centrality of the Eucharist to the church.

There are two central texts to examine here, *Lumen Gentium*, no. 8, and in addition to this conciliar teaching, John Paul II's encyclical, *Ut Unum Sint*, par. 11.

Lumen Gentium

In the first chapter of *Lumen Gentium*, on the mystery of the church, the Council states the relation of the church to the Trinitarian Persons (nos. 2–4), reviews Christ's foundation of the church (no. 5), and assembles the New Testament images and metaphors for the church (no. 6), with special attention to the church as the body of Christ (no. 7). In the last paragraph (no. 8), the Council does three things: it opens with an assertion of the unity of the church as a visible-invisible reality composed of many elements (quoted above in the introduction to this chapter); it closes with a statement of the church's mission to preach the gospel and serve Christ in the poor; and in between, it says where the one church founded by Christ is to be found today—that is to say, it asserts the unicity of the church and locates it in the Catholic church.

This [the visible society which just is the mystical body of Christ] is the one Church of Christ which in the Creed is professed as one, holy, catholic and apostolic, which our Saviour, after His Resurrection, commissioned Peter to shepherd, and him and the other apostles to extend and direct with authority, which He erected for all ages as "the pillar and mainstay of the truth." This Church con-

---

15. See the usage of the Council's *Unitatis Redintegratio*, no. 22, and the Congregation for the Doctrine of the Faith's *Dominus Iesus*, August 6, 2000, no. 17, and the Congregation's "Responses to Some Questions Regarding Certain Aspects of the Doctrine on the Church," June 29, 2007, qq. 4–5, both available at www.vatican.va.

stituted and organized in the world as a society, subsists in the Catholic Church, which is governed by the successor of Peter and by the Bishops in communion with him, although many elements of sanctification and of truth are found outside of its visible structure. These elements, as gifts belonging to the Church of Christ, are forces impelling toward catholic unity.

There are then two assertions that the Council is making. First, the church founded by Christ—one, holy, universal, and apostolic—the one church that the Lord entrusted to St. Peter, is to be found in the Catholic church. Second, many elements of gospel truth—revealed truth—and sanctification can be found outside the visible confines of the Catholic church. The full identity of the church founded by Christ and the Catholic church, in other words, does not mean that there is no ecclesial reality outside the "structure" (*compago*) of the Catholic church. It means rather that the Catholic church has a real presence beyond her visible confines, in other churches and ecclesial communities, as we shall shortly see.[16]

Is the one church established by Christ to be found *only* in the Catholic church? By implication, yes. The Council does not say it subsists anywhere else, and it will be seen why it would be impossible to say that shortly. By contrast to saying that the church is located in the Catholic church, the Council says that there are outside her only elements of truth and sanctification.[17] This reading is furthermore required by the parallel passage in the Decree on Ecumenism, *Unitatis Redintegratio*, promulgated at the same time as *Lumen Gentium* (November 21, 1964). In this

16. For the history and interpretation of this paragraph, see Karl Becker, SJ, "The Church and Vatican II's '*Subsistit in*' Terminology," *Origins* 35, no. 32 (January 19, 2006): 514–22; this article first appeared in *L'Osservatore Romano* (December 4–5, 2006). See also Francis Sullivan, "A Response to Karl Becker, S.J., on the Meaning of *Subsistit In*," *Theological Studies* 67 (2006): 395–409, and "The Meaning of *Subsistit In* as Explained by the Congregation for the Doctrine of the Faith," *Theological Studies* 69 (2008): 116–24; Christopher J. Malloy, "*Subsistit In*: Nonexclusive Identity or Full Identity?" *The Thomist* 72 (2008): 1–44, responding to Sullivan; Guy Mansini and Lawrence Welch, "*Lumen Gentium* No. 8, and *Subsistit in*, Again," *New Blackfriars* 90 (2009): 602–17, responding to Sullivan in the 2008 and 2006 *Theological Studies*. And for the authority of a witness to the proceedings that produced the paragraph, see Joseph Ratzinger, "The Ecclesiology of the Constitution *Lumen Gentium*" in *Pilgrim Fellowship of Faith*, 147, where he maintains that the idea of the Council is to assert that the church exists as a "concrete agent," a "hypostasis" capable of acting as a unit and as a whole, only in the Catholic church. There is also the first chapter of Stephen A. Hipp's excellent *The One Church of Christ: Understanding Vatican II* (Steubenville, Ohio: Emmaus Academic, 2018).

17. Saying "only" does not preclude speaking of churches and ecclesial communities as such and recognizing their salvific significance as organizations or institutions, as has been alleged.

text, the Council teaches that (1) "the unity which Christ wished to bestow" on all Christians exists only in the Catholic church, in that (2) it is only there that Christians "can benefit fully from the means of salvation," and that (3) the goods of the new covenant were given "to the apostolic college alone of which Peter is the head" (no. 3). This text makes of the Petrine office something essential to the church as established by Christ.

Read in this way, the Council is asserting the full or total identity of the church founded by Christ, the mystical body, and the Catholic church, and this is what the history of the text indicates when we inquire into the antecedents of saying that the church "subsists in" the Catholic church. The first version of the text said that the one church of Christ, the mystical body, "is" (*est*) the Catholic church, simply repeating the assertion of *Mystici Corporis*. A second version said rather that the one church of Christ is present in (*adest in*) the Catholic church, a change that works more harmoniously with granting that elements of truth and sanctification exist outside the confines of the Catholic church.

If the church of Christ is "present in" the Catholic church, however, with the implication that that that is the only place it is present in that there are but "elements" outside of it, there is no backing away from asserting the full or total identity of the church of Christ with the Catholic church as taught by *Mystici Corporis*, although saying only that it "is present" in the Catholic church can seem to suggest that. Nor does the last substitution change the teaching of *Mystici Corporis* either but rather strengthens it, where we have it that the one church "subsists in" (*subsistit in*) the Catholic church. If *subsistere* is read to mean "to stay" or "to remain," or "to continue" (the dictionary definitions), then there is not much difference from saying that the church is "present in" or "subsists in" the Catholic church. What then was the point of the change? The point resides in the technical, scholastic sense of subsisting, the sense that Joseph Ratzinger said everyone understood at the Council and supposed was the sense that was meant. In this sense, "subsisting" is said of individuals, hypostases, persons, and what is being asserted is that the one church in her full and concrete reality, able to act as one agent, is to be found only and exclusively in the Catholic church.[18] This way of stating

18. Joseph Ratzinger, "The Ecclesiology of the Constitution *Lumen Gentium*," in *Pilgrim Fellow-*

the identity of the church of Christ and the Catholic church is, therefore, a richer way of saying that the one is the other, and conveys its own quite important content—one that was touched on before in considering the church as temple and as bride and as a unitary instrument of sanctification in chapter 10. But the Council did not abandon the way *Mystici Corporis* speaks. The Decree on the Catholic Churches of the Eastern Rite, *Orientalium Eccesiarum*, published at the same time as *Lumen Gentium*, refers to "the holy and Catholic Church, which is the Mystical Body of Christ" (no. 2).[19]

The clarity of the Council's assertion grows by comparison with other ways of thinking or trying to think the church's presence today. First, does the church as founded by Christ subsist nowhere, in no body of men that calls itself Christian? Then Christ's promise that the gates of hell will not prevail against the church has not been kept (Mt 8:16). Does the church as founded by Christ continue to exist in all Christian bodies taken individually, such that it subsists in the Orthodox church, in the Catholic church, in the Lutheran church and so on? Then there are many subsistences, which is to say many churches, distinct from one another in doctrine and discipline, and the confession of the creed that the church is one is false. Does the church subsist in the ensemble of Christian bodies taken together and collected in one box—the Orthodox church and the Catholic church and the Lutheran synods, etc.? Then the church can be one, but can have no mind, because she will simultaneously hold as true contradictory doctrines and contrary practices that imply contradictory doctrines, which is precisely to be mindless and have nothing to say. But if the church has no mind, she cannot have the mind of Christ as St. Paul encouraged the Philippians to have (2:5), and the deposit of doctrine she keeps (1 Tm 6:20 and 2 Tm 1:13–14) disintegrates into unintelligibility.

Of course, if "subsists in" means nothing more than "is present in," and if the church of Christ is present in separated churches and ecclesial communions according to the elements of truth and sanctification they enjoy, then it will be a purely verbal distinction to say that the church of Christ subsists only in the Catholic church and not in the other commu-

---

ship of Faith, 147. See Stephen Hipp's detailed analysis of *Lumen Gentium*, no. 8, in chap. 2 of his *The One Church of Christ*.

19. This decree can be found in *Decrees* (ed. Tanner) 2:900–907.

nities, for the only difference will be that between "fully" and "partially" subsisting. The church of Christ will "more or less subsist" in separated churches and communions. Then we can speak of the "non-exclusive" identity of the Catholic church and the church of Christ.[20] But this supposition rather destroys the assertion of the first subparagraph of no. 8 of *Lumen Gentium* asserting the unity of the church. For if the church of Christ is fully present in the Catholic church and present by degrees in other churches and communions, whereas the Catholic church is not present in them, then there is a wedge between the Catholic church and the church of Christ, the very thing the Council means to avoid in no. 8.[21]

Such a proposal also fails to line up with how the magisterium continues to speak since the Council. The church of Christ is "concretely found" in the Catholic church, although the church of Christ—the Catholic church—is "present and operative" in separated churches and communions, and there is a "full identity" between the Catholic church and the church of Christ.[22] "Concretely found" and "operative"—this returns us the explanation of *subsistit in* that Ratzinger offers, noted above: the agent that the church of Christ is may be active in separated churches and communions, but that agent just is the Catholic church, and that is the point of saying that the church of Christ subsists there, in the Catholic church. And therefore the church of Christ subsists nowhere else, for subsistence just means identity, identifiable unity as of an individual (an "un-divid-able"). The one church can have but one subsistence.

Various post-conciliar attempts to extend the language of "subsisting" beyond the usage of the Council, whereby we will say that the church as established by Christ subsists partially or by degrees in non-Catholic churches and communions destroy the language in which the church asserts Catholic teaching about the church in continuity with *Mystici Corporis* and previous Catholic teaching on the church.

20. This is Francis Sullivan's view; see Malloy, "*Subsistit In*," for extended analysis. See also Stephen Hipp, *The One Church of Christ*, chaps. 5 and 6.

21. See Louis Bouyer, *The Church of God: Body of Christ and Temple of the Spirit*, trans. Charles Underhill Quinn (Chicago: Franciscan Herald Press, 1982), 515–22.

22. Congregation for the Doctrine of the Faith, "Responses to Some Questions Regarding Certain Aspects of the Doctrine on the Church," responses to questions 2 and 3.

Ut Unum Sint

John Paul II's encyclical on ecumenism, *Ut Unum Sint* (May 25, 1995), picks up the teaching about elements of truth and sanctification outside the confines of the Catholic church, and speaks of the relations between the church of Christ and non-Catholic communities at par. 11.[23]

> Indeed, the elements of sanctification and truth present in the other Christian Communities, in a degree which varies from one to the other, constitute the objective basis of the communion, albeit imperfect, which exists between them and the Catholic Church. To the extent that these elements are found in other Christian Communities, the one Church of Christ is effectively present in them. For this reason the Second Vatican council speaks of a certain, though imperfect communion. The Dogmatic Constitution *Lumen Gentium* (no. 15) stresses that the Catholic Church "recognizes that in many ways she is linked" with these Communities by a true union in the Holy Spirit.

Here, the imperfect communion of non-Catholic communions with the Catholic church, implied by *Lumen Gentium*, no. 15, and asserted in *Unitatis Redintegratio*, no. 3, is reasserted.[24] Because of the elements of truth and sanctification in these communities, they are themselves used by the Holy Spirit to effect salvation, as both the decree and the encyclical teach.[25] This, in fact, is the principle on which Catholic engagement in ecumenism rests.[26] However, just because the church of Christ subsists only in the Catholic church, this efficacy of non-Catholic communions for salvation is owing "to the fullness of grace and truth entrusted *to the Catholic Church*."[27] And indeed, because of these elements of truth and sanctification in non-Catholic communions, the encyclical can state that the one church of Christ "is effectively present in them." "The one church of Christ," that is to say, the *Catholic* church is present in them. The language is therefore carefully used. The one church of Christ does not

23. John Paul II, *Ut Unum Sint*, Encyclical Letter, May 25, 1995; available at www.vatican.va.

24. See also *Unitatis Redintegratio*, no. 14, on imperfect communion with Eastern churches.

25. *Unitatis Redintegratio*, no. 3.

26. See Jared Wicks, SJ, *Investigating Vatican II: Its Theologians, Ecumenical Turn, and Biblical Commitment* (Washington, D.C.: The Catholic University of America Press, 2018), 140–41.

27. *Unitatis Redintegratio*, no. 3. Not all translations have "*Catholic* Church," but it is there in the Latin. This makes it clear that that the presence of the church of Christ in separated churches and communions is not other than the presence of the Catholic church.

"subsist" in non-Catholic churches and communions, but is more or less "present" in them (according to the number of the elements of truth and sanctification they possess), and unto their efficacy in communicating salvation. This means, for instance, that when a Lutheran pastor baptizes, the Catholic church is baptizing.[28]

Taking things altogether, these two documents make plain why ecumenical dialogue is both possible and necessary for the church. It is possible because ecclesial reality really does exist outside the one Catholic church. There is something to talk about. Christians remain brothers, that is, people who can understanding one another when they speak the language of faith. It is necessary because communion among Christians and Christian communities is imperfect, contrary to the will of Christ. Furthermore, just because the elements of truth and sanctification in separated churches and communions belong to the Catholic church, the Catholic church is not only the goal of ecumenical progress, but the Catholic church is by right and duty leader of this progress.[29] On the other hand, if the church of Christ subsists in all ecclesial communities taken severally and one by one—to revisit a possibility envisaged above—then there is no point to ecumenical discussion. Each ecclesial outfit is as good as any other, and all should exist in amity and concord. Or again, if the one church of Christ subsists in all ecclesial communities taken together, there is no point to ecumenical discussion. And on both views, the doctrinal differences of the communities turn out to have no real weight or significance. Doctrine turns out to be something completely secondary, as it were, accidental to Christianity. That is, the version of what revelation is to liberal Protestantism and Catholic Modernism turns out to be true.

The ground on which ecumenical endeavor and the effort to find perfect communion make sense, moreover, also reminds us that such endeavor and effort can be successful only if they are motivated by a good will moved by grace and guided by the providence of God. For these grounds

---

28. For full analysis of these relations, see Stephen Hipp, *The One Church of Christ*, chap. 4.

29. For an examination of the charge that the Catholic church came "late" to ecumenism, see Reinhard Hütter, "Catholic Ecumenical Doctrine and Commitment—Irrevocable and Persistent: *Unitatis Redintegratio* as a Case of an Authentic Development of Doctrine," 268–311, in *Dogma and Ecumenism: Vatican II and Karl Barth's Ad Limina Apostolorum*, ed. Matthew Levering, Bruce L. McCormack, and Thomas Joseph White, OP (Washington, D.C.: The Catholic University of America Press, 2019), at 298–299.

are rooted in the conviction that, whatever the church is, she is in the first place God's work, and that therefore any effort to restore the communion of Christians will also necessarily be his work of restoration.

A Systematic Way to State the Relation: Essential and Potestative Wholes

In comparing the church to the sacrament of the Eucharist in chapter 10, the sociological and institutional communion was identified as the *signum* of the church, signifying the communion of faith and charity identified as the *res* of the church, and infallibly signifying the presence of the *res* because of the diaconal communion, where the church is considered as always and indefectibly possessing both an authoritative gospel and sacraments effective of grace, a sort of *res et sacramentum ecclesiae*.

Evidently and quite publicly, Christians are divided at the level of the *signum tantum*. But they and their ecclesial bodies can be united at the level of the communion of grace and charity, the *res*, in despite of the fact that non-Catholic communions do not always possess all the instruments of sanctification and none of them share in the unity brought about by the exercise of the Petrine office, things that belong to the *res et sacramentum* of the church.

Despite the fact that the divisions between Christians owe something to sin and not merely to the accidents of history, and therefore despite the fact that the unity of Christians is difficult to express because of the objective unintelligibility of sin, there is a way to express the relations of the Catholic church to non-Catholic churches and communities that is not entirely unsatisfactory. It requires us to distinguish kinds of wholes.

A universal whole in one which is verified in its parts with both its complete nature and with all its powers. So, animal is a universal whole relative to man and horse: the essence of animality is verified in each, and the powers of an animal, such things as the ability to eat, move, sense, and reproduce, are present in both horses and men.[30] An integral whole, on the other hand, enters into its parts neither with its entire essence nor with all its powers. Such is the human body, an organic integral whole, or a house, an accidental integral whole. An arm has neither the nature

---

30. In this paragraph, I am paraphrasing Francisco P. Muñiz, OP, *The Work of Theology*, trans. John P. Reid, OP (Washington, D.C.: Thomist Press, 1953), 1–3.

nor all the powers of the body as a whole; a roof has neither the nature nor capacities of a whole house. In between these wholes, there is the potestative whole, which is present in its parts according to its essence, but not with all the powers that flow from the essence. So, for example, the human soul exists in every organ of the body according to its essence, and the organ is therefore a human organ. But it is not present there with all its powers—it is not present in the eye with the power of hearing.

Applied to the problem of the expression of ecclesial unity, and supposing that we rightly identify communion in grace and charity as the essential character of the church, that for which everything else in the church exists, then the one church of Christ is present in the Catholic church both essentially and with all the powers with which Christ endowed and still endows it, such that we rightly say it subsists in the Catholic church. But while the essential character of the communion of grace and charity may exist in non-Catholic communities, it never exists in them with all the powers Christ wants the church to have. The church is present in them only partially potestatively.[31]

If this account of things be granted, does it make ecumenical discussion pointless? If we are already united in charity—the main thing—why bother with the work of ecumenism? The answer is that the perfection of the "diaconal communion," with all its powers of teaching authoritatively and of confecting all the sacraments, is by no means immaterial to the maintenance of charity, as we saw in chapter 10. In fact, and as is quite obvious today, without the fullness of the powers of the diaconal communion, the doctrinal and sacramental and disciplinary integrity of Christian life is seriously threatened and increasingly hard to maintain. If a Protestant minister baptizes in the name of the creator, the redeemer, and the sanctifier, has he really and truly baptized? No, he has not. And when the teaching of both the natural law and revelation on the nature of the family and what the sixth commandment requires of us is obscured, Christian identity and therefore also sharing in the charity of Christ are threatened. On the Catholic view of things, the work of ecumenism remains not simply a response to the mandate of the Lord but an increasingly urgent duty of charity itself.

31. See de La Soujeole, "The Mystery of the Church," 835–36.

Comparison and Contrast with the Ordinary
"Branch Theory" of Protestantism

According to the "branch theory" of some non-Catholic theologians, the church of Christ is treated more or less as a universal whole, and is verified as to its essence and its powers (the really necessary ones) in whatever portion of it we take. So, for instance, Kenneth Collins and Jerry Walls make it that the Reformation churches, the Orthodox, and the "Roman Church" are all parts of the one body of Christian believers, what by theological right ought to be called the "Catholic Church."[32] In the nineteenth century, E. Pusey maintained that the Catholic, Greek, and Anglican churches were three "parts" of the one church of Christ.[33] In this vein, one speaks of three (or more) ecclesial and theological "traditions," where such language suggests that they are all on the same level, all equally valuable and legitimate instantiations of "church." This view admits there are some incongruences to smooth out and difficulties to resolve. But as long as an ecclesial body accepts the one God and Father, one Lord, one Spirit, one faith, one baptism, and one church of Ephesians 4:4–7,[34] then we are all in the same box on the same revealed terms, and ought not, as Catholics do, refuse to acknowledge non-Catholic Christians as fully incorporated into the church of Christ. Catholics are reproached, in other words, for their failure both to understand the nature of the church, a theological failure in understanding scripture, and for lack of charity. This way of thinking approaches that of Catholic theologians mentioned above who want to say the church subsists in non-Catholic communions and suffers from the same difficulty as to a real ability to say that such a church really has one mind, one faith. This will be taken up again in the next section.

32. See Kenneth Collins and Jerry Walls, *Roman but Not Catholic: What Remains at Stake 500 Years after the Reformation* (Ada, Mich.: Baker Academic, 2017), xvii.

33. E. B. Pusey, *An Eirenicon: The Church of England a Portion of Christ's One Holy Catholic Church, and a Means of Restoring Visible Unity* (London: Rivington's, 1865), 97.

34. This is Pusey's checklist in ibid., 56.

Individuals: Membership

The Question of Membership

We pass from thinking about church unity at the level of communions to church unity at the level of individuals, or the question of membership in the church. This is closely related to the question of how to think the relationship between the Catholic church and non-Catholic communions. The questions illuminate each other. And the question of membership remains as important as it was in the age of Robert Bellarmine (d. 1621) and Francisco Suárez (d. 1617).[35]

Why cannot we say that all Christians belong to the one church founded by Christ in the same way? *Lumen Gentium*, no. 13, recognizes that there are different ways of belonging: "All men are called to this catholic unity [of the one people of God] ... and in different ways [*variis modis*] belong to it or are related to it [*pertinent vel ordinantur*]: the Catholic faithful, others who believe in Christ, and finally all mankind, called by God's grace to salvation."

Even if one does not belong, one is "ordered" to the church, in that God desires all men to be saved (1 Tm 2:4), and the church of Christ is the ordinary means of salvation (Acts 4:12; Eph 4:4–7).[36] The different ways of belonging are briefly described, first as to "full incorporation," in *Lumen Gentium*, no. 14: "Fully incorporated into the Church are those who, possessing the Spirit of Christ, accept all the means of salvation given to the Church together with her entire organization, and who—by the bonds constituted by the profession of faith, the sacraments, ecclesiastical government, and communion—are joined in the visible structure of the Church with Christ, who rules her through the Supreme Pontiff and the bishops."

"Full incorporation" implies by contrast partial incorporation or incorporation to some degree, and this is described in *Lumen Gentium*, no. 15: "The Church knows that she is joined in many ways [*plures rationes*] to the baptized who are honored by the name of Christian, but who do not

---

35. For Bellarmine, membership requires profession of the faith, use of the sacraments, and submission to church authority. For Suárez, it consists solely and exclusively in faith.

36. See *Lumen Gentium*, no. 14, *Unitatis Redintegratio*, no. 3, *Ad Gentes*, no. 7, and *Dominus Iesus*, nos. 20 and 22.

however profess the Catholic faith in its entirety or have not preserved unity of communion under the successor of Peter." "Joined in many ways" or on account of "many reasons" is not full and perfect membership. Why must this be insisted upon?

If all *Christians* belong in the same way and same sense to the one church of Christ, then it surely must follow that all the various *communions* and *churches*—the Catholic church and the non-Catholic churches and communions—function to insert us into that one church of Christ, which is to say that they are equally good ways of inserting us into that one church of Christ and so uniting us to Christ in the Spirit and putting us on the road to heaven.

And then all these ways, all the churches and communions, should themselves therefore be said to belong to the one church, the universal church, or be parts of it, or share in it, in the same way, and have it present in them, in the same way—how not, if the religious effect on their members of belonging to them is the same for all of them? But if all the churches and communions belong in the same sense to the one great church, in the same way, with the same effect, then the differences between them cannot be religiously or theologically significant, and cannot be worth fighting over.

And this would seem to mean that whether or not we share the same faith is not important. So, whether or not we think justification is merely extrinsically imputed is unimportant. Whether or not we think predestination is double or not is unimportant. Whether we think the Mass is a sacrifice or not is unimportant. Whether we think the consecrated host is worthy of adoration or not is unimportant. Whether we think the sacraments give grace is unimportant. Whether we think the Petrine ministry is essential to the church as founded by Christ and as understood by the First Vatican Council is unimportant.

Given the theological disarray of many of the churches and communities in the West and their inability to keep to the standard of the rule of faith today, then in fact it will turn out that whether or not we believe in the incarnation is not important. Whether or not we believe the extant text of the Bible including the Old Testament is authoritative with the authority of the word of God for what we think true about God and Christ—that will not be important, either. Whether we think marriage is a sacrament and has the same indissolubility as the relation of Christ to the church will not be important. So, whether or not we permit remarriage after divorce is not important. And also, whether or not we grant same-sex unions religious sanction is not important.

Where it is hard for ecclesial bodies to maintain clarity about the creed, then even such things as transcendence of God, the real distinction between God and the world, and the freedom with which he creates and saves become threatened with purported more ancient spiritual wisdom than the gospel and some more fundamental metaphysical truth (the "nondualism" of chapter 1). Many Christians have trouble distinguishing Christianity from "new age" spiritualities, as in fact do many baptized Catholics.[37]

In such a way, the church will be one, but it will be a hollow unity that does not mean anything because it means contradictory things. In failing to distinguish between full and partial membership, we fail to appreciate the essential functions of the diaconal communion insisted on earlier in this chapter. Failing to distinguish full and partial membership, which amounts to disregarding the fullness of the powers given to the diaconal communion, we drift into liberal Protestantism. For what liberal Protestantism and Catholic Modernism in its wake stand for is the secondary, accidental character of doctrine relative to the essential core of the church, which on this view is a relationship of *praxis* to one's neighbor and piety to God, but not one of religious assent to propositions proposed with the authority of God revealing.[38] Communion and mutual recognition of each other's Christianity as in every case perfect will be easy enough on those terms. And notwithstanding the accidental character of doctrine in such a view of things, there will, paradoxically, be established a new doctrinal standard to which all must adhere. For if it really is morally and Christianly permissible for *you* to have same-sex unions, for instance, then surely it is wrong—morally wrong—for *us* to exclude

---

37. See the Pontifical Council for Culture and the Pontifical Council for Interreligious Dialogue, *Jesus Christ: The Bearer of the Water of Life—A Christian Reflection on the New Age* (Boston: Pauline Books and Media, 2003).

38. For doctrine as accidental to the Christianity, see Jan Walgrave, *Unfolding Revelation: The Nature of Doctrinal Development* (Philadelphia: Westminster, 1972), "The Essence of Liberal Theology," 226–29, and on Protestant and Liberalism and Catholic Modernism, 229–35 and 245–53, respectively.

them. And we will be disciplined for saying they ought to be excluded. And so on.

Terminological Note

The Second Vatican Council speaks of an imperfect communion of non-Catholic churches and ecclesial bodies with the church, and coordinately with this, of full and imperfect incorporation of Christians into the church. It is not speaking of the relations of heretics and schismatics to the church. Heresy and schism name personal sins freely committed by which one separates oneself from the church.[39] A heretic rejects what he had first received as part of divine and Catholic faith, and does so culpably. A schismatic breaks communion with the church, sinning against charity. But when we are thinking today of non-Catholic Christians, we are thinking most often of people who have received their Christian faith in good human faith from their parents and communities. As they have never received the fullness of Catholic faith, they have never been in a position to reject it. Nor have they once been in communion with the Catholic church, and then broken communion with her. Hence the terms that describe them more exactly are "separated brothers and sisters."[40] Following de La Soujeole, we will say that they belong to the church as communion of grace and charity (when they are in grace), but that they belong imperfectly to the church considered as diaconal communion and so are quite visibly split from the church at the obvious level of social communion, having their own organization and law.

Conclusion

There is only one church to belong to. And this church is composed of both visible elements (for instance, the exteriority of the sacraments) and interior elements (the grace of the sacraments), as *Lumen Gentium*, no. 8, teaches. Insofar as those elements are possessed by some non-Catholic church or communion, such a group is more or less in imperfect com-

---

39. Aquinas, *ST* II-II, q. 11, a. 3, and q. 40, a. 4.

40. Charles Journet and those who follow him sometimes call such people "dissidents," and this is fine as long as it does not connote a positive act of denial or turning away.

munion with the church, and the one church is more or less present and active for salvation in that church or communion.

As to individuals, one can belong to the one church in a principally visible way, and one can belong to it in a principally invisible way. If one belongs to the church in a principally invisible way, to the communion of charity and grace, then even so the profession of faith and whatever sacraments one can avail oneself of and the works of love that charity inclines us to makes one's membership something visible, and one is identifiable as a Christian, if not a Catholic Christian. And the other way round, one can belong to the social body of the church, having been baptized, enrolled in some Catholic parish, but without charity. Even so, one still enjoys the interior grace of faith. In either case, in either very imperfect case, one belongs to the one visible-invisible church.

CHAPTER 12

THE CHURCH
IS HOLY

The holy is what is set apart from the profane. Relative to creation, the holy is the transcendent God, although originally, as we saw in chapter 6, the entire cosmos was to be a temple and Eden a microcosm of this temple for the God whom "the heaven and the heaven of heavens cannot contain" (2 Chr 2:6). Within a fallen world, the true temple of the holy God is holy church.

Objective and Subjective Holiness

The holiness of the church is both objective and subjective. Objectively, the church is holy because the sacraments are holy, scripture is sacred, the members consecrated by baptism and confirmation and perhaps by holy orders. This is the holiness of the diaconal communion, all marked by sacramental character conforming them to Christ the priest, and of the tools of this communion, word and sacrament. Subjectively, the church is holy insofar as her members are moved by charity. This is the holiness of the *res ecclesiae*, for the virtue and excellence of the church consists finally in the grace and charity of her members. This grace and charity is the proximate end of the church, whose only further end is the glory of the heaven of heavens.

The objective holiness of the church is visible in the means of holiness that the church possesses and that are in some measure visible to the eyes of those without faith. Thus, it is most visible in the Catholic church. It is more or less visible in non-Catholic churches and communions according to the elements of truth and sanctification they possess (*Lumen Gentium*, no. 8). The subjective holiness of the church is visible in the works of charity that charity provokes, the works that are traditionally counted up in the corporal and spiritual works of mercy.

Thus St. Thomas, explains that the New Law consists of more than grace and charity: "The New Law is principally the very grace of the Holy Spirit, which is given to the Christian faithful.... Nonetheless, the New Law has certain things that dispose one to the grace of the Holy Spirit, and certain things that belong to the use of this grace, which things are as it were secondary in the New Law."[1] Preaching and the sacraments dispose to grace; works of charity belong to the use of grace. And again: "it is fitting that grace flowing into us from the incarnate Word be brought down to us through certain exterior things [the sacraments], and that from this interior grace, by which the spirit subdues the flesh, certain exterior and sensible works be produced."[2] The distinction between the means of grace and the manifestation of grace in works recalls the double sense of that article of the creed where we profess to believe in the *communio sanctorum*. This can be rendered as communion of holy things—*sancta*—the communion of the holy things, the sacraments, which are commonly enjoyed. But also, it can be rendered as a communion of holy persons—*sancti*.

The Abiding Presence of Subjective Holiness in the Church

Because the church is a diaconal communion, it was argued in chapter 10, the identifiably holy institution of the church can never not be sub-

---

1. Aquinas, *ST* I-II, q. 106, a. 1.
2. Ibid., q. 108, a. 1.

jectively holy in some of its members. In this sense, there will always be "saints" in the church, men and women instinct with grace and charity. The visible church, therefore, will always be the location of a community of invisible holiness. This is part of how Catholics understand the victory of Christ. Moreover, while grace and charity are in themselves invisible, they can manifest themselves publicly and sometimes have extraordinary public and visible consequences. So, the subjective holiness of St. Francis of Assisi or of St. Catherine of Siena or of Mother Theresa of Calcutta was as it were something palpable to their associates. The respect and obedience Catholics manifest toward the objective holiness of the visible church and its hierarchical ministers spills over into a more personal love of living saints.

The constant presence of subjective holiness in the church follows not just from an ecclesiology that attends to the church as diaconal communion but is therefore also a matter of experience. Almost every serious Catholic will come to know a holy person in the church. This is a very common thing. It is a corroboration of the theoretical stance developed in chapter 10. And indeed, personally encountered holiness is often a motive for entering the church in the first place. Moreover, there have been many, as it were, public saints, acknowledged saints, in every generation of the church since its foundation. Canonization of saints today is a declaration of subjective holiness and amounts to a kind of constant witness to the abiding presence of subjective holiness in the church.

Is a Holy Church with Sinful Members Herself Sinful?

The certainty with which holy people are found in the church, however, does not eliminate the certainty that sinners will be found in the church, too. This fact of history follows also from a theological anthropology in which we are not confirmed in grace except at death, at which we have hope that the grace of perseverance will deliver us to a merciful judge. There are sinners in the church, and this, too, we know by experience, and most Catholics by their experience of themselves, and indeed, by their experience of themselves as serious sinners. Thence the question: does this fact let us say that the church herself is sinful? There are two chief answers to this question in twentieth-century ecclesiology, the answer of Charles Journet and the answer of Yves Congar.

Journet: The Church Is Entirely and Always Holy, but Her *Members* Can Be Sinners

Journet argues that what makes the church the church are such things as the indwelling Holy Spirit, the grace and headship of Christ, faith and the sacraments of faith. These objectively holy things make a holy communion of charity to which sin is alien. Insofar as the church is constituted by these things, therefore, she is sinless. And it is not *because* of sin that anyone belongs to the church. That is, sin does not make us a part of the holy church: "If one defines the Church by what precisely makes her the Church, the Body of Christ, one will hold that although she comprises numerous sinners, she is herself wholly pure and holy ... that her proper boundaries, true and precise, circumscribe only what is pure and good in her members, both the just and sinners, leaving outside of them all that is impure, even in the just."[3] The church includes only what is pure and good, and is therefore always the immaculate church and necessarily so. Thus, the members of the church as individuals may be sinful; but although they belong to the church, they do not *constitute* the church. This is the way of speaking more common to theologians and the magisterium.

Congar: The Church Is Holy in Herself, but She, the *Church*, Can Be Sinful in Her Members

Congar distinguishes four senses of the church: the church taken according to the divine principles of faith, the sacraments of faith, and hierarchical power that actively and formally constitute her; the church as the *congregatio fidelium*, the material cause of the church informed by the church taken in the first way; the church of the hierarchy—the churchmen who teach, sanctify, and govern; church as the synthesis of the foregoing three aspects.[4] In the first sense, the church is infallible and cannot sin, and, in

3. Charles Cardinal Journet, *Theology of the Church*, trans. Victor Szczurek, O. Praem. (San Francisco, Calif.: Ignatius Press, 2004), 215. I have altered the translation. For the French, see Journet, *Théologie de l'Église*, 243–44.
4. Yves Congar, OP, *True and False Reform in the Church*, trans. Paul Philibert, OP (Collegeville,

her highest determinations of rule is practically infallible.[5] If "church" means the assembly of the baptized faithful, however, the church sins. The community as a community is holy, and the community as a community does not sin. Still, the predication as such is true: the church is sinful.[6] If we could not say this, Congar says, then one would have to leave the church because of one's own personal sin: "But the church, at the same time that it is communion with Christ, is also the means of this communion … the means of pastoral help and of grace, the means of repairing the Christian life through the exercise of the power of the keys."[7]

If for Journet we can say that it is not because of sin that anyone belongs to the church, for Congar, taking the words in another way, it is indeed precisely because of sin that I belong to the church, because I need the help of the church. And there is another, very important issue for Congar. Even where no sin in the strict sense has been committed, there are "social-historical" mistakes on the part of the faithful and their pastors—missed opportunities for evangelization, inability to refresh the theological mind of the church, sticking to a narrow but unnecessary past routine, and so on. And these things damage the church and retard the fulfillment of her mission.

In the third sense, the church of churchmen, the church is sinful, just insofar as hierarchs, even in the acts of their official capacity, are vain, rash, violent, and unjust. Here, we may think of "acts of simony, nepotism, abuse of power, violent constraint, use of spiritual arms for temporal ends."[8] We can assess the differences between the two views by saying with Avery Dulles that while Journet *defines* the church, and so can include only the holy things and formal principles that make the church the church, Congar offers a *description* of the church, and such description notes the wounds of the church inflicted on her by her members.[9] When he makes a balance sheet, Jean-Hervé Nicolas agrees with Journet

Minn.: Liturgical Press, 2011), 88–92. This is a partial translation of the revised edition of 1967, a revision of the original edition of 1950.

5. *True and False Reform*, 93 and 104.

6. Ibid., 96–97.

7. Ibid., 98–99.

8. Ibid., 108. He lists also such things as Pope Honorius's indulgence to monotheletism and Pope Pius VII's alienation of the church's rights to Napoleon (105).

9. Avery Dulles, SJ, "Should the Church Repent?," *First Things* (December 1998): 38.

that the church herself is no sinner and that sin separates one from the church.[10] But personal sin, especially the sins of the leaders of the church, failures of prudence, as well as human limitations of culture and knowledge, all these things conspire to produce many "faults" throughout the church's history.[11]

Public Apology for Ecclesial Fault

It was for mentioning, expressing sorrow, and apologizing for such faults that St. John Paul II was famous (or infamous). Throughout the course of his long pontificate, the Pope addressed such matters as the Inquisition and anti-Semitism, including the silence of many Christians during the Holocaust, the crusades, the religious wars following the Reformation, the prosecution of Galileo, Catholic participation in the slave trade, oppression of ethnic groups in colonial times, condonation of dictatorships, discrimination against women, and the genocide in Rwanda, in all of which things Christians were implicated in some fashion or other.[12] This was something the church had not seen before. The Second Vatican Council had asked pardon for the sins of Catholics against unity, "pardon of God and of our separated sisters and brothers" (*Redintegratio Unitatis*, no. 7).[13] The Council also regretted the responsibility of some Christians in providing occasion for atheism and the attitudes of some Christians in opposing faith to science (*Gaudium et Spes*, nos. 19, 36), and in its declaration on non-Christian religions decried anti-Semitism (*Nostra Aetate*, no. 4).[14] But no pardon was asked for the role of Christians in these mistakes and sins.

John Paul II asked pardon, not for sin imputed to the church, for he did not impute sin to the church. But he did ask pardon for the sins of her members. And he invited Catholics, the church, to repent for such faults or sins. This was part of his intention to ready the church for the third millennium.[15] He intended a spiritual readiness in which the past

---

10. Nicolas, *Synthèse dogmatique*, 700.
11. Ibid., 701–2.
12. See Dulles, "Should the Church Repent?," 36–41.
13. So also did Pope Paul VI at the opening of the second session of the Council.
14. This text can be found in *Decrees* (ed. Tanner), 2:968–71.
15. John Paul II, *Tertio Millenio Adveniente*, Apostolic Letter, November 10, 1994; available at www.vatican.va.

would not be forgotten but atoned for, and the memories both of Catholics and the heirs of those whose forbears were harmed and sinned against cleansed.[16] The invitation for the sinless church to repent for her sinful members, after all, can surprise no thoughtful Catholic. The Lord Jesus, sinless though he was, repented—offered satisfaction—for our sins. The church also repents for the sins of her members.[17] The holiness of the church is, then, paradoxically manifested not only in Christians who repent of their own sin, but in Christians who make up in their bodies what is lacking to the sufferings of Christ (Col 1:24), that is, what is lacking to vicarious satisfaction for the sins of others after the pattern and in the power of Christ.

The fundamental theological warrant for such vicarious participation in the sufferings of Christ is the doctrine that the church is the body of Christ.[18] So, St. Paul to the Corinthians: "If one member suffers, all suffer together; if one member is honored, all rejoice together" (1 Cor 12:26). He does not qualify the kind of suffering he means, but it certainly includes the spiritual suffering of sin (1 Cor 5:2). So we all pay for debts contracted by others, even as Christ pays for the debts of all.

The Church of Reconciliation

The church exists under three conditions: in heaven, in purgatory, on earth. The communion of the saints in heaven is a final communion, and its members possess that holiness according to the degree of charity to which they were predestined before the beginning of time. The souls in purgatory are holy with a holiness that cannot be lost, but they are imperfectly holy, in that grace and charity have not wholly informed and subdued to themselves every human faculty. Holy men and women in this age are not finally holy. And in this age, they share with the souls in purgatory the need for purification from the effects of sin. In this age, we

16. Ibid., pars. 34–36, mentions especially sins against Christian unity, the use of violence in injustice. For "purification of memory," see John Paul II, *Incarnationis Mysterium*, Papal Bull, November 29, 1998, par. 11: "this calls everyone to make an act of courage and humility in recognizing wrongs done by those who have borne or bear the name of Christian"; available at www.vatican.va.

17. Nicolas, *Synthèse dogmatique*, 697.

18. See the text of the International Theological Commission, *Memory and Reconciliation: The Church and the Faults of the Past*, December 1999; available at www.vatican.va.

do this by freely done, properly satisfactory works. The poor souls are not penitents in this sense, in that they are beyond the life where both sin and merit are possible. But in another sense they are more perfect penitents insofar as their purification occupies the whole of their consciousness, and the pain of their longing for the vision of God is more intense than the charity we know now. In that respect, holy men and women in this present age are imperfect penitents: we do penance for our sins, but without the ardor of the holy souls, and it remains possible for us to fall out of charity now for a time and even for eternity.

It is also well to remember in thinking about the holiness of the church that the only member of the church who was and is perfectly subjectively holy is Mary. Every other member of the church has been or still is in some measure, whether great or small, a sinner. This means that the church can be considered above all a place of reconciliation. This reconciliation is sacramental, and indeed, has an "objective" character to it. That is how Ratzinger puts it: "the holiness of the church consists in that power of sanctification which God exerts in it in spite of human sinfulness."[19] Anscar Vonier put it the same way many years ago. The holiness of the church is "obtained through the unceasing action of the Spouse of the Church, the action of sanctifying and cleansing."[20] Paradoxically, the holiness of the church is indicated, then, by the manifest and frequent use of the sacrament of reconciliation. Part of the urgency of the question of the church's holiness today arises from the practical loss of this sacrament.

Moreover, this reconciliation brought by the sacrament ought to inform the fraternal relations of the members of the church (Mt 18:15–17), and provoke all to that humility recommended by Christ's example and the pastoral counsel of St. Paul (Phil 2:3, 5). The holiness of the church, Ratzinger says, is "the mutual support which comes ... from the fact that all of us are supported by Christ."[21] The subjective imperfection of the members means that though the holiness of the church is an indefectible gift and identifying mark of the church, for the members it declares a task. Insofar as the members' subjective participation in one mark condi-

19. Joseph Ratzinger, *Introduction to Christianity*, trans. J. R. Foster (San Francisco, Calif.: Ignatius Press, 2004), 341.
20. Vonier, *Spirit and the Bride*, 95–96.
21. Ratzinger, *Introduction*, 265.

tions their participation in the others, it follows that the other marks, too, are not only gifts but tasks: the members are always to grow in fidelity to apostolic teaching and order; they are to manifest ever more clearly the unity for which Jesus prayed; they are to make her universality coincide with the breadth of the nations.

The Holiness of the Church Is Realized in Distinct States of Life

The church as the bride who becomes mother bespeaks the responsibility not only of each Christian to conceive Christ in his heart, but also of the responsibility of each Christian to share in the maternal role of the church. Each Christian is called to bring Christians to birth by bringing Christ to birth in them. In this way, all Christians imitate Mary, the model of the church, the New Eve, mother of the savior and mother of the church, his body. The nuptial character of the relation of the church to Christ is the foundation for the different states of life within the church, which are all distinct ways of living and manifesting this nuptial reality. Here, the articulation of the church is threefold: hierarchs, laity, and religious.[22]

This articulation of the church concerns the church in her role as the means in accordance with which the states of life in themselves are a demonstration of the truth of the gospel and how it can be lived successfully. Especially, however, it serves simply to manifest her reality as an end, as the beloved bride, and such articulation is a part of the beautiful order by which God accomplishes all things (Wis 8:1, 11:20). This articulation does not come so much from any functional necessity, but is rather more purely a grace and so a sign of the superabundance of the gifts God gives to the church. Even so, the nuptial *telos* of human beings in both the natural and supernatural orders comes more fully to light because of the distinction of the states, in their mutual illumination of one another. Every human being is called to realize himself in giving himself away, wholly and completely, to other persons. The distinction of the states of life en-

22. See the distinct nuptial patterns of holiness for celibate and married Christians in John Paul II, *The Theology of the Body*, part 2.

ables us more easily to identify the created goods of human nuptiality and fecundity, human paternity and maternity, and such supernatural goods as spiritual paternity and spiritual maternity.[23]

Bishops and priests manifest the bridal reality of the church in three ways. First, following John the Baptist, they are an image of the friend of the bridegroom, who retires before the advent of the bridegroom himself (Jn 3:29–30). Second, following Paul, they are an image of the one who betroths the church to Christ (2 Cor 11:2). Third, following Christ, they are an image of the bridegroom himself insofar as they act in his person (1 Tm 3:2). This they do in discharging all three hierarchical tasks or *munera*—teaching, sanctifying, and ruling. They act in Christ's person, especially in the Eucharist, where bishops and priests quote the very words of Christ and imitate his very gestures. Doing so, they at the same time realize the mediating role of the church, the bride, in discharging the task or *munus* of sanctifying the people of God in a preeminent way. Deacons in their own order and in discharging their own functions are a sacramental sign of Christ the servant.[24] The suitability of a celibate state of life for the discharge of hierarchical tasks has long been recognized in the Latin church.

Lay men and women ordinarily fulfill their Christian vocation in marriage, and by their mutual and fruitful self-gift manifest the reality of the church as bride and mother and so her relation to Christ, the spouse. The fidelity of marriage is both a sign of the promises of Christ and is carried out only in virtue of the grace that is the object of his promises. The permanence of marriage is a sign of the eschatological character of Christ's promise and therefore of the abiding reality of the church. The monogamous character of Christian marriage is a sign at once of the universality and unity of the church and the uniqueness of Christ's saving action. The fruitfulness of marriage in both the natural and spiritual orders is itself a part of the fruitfulness of the new covenant.[25]

---

23. For the theological division and interrelation of the Christian states of life, see Hans Urs von Balthasar, *The Christian State of Life*, trans. Sister Mary Frances McCarthy (San Francisco, Calif.: Ignatius Press, 1987).

24. Congregation for Catholic Education and Congregation for the Clergy, "Basic Norms for the Formation of Permanent Deacons (1998)," no. 5; available at www.vatican.va.

25. See John Paul II, *Gratissimam Sane*, Encyclical Letter, February 2, 1994; available at www .vatican.va.

Insofar as they are entirely given over to Christ, religious, that is to say consecrated virgins and celibates, manifest the reality of the church as the one who is mother because of and without prejudice to her virginity. Married Christians manifest the unity of the love of God and the love of neighbor, but consecrated virgins show that the commandment to love God is the first and greatest. They imitate Christ. They are a witness to the truth that to possess God is to possess all good created things. In the contemporary Western world, they are an essential witness even to the existence of God.[26]

26. For a contemporary consideration and appreciation of celibacy and consecrated virginity, see Patricia Snow, "Dismantling the Cross," *First Things* (April 2015): 33–42.

CHAPTER 13

MAKING THE MYSTERY

Apostolic Church and Diaconal Communion

In chapter 10, the church was defined as a communion of faith and charity sacramentally realized by the same church taken as a diaconal communion; the church was considered as "the mystery of unity between the means of salvation and the reality of salvation."[1] We have now in this chapter to consider these means more at length, especially insofar as they consist in the ministry of the bishops, who maintain the identity of the church with the church established by Christ, the apostolic church. The apostolicity of the church consists formally in the identity of the faith of the church and the faith of the apostles. The created efficient principle of this identity is the ecclesial hierarchy, the bishops, who are the successors of the apostles.[2]

Bishops guarantee the apostolicity of the church in two ways, by word

1. De La Soujeole, "Mystery of the Church," 834.
2. *Lumen Gentium*, no. 20.

242

and by deed. The word or teaching of the hierarchy itself, however, has two components. The first component is saying what in fact God has accomplished in Christ for our salvation. Bishops declare the truth of the gospel.[3] This is a mediation, as it were, of "theoretical truth" (not in the sense of a possible truth but in the sense of what the word of God gives us to see as actual and factual). The second component is saying what should be, a declaration of what according to gospel lights is *good*. This is governing by way of a declaration and sometimes legislation of what it is good for the people of God to do.[4] It is a mediation of "practical truth." This governing discipline bears on things sacramental and moral, on things ritual and societal. There are moral determinations the hierarchy makes relative to the Ten Commandments and the celebration of the sacraments. There are ritual rules that guide the practicalities of Christian worship in an orderly way. There are social norms that regulate how bishops relate to other bishops and the pope, how bishops relate to priests, how consecrated religious life is ordered, and how the rights and duties of the baptized generally are exercised. Much of this can be found in the Code of Canon Law.[5]

But also, this governing discipline bears on things *theoretical*. For pope and bishops do not simply declare the truth, but also can bind the church to assent to the very form of the declaration they give it as something good to do. This is the highest act of governance of which the hierarchy is capable. And when the truth they declare is infallible, the act of binding is also practically infallible: that is, it cannot be wrong to assent to what we are bound by magisterial authority to assent to. Next to this highest act of governance which maintains the church in revealed truth, all other governing acts are secondary: they either make sacramental arrangements, sometimes necessary, in accord with the revealed truth; or they draw necessary moral principles from it, as from the nature of the sacrament of marriage; or they determine contingent ritual norms in accord with it; or they determine societal ordinances befitting a communion of charity.

3. Ibid., nos. 21 and 24–25.
4. Ibid., nos. 21 and 27.
5. Perhaps the most sustained treatment of the governing power of the hierarchy is that contained in Journet, *The Church of the Word Incarnate*, vol. 1, chaps. 4–5 and 7–8.

Apostolicity is guaranteed not only by theoretical and practical words, however, but also by deed, by making the sacraments.[6] For the sacraments provide the grace that is required to assent to the teaching of Christ and to keep the discipline of the church, the practical truth declared by the hierarchy.

Thus, there are distinguished three tasks that the hierarchy discharges: teaching the gospel, sanctifying Christians, and governing the people of God. These tasks are discharged in virtue of two sacred powers, powers received from Christ, namely the power of jurisdiction and the power of orders. Jurisdiction includes the competence to teach and the power to govern: to legislate, to execute policy, and judge the infraction of law.[7]

This chapter addresses, in order, the missions of Word and Spirit that made the apostles apostles; the continuation of apostolic office *via* the sacrament of holy orders; the analogy between the operation of created causes in the natural order and the operation of the sacraments that mediate grace; the mediation of revealed truth; and the interior articulation of the teaching and ruling hierarchy of the church between primate (pope) and college of bishops.

Missions of Word and Spirit

Let us begin with the obvious. The apostles and apostolic men continue to carry out the tasks of Jesus in teaching, sanctifying, and ruling verified in the New Testament. Christ teaches when he delivers the Sermon on the Mount (Mt 5–7) or the eschatological discourse (Mk 13) or teaches about the bread of life (Jn 6). He sanctifies when he forgives sin (Mk 2) and re-

---

6. *Lumen Gentium*, nos. 21 and 26.

7. Some theologians make the three tasks or *munera* coeval, all on the same level. Others fold teaching and governing into the one power of jurisdiction. For the first, see Salaverri, *De Ecclesia*, thesis three, no. 119, where the power of ruling is described as "the right of directing and obligating members of a human society to work for a common end," and the power of teaching is "the right of handing on so that those to whom it is given are required to embrace it." The threefold division is more popular now since it was adopted by *Lumen Gentium* and the new Code of Canon Law. Journet, *Church of the Word Incarnate*, 1:21–27, prefers the older division between the power of orders and the power of jurisdiction. The power to rule obviously entails the duty to obey on the part of subjects, more manifestly when it is a channeling of the *divine* governance of God's church. Does the power to teach entail the duty to believe? When the teacher is God, yes, it does. But otherwise, is there a *prima facie* duty to believer what every teacher teaches? Answering such questions determines how one thinks teaching is related to ruling.

pairs the damage caused by sin (e.g., Lk 17:11–19) and shares his body and blood. He governs the church when he chooses the Twelve (Mk 3) and sets the disciples on mission (Lk 10), when he institutes the Petrine office (Mt 16:19), determines church order (Mt 18:15–20), when he delivers the great commission (Mt 28:18–20).

The apostles and apostolic men in turn teach (see the speeches of Stephen, Peter, and Paul in Acts and the doctrinal sections of the letters of Paul). They sanctify when they baptize (Acts 2:38, 8:38), when they give the Holy Spirit by the imposition of hands (Acts 8:17, 19:6), and when they break bread (Acts 2:42). They rule when they provide for the order of Christians: first, in matters moral and temporal (see the paraenetic sections of the letters of Paul, and especially 1 Cor 5–8), when they administer property (Acts 5:1–12), and when they arrange for the support of the Jerusalem church (1 Cor 16:1–4; 2 Cor 8:1–7); and second, in matters religious, when they regulate who is to be baptized (see Peter in Acts 10:47 and the case of Cornelius), and when they regulate Christian worship (1 Cor 11:17) and determine the question of circumcision for Christians (Acts 15). In this last instance, note that the Jerusalem council not only declares what is so, that Christians need not be circumcised, but requires the church to act congruently with that truth: "it has seemed good to the Holy Spirit and to us" (Acts 15:28). Thereby they place an act of infallible governance.

We would be mistaken, furthermore, to suppose that these tasks and carrying out these tasks of teaching and sanctifying and ruling bubbled up spontaneously from Christian community life. Rather, they are grounded authoritatively in the commission of Christ and empowered by the Holy Spirit, and this is formal to the Catholic understanding of apostolic, hierarchical office discharged by the successors of the apostles, the bishops.

Just as the Lord's identity and mission were manifested at his baptism and transfiguration, his identity by the words spoken from heaven, and his own mission as Messiah by the mission of the Holy Spirit, so the mission of the apostles is manifested and established by the word of the incarnate Word and the missions of the Spirit of which they are the target. First of all, Christ chooses and commissions them: "And he went up on the mountain and called to him those whom he desired; and they came to him. And he appointed twelve, to be with him, and to be sent out to preach and have authority to cast out demons" (Mk 3:13–15). They are "with him" to learn him and learn from him; they are sent out to extend the word of the gospel of the kingdom; they have authority, for the advent of the gospel frees us from the dominion of the devil. This authority is a sort of adumbration of sacramental power. Their mission to witness to him and proclaim the kingdom and destroy the dominion of sin and evil is universalized in the great commission (Mt 28:19–20).

Second, the Holy Spirit is sent to them visibly. As to sacramental power, the Lord sends and commissions them again after his resurrection and breathes the Spirit into them, giving them the power to forgive sins and, we should understand, the power to give grace sacramentally in general (Jn 20:21–22). As to the authority to teach, the Spirit descends on them in tongues of fire on the day of Pentecost (Acts 2:1–13), so that, remembering in the Spirit what Jesus taught (Jn 14:26), they have authority to speak and teach in many tongues to all the nations of the earth, represented by the presence at Pentecost of Elamites, Medes, Persians, and so on.[8] The visible mission of the Holy Spirit brings with it invisible gifts which will be detailed in the next sections where the ministry of word and sacrament are treated. Paul, too, it should be noted, is both commissioned by the Lord and empowered by the Spirit (Acts 9:15–17; 2 Cor 11:1–5; Gal 1:12, 15–17). It is noteworthy that Peter expressly thinks of apostolic office as an office (Acts 1:20–22), a dominical institution, and one for the discharge of which he awaits the outpouring of the Spirit (Acts 1:8).

If we think in terms of apostolic responsibilities, and paying particular attention both to the example of Paul and his instruction in the pastoral letters, we can sum things up by saying that an apostle is responsible before Christ as a witness to him. He is responsible to the community he founds, the particular church he establishes by his preaching, (1) to keep its many members in the unity of faith in the gospel he preached (e.g., Gal 1:6–7; 1 Tm 6:20; 2 Tm 1:13–14, 4:2; Ti 1:9), (2) to keep its many members in mutual charity by baptism (1 Cor 1:14, 16; Ti 3:5) and by connecting them to the sacrament of charity (1 Cor 11), and (3) to keep each particular church in communion with all the other particular church-

8. For the visible mission of the Spirit, see Aquinas, *ST* I, q. 43, a. 7, ad 6. See also Dominic Legge, OP, *The Trinitarian Christology of St. Thomas Aquinas* (Oxford: Oxford University Press, 2017), 51–58.

es, which is to say he discharges a responsibility to the universal church (4) to keep it as a whole in the unity of faith and charity (1 Cor 16:1–4; 2 Cor 8:1–7; 2 Tm 4:11, 19–21; Ti 1:5, 3:15; Acts 15).

The Continuation of the Apostolic Office *via* the Sacrament of Holy Orders

These responsibilities are inherited by the successors of the apostles, the bishops, who are responsible for the unity of their own diocese and for keeping it connected to the faith and charity of the universal church.[9] "As I have been sent, even so I send you" (Jn 20:21). This entails that the apostles are given the power to commission and send even as Christ could commission and send, and there is in this word a dominical anticipation of and intention to provide successors to the apostles. The fact of this intention is corroborated by the subsequent action of the apostles themselves.

First, there is the practice of St. Paul, who in Acts 20:18–38 passes responsibility for the church at Ephesus to its elders (*presbyteroi*, 20:18) or *episkopoi* (20:28). But it is the Holy Spirit who has made them so (20:28), and their charge is the pastoral care of the flock of Christ, with special attention given to care for right doctrine (20:30). Earlier than Paul at Ephesus, there is 1 Corinthians 16:15–16, where the Corinthians are urged to be "subject" to Stephanus and "to every fellow worker and laborer." Timothy appears as Paul's deputy in 1 Corinthians 4:17. Later, there are the pastoral letters, where, by the authority of Paul, Titus is to appoint presbyters/bishops (Ti 1:5–9) and Timothy is given the list of qualifications not only for bishops but for deacons (1 Tm 3).

The text of 1 Timothy 2:2 is remarkable for its breadth of vision, where we read that "what you have heard from me before many witnesses entrust to faithful men who will be able to teach others also." So we have Paul, Timothy, those whom Timothy appoints, and "others"—perhaps a fourth generation of leaders.[10] Witness to the appointment of successors to the apostles is not confined to the Johannine and Pauline traditions,

9. Ratzinger, *Called to Communion*, 94–103.
10. Available at https://www.catholic.com/tract/apostolic-succession. See also Jerome D. Quinn, "Ordination in the Pastoral Epistles," *Communio* 8 (1981): 358–69.

but is also especially manifest in 1 Peter. The presbyters of 5:1–4 are "shepherds," and this links them up to discharging the mission of Christ the shepherd (2:25). But 5:1–4 also represents the apostle Peter as speaking to the presbyters as a *fellow* presbyter, so linking their ministry to his. Of this link, Ratzinger says: "This, in my opinion, is the strongest linking of the two offices to be found in the New Testament," and represents "a transfer of the theology of apostleship to the presbyterate."[11] The letter thus establishes a very solid linking of presbyteral/episcopal ministry to apostolic ministry and to the mission of Christ himself, "the Shepherd and Guardian of your souls" (2:25).[12]

Last, the continuation of apostolic office is sacramental. In the Holy Spirit, the late-first-century church determines that the commissioning or sending by the apostles or their collaborators of further ministers is by the laying on of hands. This is evidenced by the pastorals, where Paul lays hands on Timothy (2 Tm 1:6), presbyters lay hands on Timothy (1 Tm 4:14), and Timothy lays hands on others (1 Tm 5:22). Nothing could be less surprising than that the apostolic church found a cultic and sacramental way of signifying access to a sacramental ministry that has responsibility for the Christian cult.[13] Such congruence suggests the unfolding of what is implicated, implicit, in the original establishment of apostolic ministry.[14]

11. Joseph Ratzinger, "The Priest as Mediator and Minister of Christ in the Light of the Message of the New Testament," in his *Principles of Catholic Theology*, 279.

12. It is of course implausible to suppose that the Lord thought it likely that eleven disciples would be sufficient to make disciples of all nations (Mt 28:19). There is also a witness to the dominical intention for succession in the First Letter of Clement, in *The Epistles of St. Clement and St. Ignatius of Antioch*, trans. James A. Kleist, SJ (Westminster, Md.: Newman Bookshop, 1947), no. 44. Such indications in scripture and the Fathers do not mean that we must impute to the pre- or even post-paschal Lord a signifying of this intention that is more than implicit. We should, however, be quite clear about the fact that the late-first-century church was in a better position to discern the intentions of the Lord than we are.

13. "Sacramental ministry" is meant here in the sense picked out by Cardinal Ratzinger on the basis of such texts as Mt 10:40 and John 15:5: "a ministry … in which the human being on the basis of divine communication acts and gives what can never be given or done on the basis of human resources is in the church's tradition called a *sacrament*." See his "Biblical Foundations of Priesthood," *Origins* 20, no. 19 (October 18, 1990): 312.

14. *Episkopos* and *presbyteros* seem to be two words naming the same office. Later, *presbyteroi* will occupy an office that merely participates in the fullness of episcopal office. What can be passed on wholly can also be passed on in part.

The Analogy between Natural and Sacramental Operation

The constitution of the church as a diaconal communion in virtue of which the sacraments are celebrated was seen to be part of the solution to the problem of the indefectibility of the church in the holiness of grace and charity. The sacraments are also one of the ways bishops maintain the apostolicity of the church, for there is no assent to the word of revelation, to the witness of the apostles, without grace. Baptism, of course, is the "sacrament of faith." It is now time to explore the diaconal communion a little more closely, first as to the certainty with which grace is offered by deed in the sacraments of the New Law, and second, in the next section, how it maintains the mediation of truth by word.

The certainty with which grace is given depends in part on an understanding of sacramental causality. St. Thomas finds the categories with which to articulate the sacramental mediation of grace in what he inherits from Islamic and Christian Neo-Platonism.[15] He uses these categories first of all in understanding the emanation of things from God, that is to say, he uses them first of all in understanding creation, including the relation of creative to created causality. This understanding of divine and created action is then applied to understanding divine action in the supernatural order. So, for the natural order, God by his infinite power creates beings that are themselves causes.[16] The proper form that constitutes beings in their kind is the principle of a causal action proper to them. Animals really beget their offspring, causing their form to be communicated to new matter. Fire really causes heat in what is cold.

Second, however, the first cause is more the cause of what the second cause effects than the second cause, because he is the creator of the second cause.[17] The sun warms the stone, but God is more the cause of the

---

15. An earlier form of what follows can be found in Guy Mansini, "Ecclesial Mediation of Grace and Truth," *The Thomist* 75 (2011): 555–83, at 560–63.

16. Aquinas, *De potentia Dei*, q. 3, a. 7, in *Quaestiones Disputatae*, vol. 2, ed. P. Bazzi, M. Calcaterra, et al. (Rome: Marietti, 1949); and *ST* I, q. 103, a. 6; q. 105, a. 5. See Frederick Bauerschmidt on created causes in his *Thomas Aquinas: Faith, Reason, and Following Christ* (Oxford: Oxford University Press, 2013), 119–23.

17. Aquinas, *De potentia Dei*, q. 3, a. 7. See Proclus, *The Elements of Theology*, trans. E. R. Dodds (Oxford: Clarendon Press, 1933), propositions 56 and 70, and Aquinas's commentary on the first

stone's warmth than the sun shining on it. Third, it is impossible that any created cause can itself create, because no finite thing can possess the infinite power creation takes. Neither can a created cause be an instrument of creation, in that every instrument presupposes some matter it works on, while creation is the production of the entire being of the created thing, matter included.[18] Creation is the donation of *esse*, the act of existence, and no creature possesses that by its nature.[19] Fourth, even as true causes of being, therefore, created causes do not act simply in virtue of their proper form, but only as instruments of the first cause, God.[20] Only his nature is simply to be, and so God alone is the proportionate cause of being.

St. Thomas distinguishes two operations of an instrument: "one that belongs to it according to its proper form, another that belongs to it insofar as it is moved by an agent acting by itself [*per se*], and which goes beyond the capacity of its proper form."[21] So, it belongs to a saw to cut wood, but not to make a bench. All created causes are moved movers relative to the first cause, and in that respect are instruments. They are moved by God in acting according to their inherent form.[22] Also, however, they can be moved in such a way as to contribute to an effect beyond the proportion of their proper form. When they are moved by God in the first way only, it is convenient to call them "second causes." But when they are additionally moved by God in the second way, it is convenient to call them "instruments *stricte dicto*."[23] So, as true causes of being, created causes are instruments in this strict sense.

proposition of the *Liber de Causis, In Librum de Causis Expositio*, ed. Ceslas Pera, OP (Turin: Mariette, 1955), nos. 14 and 23–24.

18. Aquinas, *De potentia Dei*, q. 3, a. 4.

19. Essence and *esse* are really distinct in creature, for creatures are really distinct from God; see Robert Sokolowski, *The God of Faith and Reason* (Notre Dame, Ind.: University of Notre Dame Press, 1982), 41–43.

20. Aquinas, *De potentia Dei*, q. 3, a. 7. See J. H. Nicolas, OP, "L'origine première des choses," *Revue Thomiste* 91 (1991): 181–218.

21. Aquinas, *De veritate*, q. 27, a. 4 and a. 7, in *Quaestiones Disputatae*, ed. Raymond Spiazzi, OP (Rome: Marietti, 1949). On the universal instrumentality of created causes relative to being, see Bernard Lonergan, *Grace and Freedom: Operative Grace in the Thought of St. Thomas Aquinas* (New York: Herder and Herder, 1971), 80–84.

22. Aquinas, *ST* I, q. 105, a. 5, ad 3: God not only gives things their forms, by which they are real causes, "but also conserves them in being, and applies them to act, and is the end of all action."

23. For this convention, see, e.g., Benoît-Dominique de La Soujeole, OP, "Le mystère de la prédication," *Revue Thomiste* 107 (2007): 355–74.

This understanding of God's causality relative to the created order can be applied point by point to the supernatural order of sacramental grace. First, the Lord makes his apostles causes of grace. Baptism gives a share in the divine life in that it inserts the baptized into the paschal mystery, and the Lord tells the disciples to baptize. For St. Thomas, baptism and the sacraments are themselves simply particular causes applying the universal cause of the Lord's passion to the individual.[24] And if the sacraments are causes, so also are the ministers of the sacraments, the ministers that make them happen or "confect" them.[25] Just as the power of baptism to conform us to Christ's death and unite us to him, the power of which St. Paul speaks (Rom 6:2–5), can be re-registered in the language of causality—universal and particular, principal and instrumental—so also can the working of the ministers.[26] Both the sacraments and their ministers are strictly instrumental causes of grace.

Second, in what the ministers bring to sacramental activity that is within the proportion of their proper form—speaking, pouring water, anointing with oil—God even here is more the cause of what they do than they are. But third, it is impossible that they be given a proper form in virtue of which they could as second causes cause grace, for grace is by definition a share in divine life (2 Pt 2:4), and no created thing, no thing whose nature is not the divine nature, can by its nature produce what belongs to this other, incomparably higher, nature.[27] Fourth and finally, what they cannot do as second causes, they can do as instrumental causes.[28] These doings, these actions, result in a share of the divine life,

24. Aquinas, *ST* III, q. 49, a. 1, ad 4; q. 61, a. 1, ad 3.

25. For the development of St. Thomas's thought on sacramental causality, see chap. 3 of John F. Gallagher, *Significando Causant: A Study of Sacramental Efficiency* (Fribourg: Fribourg University Press, 1965), a dissertation directed by J.-H. Nicolas, OP. See also Blankenhorn, OP, "The Instrumental Causality of the Sacraments."

26. Bernhard Blankenhorn, OP, "The Place of Romans 6 in Aquinas's Doctrine of Sacramental Causality: A Balance of History and Metaphysics," in *Ressourcement Thomism: Sacred Doctrine, the Sacraments, and the Moral Life* (Washington, D.C.: The Catholic University of America Press, 2010), 136–49.

27. See Aquinas, *ST* I-II, q. 112, a. 1; III, q. 64, a. 1.

28. As long as grace was thought by Aquinas to be created, then the instrumental causality of the sacraments terminated in sacramental character or some disposition to grace but not in grace itself, and this was the position of the commentary on the *Sentences*; when grace was no longer conceived so, the way was open to assert an instrumental efficient causality that terminated in grace itself. See Gallagher, *Significando Causant*, 87–90, 111–12, and 114. For the same point relative to the causality of the humanity of Christ, see J.-P. Torrell, OP, "La causalité salvifique de la resurrec-

something beyond the capacity of any created cause to effect of its own nature and power, even when that nature and power are moved, as they must be moved, by God.[29]

The sacramental ministers of the church are instruments in the strict sense. God can create causes whose native forms, making them what they are, enable them to act in the ways specific to their nature, effecting those things within the compass of their native power. This is the notion of a second cause. Just as he cannot create a cause whose nature it is to create, however, so he cannot create a cause whose *nature* it is to recreate humanity and to make us *consors divinae naturae*, "sharers of the divine nature" (2 Pt 1:4). Such causes, the sacraments and the ministers thereof, are purely instruments. While no creature can be even an instrument of creation, however, some creatures may be instruments of the re-creation of human nature.[30] It is just because of their purely instrumental nature, moreover, that the ministers (like the sacraments) ensure the indefectibility of the church in grace. If they were *second* causes, we would have no such assurance. But instruments, where they are *God's* instruments, are more trustworthy.

The analogy between the causal order of creation and the causal order of re-creation in grace is exact, and does really give intelligibility to the sacramental mediation of grace. As created causes are instruments of the first cause relative to the production of being, so sacraments and sacramental ministers are instruments of God and Christ relative to the production of grace. The first proposition of the *Liber de Causis* holds good here, too. When we are touched in the sacrament, we are touched more by Christ than by any priest, and the holiness of the church is constantly and certainly renewed.[31]

---

tion du Christ selon saint Thomas," *Revue Thomiste* 96 (1996): 188. See M.-Benôit Lavaud's foundational study, "Saint Thomas et la causalité physique instrumentale de la sainte humanité et des sacrements," *Revue Thomiste* 32 (1927): 292–316, at 304 and 308–13.

29. Aquinas, *De potentia Dei*, q. 3, a. 7; *ST* III, q. 62, a. 1.

30. An instrument acts on a material out of which the principal agent makes something; see Aquinas, *ST* I, q. 45, a. 5. In the re-creation of man in the order of redemption, however, man himself is the preexisting material.

31. The imagination of all causality as mechanical, as a matter of three-dimensional things moving one another about, obstructs the appropriation of the medieval appropriation of causal mediation. Materialism makes it difficult to think how things can be interior to one another otherwise than as little parts within bigger parts.

In this way, the Augustinian dogmatic theology of sacramental character is inserted into a properly systematic theology.[32] What St. Augustine and subsequent tradition affirmed as character, St. Thomas understood as the instrumental power of the ministers of the New Law. The sacraments of baptism, confirmation, and orders have two effects: they give grace, the *res* of the sacrament, and they give an intermediate reality and sign (*res et sacramentum*), the character. Character stands between the visible sign of the sacramental word and action (*sacramentum tantum*), and grace. Sacramental character is a sign relative to grace; relative to the visible sign, it is a thing. St. Thomas understands it as instrumental power: that is, it makes whoever receives these sacraments able to place valid and effective sacramental acts.[33] Baptismal character enables the recipient to offer the sacrifice of the Mass in communion with the priest. Sacerdotal character enables the priest to confect the Eucharist, to change bread and wine as an instrument of Christ into the true body and blood.[34] And in order to do this, in order really to make the baptized capable of offering the sacrifice and in order to make a priest a true instrument of Christ the priest, character conforms the recipient of these sacraments to Christ.[35] This conformation, as it were, fits the instrument to the hand of Christ, the principal agent of the sacramental act, the way the handle of a saw fits the tool to a man's hand. The historical action of Christ on the cross gives grace causally, and therefore conforms the recipient to him, insofar as effects share the likeness of their causes. So also the minister is conformed to Christ in the sacrament of ordination *via* the character. Now, the grace the sacraments impart can be lost by falling into serious sin. But the characters of baptism, confirmation, and holy orders cannot be lost. The permanent effects of these sacraments explain why they cannot be repeated. Historically, the fact that they cannot be repeated led in part to the recognition of their permanent effect.

32. For texts of St. Augustine, see Jean Galot, SJ, *La notion du caractère sacramental: étude de théologie médiévale* (Paris: Desclée de Brower, 1956).

33. Aquinas, *ST* III, q. 63, a. 2, co.

34. Ibid., q. 72, a. 3, ad 2: "an instrument receives its instrumental power in two ways: in receiving the form of an instrument, and when the principal agent uses it to work."

35. Ibid., q. 63, a. 3, co. and ad 2.

The Mediation of Revealed Truth

Bishops maintain the apostolicity of the church by word and by deed. We have just considered sacramental deed; now for words. The sanctifying activity of apostolic ministry just considered can be considered the final end of apostolic teaching in that it fashions and maintains the communion of charity. But the sacraments, while they give the grace necessary to assent to the creed in faith, also presuppose the creed, so that we know what we are doing when we receive them. In that sense, the sacraments presuppose faith. And in that way, teaching is more fundamental than sanctifying and governing, as Robert Sokolowski says, "in the sense that it establishes the possibility of the other two."[36]

So, sharing divine truth is ordered to sharing divine life (Jn 14:6). Just in order to prosecute the goals of sharing in truth so as to share in life, moreover, apostolic ministers are also given authority to govern and provide for such good order of their church that the gospel can be regularly preached and the sacraments fruitfully received.[37]

The Problem with Sustaining Apostolic Teaching

Because of the purely instrumental nature of the priest's or bishop's role in making the sacramental event happen, whether of the Mass or the sacrament of reconciliation or the sacrament of holy orders and so on, it does not matter for the success of the event whether the priest or bishop is in the state of grace and moved by charity or not.[38] A rusty hammer gets the nail in the board just as well as a clean and well-kept one. And likewise, baptismal character fits a man to receive the sacramental grace offered in the sacraments, as long as he interposes no obstacles to the finality of the sacramental action.[39]

While sacramental mediation is the mediation of an action, of a doing, of an efficiently worked change in some subject, the mediation of

36. Robert Sokolowski, "The Identity of the Bishop," in his *Christian Faith and Human Understanding: Studies on the Eucharist, Trinity, and the Human Person* (Washington, D.C.: The Catholic University of America Press, 2006), 118.

37. Ibid.

38. Aquinas, *ST* III, q. 64, a. 5, co.

39. As he would with penance, if he had no faith; as he would with taking Communion, if he were in mortal sin.

word is the mediation not of changing but of *showing* the real, the mediation of displaying how things are.[40] Displaying is not doing. However, just as we say that God warms the rock in the sun's warming, we can say here too that God teaches in the teaching of any created teacher, angelic or divine, and is to be considered more the author of a true teaching than the created teacher. This is because the truth of any created thing is a participation in uncreated truth, and the publication of any such truth by man or angel is a participation in that manifestation of the truth that is the proceeding of the Word from the Father.[41] Furthermore, the church's mediation of truth concerns the mediation of revealed truth. Therefore, just as the sacramental doings of the church are such that they can properly be the doings only of God, so the teachings of the church are such that they can properly be the teachings only of God. Just so, when the gospel is proclaimed, we hear Christ more than we do some evangelist.[42]

Can we therefore press into service here the categories already used for sacramental mediation? We cannot. Sacramental mediation is strictly and exclusively instrumental, but the mediation of word effected in proclaiming and preaching is not. To be sure, ministers of the word are like an instrument in two ways. First, they are not themselves in possession of the truth they preach except they be elevated by a supernatural form, the light of faith, to assent to the creed. Second, their preaching of the exterior word is not of itself sufficient to produce faith in the hearer apart from the "interior word" of the Holy Spirit.[43] Ministers of the word, however, rather share the *ratio* of a second cause. Their own agency, their own personal understanding and prudence are more engaged in preaching (and governing) than in confecting the sacraments, and having received by

40. An altered form of what follows in this section can be found in Guy Mansini, "Ecclesial Mediation of Grace and Truth," 563–66 and 573–78.

41. Aquinas, *Commentary on the Gospel of John*, trans. James A. Weisheipl, OP, and Fabian R. Larcher, OP (Albany, N.Y.: Magi Books, 1980), chap. 1, lect. 1, no. 33, speaks of the absolute Word "by participation in whom all who have a word are said to be speaking." For the Word as the interior teacher because the creator of the light of the mind, see Augustine, *The Teacher*, trans. Robert Russell, OSA, FOTC 59 (Washington, D.C.: The Catholic University of America Press, 1968), chap. 11, no. ii, and chap. 12, no. 40. See also Aquinas, *De veritate*, q. 11, a. 1. See Dt 1:17, where the judgment of the judge is God's judgment.

42. See Aquinas, *ST* III, q. 42, a. 4, ad 1, quoting St. Augustine. See the texts of Augustine to this effect in Domenico Grasso, SJ, *Proclaiming God's Message: A Study in the Theology of Preaching* (Notre Dame, Ind.: University of Notre Dame Press, 1965), 26–29.

43. See de La Soujeole, "Le mystère de la predication," 357–59.

faith the words of faith, they subsequently speak them according to the power of their own proper form.[44] As engaging more of the minister's personal agency, the mediation of the word is in that respect more fragile than the mediation of grace; it can be undone or impeded by ignorance and stupidity, by negligence, laziness, and vanity as the mediation of sacramental grace, just in itself, cannot.[45] For just this reason, when we receive the sacraments at the hands of a sinful priest, we really do receive the sacrament and grace. The sacraments work *ex opere operato*, and not from the personal holiness or goodness of the priest. But when we hear what purports to be the word of God from an ignorant or lazy or vain priest or bishop, we cannot be sure we are hearing the word of God. What an individual minister can assuredly do as a minister of grace, he does not always assuredly do as a minister of the word. What recourse do we have for understanding how it is that the church abides in gospel truth?

The Insufficiency of Purely Human Quotation

When we want to understand the mediation of grace and the supernatural efficiency of God, we have as a foil God's efficiency in creation. Instruments in the causality of being can serve as a foil to instruments in the causality of grace. When we come to the mediation of the word, however, there is no "natural" word of God, no natural speaking of God, which can be played off against his supernatural speaking. God's speaking to us in such a way that he reveals himself as speaker is always supernatural, at least in the sense that it is always an encounter with his own freedom.[46] The book of scripture is sometimes compared to the book of nature, but creation, although it occurs by the Word of God, is not in itself a word—it is not a speaking.[47] Or again, God can be said to promulgate

44. For just this view, see Augustine Rock, OP, *Unless They Be Sent: A Theological Study of the Nature and Purpose of Preaching* (Dubuque, Iowa: Wm. C. Brown Co., 1953), 137–39, who wants to say that ministers of the word are more to be considered instruments in preaching than in administering the sacraments, on the ground that more of their personal reality is engaged.

45. On the other hand, the mediation of sacramental grace can be impeded by the unavailability of holy orders, while the ability of every Christian to witness to the word of God can still be exercised. So the gospel was preserved in Japan without benefit of clergy in the seventeenth and eighteenth centuries.

46. This is so even if the content of the speaking is not supernatural.

47. For a recent and authoritative statement of the comparison, see Benedict XVI, *Verbum Domini*, par. 7. Aquinas finds the comparison useful; see his *Super Epistolas S. Pauli Lectura*, ed.

the natural law by the very positing of human nature, the very presenting of human nature to human mind. But this is very different from the commandments given to Moses.

God speaks naturally to angels in creating them, for he creates them as actually understanding according to the natural species proportionate to their intellects,[48] but God does not similarly naturally speak to us in creating us. God spoke preternaturally and supernaturally to Adam in creating *him*, for both naturally and supernaturally knowable truths were instilled in his intellect at his creation.[49] Adam was then to teach others.[50] God more than spoke to the second Adam in the creation of the humanity assumed by the Word, for Christ the man was both *comprehensor* and *viator*—that is, he beheld the intelligibility of divinity itself even in the condition of a wayfarer in time.[51] The second Adam then taught in words what he beheld in vision.[52] It is the conditions of his teaching *abiding* as universally available that we are looking for.

We may think that this is easy to understand. After all, once they are written down and their reception recorded (a necessary determinant of what they meant), cannot we simply repeat his words just as we repeat anyone else's? What problem can there be? According to St. Thomas, God addresses us "immediately" through scripture,[53] and we might think that the stability and "quotability" of the word of God, as of any other word, would make it possible to be read intelligently and paraphrased accurately by anyone who understood the human language it is written in. Robert Sokolowski has devoted considerable attention to quotation as a presentational form of truth. The words and syntax of a speaker are

Raphael Cai, OP, 8th rev. ed. (Rome: Marietti, 1953), I, *Super Primam Epistolam ad Corinthios Lectura*, c. 1, lect. 3, no. 55. But strictly, creating is not speaking and creatures are words of God only metaphorically; see *De veritate*, q. 4, a. 2, and *Super Epistolas S. Pauli Lectura*, II, *Super Epistolam ad Hebraeos*, c. 1, lect. 1, no. 15. In the *Lectura super Evangelium S. Ioannis*, ed. R. Cai, OP (Rome: Marietti, 1952), c. 1, lect. 5, nos. 135–36, the creation is the effect of the Word, and a manifestation of the Word, but is not said to be itself a word. See Francis Martin, "Revelation as Disclosure: Creation," in *Wisdom and Holiness, Science and Scholarship: Essays in Honor of Matthew L. Lamb*, ed. Michael Dauphinais and Matthew Levering (Naples, Fla.: Ave Maria University, 2007), 205–47.

48. Aquinas, *ST* I, q. 55, a. 2, and q. 107, a. 2.

49. Ibid., q. 94, a. 3.

50. Ibid.

51. Aquinas, *ST* III, q. 9, a. 2.

52. Ibid., a. 3.

53. Aquinas, *Super Secundam Epistolam ad Timotheum Lectura*, c. 3, lect. 3, no. 126.

a manifestation of his personal authority as an agent of truth, someone responsibly and truthfully bringing the intelligibility of the real to light. Quotation, Sokolowski says, can reactualize the authority of the original speaker and make it present to us again. There can be a sort of "resuscitation" of the personal agency of someone who has died when they are quoted.[54] The authority of that speaker as an agent of truth is again made present. Think of Gregory Peck or Sam Waterston or Daniel Day-Lewis revivifying Lincoln.

Furthermore, it is not just that the church possesses a text that can be read and read again, quoted and paraphrased. The church's tradition includes nonwritten things, too, things that frame the writing so that it can be quoted judiciously, read aright. Revelation is also mediated, in other words, by the traditioning of prayers, worship, sacraments, creeds, church orders, sacred art and music, and so on.

However, the stability and quotability of the written word, and even within the context of the other things within the tradition of the church, do not meet all the issues that arise in thinking about the transmission even of purely human speaking, in purely human traditions. Alasdair MacIntyre contrasts the philosophical practices of Kant and Plato.[55] Kant exhorts each of us to dare to think for himself. Plato rather shows us that the truth is successfully pursued only in conversation. MacIntyre recalls the stricture on writing that Plato's Socrates makes in the *Phaedrus*.[56] Written words cannot defend themselves in the contest of interrogation, but always say only the same thing; furthermore, a writer cannot be sure they will always get into the right hands (275d–e).[57] Only the discourse written in the soul can defend itself (276a), and Socrates concludes that a wise man will never commit his serious thoughts to pen and paper. Writing on paper is related to writing on the soul the way playful gardening is to serious farming (276b). Writing on the soul is a matter of dialogue; it is the way of the live, disciplined conversation that produces disciples. We could conclude therefore that no one will commit his serious thoughts to

54. Sokolowski, *Phenomenology of the Human Person*, 76.

55. Alasdair MacIntyre, "Some Enlightenment Projects Reconsidered," in his *Ethics and Politics* (Cambridge: Cambridge University Press, 2006), 172–85.

56. Ibid., 177–78.

57. Plato, *Phaedrus*, trans. R. Hackforth, in *Plato: The Collected Dialogues*, ed. Edith Hamilton and Huntington Cairns, Bollingen Series LXXI (Princeton, N.J.: Princeton University Press, 1961).

paper unless (1) he can write what the words mean also on the soul, and (2) he can ensure that his written words do not fall into the wrong hands, and (3) he can remain with them so as to be able to defend them, answering the questions they provoke.

God has, of course, committed his serious thoughts to paper. This is a once-for-all-time commission, moreover. Revelation is closed with the "death of the last apostle," for it is closed with the mission of the enfleshed Word of Christ to the people of Israel and its renewed form in the nascent church. God has, as it is usually put, nothing more to say to us that is not already spoken in this incarnate Word, because his Word contains the expression of the entire intelligibility of the economy of salvation and his assumed humanity and human life express it for us. But if he has committed his "serious thoughts" to paper, then doubtless the conditions of doing this responsibly, conditions articulated in the *Phaedrus*, will therefore be strictly met, although perhaps in ways Plato could not have imagined.

Meeting the First Condition

St. Thomas supposes that the oral teaching of the gospel, the oral teaching our Lord practiced, is superior to any other kind, in that it more readily imprints its message on the heart of the hearer.[58] There is also another kind of "writing" that meets the first condition. The New Law fulfills the promise of Jeremiah 31:33 and is written on our hearts. About this St. Thomas says: "that which is preponderant in the law of the New Testament, and whereon all its efficacy is based, is the grace of the Holy Spirit, which is given through faith in Christ. Consequently the New Law is chiefly the grace itself of the Holy Spirit."[59] St. Thomas grants that we also need instruction "both by word and writing" as to what we are to believe and do. Still, "the New Law is in the first place [*principaliter*] a law that is inscribed on our hearts" and only secondarily something written.[60] Part of Christ's excellence as a teacher, moreover, consists in his capacity to write on the heart in this way.[61]

This ability to write on hearts by the Spirit is in addition to the pow-

---

58. Aquinas, *ST* III, q. 42, a. 4, ad 2.
59. Ibid., I-II, q. 106, a. 1 (Old Blackfriars translation, altered).
60. Ibid.; see 2 Cor 3:3.
61. Aquinas, *ST* III, q. 42, a. 4, co.

er of his oral teaching, which consists in the miracles that confirm it, his superior ability to persuade, and his authority.[62] He writes both within and without. The writing from within, grace and charity and the gifts that accompany them, serves to the right hearing and interpretation of the exterior word of preaching and later to the right reading of the New Testament, whose "secondary" nature relative to grace and charity does not mean it does not have to be preserved in the integrity of its truth.

The sacramental mediation of grace thus comes to ensure the genuineness of the mediation of Christ's truth, for the writing on the heart just spoken of is accomplished through the sacraments.[63] Thus there is a circle. The "secondary" writing of the precepts, parables, and actions of Christ disposes us to grace, and the grace of the sacraments enables us to understand and affirm the words of and teaching of Christ.

Meeting the Second Condition

Plato's Socrates also insisted that the author be able to keep his book from falling into the wrong hands. It is only too obvious that the Bible is read outside the church and by a regularly unbelieving academy. It is also evident, however, that the Bible soon ceases to be the Bible in the academy. Essential to apprehending the Bible as what it is is apprehending it in its unity. Being and unity, however, are convertible. Once its unity is forgotten or denied, it no longer exists as the book it is taken to be in the church.[64] It rather disintegrates into many books, and the many books sometimes fragment into many sources. There therefore seems to be a sort of "self-destruct" routine built into the Bible. When it falls into the wrong hands, it falls apart. The modern academy may be reading ancient literature of this that or the other century or millennium, people, land, or culture. But it is not reading the Bible.

62. Ibid., a. 1, ad 2. For the oral teaching of Christ, see Kevin White, "Aquinas on Oral Teaching," *The Thomist* 71 (2007): 205–28.

63. J. Mark Armitage, "Why Didn't Jesus Write a Book? Aquinas on the Teaching of Christ," *New Blackfriars* 89 (2008): 337–53, at 342–43.

64. See Benedict XVI, *Verbum Domini*, par. 39: "Viewed in purely historical or literary terms, of course, the Bible is not a single book, but a collection of literary texts composed over the course of a thousand years or more, and its individual books are not easily seen to possess an interior unity; instead, we see clear inconsistencies between them." The unity of the Bible is a function of its relation to the Word, Christ (ibid.).

Meeting the Third Condition

There remains the third condition of Plato's Socrates, that an author remain with his text in order to defend it and answer questions put to it. For there will be questions. Reading, preaching, and teaching the word of God is always a matter of interpretation. Sometimes interpretation involves no more than deciding how to inflect a sentence, or where to pause for emphasis. Sometimes interpretation involves drawing inferences, connecting one text to another within the Bible, distinguishing words and realities in answering questions the text evokes. Sometimes interpretation arises from the connatural knowledge that the love of holy things produces. Sometimes interpretation means asking the written word of God questions a surrounding culture with its presuppositions and mores brings to it.[65] And where some culture has what purports to be as comprehensive an account of reality as does the Bible, as was the Neo-Platonism of the fourth century, the newly discovered Aristotelianism of the thirteenth century, or the German Idealism of the nineteenth century, interpretation can be fundamental and thoroughgoing. All such interpretations, large or small, are developments of doctrine.

It was Newman's part in the *Essay on Development* to show us how inevitable and necessary developments are.[66] In the main, moreover, they are happy things, for the word of God cannot return to him empty but accomplishes his purpose (Is 55:11); it is "living and active, sharper than any two-edged sword," discerning our thoughts and intentions (Heb 4:12). Moreover, the foolishness of the word of Christ crucified is wiser than the wisdom of the Greeks (1 Cor 1:21–25), and the knowledge of God in Christ is something to which every thought can be taken captive (2 Cor 10:5). We know, furthermore, the entire legitimacy of developments from the word of God. For one thing, they are foreshadowed and anticipated within the word of God itself, in the very history of its constitution.[67]

---

65. *Dei Verbum*, no. 8, counts three distinct engines of development, which I render as follows: "from the contemplation and study of the faithful … from the intimate understanding faithful experience of spiritual things, and from the preaching of those … who have received the certain charism of truth [bishops]." As to the second thing, the Council says, not that spiritual things are experienced, but that an *understanding* of them is experienced. Aquinas adverts to this understanding from becoming like what one loves in *ST* II-II, q. 45, a. 2.

66. Newman, *An Essay on the Development of Christian Doctrine*, chap. 2, sec. 1.

67. R. Francis Martin, "*Sacra Doctrina* and the Authority of its *Sacra Scriptura* according to

For another thing, there is the fact that the word of God comes to us in both Hebrew and Greek. The word of God that first came to us in Hebrew can *also* come to us in Greek.[68] The word of God, while it can come to us only in some determinate human language, is something that transcends and can be expressed in all languages.[69] As has been said, Christianity is a religion of the word, but not a religion of the book.[70]

This is important for our confidence not only in theological argumentation that does not take place in Hebrew or Greek, but also for our confidence in magisterial teaching, and this was expressly recognized at the time of the Humanist and Reformation criticism of the Vulgate.[71] The fact that the one word of God can be rendered in many languages is a sort of foreshadowing of the development of doctrine. For to unfold what is implicit in the word of God is to interpret, and to interpret is to translate. And the other way around—to translate is to interpret, to interpret is to unfold.

In addition to the happy interpretations and translations of the word of God, however, there are also possible corruptions—that is, interpretations that fail accurately to state what God means by the word he has spoken to us, purported developments that do not develop but distort. It is because of this that the author of scripture must somehow remain with it if it is not to disappear into an impenetrable fog of human chatter, such that what was once revealed becomes again concealed, in which case no true and divine revelation was ever made.

St. Thomas," *Pro Ecclesia* 19 (2001): 84–102. For development across the testaments, see Cardinal Newman, *An Essay on Development*, chap. 2, sec. 1.

68. As is well known, the Septuagint was taken to be authoritative in its own right—not just as quoted by the New Testament—and was itself considered to be an inspired text.

69. Benedict XVI, *Verbum Domini*, par. 115, asserts the translatability of the Bible. See Aquinas, *ST* I, q. 29, a. 3, ad 1, where he argues from the introduction of the nonscriptural word "person" into the language of the church to the possibility of the translation of scripture: "Si ... oporteret de Deo dici solum illa, secundum vocem, quae sacra Scriptura de Deo tradit, sequeretur quod nunquam in alia lingua posset aliquis loqui de Deo, nisi in illa in qua primo tradita est Scriptura veteris vel novi Testamenti."

70. Benedict XVI, *Verbum Domini*, par. 7; and par. 38, on transcending the letter: "the word of God can never simply be equated with the letter of the text. To attain to it involves a progression and a process of understanding guided by the inner movement of the whole corpus, and also has to become a vital process."

71. Michael C. Legaspi, *The Death of Scripture and the Rise of Biblical Studies* (Oxford: Oxford University Press, 2010), 14, reports the position of Pierre Cousturier (d. 1537): "In dislodging the Vulgate, Cousturier argued, he [Erasmus] was not simply questioning the authority of a translation, he was undermining scripture itself."

When St. Thomas thinks about the capacities of preachers to transmit the word of God, he invokes the gifts of the Holy Spirit and the light of prophecy. The gifts of the Holy Spirit, which include wisdom and knowledge, are given to all by baptism and confirmation. They are given also by orders, in such a way that they amount to *gratiae gratis datae*, in virtue of which the common good of the church is served by public witness and ministry. For just this reason, St. Thomas says, St. Paul mentions the *"word* of wisdom and knowledge" (1 Cor 12:8), as the gifts of wisdom and knowledge can be given in such fullness that they enable teaching others.[72] In this way are they given to prelates.[73]

Furthermore, the light of prophecy is given also for interpretation of scripture—answering questions put to the text that the text itself does not answer in so many words. So prophetic light was given to the apostles by Christ (Lk 24:45) so that they might expound the sense of the Old Testament.[74] Such prophetic light continues to be given for the interpretation of scripture, such that "they are interpreted in the same spirit in which they have been written."[75]

Therefore, when the bishops quote Christ or otherwise proclaim the scriptures, they are speaking the Word of God with an authority not only envisaged in the past but also now conferred by the sacrament and with it an enhanced ability so to speak the Word of God, according to that word of the Lord: "the Holy Spirit, whom the Father will send in my name, he will teach you all things and bring to your remembrance all that I have said to you" (Jn 15:26), and "when the Spirit of truth comes, he will guide you into all the truth" (Jn 16:12).

The problem of the certain mediation of gospel truth nonetheless remains. No bishop possesses such gifts, the gifts of the Holy Spirit or some share in prophetic light, inalienably, in the way an ordained person inalienably possesses the ability to confect the sacraments. We know this

---

72. Aquinas, *ST* I-II, q. 68, a. 5, ad 1, and q. 111, a. 4, ad 4.

73. Ibid., II-II, q. 177, a. 2; see also q. 45, a. 5, co. and ad 2.

74. Ibid., q. 173, a. 2. Presumably, they are enabled to read the Old Testament Christologically, as Christ does to the disciples on the road to Emmaus.

75. Aquinas, *Super Primum Epistolam ad Corinthios Lectura*, cap. 14, lect. 1, no. 813: "eodem spiritu interpretae sunt quo editae sunt." See also *Super Epistolam ad Romanos Lectura*, c. 12, lect. 2, no. 978, and *SCG* III.154. See Matthew Lamb's introduction to his translation of Aquinas's *Commentary on Saint Paul's Epistle to the Ephesians* (Albany, N.Y.: Magi Books, 1966), 7–8, and esp. n115 and n118.

first of all from the history of the church, which is no stranger to wicked and heretical bishops. Second, the light of prophecy or any participation therein is a charismatic gift, and of itself not stable. Third, we know that the gifts of the Holy Spirit are lost with the loss of charity.

While each bishop individually in interpreting the word of God remains a fallible second cause, as noted above, they cannot all of them together fail to interpret correctly, fail to recognize which developments are legitimate and true, and which purported developments are corruptions. No individual bishop is therefore an instrumental cause of correct interpretation, the way a prophet or hagiographer could be such an instrument, delivering that message and only that message God chooses. Still, all together they exercise that more than moral agency verified in the unity of the church through the mission of the Holy Spirit to the one bride and body of Christ.[76] When they exercise it in this way, in communion with one another and with the pope, they cannot fail to keep the church in the truth of the gospel word.

A College with a Primate

Collegial Infallibility

We are now in view of a solution to the question of how the word of God abides. While each individual bishop is fallible, the entire body of bishops, like the entire church, is not. And this is in fact the teaching of the church. The bishops in communion with the pope who teach on matters of faith and morals cannot be mistaken, and this is so whether they are scattered throughout the world or gathered in council.[77] This is how the active members of the diaconal communion, those charged with public preaching and teaching, maintain the church in the truth of the gospel, which is to say, maintain the truth of the gospel from age to age. When

---

76. Yves M. J. Congar, OP, *La foi et la théologie* (Tournai: Desclée and Co., 1962), no. 42: "The principle of indefectibility in the faith is not personal, not even for the pope, in the sense that it would be given to an individual just as such. It is given to the *Church* as such and in its unity. But the Church is concentrated, is personalized, and, in that sense, is represented in its heads and most particularly in the successor of Peter, the prince of the apostolic college. The thesis of the testimony of the Holy Spirit needs to be restored to its true 'place': the subject of this testimony is the Church as such, animated as a whole by the Holy Spirit."

77. *Lumen Gentium*, no. 25.

the entire body of the episcopate so teaches, we have verified an instance in which the church acts as an agent, in which her personality as something more than moral, as particularly expressed in those who discharge a care for the church in virtue of the commission of Christ and the grace of the Holy Spirit, comes to expression. When we have such authoritative teaching for the whole church, for all Christians, there is a sort of demonstration that the church of Christ subsists in the Catholic church (*Lumen Gentium*, no. 8).

As to its content, such teaching is nothing more than an expression or interpretation of the original word of God, and does nothing but make it present once again in circumstances other than that of the time when revelation was closed. Thus, it shares the authority of that original word. It is not a new word of revelation, but something old brought forth in new light. Because it shares the authority of the old, it is said by both Vatican councils to be "irreformable," which means nothing except that its authority is that of the original word of God and therefore does not depend on the agreement of those who hear it, or the consent of the church as a whole subsequently responding to it.[78]

When the bishops teach doctrine with the authority of the word of God they have also the power to require public assent to it. That is the force of the canons with which the highest teaching is formulated. So at Nicaea: "But those who say that the Son of God is subject to change or alteration, the catholic and apostolic Church *anathematizes*." That is, the church excludes such men from her communion. Or at Second Constantinople (553), with what became the standard form in the passive voice: "If anyone says that the Word of God who works miracles is one thing and the Christ who suffered is another … *let him be anathema* [*anathema sit*]." If he does not publicly confess what is taught, he is excluded from communion. So two things are going on: there is first a formulation and declaration of some truth of revelation that is seen in the word of God and the church's tradition of it; second, there is a direction for action such that, if someone does not confess the truth so formulated, the church is to treat him as an outsider. This second thing is a matter of governing. It is the highest of all the acts of governing, for it sets the boundaries of ecclesial

78. Ibid.; see *Pastor Aeternus*, chap. 4.

communion, and contains within itself all lesser acts of jurisdiction as listed in the introduction to this chapter. Therefore, just as the declaration of
the word of truth is within the compass of the college of bishops, so also is
the declaration of the word that rules and governs. As the teaching authority of the college is supreme, so its ruling authority is also supreme.[79]

Catholic teaching on the supreme authority by which the church is
maintained in the truth and governed, however, does not speak only of
the college of bishops, but also particularly and individually of the primate of this college, the bishop of Rome, and recognizes that he, too, can
teach infallibly and exercise supreme ruling authority in the church.[80] Is
this a matter of redundancy? Is it like having a second computer on board
the spacecraft in case the first fails? No, the Petrine office is more organi-
cally related to the functioning of the college of bishops. This will become
plain shortly after a brief review of the data of the New Testament and the
dominical institution of Petrine office.

Reviewing the Biblical Data on Peter

The New Testament warrant for the Petrine office is abundant. It is not
just that it is hard not to run into Peter just about everywhere in the New
Testament; it is hard not to run into him as exercising a special office within the company of the Twelve. All the Gospels bear witness to his unique
position, and he is himself the chief witness behind the Gospel of Mark.[81]
And what a witness he is! All four Gospels record his paradigmatic in-
sertion into the unfolding of the paschal mystery, the sinner who cannot
keep his word never to fail in faithfulness to Jesus (Mt 26:33; Mk 14:29; Lk
22:33; Jn 13:37) but who denies him three times (Mt 26:69–75; Mk 14:66–
72; Lk 22:54–62; Jn 18:17, 25–27). John recounts in detail his rehabilitation
after the resurrection (Jn 21:15–19). It cannot surprise us that some see the
work of reconciliation as central to the discharge of the Petrine office.[82]

In Mark and Luke, Peter acts as the spokesman of the Twelve at Cae-

79. *Lumen Gentium*, nos. 21 and 27.

80. With regard to the pope, *Lumen Gentium* repeats the teaching of *Pastor Aeternus*, chap. 4,
of the First Vatican Council. For the pope's supreme governing authority, see *Pastor Aeternus*, chap.
3, and *Lumen Gentium*, nos. 21 and 27.

81. There is no good reason to set aside the witness of Papias, Irenaeus, and others to Peter's
relation to the Gospel according to Mark.

82. Ratzinger, *Called to Communion*, 64–65.

sarea Philippi (Mk 8:29; Lk 9:20); in Matthew he is expressly commissioned as the rock (Mt 16:18), and John records an equivalent scene at the end of the bread of life discourse (Jn 6:68–69). Then there is the Lord's prayer for Peter in Luke, that he "strengthen" his brothers (Lk 22:31–32); Jesus takes thought for Peter and his place in the church at the very hour of his passion. Peter's prominence in Acts (e.g. Acts 1:15, 2:14, 5:1–11, 15:7–11) is therefore no surprise, nor his teaching about church office in 1 Peter 5:1–5. Not only the express words of the Lord in Matthew and Luke, therefore, but the church's acceptance of Peter's preeminence give a first answer as to why there is a primate: it is because the Lord Jesus wanted one for the service of the church.

Why the College Needs a Primate

Why is the primacy of the pope a good thing? Why is it not just a redundancy? What is its organic connection to the successful operation of the college, of episcopal office? There is the argument for monarchy from political philosophy; but there is also something more properly theological to say. At first, we may think that the articulation of the hierarchy is explained by saying that it is the bishops who have care of local churches and the pope who has care of the universal church. Just as the unity of a local church comes to expression in one bishop, so the unity of the universal church comes to expression in the pope. For, it might be argued, the unity of the universal church cannot come to fitting expression in a *multitude*, and that is what the college of bishops is. This is good as far as it goes. It does not go far enough. If bishops *can* act together as one body for the whole, we do not yet see the organic, necessary connection of the primate to the college.

There is first the question as to why it is good that a *local* church comes to expression in one bishop. Why can there be only one bishop in a place? Ratzinger's argument for what Ignatius of Antioch celebrates in his letters is very good here. It has to do with the nature and signification of the nature of the Eucharist. The Eucharist makes all who celebrate it one body in Christ, and it has to bear this meaning on its face. I put Ratzinger's argument as follows.

Of old, each regular Sunday Eucharistic celebration is for all and open to all Christians of one locality. The celebration is not the celebration of a private club or voluntary association of men. So to speak, an invitation to Sunday Mass comes with baptism. Of its nature, the sacrament of charity has to be accessible to all Christians of a place. It has, therefore, and in that sense, to be public. Christ did not shed his blood for a few, but for all, and the memorial of his sacrifice has to respect that fact in the hospitality it offers to all. Therefore, ideally—and this was often realized in the first centuries of the church—there is one Sunday Mass, one Eucharistic celebration in a town or neighborhood. But the one Eucharist wants one president, one gatekeeper ensuring that Eucharistic hospitality is an ordered hospitality.[83] The one president, furthermore, if he really presides at the celebration with authority, must also preside over the community itself, all of whose members have access to the one celebration. So, the one president of the assembly is the one (or chief) pastor of the place.[84] "A Church understood eucharistically is a Church constituted episcopally."[85]

Evidently, care for the sanctification and ordering of a community presupposes teaching: even within the Eucharist, the breaking of the bread is preceded by the breaking of the Word (just as in Lk 24). And now, we get insight into why it must be that a bishop take up care not just for his own local church but succeeds to an apostolic concern for all the churches, something that was noted above in reviewing the New Testament evidence about apostolic and post-apostolic ministry.

If the teaching of an individual bishop is in principle fallible, and if it is only all the bishops that, when they teach the same thing, are certainly mediating the truth of the gospel, then each episcopal teacher must attend to all episcopal teachers—that is, he has to have a concern for the whole. This duty is founded on his immediate duty for his own church; his church will be in the truth only if he is *also* concerned for the whole. And without this concern for the whole, unless bishops succeed to this part also of apostolic office, it will be hard not to think of the church as a federation of local churches.[86]

The question then becomes how this concern can be exercised practically, or whether there really is a way for it to be exercised at all. In the an-

83. The contemporary practice of "concelebration," where many priests exercise their priesthood in common at a single Mass was unknown to the early church.
84. See Ratzinger, *Called to Communion*, 77–79, for this argument.
85. Ibid., 79.
86. Ibid., 83–85.

cient church, it was evidently hard for sees, especially more remote ones, to keep up. There are letters of communion and lists of churches a bishop is in communion with.[87] That is, there are lists of the gatekeepers of other local Eucharistic assemblies whose teaching is recognized as orthodox. But it is far easier, and in the end, must be possible, to attend to only one see. And so it was; in the ancient church it was enough to claim communion with the Apostolic See, with Rome, to prove that one still remained in the truth and so in the catholic (universal) church.[88] And this is a recognition of the Roman bishop's responsibility as the universal gatekeeper of the church.

Nor should we think this is a late realization. When the canon of the New Testament is agreed on as a norm of orthodoxy, it is itself a norm that comes late to the church's concern to remain in the gospel truth. However, recognizing in Rome the touchstone of truth is something *older* than the canon of the New Testament.[89] St. Irenaeus is a remarkable witness to this truth in the second century: it is necessary for every particular church to agree doctrinally with "the very great, the very ancient, and universally known church," the church of Rome, "on account of its pre-eminent authority."[90]

The fact of the Petrine office is given to us in Matthew 16. The *convenientia* of the Petrine office is conveyed in two other places. First of all, it is a fittingness installed by the divine law and wisdom, a fittingness extraordinarily apt for a church so intimately tied to the Eucharist. We see this in John 6: just as the Eucharist of which the Lord speaks at the end of this chapter is the sacrament that makes the church and makes the church one, so it is Peter at the end of that chapter who confesses his faith both in the Lord and therefore in his Eucharistic teaching: "'Lord, to whom shall we go? You have the words of eternal life'" (Jn 6:68). How right, therefore, that Peter and his successors should have the charge of maintaining the unity of the church, just as, as a matter of historical fact, they have especially concerned themselves with the true doctrine of the Eucharist, from the time of Berengarius and his purely symbolic view of the Christ's

87. Ludwig Hertling, SJ, *Communio: Church and Papacy in Early Christianity*, trans. Jared Wicks, SJ (Chicago: Loyola University Press, 1972 [1943]), 29–35 and 47–55.

88. Hertling, *Church and Papacy*, 65–69.

89. Ratzinger, *Called to Communion*, 70.

90. Irenaeus, *Against Heresies*, III.3.

presence, reproved by Pope Gregory VII, to that of Paul VI, reproving the modern theory of trans-signification.[91]

Second, the same connection is established at the Last Supper in Luke 22:31–32: "Simon, Simon, behold, Satan demanded to have you, that he might sift you like wheat, but I have prayed for you that your faith may not fail; and when you have turned again, strengthen your brethren." The malice of Satan recalls the gates of hell of Matthew 16:18, the powers of which will not destroy the church built on Peter's faith. The primacy is indicated in that Peter is to strengthen his brethren. And the context is once again Eucharistic, about which Pope Benedict XVI says:

> This contextualization of the Primacy of Peter at the Last Supper, at the moment of the Institution of the Eucharist, the Lord's Pasch, also points to the ultimate meaning of this Primacy: Peter must be the custodian of communion with Christ for all time. He must guide people to communion with Christ; he must ensure that the net does not break and consequently that universal communion endures. Only together can we be with Christ. Who is Lord of all.[92]

Conclusion

The human mediation of the truth of Christ by erring, forgetful, and sinful men may make this mediation seem frail. Considering this mediation in its entirety, however, and the extent to which it has been unfolded in the teaching of the church, may enable us to share some of St. Thomas's confidence. Responding to the objection that Christ should not have entrusted the mission to the Gentiles to his disciples but himself have taught them, he says that "it bespeaks not a lesser power but a greater power to do something through others than by oneself. And therefore, the divine power of Christ is shown most of all in this, that he conferred on his disciples such great power in teaching, that they converted to Christ even the nations that had heard nothing of him."[93] Just as in the sacramental order the divine and original cause of grace can make true instrumental causes of others, so in the order of the manifestation of truth, the divine teacher can make others successful teachers.

91. See Paul VI, *Mysterium Fidei*.
92. Benedict XVI, "General Audience of June 7, 2006"; available at www.vatican.va.
93. Aquinas, *ST* III, q. 42, a. 1, ad 2 (my translation).

CHAPTER 14

THE CATHOLIC MISSION
OF THE CHURCH

The kingdom of God of which the church is a harbinger is evidently a kingdom that in some way includes the whole of humanity (Mt 25:31, Dn 7:13–14). The messianic people of God is to be an all-inclusive people, and the church is commissioned to make this happen with the authority of the risen Christ (Mt 28:18–20). In the power of the Spirit, she begins to do so on Pentecost, where representatives of all the nations are gathered (Acts 2:9–11). The urgency with which she takes up her mission is generated by her knowledge that God wills all men to be saved (1 Tm 2:4) and that the name of Jesus is the only name by which we can be saved (Acts 4:12), in that he is the single and sole mediator between God and man (1 Tm 2:5).

Evidently, the work of the church to convert all men and every nation is not complete. The following questions therefore arise. First, what are the prospects for salvation, abstractly considered, for those who do not know the name of Jesus? Second, what is the role of non-Christian religions in the salvation of non-Christians? Third, does the missionary work of the church really enhance the chances for the salvation of those she evangelizes? That is, does being a Christian make any difference to one's chance for salvation? Fourth, what should the church expect from the non-Christian cultures and nations and states in which she will continue to exist for the foreseeable future? Fifth, how can we better specify the role the *church* plays in the salvation of non-Christians?

The Prospects for Salvation of Non-Christians Absolutely Considered

The dictum first formulated by St. Cyprian in the West and Origen in the East that outside the church there is no salvation—*extra ecclesiam nulla salus*—was applied to those in the church who subsequently and culpably left. It was not a teaching about the prospects for salvation of those who had never heard the gospel.[1] Justin Martyr supposed that any man who lived by the *logos spermatikos*, the seed of the Word implanted in him, would by following the natural law cooperate with God for his own soul's salvation.[2]

The official teaching of the church since the nineteenth century is that non-Christians may be saved. According to Pius IX, invincible ignorance of the true religion is no sin.[3] If such invincibly ignorant men keep the natural law and are disposed to obey God, they may be aided by grace unto attaining eternal life.[4] This teaching was repeated by the Second Vatican Council, which nonetheless insisted that the missionary mandate given the church by Christ is to be obeyed.[5] And if men invincibly ignorant of the true religion are saved, they are saved by the grace of Christ which is always somehow ecclesially mediated.[6] If one is culpably outside the church, he cannot be saved because of the grave sins of either

---

1. For the history involved, see Francis A. Sullivan, SJ, *Salvation Outside the Church? Tracing the History of the Catholic Response* (New York: Paulist Press, 1992).

2. The Second Vatican Council's *Ad Gentes*, no. 11, invokes this theme. For Justin, see the First Apology, c. 46, and the Second Apology, c. 14, in ANF 1.

3. Pius IX, *Singulari Quadam*, Papal Allocution, December 9, 1854; available at https://novusordowatch.org/pius9-singulari-quadam/.

4. Pius IX, *Quanto Conficiamur Moerore*, Encyclical Letter, August 10, 1863; available at http://www.papalencyclicals.net/pius09/p9quanto.htm. God does not condemn to hell any who have not freely sinned.

5. *Lumen Gentium*, nos. 16 and 17; *Ad Gentes*, no. 7.

6. See *Dominus Iesus*, according to which salvation is always Christological (nos. 11–12 and 14) and always ecclesial (no. 20).

heresy or schism or both; but anyone who is saved is saved through the church, even if one is outside her visible bounds. The church is, then, as the Council says, "the universal sacrament of salvation."[7]

This she can be for all non-Catholic *Christians*, insofar as their communities possess elements of truth and sanctification belonging to the church established by Christ, as was said in chapter 11. As to *non*-Christians, we will see in the last section of this chapter the role the church plays in their salvation.

The Role of Non-Christian Religions in the Salvation of Non-Christians

A Word about Judaism

The Jews are included in the Second Vatican Council's Declaration on Non-Christian Religions, *Nostra Aetate* (October 28, 1965).[8] The Council recognizes "the common spiritual patrimony" shared by Christians and Jews (no. 4). This patrimony includes the sure word of revelation contained in the Old Testament and, we might add, the many forms of life and prayer it has sustained and such things as the respect Jews and Christians cultivate for women. Notwithstanding the role some Jewish leaders played in the death of Jesus, the Council teaches that Jews are not rejected or accursed by God (no. 4). They remain dear to God, who does not repent of his gifts (Rom 11:29). Moreover, the church's faith begins with the patriarchs, Moses, and the prophets, and Israel's history foreshadows the church (no. 4). In this light, Judaism is not a non-Christian religion so much as the religion that is on the way to being the Christian religion, and this by the positive intention and will and revelation and action of God, even if the Jews do not recognize this. Insofar as there is no culpable rejection of the gospel, therefore, we may suppose that God remains faithful to the covenants with Abraham and Moses, and that practicing the Jewish religion is pleasing in his sight and rewarded with grace and blessings.[9]

7. *Lumen Gentium*, no. 48.
8. The Declaration can be found in *Decrees* (ed. Tanner), 2:968–71.
9. Aquinas, who asserts that Israel's election is permanent, following Rom 11:29, also holds that the practice of Jewish ceremonial rites is now forbidden by God and that worshipping according to

The Magisterium on the Role of Non-Christian Religions in Salvation

We are concerned in this section rather with all the other non-Christian religions, none of which is the result of the positive intention and will and revelation and action of God in history. That they are not the result of his will and intention is something easily known from the New Testament, which consigns the worship of pagans to the worship of idols and demons (1 Cor 8:4; Gal 4:8). That they are not the result of his will and intention is, moreover, the teaching of the Second Vatican Council. In its Declaration on Religious Freedom, *Dignitatis Humanae* (December 7, 1965), it asserts that God himself reveals how we may be saved in Christ (no. 1).[10] Then it adds this:

> We believe that this one and only true religion [*unicam veram religionem*] subsists in [*subsistere in*] the Catholic and Apostolic Church, to which the Lord Jesus entrusted the task of spreading it to all men saying to the apostles: "Therefore go forth and teach the nations, baptizing them in the name of the Father and of the Son and of the Holy Spirit, teaching them to observe all that I have commanded you" (Mt 28:19–20).[11]

If the Catholic church is the one and only true religion, then the other religions are not true, and therefore cannot have been willed and intended by God.

It is noteworthy that the same language used for identifying the church of Christ, saying that it subsists in the Catholic church, is used for identifying the only true religion. If there are elements of the church of Christ outside the visible confines of the Catholic church (*Lumen Gentium*, no. 8), are there elements of true religion outside the visible con-

---

those rites whose purpose was to prefigure is now death-dealing as the prefigured has arrived. See for instance *ST* I-II, q. 103, a. 4, co., and q. 104, a. 3, co. But in II-II, q. 10, a. 11, he speaks as if even *now* Jewish worship presents to Christians what we worship "*quasi in figura*," and this seems to call for a revaluation of Jewish worship and the admission that God intends it even now to achieve some share in the life of Christ, of the church. See Bruce Marshall, "Christ and Israel: An Unsolved Problem in Catholic Theology," in *The Call of Abraham: Essays on the Election of Israel in Honor of Jon D. Levenson*, ed. Gary A. Anderson and Joel S. Kaminsky (Notre Dame, Ind.: University of Notre Dame Press, 2013), 345–46.

10. The Declaration can be found in *Decrees* (ed. Tanner), 2:1001–11.

11. I have slightly modified the translation.

fines of the church in non-Christian religions? The conciliar documents do not say this. Non-Christian religions are not related to Christianity in the way that non-Catholic Christian communions are related to the Catholic church. To think so would suppose that all religions are seeking a univocally defined "salvation." Discovering that one is indistinct from the All that is One of absolute reality and consciousness accessed in a mystical experience, however, is not at all the same as the perfection of one's inalienable personhood in Trinitarian communion with God. On the other hand, the conciliar documents recognize that there are true and good things in non-Christian religions. According to *Nostra Aetate*, the church "rejects nothing of those things which are true and holy in these religions" (no. 2). After all, in that God is absolute and infinite and creative truth and goodness, whatever there is in the heart of man that is true and good, and whatever there is in any culture or religion that is true and good comes from God. This takes up what *Lumen Gentium* says of the good things to be found in various non-Christian rites and cultures, goods that are "saved from destruction" and "raised up and brought to completion to the glory of God" and "the confusion of the devil" (no. 17). This is repeated in *Ad Gentes* (no. 9).

This same theme is echoed by Paul VI in 1975 in *Evangelii Nuntiandi*, which however denies that non-Christian religions as such establish a positive relation with God as does Christianity, and rather characterizes them as having their arms raised to heaven.[12] That is to say, they are the products of the human search for God, but not God's gift to man—their arms are lifted up but their hands are empty of divine gifts.[13]

The same line is taken by John Paul II in *Redemptor Hominis* (1979), par. 6, and in *Redemptoris Missio* (1990), pars. 28–29.[14] John Paul II speaks there both of the "seeds of the Word" in non-Christian religions, and of the Spirit producing good things in these religions of mankind.

12. Paul VI, *Evangelii Nuntiandi*, Apostolic Exhortation, December 8, 1975, par. 53: "In other words, our religion effectively establishes with God an authentic and living relationship which the other religions do not succeed in doing, even though they have, as it were, their arms stretched out towards heaven" (available at www.vatican.va).

13. See Henri de Lubac, SJ, "The Pagan Religions and the Fathers of the Church," in his *The Church: Paradox and Mystery*, trans. James R. Dunne (New York: Alba House, 1969), 69–95.

14. John Paul II, *Redemptoris Missio*. See also *Redemptor Hominis*, Encyclical Letter, March 4, 1979; available at www.vatican.va.

But producing good things in a religion is not the same thing as producing the religion. It is difficult to say that John Paul II moves beyond what Paul VI has said.[15] And this line is repeated in *Dominus Iesus*, par. 21, which forbids us to think that the scriptures of non-Christian religions are inspired, although they certainly can contain many truths (par. 8), or that their rites are divinely instituted or efficacious of themselves for salvation (par. 21). They are not other "ways" of salvation alongside the way of Christianity (par. 21).

Therefore, taken as the religions they are, in their integrity and unity, they play no role in salvation at all—a "salvation," moreover, that may be conceptually quite foreign to them. This neither denies the presence of truths, religious truths in them, nor the possible moral goodness, and, as such, pleasingness before God, of their rites. For it is possible that their rites retain something of the sacramentality enjoined by the natural law in such things as sacrifices.[16] In assessing the religious worth of non-Christian religions, then, each item, each rite, each custom, each tradition within them has to be examined in itself.

When some religious truth or practice is found to be sound and therefore possibly conducive to salvation (we say possibly, for we are outside the sphere of direct revelation at this point), then the effectiveness of such truths or practices will be that of instruments of the saving power of Christ, of his death and resurrection. For if we say that the true and good things in non-Christian religions are "seeds of the Word," the Word has always been freely destined to be and is now the incarnate Word. But according to St. Thomas, the power of Christ's humanity is in touch with all times and places because the divine power is so in touch.[17] And he is the one mediator between God and man (1 Tm 2:5). Moreover, Christ is always and inalienably the head of the church, and where he acts, the church also acts. Wherever or whenever some non-Christian is being saved, therefore, the church remains, as the Council taught, "the universal sacrament of salvation" (*Lumen Gentium*, no. 48).[18]

15. Contrary to what Sullivan maintains in chap. 11 of his *Salvation Outside the Church?*

16. See Aquinas, *ST* I-II, q. 103, a. 1, and II-II, q. 85, a. 1. For an analogical conception of sacraments suitable for understanding non-Jewish and non-Christian sacraments, see de La Soujeole, OP, "The Importance of the Definition of Sacraments as Signs," 127–35, esp. 130–34.

17. Aquinas, *ST* III, q. 56, a. 1, ad 3, and q. 49, a. 1, ad 2.

18. See Hipp, *The One Church of Christ*, 159–61, and Thomas Joseph White, OP, "The

Why Non-Christian Religions Just as Such Play No Role in Salvation

A non-Christian religion may of course make its adherents more serious and thoughtful persons. It may make them more morally alert, readier to hear the gospel, supposing their attachment to it does not close their ears and narrow their hearts. There is no general rule to lay down here.[19] Even so, just as such, non-Christian religions play no positive role in the salvation of their adherents. We can see why this must be so if we briefly examine the thesis that men hear the word of God in the writings of other religions. If they do, it seems we must concede that these other religions are also ways of salvation. There are dogmatic and systematic objections to this proposal, however.

First, dogmatically, the teaching of the New Testament is not favorable to this proposal as we have previously seen. In Acts, after Paul has healed a cripple and the priest of Zeus and the people want to offer sacrifice to him and Barnabas, he addresses the men of Lystra in Acts 14:15–17:

We also are men, of like nature with you, and bring you good news, that you should turn from these vain things to a living God who made the heaven and the earth and the sea and all that is in them. In past generations, he allowed all the nations to walk in their own ways; yet he did not leave himself without witness, for he did good and gave you from heaven rains and fruitful seasons satisfying your hearts with food and gladness.

Three comments are in order. First, in the past, God left the nations to go their own ways. "Their own ways" are human ways, not divine ways. That is, God did not give these nations a divine religion; he did not institute a way of salvation for them. He allowed them to walk in these ways, but it is safe to say that insofar as these ways suffered the distortion of superstitions and the deformations of bad morals, he certainly did not want them to do so.[20] Second, the religion that the men of Lystra in fact have, with

---

Universal Mediation of Christ and Non-Christian Religions," *Nova et Vetera* (English edition) 14 (2016): 179–84 and 187–90.

19. Newman thought that what he called the "Natural Religion" of mankind made men ready to hear the gospel; see *Grammar of Assent*, 267–69 (415–18).

20. So for the Fathers and St. Thomas, "non-Christian religions" are forms of idolatry; there is no such thing as a "natural religion" that would be as it were neutral or ready to be determined positively by revelation. The religion of the old people of God as of the new are willed by God;

temples and sacrifices to Zeus and Hermes (see 14:11–13) is vain, which is to say, useless. That is, in what is proper and distinctive to it, it does not profit a man unto salvation. What is vain and useless for salvation, therefore, would include such writings as the *Theogony* of Hesiod and other pagan Greek religious literature. It claims divine authority, inspired by the Muses, but is nothing more than part of the human way in which the Greeks walk. Third, in the past, not giving them his own way, leaving them in their own ways, God nonetheless left them with a witness to himself. It is not a witness recorded in Hesiod. Rather, it is the witness of nature, of creation, by which men could know him, as Paul says in Romans 1. In Acts 17:24–30, where Paul addresses the Athenians, there is added the injunction that, in the times of the ignorance of the true God, men should indeed have sought God "in the hope that they might feel after him and find him." They would do so, presumably, on the basis of the witness to God he gives himself in creation and the good things of the earth, whence, Paul says, "he is not far from each one of us, for 'in him we live and move and have our being,'" quoting the poet (Acts 17:27–28).

Second, if we consider non-Christian scripture more systematically, it is useful to distinguish between telling someone something and causing him to be informed about something. If John tells me that S is P, and truly, then God is causing me to be informed that S is P, because God is the creator of John and John-as-speaking. But this does not mean that God is telling me that S is P. Telling requires going bail for the assertion, taking responsibility for it, personally warranting it. So, John is telling me, but God is not, that S is P.

Now some people, including Jacques Dupuis, want to say that God's word is in other, non-Christian (and non-Jewish) scriptures. Dupuis calls this a "hidden" or secret word.[21] A secret word is like being informed that S is P without knowing who the ultimate, original informer is. George sends a message to John *via* Paul, without telling John that it is his,

---

whatever other religion we see is the work of demons. *Lumen Gentium*, no. 16, allows for this. See also *Lumen Gentium*, no. 17, and *Ad Gentes*, no. 9, for mention of the devil. See Bruce Marshall, "Religion and Election: Aquinas on Natural Law, Judaism, and Salvation in Christ," *Nova et Vetera* (English edition) 14 (2016): 71–78 and 102–3.

21. Jacques Dupuis, SJ, *Toward a Christian Theology of Religious Pluralism* (Maryknoll, N.Y.: Orbis Books, 1997), 250.

George's message, and without telling John that Paul is his, George's, messenger. The idea, then, is that God speaks openly in the Old and New Testaments, but that he speaks secretly in, say, the Koran. If I am a Christian and if I think God is speaking—wherever and however I hear it, secretly or openly—my response must be that of faith. If I think God is saying S is P, I must believe it, and on the ground he is telling me.

On what ground, however, do I think God is telling me something in the Upanishads or the Koran? Mostly, it seems to be an argument from antecedent probability. God is good. There are lots and lots of Muslims and Hindus. Therefore, it cannot be that he has not spoken to them, provided for them and their salvation in some positive way, a way actually within their historical and cultural reach, which is to say, in and by means of their own religion.

But if I think God is speaking in the writings of these other religions, then as mentioned, there is some *prima facie* duty on my part to appropriate it by faith. If there is any discrepancy between what he is purported as saying there and what he says in the Old and New Testaments, however, I measure the purported saying against the standard of my own scripture, which I know by divine and Catholic faith to be God's open word, addressed to all.

It turns out, then, that the purported revelation, the purported secret word, is useless. It will turn out I accept only the things I already know God has said, known from the church's scripture. I will reject the anti-Trinitarian and anti-Christological parts of the Koran. The other things, insofar as they agree with the Old and New Testaments, I can accept. But also, I must come to a judgment relative to the worth of non-Christian scriptures for non-Christians. If I think that religious truth has any bearing on salvation, I shall have to admit that the Koran— just because of its anti-Christian parts—is as a whole useless for salvation, even for those who think it is the word of God.

Suppose the Koranic revelation says more things, other things than the Bible does, things that may, for all I can see, be compatible with what is contained in scripture but do not contradict it. Will I accept these other things by faith? Only on the supposition of the inerrancy of the Koran, which depends on the supposition that the whole of it is divinely inspired, like the Bible. So, no, I will not accept these other things. Because

I know the Koran to be erroneous in its anti-Christian parts bearing on Christ and the Trinity, I cannot trust that any of it is inspired.

So it does not seem really possible to excise contradictions of Christ from the scriptures of other religions, but still understand the scriptures of other religions as complementary to our own. We return to an insight of Newman's. In Christianity, revelation comes to us *as* revelation. So also does it in Islam. But they are incompatible wholes; so one must choose.[22]

Concluding Balance

For St. Augustine, "non-Christian religions" are the work of demons and forms of idolatry, and the same is true for St. Thomas.[23] For St. Thomas, there is no such thing as a "natural religion" that would be as it were a neutral work of reason and ready to be determined positively by revelation.[24] The religion of the old people of God as of the new are willed by God; whatever other religion we see is the work of demons. Augustine and Thomas are simply following St. Paul here (1 Cor 8, 10:20–21; Gal 4:8). Of course, neither *Nostra Aetate* nor *Lumen Gentium* (nos. 16 and 17) nor *Ad Gentes* (no. 9) say simply and without qualification that non-Christian religions are the work of demons. *Lumen Gentium* notes the deformations of man's religious sense worked by the devil. It does not speak of the possibility that the whole of some religion is the devil's work, although this possibility is not explicitly foreclosed. However, there are important differences between the religions of Greece and Rome, elaborated in a climate much beholden to a living consciousness of demons and their power and prerogatives, and the religions the Council must think of, Buddhism and Hinduism, vast cultural empires as they are of religious thought and practice and not without high philosophical aspirations. So, for both conciliar documents, there can be good things, true teachings, and good practices "in" non-Christian religions, and they leave it at that. It is left to John Paul II to teach that God "can make himself present in many ways, not only to individuals but also to entire peoples through their spiritual riches, of which their religions are the main and essential

22. See Joseph DiNoia, *The Diversity of Religions* (Washington, D.C.: The Catholic University of America Press, 1992).

23. St. Augustine, *The City of God* VIII.8.17–23, VIII.21.6; Aquinas, *ST* II-II, q. 94, a. 4.

24. Marshall, "Religion and Election," 71–78 and 102–3.

expression" (*Redemptoris Missio*, par. 55).[25] And that seems to be as close as we can get to the truth of this difficult matter.

Does Belonging to the Church Make Any Real Difference before God?

How Did This Question Ever Come to Be Asked?

Because scripture and tradition are so very clear about the missionary mandate of the church, and on the supposition that it makes a real difference to a person's chance of salvation, and even when the abstract possibility is granted of salvation without hearing the gospel—Pius IX's teaching did nothing to inhibit the enormous missionary activity of the nineteenth century—it may be asked however it came to be that the question of this section could be asked.[26] There are two answers to this.

First, the abstract possibility was turned into a more determinate likelihood. There have more recently been three ways to make this turn. We have just seen one of them, the effort to find in non-Christian religions just as such ways of salvation. If it is not simply a matter of these religions having good things *in* them but rather that just as such they are ways of salvation, then it does not seem to be so important to belong to the church and confess Christ's name.

The effort to relativize religious difference also follows from the theological anthropology of Karl Rahner, which we can consider as a second way to turn the abstract possibility of salvation for non-Christians into a likelihood.[27] Rahner believed that the human being is always already in-

25. The International Theological Commission in "Christianity and the World Religions" (1997) concludes that despite the deformations of sin and the devil (no. 85), and despite the fact that not everything in them is necessarily salvific, it is possible to think that non-Christian religions "exercise as such a certain salvific function," helping man to his ultimate end (no. 84), and acting even as a *praeparatio evangelii* (no. 85). This seems hardly different from saying that they exercise "a salvific function" because of the good things "in" them—a position that seems safely abstract and vague enough. "Christianity and the World Religions" is available at www.vatican.va.

26. See Ralph Martin, *Will Many Be Saved: What Vatican II Actually Teaches and Its Implications for the New Evangelization* (Grand Rapids, Mich.: Eerdmans, 2012), and Matthew Ramage, "*Extra Ecclesiam Nulla Salus* and the Substance of Catholic Doctrine: Towards a Realization of Benedict XVI's 'Hermeneutic of Reform,'" *Nova et Vetera* (English edition) 14 (2016): 295–330.

27. In fact, Dupuis's work is a development of Rahner's theology of the salvific role of non-Christian religions. See Karl Rahner, "Christianity and the Non-Christian Religions," 97–134,

volved with God in the performance of his distinctively human acts of knowledge and love. What does it mean to know the material object we see and touch by the senses? To know it is to know it as a kind of being, and we do this only by projecting the deliverances of our senses against the horizon of being that our intellectual dynamism is always actively oriented to. In other words, the human being has always a "pre-apprehension" (*Vorgriff*) of being as a transcendental condition of the possibility of knowing any of the beings of our experience and of which beings we speak in the categories or concepts of which we are conscious. We are "thematically" conscious of these many beings—that is, we are conscious of them as objects. We are "unthematically" conscious of the pre-apprehension of being—that is, we are really conscious of it but not as of an object like the bread or the butter, the gardener or garden hose.

The pre-apprehension of being in its unlimited breadth, moreover, is also at the same time an always operative ordination unto absolute being, unto God. Thus it is that we cannot know the least thing in the world, the most trivial material object, without having to do with God. Well and good. We might be reminded of St. Augustine and St. Bonaventure in their teaching that we cannot recognize just acts and just men as just without the influence of the divine idea, the divine rule, of justice. Giving a metaphysical analysis of the Kantian critical problem, Rahner remains in recognizably Christian philosophical territory.[28] To know the things of the world involves some kind of knowing or being-unto God as one of the conditions of this knowledge.

In the order of freedom, furthermore, we respond in love to no finite good, according to Rahner, unless we are also responding to the absolute good. Knowing finite being is borne up by a dynamic orientation to absolute being, and loving finite goods is similarly sustained by a dynamic orientation to God. At this point, notice how different our engagement with God is by comparison with our engagement with another human being. I know another human being through the concepts evoked by the language we speak; I know him "categorially" and "historically," which is

in his *Theological Investigations*, vol. 5, trans. Karl-H. Kruger (London: Darton, Longman and Todd, 1966), and his *Foundations of Christian Faith*, 311–21.

28. This analysis is the goal of Rahner's as expressed in his *Spirit in the World*, trans. William Dych (New York: Herder and Herder, 1968).

to say as an object in the world and in time. But I know God not only categorially in some metaphysical system or religious language so as to be able to speak of him and think of him expressly and as an object; I know him and respond to him *also* on the transcendental level, and I can do this without even knowing conceptually and in the ordinary categories of thought that I am doing this.[29]

There is another step to take. In the actual world, God has destined human beings to the supernatural end of seeing him face to face and loving him in the power of his own love. This divine decision, according to Rahner, conditions our subjectivity, our knowing and loving, from the first instant we exist. This *a priori* conditioning of subjectivity (that is, a conditioning prior to any exercise of our mind and will) as ordered to the God of grace Rahner calls the "supernatural existential." The supernatural existential is not conceived in the old scholastic categories of grace, habitual and actual, prevenient and consequent. It is conceived after the pattern of the "existentials" that Martin Heidegger recognized, such factors determining the exercise of our freedom as "thrownness" (our originally already being conditioned by a determinate place and time not of our own choosing) or "being unto death" (our always subliminal awareness of our mortality). The supernatural existential amounts in practice to a constant offer of grace that conditions our human freedom, an availability of grace ready to be given to us.[30]

It is in fact given to a human being when he responds rightly to some finite good, for then he is necessarily also responding to the God of grace, the God as Christians know him to be, even if he knows nothing of this God expressly and conceptually. When he does so respond in a morally upright and conscientious way to a created good, he becomes really if anonymously and unbeknownst to himself a Christian.[31] We seem at this point to be in the territory St. Thomas delineated when he taught that with the first use of reason, if a human being orders himself morally to a due end, he receives the remission of original sin by grace.[32]

29. For the distinction between the transcendental and the categorical, see Rahner, *Foundations of Christian Faith*, 31–39, and as bearing on salvation, 153–62.

30. For the supernatural existential, see Rahner, *Foundations of Christian Faith*, 126–33.

31. For anonymous Christians, see Rahner, "Anonymous Christians," in *Theological Investigations*, vol. 6, trans. Karl-H. and Boniface Kruger (Baltimore: Helicon Press, 1969), 390–98.

32. *ST* I-II, q. 89, a. 6.

Just because of his sharp distinction between the transcendental and categorical levels of conscious subjectivity, however, Rahner is very liberal about the kind of categorical, conceptually characterized act that can include a positive transcendental response to the God of grace. In the order of revelation and salvation, the only adequate and wholly successful categorical—that is, historical and sense-perceivable—manifestation of the saving truth of God is Jesus of Nazareth in his life, death, and resurrection. When we confess Jesus as the Christ in a sincere love of God, then our categorical and transcendental responses to God are in harmony.[33]

But Rahner tended to hollow out the necessary connection between an adequate and saving "transcendental" response to God and its "categorical" expression in Jesus of Nazareth. It is possible to make an adequate response to the saving God in the absence of any conceptual knowledge of and conscious commitment to Jesus. We can make an adequate transcendental response to the Christian God of grace through the categories of Hinduism or Buddhism and even as an atheist.

We respond in a transcendentally adequate way to the God of grace when we follow our conscience. And we do so even if our conscience is erroneous.

We must consider the immeasurable distance … between what is objectively wrong in moral life and the extent to which this is really realized with subjectively grave guilt.… We will not hold it to be impossible that grace is at work, and is even being accepted, in the spiritual, personal life of the individual, no matter how primitive, unenlightened, apathetic and earth-bound such a life may at first sight appear to be.[34]

The infinite mystery of God can "come close to us," as Rahner liked to say, and be hung on the most unlikely "categorical" hook, religious or moral.

---

33. On Christ as the "absolute savior" and summit of categorical, historical revelation, see Rahner, *Foundations of Christian Faith*, 192–95.

34. Rahner, "Christianity and the Non-Christian Religions," 124–25. See also his "On the Importance of Non-Christian Religions for Salvation," 288–95, in *Theological Investigations*, vol. 18, trans. Edward Quinn (New York: Crossroad, 1983), 294: "even false and debased religious objectivity can be a way of mediating a genuine and grace-given transcendentality of man." For some critical remarks on Rahner's understanding of conscience, see Reinhard Hütter, *John Henry Newman on Truth & Its Counterfeits: A Guide for Our Times* (Washington, D.C.: The Catholic University of America Press, 2020), 83–85.

In the end, therefore, Rahner embraced a sort of optimism about the chances of salvation that applied fairly universally in time and space:

It is senseless to suppose cruelly … that nearly all men living outside the official and public Christianity are so evil and stubborn that the offer of supernatural grace ought not even to be made in fact in most cases …. It is furthermore impossible to think that this offer of supernatural, divinizing grace made to all men on account of the universal salvific purpose of God, should in general (prescinding from a relatively few exceptions) remain ineffective in most cases on account of the personal guilt of the individual…. we do have every reason for thinking optimistically of God and his salvific will which is more powerful than the extremely limited stupidity and evil-mindedness of men…. We have every right to suppose that grace has not only been offered even outside the Christian Church (to deny this would be the error of Jansenism) but also that, in a great many cases at least, grace gains the victory in man's free acceptance of it, this being again the result of grace.[35]

Rahner presented this sort of theorizing as a sort of commentary on and implication of *Lumen Gentium*, no. 16. As Ralph Martin points out, however, Rahner never cited or took into account the conciliar teaching that people who do not know Christ or God "more often" go astray in their thinking about God, deceived by the devil, just as is taught in Romans 1.[36]

Part of the appeal of Rahner's proposal resided in the very genius of that appellation, "anonymous Christian." "What's in a name?," we may ask. If one can be anonymously and namelessly a Christian in a non-Christian religion, is it so important to name God the way Christians do, to name the Trinity and Christ, and bother with evangelization and the church? Still, that does not completely explain why Rahner's theology had the negative impact it did on missionary activity, while Pius IX's teaching did not. Are they not both assertions of the bare possibility of the salvation of non-Christians? That is what Pius's assertion is. But Rahner's theory, grounded in his anthropology, rather introduced the idea that being an anonymous Christian is the default position for human beings. The infinite mystery of God has come so close to us transcendentally in grace that we are, as it were, already home. It does not matter that

35. Rahner, "Christianity and the Non-Christian Religions," 123–24.
36. Martin, *Will Many Be Saved?*, 107.

Rahner himself did not intend to unplug the missionary activity of the church. But in fact, that is what happened, and the popular reception of Rahner amounted to a view in which all religions are more or less equal as vehicles of salvation, even if not as adequate expressions of the truth of revelation.[37]

A third way to make it seem that belonging to the church makes no real difference before God is the soteriology of Hans Urs von Balthasar, who passionately defended the proposition that we may hope that all men may be saved.[38] His own hope for this was founded on his soteriology, according to which the alienation and "distance" that sin makes between the sinner and God is always already included in the greater inner-Trinitarian distance between Father and Son, who nonetheless remain one in the unity of the divine essence and in their mutual love for one another.[39] As it were, there is a more fundamental, more powerful distance installed in God by the Trinitarian processions than the distance sin effects. And if there remained some unforgiven and unreconciled sin in some creature, then the creature would turn out to be greater than God; the creature would turn out to be more powerful than God; the creature would turn out to be capable of making a more profound distinction and erect a greater "distance" than the divine distance between Father and Son. However far the sinner places himself from God, the incarnate Son of God can go farther to catch him up again; he can go farther because all the "distances" of whatever distinction whatsoever, including the distinction and distance of sin, are surpassed by the Trinitarian distance between Father and Son.

On this view, then, *not* to hope that all will be saved, will involve us in thinking contrary to God himself. And we may argue thus: if we can hope that all will be saved, then we must think that possible; it is therefore a *possible* good; and if we think that the all-powerful God will not realize this good, a good entirely possible for him to effect, a good touching the

---

37. Joseph Ratzinger criticizes Rahner for flattening out the differences between religions in *Truth and Tolerance*, 17. He offers a more general criticism of Rahner's theology of which "anonymous Christianity" is a part in *Principles of Catholic Theology*, 161–71.

38. Hans Urs von Balthasar, *Dare We Hope "That All Men Be Saved"?* with a *Short Discourse on Hell*, trans. David Kipp and Lothar Krauth (San Francisco, Calif.: Ignatius Press, 1988).

39. See, e.g., Hans Urs von Balthasar, *Theo-Drama: Theological Dramatic Theory*, vol. IV: *The Action*, trans. Graham Harrison (San Francisco, Calif.: Ignatius Press, 1994), 319–67.

eternal happiness of his own creatures, we turn him into a mere shadow of the God whose mercy, as we know, lasts for a thousand generations. As with Rahner, von Balthasar would be disturbed to think his hope that all may be saved, founded as it is on his inner-Trinitarian soteriology, takes the wind out of the sails of the church's missionary activity. But of course it does, and very much reduces the urgency of belonging to the church. Beside the three ways of relativizing the importance of belonging to the church advanced by Dupuis, Rahner, and von Balthasar, there is also one other factor that should be considered.

The course of post-Enlightenment thought in the West has been to make it ever more philosophically implausible, and ever more impolitic and impolite, to claim to know any moral or religious truth. I can know what feels right for me, but I cannot know what is true for everyone. In fact, the claim so to know such truths and to speak them as calling on all men to assent to them is a sort of violence. Did not conflicting claims about the supernatural lead to overt violence in the "wars of religion"?[40] And just in order to get rid of such violence inviting appeals to the supernatural, Europe needed first to get rid of appeals to the *natural*.[41] The positivism of Thomas Hobbes comes to the aid of those who wish to escape Christianity in all its forms. We know what the empirical sciences can tell us. But we do not know natures. And so we do not know the finalities of natures, even our own nature. And so we do not know even the natural moral law.

But absolute moral norms presuppose the knowledge of natures. And such knowledge is propaedeutic to recognizing supernatural claims on our nature by the God who made us. It is all one package. And whenever a Christian proposes either some universal norm of morality or the universal claim of the truth of the gospel, he denies the cogency of the Enlightenment denial of this package. He is close to practicing violence on Locke and Hobbes and all their intellectual heirs, which is most of the West today.

40. Rather was religion often hijacked for the interests of the budding nation-states of Europe; see David Bentley Hart, *Atheist Delusions: The Christian Revolution and Its Fashionable Enemies* (New Haven, Conn.: Yale University Press, 2009), chap. 8.

41. Pierre Manent, "Christianity and Democracy," in *Modern Liberty and Its Discontents*, ed. and trans. Daniel J. Mahoney and Paul Seaton (Lanham, Md.: Rowman and Littlefield, 1998), 97–115, at 101–3.

Christians feel this. They feel afraid to speak the gospel and what it requires publicly, which just is the task of evangelization. But thanks be to God, as Dupuis, Rahner, and von Balthasar assure us in despite of themselves, we do not have to worry about any soul's salvation no matter how far from the church it may be. It will be saved by some other way of salvation than Christianity (Dupuis). Or it will be anonymously Christian (Rahner). Or we have good and consoling hope that it will be saved, no matter how unlikely that may seem, because God has already reconciled all sinners to himself in virtue of the greater power of the mystery of the Trinity compared with the power of evil (von Balthasar). The various post-conciliar takes on the realization of salvation for all unstring the bow of evangelization, and the ordinary cowardice and laziness of Christians have their day.

Answering the Question

The true answer to the question of this section is that, to be sure, belonging to the church makes a huge difference to the prospects of our salvation before God, and makes a huge difference for those whom we love. There is first of all our dogmatic knowledge of this fact, insofar as we ask ourselves why God became man. Not for sorting out some minor misunderstanding. Not for undoing some penultimate evil. Rather, for conquering the radical hatred of God and his love induced by human pride, which is to say, for undoing sin, enmity with God (Rom 5:8, 8:7); and for overcoming the consequences of sin, death (Rom 6:23), and the everlasting death of hell.

The true answer supposes what the church has always supposed, that this overcoming of sin, death, and the devil happens in history, and only there, and is not the annunciation of an always already and eternally enacted drama of alienation and reconciliation, of obedience and humility, within God. The true answer therefore takes seriously the possibility of hell. The drama of human history is certainly made more dramatic by the divine call to a strictly supernatural end, where we are sons and daughters of God, brothers and sisters of Christ, and bound by the charity of the Holy Spirit to all who are saved: we play for stakes beyond any happiness we could possibly imagine we could acquire in this life. But also, the drama depends on our own free cooperation with grace. The freedom to cooperate or not, this is inalienable, and cannot be excised from our humanity in this life without our ceasing to be human.[42] We cannot possibly be everlastingly subject to the state of beatitude if we are not possibly everlastingly subject to the state of hell. Thus, that we can fail to cooperate is a real possibility, and persistence in such failure means eternal alienation from God, and a condition in which every man like us so alienated is our enemy, in an everlastingly antagonistic wailing and gnashing of teeth.

The gift of grace, the gift of God as friend, has to be able to be rejected, or else it is not a gift, and cannot be received as a gift. But the rejection does not mean annihilation, for while it is in our power to kill our body, it is not in our power to make our soul disappear, nor is it within the power of God as governed by the wisdom with which he has created us to dismantle it, for according to this wisdom the soul is a created but intrinsically everlasting testament to his own being and goodness. The soul is naturally immortal, and God does not wreck the natures he has created.[43]

The mission of Christ is therefore to save us from a really and truly possible-for-us hell and open for us the gates of heaven. This mission of Christ, however, includes and *cannot* be divorced from his establishment of the church. In entering our history just so as to reorient it and point it toward his Father, he necessarily makes those who believe in him the members of the body of which he is the head, and he necessarily erects a temporal temple of grace, the antechamber to the glory of the eternal tent, and he necessarily makes of his people the beautiful bride of the wedding of heaven. If we say that the church is not so important, then his mission is not important. The church just is the abiding availability of the merit of his cross, the truth about sin, the news about forgiveness, which we could have in no other way. The church is the only place where, in fact, we truly understand the gravity of sin and its damage to us made in the image of God and how it dishonors God and evacuates the creation of its meaning and purpose. And correlatively, it is the only place where we understand what the promise of glory entails, and how purely a gift of grace it is. Therefore, if we have any of our wits about us at all, we must do everything in our power to discern the true religion, and within Chris-

42. See the *Catechism of the Catholic Church*, no. 1033.
43. Aquinas, *ST* I, q. 75, a. 6.

tianity, to discern the place where the church of Christ abides, and once having figured that out, to become true and true ecclesial men and women, true and true persons who would give their life for the church even as did originally and foundationally Christ himself.

Second, there are some systematic considerations as well. For one thing, thinking of Rahner, there is the question of the dependence of our morally significant action on "categorical" knowledge, the conceptual knowledge of persons and objects within the world and of goods suitable for man to pursue and of virtues perfective of our nature. The transcendental exercise of our faculties of will and intellect is something deduced by Kant and his followers. It is an exercise we are not conscious of in the way we are conscious of the furniture in the room, the persons in line at the grocery checkout, the kinds of action that are friendly or hostile to other persons, and so on. But morally significant action is conscious action. It is action informed by conscious knowledge of the object of the act—what we are doing—and the end for which we are acting, that is, why we are doing it.[44] Apart from acts of justice, temperance, courage, and so on informed by such knowledge, there is no moral progress and we are not in moral motion. Therefore, to be on the road to salvation, we have to be in the truth made known to us in the gospel. We have to be in this truth to know the way to the life, to Christ who is all three (Jn 14:6). We are in this truth fully only insofar as we know and assent to the articles of the creed. We are not fully in it if all we know is that God exists and that he rewards those who seek him. It is a good thing to know he exists and rewards those who seek him, but it is not knowing the way to seek him, and it does not put us on the way, which is Christ and him alone.

Our responses to finite goods surely depend on our nature as oriented to an infinite horizon of truth and goodness, and in fact to the good God. There are no responses to participated goods known as good unless we are ordered to the unparticipated, infinite good. And that is part of the truth of working out the transcendental conditions of the possibility of our morally significant action as we engage the goods and persons and respond to the personal actions we encounter throughout the day.

---

44. See Aquinas, *ST* I-II, q. 18, aa. 2 and 4. See at length Michael Sherwin, *By Knowledge and By Love: Charity and Knowledge in the Moral Theology of St. Thomas Aquinas* (Washington, D.C.: The Catholic University of America Press, 2005).

But not a single one of these responses to created goods just as such and in their determinate "categorical" form is a response to the infinite good of God himself, and that is so even if I risk my own bodily good for the good, bodily or spiritual, of another human person. Nor does a constant supernatural presence of God to us in a constant offer of grace, Rahner's "supernatural existential," make it so. No, to respond to God, I have to think of God. To love *him*, I have to know *him*, not transcendentally, but *categorically*, conceptually.[45] Doubtless the Christian wants his engagements with all persons to be governed by godly charity. But this will be so only if he knows the first of the two great commandments, and puts everything he does—knowingly, consciously—under its aegis. Morally and religiously perfective responses to God are responses to God known as God; they are not some transcendentally automatic machinery clicking and clacking away behind our engagements with the persons and things of the world. Where everything is baptized as a response to God, baptism ceases to consecrate anything and loses any meaning.

Doubtless it is difficult, as the church has always recognized, to come to a true knowledge of God apart from revelation. In the absence of revelation, we can be deceived by the devil and exchange the truth about God for a lie and worship the creature instead of the creator (Rom 1:21, 25). The Council teaches, in fact that this "more often" happens than not (*Lumen Gentium*, no. 16). And in the modern world, it adds that without God, some are tempted to despair. As neither of these states of affairs conduces to salvation, the Council's teaching in fact provokes a kind of urgency for the work of evangelization, and not the confident expectation that most men will be saved apart from the gospel and a conscious response to it.[46] Thus, notwithstanding the fact that grace is offered to every man, even those who do not know God, the Council is saying that the conditions favoring *cooperation* with that grace often do not exist.[47]

---

45. Aquinas, *ST* II-II, q. 1, aa. 2 and 7. We must believe at least that God exists and that he cares for us, following Heb 11:6.

46. Martin, *Will Many Be Saved?*, 107, observes that while Rahner often appeals to *Lumen Gentium*, no. 16, the first and second part of it, he never mentions the third part on the deformation that sin works in non-Christian religious apprehension. In the end, the "categorical" is just not very important for him.

47. For the importance of reviving the distinction between operative and cooperative grace in thinking things through here, see White, "The Universal Mediation of Christ," 177–98.

If to Rahner it must be said that we have to have categorical knowledge of God to make morally and religiously significant responses to him, then in the second place and to Dupuis, it must be said that we have to have the *right* categories to think of God and refer ourselves and our actions to him. The correct categories are the revealed ones. There are the ones of natural knowledge, too, worked out preeminently in our experience of the moral law and our conscience, and especially, alas, our experience of moral failure. But ordinarily for most men, this natural knowledge has to be corrected by revelation. The revealed concepts and categories that disclose the nature of divinity and the divine Persons to us have a shape to them, however, a shape that excludes other shapes. The God of Moses is not Baal or Moloch or Aristotle's first unmoved mover. The Father of our Lord Jesus Christ is not Jupiter or Saturn. The Trinity is not the first three hypostases of Plotinus, or the triad of Brahma, Vishnu, and Shiva. The names matter, for they name quite incompatible ways of thinking about divinity. And this seems to stand in the way of finding in Jacques Dupuis's proposals a satisfying way to relate non-Christian religions to Christianity.

There is a third and last systematic remark to make *apropos* of von Balthasar. Beyond whatever Trinitarian problems there are in his soteriology which allows us to hope that a sinful "no" may be turned into an acceptable "yes," there is a problem for theological anthropology. The arena in which salvation is won or lost is history, although it seems hardly necessary to say this to von Balthasar. But then again, it is to be emphasized that history is for *this* life. After this life, there is no history, not because of some arbitrary decree of God closing the shop for business at the end of the day, but because of the nature of man. We must not think of ourselves after death as living the way the movies depict souls after death, as having moved to a more ethereal neighborhood and continuing to be able to act and choose. Choice is for this life, and changing choices, rechoosing, is bound up with changeable emotions ordered to different ends differently conceived. This depends on bodiliness.[48] Choice depends on our affec-

---

48. For the impossibility of postmortem change of mind or "conversion" for those alienated from God, see Aquinas, *Summa Contra Gentiles* IV.95, trans. Charles J. O'Neil (Notre Dame, Ind.: University of Notre Dame Press, 1975). Change of mind is possible in this life, but it is a possibility bound up with changeable emotions and dispositions unto a determinate end, which depend on

tive responses to things and persons and courses of action. And affectivity is a conjoint affair of body and soul. Just as the poor souls in purgatory are passive, and cannot place either sinful or meritorious acts, so also are those worthy of damnation similarly passive. Their final choice of their end has been made.

Strictly, von Balthasar envisages a final choice to be made in death or at death, and not after it.[49] Whether at death or (for other theologians) after death, the question is why God cannot supply some kind of help to enable those worthy of damnation to choose again. As long as we are not thinking of the ordered, orderly power of God, we may suppose that God can do whatever contains no internal contradiction. But the price of fixing things in this way, envisioning a choice quite unlike the choices of this life, is that the very natures God creates seem to lose density and reality. They never are let to operate in the way for which they were designed, and designed by … well, God himself. These are natures, after all, created in the wisdom of God. Fixing up the nature of a person so he can say "yes" even though, by the due course of his life, and according to the capacity of its nature, he said what would naturally be a final "no" makes what is supposed to be dramatic into a nondrama, a sort of fantasy land where there are no rules because there are no natures and creation was not really serious.

If the proposals of Rahner, Dupuis, and von Balthasar are unsatisfactory for thinking about what difference it makes to belong to the church, then a certain urgency returns to our thinking about our own salvation and the salvation of those we love and the salvation of those we do not know but should be concerned about if we take Matthew 28:18 seriously. We have to get on Christ's way. For of course it makes a difference to our own soul's salvation insofar as we have access to, understand, and share in the sacraments knowledgeably and with devotion. They give grace. They give it certainly. If we think that we do not need grace or the certain assurance of how to avail ourselves of it, we are not thinking that God is calling us to an end, himself, above what we could naturally attain to.

<hr/>

bodiliness. See John Lamont, "The Justice and Goodness of Hell," *Faith and Philosophy* 28 (2011): 152–73, at 167–68.

49. See Joshua Brotherton, "The Possibility of Universal Conversion in Death: Temporality, Annihilation, and Grace," *Modern Theology* 32 (2016): 307–24.

And of course it makes a difference to our own soul's salvation in accordance with how we understand the natural moral law and its demands, which we are unlikely to do fully and accurately while still in our sin, and it makes a difference in accordance with how we know the demands of gospel charity, the intelligibility of which we cannot grasp until we know the condescension of God and the work of Christ. And of course it makes a difference to our own soul's salvation in accordance with how we cooperate with grace and install the virtues God offers us with this grace and so drive out spiritual laziness, overcome unchastity, depotentiate pride and vanity, hate lies, and stand up to the devil.

The dogmatic and systematic reflections add up: we know that the drama of salvation is so desperate that it called for its best remedy what only the divine wisdom could plan and what only the divine power could execute, namely the death and resurrection of his incarnate Son; and we know theologically and anthropologically that our chances of knowing God's goodness and his providence easily and accurately apart from the gospel are slight and that our chances of conforming ourselves to the divine will and cooperating with a real but only secretly given grace are similarly slight; and we know, finally, that as far as our best lights give us to see, we finish our freedom and our destiny for good or for ill in this life, which is short, and that if there is an acceptable time, it is now, and if there is a day of salvation, it is today (2 Cor 6:2). So, yes, belonging to the church makes a real difference to the prospect of our salvation. And the salvation of those we love. And the salvation of all those to whom the church is sent to preach and baptize.

As for non-Christians who remain non-Christians, the Council certainly implies that there is some role the church plays in their salvation by asserting the possibility of their salvation (*Lumen Gentium*, no. 16) and declaring the church to be the universal sacrament of salvation (no. 48). Before addressing that question head-on, however, account should be taken of an important conditioning factor of the church's salvific activity, and that is her relation to the world and the political order.

Church and World

The Tension between Church and World

In 1935, in a chapter entitled "The Burden of the Church," Anscar Vonier wrote in his *The Spirit and the Bride* that if being a Christian did not require us to live with our brothers in Christ, and that if it is enough to be a spiritual Christian, mystically and invisibly with Christ, then being a Christian would provoke no reaction or resentment or resistance in the world.[50] But, he continued: "let there be a group of men to whom the same truths concerning Christ are a bond of unity, are as the breath of life, then the benevolent tolerance of the outsider will suddenly become fierce enmity." Once the world realizes that the church is "one compact spiritual society," "an organized force," there will be hostility and, betimes, persecution. "It is certain that at no time, even in the days of Nero, would Christians have been persecuted if they had not been dreaded, if they had not stood in the way of someone's ambition or folly."[51] The opprobrium of the world is provoked all the more when it is realized that "the Christian attributes to his Church a sort of divinity which he would never dare to arrogate to himself … His Church is to him an absolute reality, though he himself may be imperfect and incomplete in grace."[52] Whence the great scandal, furthermore, in that while the world may credit this or that or the other Christian with leading a holy life, the church herself will be seen to be a great failure, "full of all abominations," and "no one will be found, in these days, outside Catholicism, who will speak well of the Church."[53]

So, whatever society or state into which the church is introduced fears it as pretending to be an "absolute reality," public and organized, and mocks it, as failing to live up to its own self-professed obligations. Writing in 2017, Thomas Joseph White makes a similar observation: "The ancient Roman emperors who killed the Christians were prescient: when Christian revelation is taken seriously, it does change everything. Because human culture functions concretely under the effects of original and per-

50. Vonier, *Spirit and the Bride*, 3.
51. Ibid., 4.
52. Ibid., 5.
53. Ibid., 5–6.

sonal sin, there are many forms of collective blindness operative at the heart of every human society, no matter how noble or venerable."[54] Such tension can be observed throughout history, not least in the Christian age of Europe (remember Frederick II and Philip the Fair), especially in the nineteenth century in Europe (e.g., Emperor Joseph II of Austria), now in the twenty-first century in China, and also in the United States, where there are constant conflicts over legalized abortion, the nature of marriage, and the requirements of sexual morality. Moreover, if the church finds herself ever more alienated not only from what the liberal modern state permits, but also from what many insist must be agreed upon by all its citizens, then failure so to agree publicly may be counted by some as some form of violence. We meet once again the tension between modern Western society and the church's articulation of the natural law and "absolute norms" of morality.

An Unavoidable Tension

The tension between the church and the world is unavoidable, for the world is in such a condition—the condition of the Fall—that we must expect the church to come into conflict with it. In the first place, if we take "world" in its Johannine sense, then we refer to something touched by sin, as was just mentioned. The world in this sense is not simply somewhat mangled in its social orderings, a place where men *de facto* deform the image of God in which they were created. This "world" is in fact more actively and energetically opposed to Christ and therefore to the church than we can comfortably acknowledge today. The words of the Lord in John 15:18, however, are explicit: "If the world hates you, know that it has hated me before it hated you." And in the next verse: "I chose you out of the world, therefore the world hates you."

In the second place, there is the church's obligation by divine law to evangelize and so to publish revealed truth and establish itself in every land and nation. It is an obligation, as it were, to make itself obnoxious to the world just insofar as the world is the empire of Satan. Indeed, evan-

---

54. Thomas Joseph White, OP, *The Light of Christ: An Introduction to Catholicism* (Washington, D.C.: The Catholic University of America Press, 2017), 225.

gelizing and establishing itself is not, as it were, a negotiable item in the church's inventory of duties. "Go, therefore ..."

Just because this obligation is founded in divine positive law, the law given by Christ to declare the truth, it engages and satisfies the corresponding natural law implanted in every man to seek the truth, especially the truth concerning God.[55] And just because of this natural law obliging man to *seek* the truth about God, he has a natural right to listen to the evangelist and to help construct that freely constituted organization— the church—that answers to and fulfills his natural duty.[56] This freedom belongs both to individuals and to the communities they have also a right to form.[57]

In turn, the state is obliged by the same natural law to pose no impediment either to evangelist and church or to those who seek the truth with a sincere heart.[58] Insofar as society and the state recognize the right of all men to seek the truth according to their own lights, things are happy. But there have been, and are, many places where this is not the case, for instance, China and Saudi Arabia and many lands where Islamic law denies this right.

It is also true that the state just as such has an obligation to recognize and discharge its *own* duty to God, to recognize his existence and honor him by obeying the natural law, as St. Augustine maintained in *The City of God*, and as the church still continues to teach.[59] Religious matters and all the more matters of the true religion belong to the public square and should be publicly celebrated, despite the new arrangement prosecuted by the modern liberal state. Catholics should remember their history and those political orders, just and humane and by no means in principle oppressive of the rights of others, that were legally and officially Catholic. This is not a teaching that is likely to be put into effect in the modern

---

55. Aquinas, *ST* I-II, q. 94, a. 2. See Cajetan Cuddy, OP, "Thomas Aquinas on the Bible and Morality: The Sacred Scriptures, the Natural Law, and the Hermeneutic of Continuity," in *Toward a Biblical Thomism: Thomas Aquinas and the Renewal of Biblical Theology*, ed. Piotr Roszak and Jörgen Vijgen (Pamplona: Eunsa, 2018), 173–98.

56. See *Dignitatis Humanae*, no. 3.

57. Ibid., no. 4. See White, *The Light of Christ*, 258.

58. *Dignitatis Humanae*, nos. 4 and 6.

59. Ibid., no. 3. See Augustine, *The City of God* XIX.23, esp. 705–6.

West any time soon. But the teaching is important in thinking out fully the relations of church and state. Part of what the state owes in justice to God is to respect the right of its people to make Catholicism the official or at least privileged religion of the polity, should circumstances warrant, without prejudice to the religious freedom of all the citizens.[60]

Contemporary Prospects

At the time of the Second Vatican Council, it was possible to envisage a close cooperation between the church and modern liberal states insofar as both recognized the natural rights of men and the common good of society, part of which consists in seeking the truth about God, and also insofar as both favored those citizens who sought and found it. This prospect was enshrined in *Gaudium et Spes*. Since the Council, the world has gone in an ever more secular way, where the church and modern Western states disagree even over the nature of such basic institutions as marriage.[61] The church in such states may expect her right to proclaim the moral truth about such things as marriage and sexual morality increasingly disparaged and even denied, if not by law then at least by custom.

In other lands, however, there is a greater appreciation and recognition of the natural law, and the state comes to the defense of marriage and sexual morality. This is true, for instance, in some places in Africa. Here, the church can envisage a better prospect than seems to be in view in Europe and North America, and there is a happier prospect for public cooperation of the church with the state for the common good of society.

The Salvation of Non-Christians

In one way, it is very obvious what the role of the church is in the salvation of non-Christians. The church offers prayers for them, especially the sacrifice of the Mass. So Pius XII in *Mystici Corporis* (par. 44):

---

60. See *Dignitatis Humanae*, no. 6, and White, *The Light of Christ*, 253. For the idea of a "secular Christendom," see Journet, *The Church of the Word Incarnate*, 1:214–20.

61. See Thomas Joseph White, OP, "Gaudium et Spes," in *The Reception of Vatican II*, edited by Matthew L. Lamb and Matthew Levering (Oxford: Oxford University Press, 2017), 113–43, esp. 123–25 and 134–35.

Our Savior ... wills to be helped by the members of His Body in carrying out the work of redemption. That is not because He is indigent and weak, but rather because He has so willed it for the greater glory of His spotless Spouse. Dying on the Cross He left to His Church the immense treasury of the Redemption, towards which she contributed nothing. But when those graces come to be distributed, not only does He share this work of sanctification with His Church, but He wills that in some way it be due to her action. This is a deep mystery, and an inexhaustible subject of meditation, that the salvation of many depends on the prayers and voluntary penances which the members of the Mystical Body of Jesus Christ offer for this intention and on the cooperation of pastors of souls and of the faithful, especially of fathers and mothers of families, a cooperation which they must offer to our Divine Savior as though they were His associates.

In the Fourth Eucharistic Prayer, there is offered to God the body and blood of the Lord, the acceptable sacrifice, "which brings salvation to the whole world." It is offered not just for the entire people of God but "for all who seek you with a sincere heart." It is not just the priest who offers, of course, but the church.

In the offering of the Mass, as we saw in chapter 8, the church actualizes her deepest reality, and brings to the fore her truest identity. She "cooperates" with Christ for the salvation of many, as Pius puts it. How can this cooperation be more exactly specified? How more exactly does the mission of the church share in and actualize the mission of Christ? One possible way was noted above when magisterial teachings on this issue were reported. The universal mediation of the humanity of Christ was there acknowledged. If he uses good things and true things in non-Christian religions to effect salvation, however, he must nonetheless do so as head of the church. There is also another way.

Joseph Ratzinger addressed this issue in a remarkable essay some sixty years ago.[62] The church shares in the mission of Christ insofar as Christ's mission itself is one of vicarious representation. Just as Christ identifies himself with the Suffering Servant of Isaiah, and takes up a "pro-existence" in suffering unto God for the salvation of all who are being saved, so also must the church. This "pro-existence" is already verified in Abraham and Moses in the Old Testament. Moses stands for the righteous and

62. Joseph Ratzinger, "Vicarious Representation," trans. Jared Wicks, SJ, in *Letter & Spirit* 7 (2011): 209–22.

risks his friendship with God to turn away his wrath from the cities of the plain (Gn 18). Moses offers himself in place of the people after their apostasy at Sinai (Ex 32:32). This way of existence unto God and for his people is appropriated by Elijah on Mt. Horeb/Sinai (1 Kgs 19). Most signally, this role of representing and standing in for the sinful multitude, the role of the Suffering Servant, defines Jesus from the outset of his mission at his baptism (Mk 1:11); it is reasserted at the transfiguration (Mk 9:7), where he discusses his passion with Moses and Elijah (Lk 9:31); it is repeated at the Last Supper (Mk 14:23–24) and so interprets Calvary. It is acknowledged by St. Paul when he characterizes Christ as the second Adam (Rom 5:12–21; 1 Cor 15:45–49).

Ratzinger maintains that this reality of vicarious representation is the key to understanding both the mission of the church and her absolute character. If there are many who are saved beyond the visible confines of Christianity, they are not saved apart from the church, for her mission is simply the extension of Christ's, and she takes on this mission when she eats the body and drinks the blood.[63] When the Lord says "Do this!," he means to include his very action of laying down one's life for others. This is to say that she cannot realize her own reality as church without being for others, the others that really are other and not Christian, but whom she can represent, just as the Lord represented Christians "while we were yet in our sins" (Rom 5:8). So also, in Romans 9–11, Israel and the church of the Gentiles are not isolated entities, but affect one another, and what one does serves to the salvation of the other.

What goes for the church goes for the individual Christian. St. Paul expressly takes on this "pro-existence" in Romans 9:3: "For I could wish that I myself were accursed and cut off from Christ for the sake of my brethren." And "if one man has died for all, then all have died" (2 Cor 5:14). It was argued above that belonging to the church gives the greatest advantage for our own hope of salvation, and this is true. But we cannot wholly belong to the church and take on her identity without taking on the same kind of "pro-existence," without being ourselves ready vicariously to represent and so to suffer in the world for others. This, Ratzinger thinks, is a more just solution to the question of the salvation

63. Ibid., 213.

of non-Christians that imputing to them some secret desire, unknown to themselves, for Christianity.

This hope for others does not obviate the responsibility that others have to seek the truth and do it, freely to live for God according to their lights. But it makes less urgent the theoretical task of figuring out the relations of other religions to Christianity or how non-Christian religious practices lead to Christian salvation and returns us to the practical task of our own Christian living.

Taking on this identity of vicarious representation, "one will thereby understand in a fresh way the meaning of the church's absolute value and how it is strictly necessary for salvation. One will realize that being Christian is being-for-the-others and one does not have to deny that in many respects this is a burden, which though is the holy burden of serving humanity as a whole."[64] And again:

For the church to be the means of salvation for all, it does not have to extend itself visibly to all, but has instead its essential role in following Christ, who is uniquely "the one," and therein the church is the little flock, through which God however intends to save "the man." The church's service is not carried out *by* all human beings, but is indeed carried out *for* all of them.[65]

The fact that the individual Christian and the church as a whole share in the redemptive work of Christ by representing all men in suffering and suffering for all men is moreover a sort of demonstration of the truth of Christianity, as it shows it to fulfill what we should expect to see in the religious economy of the world and even before we consider the word of Christian revelation. The work of vicarious suffering does not replace the work of evangelization and is rather a sort of proof of the truth of the gospel message: the life of the messenger is congruent with the content of the message. Where this is not the case, the message cannot be believed.

Cardinal Newman thought it a law inscribed within human nature and demonstrated in the course of the world that we are indeed called on "to bear one another's burdens." This does not obviate the incommunicable responsibility each man must take for his own conduct. "The final burden of responsibility when we are called to judgment is our own,"

64. Ibid., 218.
65. Ibid.

he writes.[66] But there is a "vicarious principle" at work in the world, the principle of representation in Ratzinger's words, such that we who are sinners and needy depend on the good works of good men done for us even unbeknownst to us. Among the means "by which we are prepared for that judgment are the exertions and pains taken in our behalf by others."[67] "We all suffer for each other, and gain by each other's sufferings; for man never stands alone here, though he will stand by himself one day hereafter; but here he is a social being, and goes forward to his long home as one of a large company."[68] What Christianity adds to this law of vicarious suffering and representation is that now we know whose law it is and where it is perfectly fulfilled. "Bear one another's burdens," St. Paul says, "and so fulfill the law of Christ" (Gal 6:2).

Christians and the church save the world, insofar as they do, by praying for and by suffering for it. We should expect no other answer, so Christological, so evangelical, as it is. This does not tell us how many will be saved. It only specifies how the church shares in the work of the salvation of non-Christians.

66. Newman, *Grammar of Assent*, 261 (405).
67. Ibid.
68. Ibid., 261 (406).

CHAPTER 15

THE HEAVENLY CITY

In chapter 3, Jesus' preaching of the kingdom was described as a church-founding action. In chapter 10, the church was described, following *Lumen Gentium*, no. 1, as a sign and instrument of union with God and of the unity of the human race. If the fullness of the kingdom of God means union with God in glory together with the unity of all those predestined to salvation with one another, then we can take the church now as a sacrament of the kingdom. The church is an imperfect sign of the kingdom, especially insofar as on her pilgrim way her members are sinful, and yet still she is an instrument of the salvation of those who will belong to the kingdom eternally.

Even if the church is but an imperfect sign of the kingdom, however, she nevertheless anticipates the nature of the kingdom in a remarkable way, a way that tells us something of the final destiny of man. This anticipation has already been registered in what has been covered in this book, especially in chapters 6, 8, 11, and 13. According to chapter 6, the Holy Spirit dwells in each Christian as in a temple and in the community of Christians as in a temple, and this gives the church an identity which is more than moral, more than an agreement of minds and hearts. Such a union is certainly "personal." But the union of the church is personal in a more intense way, in a supernatural way. It is personal insofar as it unites persons, to be sure; it is personal, because the unity of these persons *is* a Person. In chapter 8, the unity of the body of Christ was once again seen to be more than moral. It is mystical, and its superpersonal character relative to its members is located in Christ, the head, such that by his grace all have his mind and imitate his charity. In chapter 11, the more-than-moral unity of the church was manifest insofar as, according to *Lumen Gentium*, no. 8, the church of Christ is said to subsist in the Catholic church. In this way, she possesses a mode of being like that of an agent or person. The understanding of her Marian motherhood (chapter 7) is better achieved. And in chapter 13, this kind of more than moral, superpersonal because supernatural, identity of the church in Christ through the Spirit was the solution to the question of the agency of the church as such in giving grace through the sacraments as well as in authoritatively guarding and unfolding the truth of the gospel. Here, the agency of the church is especially exercised on her behalf by the hierarchy.

It is just this kind of supernatural union, a union that is *of* persons, above *human* persons but still personal with the personal reality of the *divine* Persons, that characterizes the kingdom of God, the kingdom of heaven—the kingdom of our final destiny. But it is this kind of union that the church realizes now in time, and so even now, we have a promise and foretaste of our heavenly estate. This is not a church that reason could anticipate (chapter 1), but it is a church in which the splendor of man's conscience is guarded and shines out.

The supernatural union of the final kingdom, the kingdom of heaven, is a properly Trinitarian union, and in three ways. First, it is Trinitarian in virtue of the Holy Spirit, who plays the same role in the kingdom as he does in the Trinity itself. In the kingdom, the Holy Spirit unites created persons to one another by their love and by dwelling in them in the same way as he unites Father and Son in the Trinity. Second, it is Trinitarian in virtue of the Word, who by his incarnation will give us all to share in the divine Wisdom insofar as we behold it in vision. And this Wisdom, spoken by the Father in begetting his Son, will eternally and perfectly direct the drive of Christian love under the impulse of the Spirit. Third, it is Trinitarian in virtue of the unity of Father, Son, and Spirit in one essence, which, when the persons dwell in us when we dwell in our heavenly mansions, gives our natural union to one another as human beings a more than natural guarantee.[1] The union is Trinitarian because that is the original union of Persons, and the last union than which there is no better, and persons made in the image of God do not find what they were made for until they perfectly imitate it by sharing in the knowledge and love of God insofar as it is a knowledge and love that flower in Word and Spirit.

But as the previously mentioned chapters give us to know, the church realizes this Trinitarian union in some measure even now. And she must share in it, as she is the instrument by which it is propagated in time so as to include all who are being saved. In this light, moreover, the unity of the divine plan of salvation is apparent. It is a unity the beauty of which makes the act of faith now almost spontaneous and renders charity easy. For in the first place, the procession of the Son from the Father and of the Spirit from both is the model of the procession of the world from God in wisdom and love. The created world in its original constitution imitates the procession of Son and Spirit and is therefore fitted to be the place of the introduction of Son and Spirit into the world through their missions. The mission of the Son achieves our redemption through the humanity of Jesus. The mission of the Spirit completes the work of Christ by dwelling in our hearts with the gifts of grace and charity Christ merited. The Trinity is the term from which the world and all its wonders comes forth in the orders both of creation and of salvation.

Likewise, in the second place, the Trinity is the term to which all is ordered, where those who are saved share in the life of the Trinity, conformed to the Son and moved by the Spirit in all their knowledge and love both of God and of one another, as has been pointed out in these concluding pages.[2] Also, in the third place, the Trinitarian order of distinction in unity, the sort of union of persons that is original in the uncreated God, this order marks the pattern and is the very way the pilgrim church makes her way toward God. In making our way to heaven, we become more personal insofar as we let ourselves be completed in the

---

1. See Henri de Lubac, SJ, *Catholicism: Christ and the Common Destiny of Man*, trans. Lancelot C. Sheppard and Sister Elizabeth Englund, OCD (San Francisco, Calif.: Ignatius Press, 1988), 112–19.

2. For the *exitus-reditus* pattern of creation and its return to God based on the divine processions of Son and Spirit and their missions in the economy of salvation according to Aquinas, see Dominic Legge, OP, *The Trinitarian Christology of St. Thomas Aquinas* (Oxford: Oxford University Press, 2016), 12–14.

order of knowledge by sharing the mind of Christ and in the order of love by acting always in the charity of the Holy Spirit. The world is the place for making persons perfect because it is the place where they get bound up with the divine Persons. We do this, however, just insofar as we are members of the body of Christ (chapter 8), Marian in our relation to Christ (chapter 7) and so holy (chapter 12), insofar as we are stones in the temple built by the Messiah (chapter 6), and so belong to the messianic people (chapter 5). We do this, in other words, insofar as we belong to the church.

The heavenly and the earthly realization of Trinitarian union shared out to created persons in the kingdom and the church is so much the same thing that in this life longing for heaven is longing for the perfection of the church, and fear of final loss is fear of losing the charity that makes the church one. The ancient hymn, *Urbs beata Jerusalem*, celebrates both together.

> Blessed City, Heavenly Salem,
> Vision dear of Peace and Love,
> Who, of living stones upbuilded,
> Art the joy of Heav'n above,
> And, with angel cohorts circled,
> As a Bride to earth dost move!
> Many a blow and biting sculpture
> Polish'd well those stones elect,
> In their places now compacted
> By the Heavenly Architect,
> Who therewith hath will'd for ever
> That His Palace should be deck'd.
> Christ is made the sure Foundation,
> And the precious Corner-stone,
> Who, the two-fold walls surmounting,
> Binds them closely into one:
> Holy Sion's help for ever,
> And her confidence alone.[3]

---

3. This is the John Mason Neale translation.

SELECTED BIBLIOGRAPHY

Achtemeier, Elizabeth. "Exchanging God for 'No Gods': A Discussion of Female Language for God." In *Speaking the Christian God: The Holy Trinity and the Challenge of Feminism*, edited by Alvin F. Kimel, Jr., 1–16. Grand Rapids, Mich.: Eerdmans, 1992.

Aquinas, Thomas. *Scriptum Super Libros Sententiarum*. Edited by P. Mandonnet. 4 vols. Paris: Lethielleux, 1929–47.

———. *Summa Theologica*. Translated by the English Dominican Province. 5 vols. New York: Benziger Bros., 1948.

———. *Quaestiones Disputatae de Potentia Dei*. In *Quaestiones Disputatae*, vol. 2. Edited by P. Bazzi, M. Calcaterra, et al. Rome: Marietti, 1949.

———. *Quaestiones Disputatae de Veritate*. In *Quaestiones Disputatae*, vol. 1. Edited by Raymond Spiazzi, OP. Rome: Marietti, 1949.

———. *Lectura super Evangelium S. Ioannis*. Edited by R. Cai, OP. Rome: Marietti, 1952.

———. *Summa theologiae*. Torino: Marietti, 1952.

———. *Super Epistolas S. Pauli Lectura*. 2 vols. Edited by R. Cai. Eighth edition. Rome: Marietti, 1953.

———. "In salutationem angelicam exposition." In his *Opuscula Theologica*, vol. 2: *De re spirituali*. Edited by M. Calcaterra. Rome: Marietti, 1954.

———. *In Librum de Causis Expositio*. Edited by Ceslas Pera, OP. Turin: Marietti, 1955.

———. *Commentary on Saint Paul's Epistle to the Ephesians*. Translated by Matthew Lamb. Albany, N.Y.: Magi Books, 1966.

———. *Summa Contra Gentiles*. Book IV. Translated by Charles J. O'Neil. Notre Dame, Ind.: University of Notre Dame Press, 1975.

———. *Commentary on the Gospel of John*. Translated by James A. Weisheipl, OP, and Fabian R. Larcher, OP. Albany, N.Y.: Magi Books, 1980.

Aristotle. *The Basic Works of Aristotle*. Edited by Richard McKeon. New York: Random House, 1947.

Armitage, J. Mark. "Why Didn't Jesus Write a Book? Aquinas on the Teaching of Christ." *New Blackfriars* 89, no. 10 (2008): 337–53.

Auer, Johann. *The Church: The Universal Sacrament of Salvation.* Translated by Michael Waldstein. Washington, D.C.: The Catholic University of America Press, 1993.

Augustine. *The City of God.* Translated by Marcus Dods. New York: Modern Library, 1950.

———. *Holy Virginity.* Translated by John McQuade, SM. In *Saint Augustine: Treatises on Various Subjects.* FOTC 27. Edited by Roy J. Deferrari. Washington, D.C.: The Catholic University of America Press, 1955.

———. *The Teacher.* Translated by Robert Russell, OSA. FOTC 59. Washington, D.C.: The Catholic University of America Press, 1968.

———. *Tractates on the Gospel of John.* In Nicene and Post-Nicene Fathers (First Series) 7, edited by Philip Schaff. Grand Rapids, Mich.: Eerdmans, 1986.

———. *Essential Sermons.* Translated by Edmund Hill, OP. Hyde Park, N.Y.: New City Press, 2007.

———. *The Trinity.* Second edition. Translated by Edmund Hill, OP. Hyde Park, N.Y.: New City Press, 2012.

Balthasar, Hans Urs von. *The Christian State of Life.* Translated by Sister Mary Frances McCarthy. San Francisco, Calif.: Ignatius Press, 1987.

———. *Dare We Hope "That All Men Be Saved"?* with a *Short Discourse on Hell.* Translated by David Kipp and Lothar Krauth. San Francisco, Calif.: Ignatius Press, 1988.

———. *Theo-Drama: Theological Dramatic Theory*, vol. III: *Dramatis Personae: Persons in Christ.* Translated by Graham Harrison. San Francisco, Calif.: Ignatius Press, 1992.

———. *Theo-Drama: Theological Dramatic Theory*, vol. IV: *The Action.* Translated by Graham Harrison. San Francisco, Calif.: Ignatius Press, 1994.

Barton, John. "Biblical Studies." In *The Blackwell Companion to Modern Theology*, edited by Gareth Jones, 18–33. Oxford: Blackwell, 2007.

Bauckham, Richard. *Jesus and the Eyewitnesses: The Gospels as Eyewitness Testimony.* Grand Rapids, Mich.: Eerdmans, 2006.

———. *Jesus: A Very Short Introduction.* Oxford: Oxford University Press, 2011.

Bauerschmidt, Frederick. *Thomas Aquinas: Faith, Reason, and Following Christ.* Oxford: Oxford University Press, 2013.

Beale, G. K. *The Temple and the Church's Mission: A Biblical Theology of the Dwelling Place of God.* Downers Grove, Ill.: InterVarsity Press, 2004.

Becker, Karl, SJ. "The Church and Vatican II's *'Subsistit in'* Terminology." *Origins* 35, no. 32 (January 19, 2006): 514–22.

Bellarmine, Robert. *De controversiis Christianae fidei adversus hujus temporis haereticos.* Tomus secundus. *Prima controversia generalis de conciliis et Ecclesia militante. Liber Tertius, de Ecclesia militante.* Rome: Ex typographia Giunchi et Menicanti, 1836.

Benoît, Pierre, OP. "Body, Head and *Pleroma* in the Epistles of the Captivity." In his *Jesus and the Gospel*, translated by Benet Weatherhead, 2:51–92. New York: Herder and Herder, 1973.

————. "Reflections on 'Formgeschichtliche Methode.'" In his *Jesus and the Gospel*, translated by Benet Weatherhead, 1:11–45. New York: Herder and Herder, 1973.

Bergsma, John, and Brant Pitre. *A Catholic Introduction to the Bible: The Old Testament*. San Francisco, Calif.: Ignatius Press, 2018.

Blankenhorn, Bernhard, OP. "The Instrumental Causality of the Sacraments: Thomas Aquinas and Louis-Marie Chauvet." *Nova et Vetera* (English edition) 4, no. 2 (2006): 255–93.

————. "The Place of Romans 6 in Aquinas's Doctrine of Sacramental Causality: A Balance of History and Metaphysics." In *Ressourcement Thomism: Sacred Doctrine, the Sacraments, and the Moral Life*, edited by Reinhard Hütter and Matthew Levering, 136–49. Washington, D.C.: The Catholic University of America Press, 2010.

Bornkamm, Günther. "MUSTERION." In *Theological Dictionary of the New Testament*, vol. 4. Edited by Gerhard Kittel. Grand Rapids, Mich.: Eerdmans, 1965.

Bouyer, Louis. *The Church of God: Body of Christ and Temple of the Spirit*. Translated by Charles Underhill Quinn. Chicago: Franciscan Herald Press, 1982.

————. *Rite and Man: Natural Sacredness and Christian Liturgy*. Translated by M. Joseph Costelloe, SJ. Notre Dame, Ind.: University of Notre Dame Press, 1963.

Brotherton, Joshua. "The Possibility of Universal Conversion in Death: Temporality, Annihilation, and Grace." *Modern Theology* 32 (2016): 307–24.

Burridge, Richard. *What Are the Gospels? A Comparison with Graeco-Roman Biography*. Cambridge: Cambridge University Press, 1992.

Calvin, John. *Institutes of the Christian Religion*. 2 vols. Seventh edition. Translated by John Allen. Philadelphia: Presbyterian Board of Christian Education, 1936.

Carroll, E. R. "Mary, Blessed Virgin, II: Mary, Blessed Virgin, Devotion to." *New Catholic Encyclopedia*, 9:364b–368a. Second edition. Farmington Hills, Mich.: Thomas Gale, 2002.

Catechism of the Catholic Church. Second edition. New York: Doubleday, 2003.

Clement of Alexandria. *The Instructor* (*Paedagogus*). In ANF 2, edited by Alexander Roberts and James Donaldson. New York: Charles Scribner's Sons, 1905.

Clement of Rome. *The Epistles of St. Clement of Rome and St. Ignatius of Antioch*. Translated by James A. Kleist, SJ. ACW 1. Westminster, Md.: Newman Bookshop, 1946.

Cole, W. J. "Mary, Blessed Virgin, II: Spiritual Maternity of Mary." In *New Catholic Encyclopedia*, 9:352a–354a. Second edition. Farmington Hills, Mich.: Thomas Gale, 2002.

Collins, Kenneth, and Jerry Walls. *Roman but Not Catholic: What Remains at Stake 500 Years after the Reformation*. Ada, Mich.: Baker Academic, 2017.

Congar, Yves, OP. *Christ, Our Lady and the Church*. Translated by Henry St. John, OP. Westminster, Md.: Newman Press, 1957.

————. *The Mystery of the Temple, Or, The Manner of God's Presence to His Creatures from Genesis to the Apocalypse.* Translated by Reginald F. Trevett. Westminster, Md.: Newman Press, 1962. The French edition appeared in 1958.

————. "The Idea of the Church in St. Thomas Aquinas." In his *The Mystery of the Church*, 97–117. Translated by A. V. Littledale. Baltimore, Md.: Helicon Press, 1960.

————. *La foi et la théologie.* Tournai: Desclée, 1962.

————. *Tradition and Traditions.* Translated by Michael Naseby and Thomas Rainborough. New York: Macmillan, 1966.

————. *L'Église de saint Augustin à l'époque modern.* Paris: Cerf, 1970.

————. *True and False Reform in the Church.* Translated and with an Introduction by Paul Philibert, OP. Collegeville, Minn.: Liturgical Press, 2011.

Congregation for Catholic Education and Congregation for the Clergy. "Basic Norms for the Formation of Permanent Deacons." 1998. Available at www.vatican.va.

Congregation for the Doctrine of the Faith. "Declaration in Defense of the Catholic Doctrine of the Church." June 24, 1973. Available at www.vatican.va.

————. "Letter to the Bishops of the Catholic Church on Some Aspects of the Church Understood as Communion." May 28, 1992. Available at www.vatican.va.

————. "Declaration on the Unicity and Salvific Universality of Jesus Christ and the Church." August 6, 2000. Available at www.vatican.va.

————. "Responses to Some Questions Regarding Certain Aspects of the Doctrine on the Church." June 29, 2007. Available at www.vatican.va.

Cuddy, Cajetan, OP. "Thomas Aquinas on the Bible and Morality: The Sacred Scriptures, the Natural Law, and the Hermeneutic of Continuity." In *Toward a Biblical Thomism: Thomas Aquinas and the Renewal of Biblical Theology,* edited by Piotr Roszak and Jörgen Vijgen, 173–98. Pamplona: Ediciones Universidad de Navarra, 2018.

Daguet, François, OP. *Théologie du dessein divine chez Thomas d'Aquin: Finis omnium Ecclesia.* Paris: Vrin, 2003.

Daniélou, Jean, SJ. *The Presence of God.* Translated by Walter Roberts. Baltimore, Md.: Helicon, 1959.

————. *From Shadows to Reality: Studies in the Biblical Typology of the Fathers.* Translated by Dom Wulstan Hibberd. Westminster, Md.: Newman Press, 1960.

De La Soujeole, Benoît-Dominique, OP. *Le sacrement de la communion. Essai d'ecclésiologie fondamentale.* Paris: Cerf, 1998.

————. "Le mystère de la predication." *Revue Thomiste* 107, no. 3 (2007): 355–74.

————. "The Economy of Salvation: Entitative Sacramentality and Operative Sacramentality." *The Thomist* 75, no. 4 (2010): 537–53.

————. "The Importance of the Definition of Sacraments as Signs." In *Ressourcement Thomism: Sacred Doctrine, the Sacraments, and the Moral Life,* edited by Reinhard Hütter and Matthew Levering, 127–35. Washington, D.C.: The Catholic University of America Press, 2010.

————. "The Mystery of the Church." *Nova et Vetera* (English edition) 8, no. 4 (2010): 827–37.

————. *Introduction to the Mystery of the Church.* Translated by Michael J. Miller. Washington, D.C.: The Catholic University of America Press, 2014.

De Lubac, Henri, SJ. "The Pagan Religions and the Fathers of the Church." In his *The Church: Paradox and Mystery,* translated by James R. Dunne, 69–95. New York: Alba House, 1969.

————. *The Motherhood of the Church.* Translated by Sr. Sergia Englund, OCD. San Francisco, Calif.: Ignatius Press, 1982.

————. *The Splendor of the Church.* Translated by Michael Mason. San Francisco, Calif.: Ignatius Press, 1986.

————. *Catholicism: Christ and the Common Destiny of Man.* Translated by Lancelot C. Sheppard and Sister Elizabeth Englund, OCF. San Francisco, Calif.: Ignatius Press, 1988.

DiNoia, Joseph A. *The Diversity of Religions.* Washington, D.C.: The Catholic University of America Press, 1992.

Dulles, Avery, SJ. "The Church According to Thomas Aquinas." In his *A Church to Believe In: Discipleship and the Dynamics of Freedom,* 149–69. New York: Crossroads, 1982.

————. *The Assurance of Things Hoped For: A Theology of Christian Faith.* New York: Oxford University Press, 1994.

————. "Should the Church Repent?" *First Things* (December 1998): 36–41.

Dupuis, Jacques, SJ. *Toward a Christian Theology of Religious Pluralism.* Maryknoll, N.Y.: Orbis Books, 1997.

————. *The Christian Faith: In the Doctrinal Documents of the Catholic Church.* Seventh edition. New York: Alba House, 2001.

Eliade, Mircea. *The Sacred and the Profane: the Nature of Religion.* Translated by Willard Trask. New York: Harcourt, Brace and World, 1959.

Extraordinary Synod of 1985. "Final Report." Available at https://www.ewtn.com/library/CURIA/SYNFINAL.HTM.

Farkasfalvy, Denis, O. Cist. *Inspiration and Interpretation: A Theological Introduction to Sacred Scripture.* Washington, D.C.: The Catholic University of America Press, 2010.

Feuillet, André Feuillet. "L'Eglise plérôme du Christ d'après Ephés., I, 23." *Nouvelle Revue Théologique* 78 (1956): 449–72 and 593–610.

Francis, Pope. *Evangelii Gaudium.* Apostolic Exhortation. November 24, 2013. Available at www.vatican.va.

Fulgentius of Ruspe. "To Peter on Faith." In *Fulgentius: Selected Works.* FOTC 95. Translated by Robert B. Eno, SS. Washington, D.C.: The Catholic University of America Press, 1997.

Gallagher, F. *Significando Causant: A Study of Sacramental Efficiency.* Fribourgh: Fribourgh University Press, 1965.

Galot, Jean, SJ. *La notion du caractère sacramental: étude de théologie médiévale.* Paris: Desclée de Brower, 1956.

Gambero, Luigi. *Mary and the Fathers of the Church: The Blessed Virgin Mary in Patristic Thought*. Translated by Thomas Buffer. San Francisco, Calif.: Ignatius Press, 1991.

Garrigou-Lagrange, Reginald, OP. *De Revelatione per Ecclesiam Catholicam Proposita*. 2 vols. Rome: Ferrari, 1950.

Gerhardsson, Birger. *The Reliability of the Gospel Tradition*. Peabody, Mass.: Hendrickson, 2001.

Grasso, Domenico, SJ. *Proclaiming God's Message: A Study in the Theology of Preaching*. Notre Dame, Ind.: University of Notre Dame Press, 1965.

Hamer, Jerome, OP. *The Church Is a Communion*. New York: Sheed and Ward, 1964.

Hart, David Bentley. *Atheist Delusions: The Christian Revolution and Its Fashionable Enemies*. New Haven, Conn.: Yale University Press, 2009.

Hauck, Friedrich. "KOINOS." In *Theological Dictionary of the New Testament*, vol. 3, edited by Gerhard Kittel. Grand Rapids, Mich.: Eerdmans, 1965.

Hebert, A. G. *The Throne of David: A Study of the Fulfillment of the Old Testament in Jesus Christ and His Church*. New York: Morehouse-Gorham Co., 1941.

Heim, Maximillian Heinrich. *Joseph Ratzinger: Life in the Church and Living Theology. Fundamentals of Ecclesiology with Reference to Lumen Gentium*. Translated by Michael J. Miller. San Francisco, Calif.: Ignatius Press, 2007.

Hengel, Martin. "The Titles of the Gospels and the Gospel of Mark." In *Studies in the Gospel of Mark*, translated by John Bowden, 64–84. Philadelphia: Fortress Press, 1985.

Hertling, Ludwig, SJ. *Communio: Church and Papacy in Early Christianity*. Translated by Jared Wicks, SJ. Chicago: Loyola University Press, 1972.

Hildebrand, Dietrich von. *Christian Ethics*. Chicago: Franciscan Herald Press, 1953.

Hipp, Stephen A. *The One Church of Christ: Understanding Vatican II*. Steubenville, Ohio: Emmaus Academic, 2018.

Hubert, Henri, and Marcel Mauss. *Sacrifice: Its Nature and Function*. Translated by W. D. Hall. London: Cohen and West, 1964.

Hütter, Reinhard. "Catholic Ecumenical Doctrine and Commitment—Irrevocable and Persistent: *Unitatis Redintegratio* as a Case of an Authentic Development of Doctrine." In *Dogma and Ecumenism: Vatican II and Karl Barth's Ad Limina Apostolorum*, edited by Matthew Levering, Bruce L. McCormack, and Thomas Joseph White, OP, 268–311. Washington, D.C.: The Catholic University of America Press, 2019.

———. *John Henry Newman on Truth & Its Counterfeits: A Guide for Our Times*. Washington, D.C.: The Catholic University of America Press, 2020.

Ignatius of Antioch. *The Epistles of St. Clement of Rome and St. Ignatius of Antioch*. Translated by James A. Kleist, SJ. ACW 1. Westminster, Md.: Newman Bookshop, 1946.

International Theological Commission. "The Consciousness of Christ concerning Himself and His Mission." In *International Theological Commission: Texts and Documents*, edited by Michael Sharkey. San Francisco, Calif.: Ignatius Press, 1989.

————. "Christianity and the World Religions." 1997. Available at www.vatican.va.

————. "Memory and Reconciliation: The Church and the Faults of the Past." December 1999. Available at www.vatican.va.

Irenaeus of Lyon. *Against Heresies.* In ANF 1, edited by Alexander Roberts, James Donaldson, and Arthur Cleveland Coxe. New York: Cosimo Classics, 2007.

Isaac de l'Étoile (Isaac of Stella). *Sermons III.* Sources Chrétiennes 339. Paris: Cerf, 1987.

John Chrysostom. *Baptismal Instructions.* ACW 31. Translated by Paul W. Harkins. Westminster, Md.: Newman Press, 1963.

John Paul II, Pope. *Redemptor Hominis.* Encyclical Letter. March 4, 1979. Available at www.vatican.va.

————. *Salvifici Doloris.* Apostolic Letter. February 11, 1984. Available at www.vatican.va.

————. *Redemptoris Mater.* Encyclical Letter. March 25, 1987. Available at www.vatican.va.

————. "Address to the Bishops of the United States of America." September 16, 1987. Available at www.vatican.va.

————. *Redemptoris Missio.* Encyclical Letter. December 7, 1990. Available at www.vatican.va.

————. "Address to the Roman Curia." December 20, 1990. Available at www.vatican.va.

————. *Pastores Dabo Vobis.* Apostolic Exhortation. March 15, 1992. Available at www.vatican.va.

————. *Gratissimam Sane.* Apostolic Letter. May 2, 1994. Available at www.vatican.va.

————. *Tertio Millenio Adveniente.* Apostolic Letter. November 10, 1994. Available at www.vatican.va.

————. *Ut Unum Sint.* May 25, 1995. Available at www.vatican.va.

————. *The Theology of the Body: Human Love in the Divine Plan.* Boston: Pauline Books and Media, 1997.

————. *Fides et Ratio*, Encyclical Letter. September 14, 1998. Available at www.vatican.va.

————. *Incarnationis Mysterium.* Papal Bull. November 29, 1998. Available at www.vatican.va.

————. *Ecclesia de Eucharistia.* Encyclical Letter. April 17, 2003. Available at www.vatican.va.

Journet, Charles. *The Church of the Word Incarnate*, vol. 1: *The Apostolic Hierarchy.* Translated by A. H. C. Downes. New York: Sheed and Ward, 1955.

————. *Théologie de l'Église.* Paris: Desclée De Brouwer, 1958.

————. *Theology of the Church.* Translated by Victor Szczurek, O. Praem. San Francisco, Calif.: Ignatius Press, 2004.

Justin Martyr. *Dialogue with Trypho* and *Second Apology.* In ANF 1, edited by Alexander Roberts, James Donaldson, and Arthur Cleveland Coxe. New York: Cosimo Classics, 2007.

Kasper, Walter. "The Church as a Universal Sacrament of Salvation." In his *Theology and Church*, translated by Margaret Kohl, 111–28. New York: Crossroad, 1989.

Keenan, Dennis King. *The Question of Sacrifice*. Bloomington: Indiana University Press, 2005.

Kelber, Werner. *The Kingdom in Mark*. Philadelphia: Fortress, 1974.

La Potterie, Ignace de. "Le Christ, Plérôme de l'Église, Ep 1:22–23." *Biblica* 58 (1977): 500–524.

Lamont, John. "The Justice and Goodness of Hell." *Faith and Philosophy* 28, no. 2 (2011): 152–73.

Lavaud, M.-Benôit. "Saint Thomas et la causalité physique instrumentale de la sainte humanité et des sacraments." *Revue Thomiste* 32 (1927): 292–316.

Legaspi, Michael C. *The Death of Scripture and the Rise of Biblical Studies*. Oxford: Oxford University Press, 2010.

Legge, Dominic, OP. *The Trinitarian Christology of St. Thomas Aquinas*. Oxford: Oxford University Press, 2017.

Levenson, Jon D. "The Temple and the World." *Journal of Religion* 64, no. 3 (1984): 275–98.

———. *Sinai and Zion: An Entry into the Jewish Bible*. San Francisco, Calif.: Harper and Row, 1987.

———. *The Death and Resurrection of the Beloved Son: The Transformation of Child Sacrifice in Judaism and Christianity*. New Haven, Conn.: Yale University Press, 1993.

Ligier, Louis, SJ. "The Question of Admitting Women to the Ministerial Priesthood." *L'Osservatore Romano* (English edition) (March 2, 1978): 5. Available at https://www.ewtn.com/catholicism/library/question-of-admitting-women-to-the-ministerial-priesthood–10122.

Lonergan, Bernard, SJ. *De verbo incarnato*. Rome: Gregorian University, 1961.

———. *Grace and Freedom: Operative Grace in the Thought of St. Thomas Aquinas*. New York: Herder and Herder, 1971.

———. *Method in Theology*. Second edition. New York: Herder and Herder, 1972.

Luther, Martin. *On the Papacy*. Translated by Eric W. and Ruth C. Gritsch. In *Luther's Works*, vol. 39, edited by Eric Gritsch. Philadelphia: Fortress Press, 1970.

Lyonnet, Stanislaus, and Leopold Sabourin. *Sin, Redemption, and Sacrifice: A Biblical and Patristic Study*. Rome: Biblical Institute Press, 1970.

MacIntyre, Alasdair. "Some Enlightenment Projects Reconsidered." In his *Ethics and Politics*. Cambridge: Cambridge University Press, 2006.

Malloy, Christopher J. "*Subsistit In*: Nonexclusive Identity or Full Identity?" *The Thomist* 72, no. 1 (2008): 1–44.

Manent, Pierre. "Christianity and Democracy." In *Modern Liberty and Its Discontents*. Edited and translated by Daniel J. Mahoney and Paul Seaton. Lanham, Md.: Rowman and Littlefield, 1998.

Mansini, Guy. "Ecclesial Mediation of Grace and Truth." *The Thomist* 75, no. 4 (2011): 555–83.

Mansini, Guy, and Lawrence Welch. "*Lumen Gentium* No. 8, and *Subsistit in*, Again." *New Blackfriars* 90 (2009): 602–17.

Marion, Jean-Luc. "Sketch of a Phenomenological Concept of Sacrifice." In his *The Reason of the Gift*, translated by Stephen E. Lewis. Charlottesville: University of Virginia Press, 2011.

Maritain, Jacques. *The Degrees of Knowledge*. Translated by Gerald B. Phelan. New York: Charles Scribner's Sons, 1959.

Marshall, Bruce. "Christ and Israel: An Unsolved Problem in Catholic Theology." In *The Call of Abraham: Essays on the Election of Israel in Honor of Jon D. Levenson*, edited by Gary A. Anderson and Joel S. Kaminsky, 330–50. Notre Dame, Ind.: University of Notre Dame Press, 2013.

———. "Religion and Election: Aquinas on Natural Law, Judaism, and Salvation in Christ." *Nova et Vetera* (English edition) 14, no. 1 (2016): 61–125.

Martin, R. Francis. "Sacra Doctrina and the Authority of its *Sacra Scriptura* according to St. Thomas." *Pro Ecclesia* 19, no. 1 (2001): 84–102.

———. "Revelation as Disclosure: Creation." In *Wisdom and Holiness, Science and Scholarship: Essays in Honor of Matthew L. Lamb*, edited by Michael Dauphinais and Matthew Levering, 205–47. Naples, Fla.: Sapientia Press of Ave Maria, 2007.

Martin, Ralph. *Will Many Be Saved? What Vatican II Actually Teaches and Its Implications for the New Evangelization*. Grand Rapids, Mich.: Eerdmans, 2012.

Meinert, John M. *The Love of God Poured Out: Grace and the Gifts of the Holy Spirit in St. Thomas Aquinas*. Steubenville, Ohio: Emmaus Academic Press, 2018.

Meyer, Ben F. *The Church in Three Tenses*. New York: Doubleday, 1971.

———. *The Aims of Jesus*. London: SCM Press, 1979.

Milbank, John. "Stories of Sacrifice: From Wellhausen to Girard." *Theory, Culture, and Society* 12, no. 4 (1995): 15–46.

Morerod, Charles, OP. *The Church and the Human Quest for Truth*. Washington, D.C.: The Catholic University of America Press, 2008.

Muñiz, Francisco P., OP. *The Work of Theology*. Translated by John P. Reid, OP. Washington, D.C.: Thomist Press, 1953.

Newman, John Henry. *Apologia pro Vita Sua* (1865). London: Longmans, Green, and Co., 1908.

———. "Letter to the Duke of Norfolk." In his *Certain Difficulties Felt by Anglicans on Catholic Teaching Considered*, vol. 2. London: Longmans, Green, and Co., 1896.

———. *An Essay in Aid of a Grammar of Assent*. Edited by I. T. Ker. Oxford: Clarendon Press, 1985.

———. *An Essay on the Development of Christian Doctrine*. Sixth edition. Notre Dame, Ind.: University of Notre Dame Press, 1989.

Nichols, Aidan, OP. *Lovely, Like Jerusalem: The Fulfillment of the Old Testament in Christ and the Church*. San Francisco, Calif.: Ignatius Press, 2007.

Nicolas, Jean-Hervé, OP. "L'origine première des choses." *Revue Thomiste* 91, no. 2 (1991): 181–218.

———. *Synthèse dogmatique: de la Trinité à la Trinité*. Paris: Beauchesne, 2012.

O'Carroll, Michael. *Theotokos: A Theological Encyclopedia of the Virgin Mary*. Wilmington, Del.: Michael Glazier, 1982.

Pagé, Jean-Guy. *Qui est l'Église?*, vol. 1: *Le mystère et la sacrement du salut*. Montréal: Bellarmin, 1977.

Panikulam, George. *Koinônia in the New Testament: A Dynamic Expression of Christian Life*. Rome: Biblical Institute Press, 1979.

Pascal, Blaise. *Pensées*. Translated by W. F. Trotter. New York: E. P. Dutton and Co., 1958.

Paul VI, Pope. "Speech Closing the Third Session of the Second Vatican Council." November 21, 1964. Available at www.vatican.va.

———. *Mysterium Fidei*. Encyclical Letter. September 3, 1965. Available at www .vatican.va.

———. *Evangelii Nuntiandi*. Apostolic Exhortation. December 8, 1975. Available at www.vatican.va.

Pitre, Brant. "Jesus, the New Temple, and the New Priesthood." *Letter & Spirit* 4 (2008): 47–83.

———. *Jesus the Bridegroom: The Greatest Love Story Ever Told*. New York: Image, 2014.

———. *The Case for Jesus: The Biblical and Historical Evidence for Christ*. New York: Image, 2016.

Pius IX, Pope. *Singulari Quadam*. Papal Allocution. December 9, 1854. Available at https://novusordowatch.org/pius9-singulari-quadam/

———. *Quanto Conficiamur Moerore*. August 10, 1863. Available at www .papalencyclicals.net.

Pius XII, Pope. *Mystici Corporis*. Encyclical Letter. June 29, 1943. Available at www .vatican.va.

———. *Mediator Dei*. Encyclical Letter. November 20, 1947. Available at www.vatican .va.

———. *Humani Generis*. Encyclical Letter. August 12, 1950. Available at www .vatican.va.

Plato. *The Collected Dialogues*. Edited by Edith Hamilton and Huntington Cairns. Bollingen Series LXXI. Princeton, N.J.: Princeton University Press, 1961.

Pontifical Biblical Commission. *Sancta Mater Ecclesia*. April 21, 1964. Available at www.vatican.va.

Pontifical Council for Culture and the Pontifical Council for Interreligious Dialogue. *Jesus Christ: The Bearer of the Water of Life—A Christian Reflection on the New Age*. Boston: Pauline Books and Media, 2003.

Portalié, Eugène. "Dogma and History." In *Defending the Faith: An Anti-Modernist Anthology*, edited and translated by William H. Marshner. Washington, D.C.: The Catholic University of America Press, 2017.

Proclus. *The Elements of Theology*. Translated by E. R. Dodds. Oxford: Clarendon Press, 1933.

Pusey, E. B. *An Eirenicon: The Church of England a Portion of Christ's One Holy Catholic Church, and a Means of Restoring Visible Unity.* London: Rivington's, 1865.

Quinn, Jerome D. "Ordination in the Pastoral Epistles." *Communio* 8 (Winter 1981): 358–69.

Rahner, Karl, SJ. "*Theos* in New Testament." In *Theological Investigations*, 1:79–148, translated by Cornelius Ernst. London: Darton, Longman, and Todd, 1963.

———. *Spirit in the World.* Translated by William Dych, SJ. New York: Herder and Herder, 1968.

———. "Anonymous Christians." In his *Theological Investigations*, 6:390–98. Translated by Karl-H. and Boniface Kruger. Baltimore, Md.: Helicon Press, 1969.

———. *Foundations of Christian Faith: An Introduction to the Idea of Christianity.* Translated by William V. Dych. New York: The Seabury Press, 1978.

Ramage, Matthew. "*Extra Ecclesiam Nulla Salus* and the Substance of Catholic Doctrine: Towards a Realization of Benedict XVI's 'Hermeneutic of Reform.'" *Nova et Vetera* (English edition) 14, no. 1 (2016): 295–330.

Ratzinger, Joseph. "Importance of the Fathers for the Structure of Faith." In his *Principles of Catholic Theology: Building Stones for a Fundamental Theology*, translated by Sister Mary Frances McCarthy, SND, 133–52. San Francisco, Calif.: Ignatius Press, 1987.

———. "The Priest as Mediator and Minister of Christ in the Light of the Message of the New Testament." In his *Principles of Catholic Theology: Building Stones for a Fundamental Theology*, translated by Sister Mary Frances McCarthy, SND, 267–84. San Francisco, Calif.: Ignatius Press, 1987.

———. *Eschatology: Death and Eternal Life.* Translated by Michael Waldstein. Washington, D.C.: The Catholic University of America Press, 1988.

———. "Biblical Foundations of Priesthood." *Origins* 20, no. 19 (October 18, 1990): 312.

———. *Called to Communion: Understanding the Church Today.* Translated by Adrian Walker. San Francisco, Calif.: Ignatius Press, 1996.

———. *Introduction to Christianity.* Translated by J. R. Foster. San Francisco, Calif.: Ignatius Press, 2004.

———. "The Unity and Diversity of Religions: The Place of Christianity in the History of Religions." In his *Truth and Tolerance: Christian Belief and World Religions*, translated by Henry Taylor, 15–44. San Francisco, Calif.: Ignatius Press, 2004.

———. *Pilgrim Fellowship of Faith: The Church as Communion.* Translated by Henry Taylor. San Francisco, Calif.: Ignatius Press, 2005.

———. "Thoughts on the Place of Marian Doctrine and Piety in Faith and Theology as a Whole." In his *Mary: The Church at the Source*, with Hans Urs von Balthasar, translated by Adrian Walker. San Francisco, Calif.: Ignatius Press, 2005.

———. *God's Word: Scripture, Tradition, Office.* Edited by Peter Hünermann and Thomas Söding. Translated by Henry Taylor. San Francisco, Calif.: Ignatius Press, 2008.

————. "Vicarious Representation." Translated by Jared Wicks, SJ. *Letter & Spirit* 7 (2011): 209–22.

Ratzinger, Joseph/Pope Benedict XVI. "General Audience of March 15, 2006." Available at www.vatican.va.

————. "General Audience of March 22, 2006." Available at www.vatican.va.

————. "General Audience of June 7, 2006." Available at www.vatican.va.

————. "General Audience of November 22, 2006." Available at www.vatican.va.

————. *Sacramentum Caritatis.* Apostolic Exhortation. February 22, 2007. Available at www.vatican.va.

————. *Spe Salvi.* Encyclical Letter. November 30, 2007. Available at www.vatican.va.

————. *Jesus of Nazareth: From the Baptism in the Jordan to the Transfiguration.* Translated by Adrian Walker. New York: Doubleday, 2007.

————. *Verbum Domini: The Word of God in the Life and Mission of the Church.* Vatican City: Libreria Editrice Vaticana, 2010.

————. *Jesus of Nazareth: Holy Week.* Translated by Adrian Walker. San Francisco, Calif.: Ignatius Press, 2011.

Rikhof, Herwi. "Thomas on the Church." In *Aquinas on Doctrine: A Critical Introduction,* edited by Thomas G. Weinandy, Daniel A. Keating, and John P. Yocum, 199–223. London and New York: T and T Clark International, 2004.

Rock, Augustine, OP. *Unless They Be Sent: A Theological Study of the Nature and Purpose of Preaching.* Dubuque, Iowa: Wm. C. Brown Co., 1953.

Ross, James F. *Introduction to the Philosophy of Religion.* London: Macmillan, 1969.

————. "Ways of Religious Knowing." In *The Challenge of Religion: Contemporary Readings in Philosophy of Religion,* edited by F. Ferré et al. New York: Seabury, 1982.

Salaverri, Ioachim, SJ. *De Ecclesia.* In his *Sacrae Theologiae Summa iuxta Constitutionem Apostolicum "Deus scientiarum Dominus,"* part I: *Theologia Fundamentalis: Introductio in Theologiam.* Madrid: Biblioteca de Autores Cristianos, 1952.

————. *On the Church of Christ.* In *Sacrae Theologiae Summa,* IB. Translated by Kenneth Baker, SJ. Ramsey, N.J.: Keep the Faith, 2015.

Sanders, E. P. *Jesus and Judaism.* Philadelphia: Fortress Press, 1985.

Schlier, Heinrich. "The Pauline Body Concept." Translated by Lawrence E. Brandt. In *The Church: Readings in Ecclesiology,* edited by Albert LaPierre, Bernard Verkamp, Edward Wetterer, and John Zettler, 44–58. New York: P. J. Kenedy and Sons, 1963.

Schnackenburg, Rudolf. *The Church in the New Testament.* New York: Herder and Herder, 1965.

————. *God's Rule and Kingdom.* Second edition. New York: Herder and Herder, 1968.

Scruton, Roger. *Beauty: A Very Short Introduction.* Oxford: Oxford University Press, 2011.

————. *On Human Nature.* Princeton, N.J.: Princeton University Press, 2012.

————. *The Soul of the World.* Princeton, N.J.: Princeton University Press, 2016.

Sherwin, Michael, OP. *By Knowledge and By Love: Charity and Knowledge in the Moral Theology of St. Thomas Aquinas.* Washington, D.C.: The Catholic University of America Press, 2005.

Smith, William Robertson. *The Religion of the Semites.* New York: Meridian Books, 1956.

Snow, Patricia. "Dismantling the Cross." *First Things* (April 2015): 33–42.

Sokolowski, Robert. *Presence and Absence: A Philosophical Investigation of Language and Being.* Bloomington, Ind.: Indiana University Press, 1978.

———. *The God of Faith and Reason.* Notre Dame, Ind.: University of Notre Dame Press, 1982.

———. "The Identity of the Bishop." In his *Christian Faith and Human Understanding: Studies on the Eucharist, Trinity, and the Human Person.* Washington, D.C.: The Catholic University of America Press, 2006.

———. *Phenomenology of the Human Person.* Cambridge: Cambridge University Press, 2008.

Sullivan, Francis A., SJ. *Salvation Outside the Church? Tracing the History of the Catholic Response.* New York: Paulist Press, 1992.

———. "A Response to Karl Becker, S.J., on the Meaning of *Subsistit In.*" *Theological Studies* 67, no. 2 (2006): 395–409.

———. "The Meaning of *Subsistit In* as Explained by the Congregation for the Doctrine of the Faith." *Theological Studies* 69, no. 1 (2008): 116–24.

Summa Sententiarum Septem Tractatibus Distincta. Patrologia Latina 176. Edited by J.-P. Migne. Paris, 1844–55.

Tanner, Norman, P., SJ. *The Decrees of the Ecumenical Councils.* 2 vols. London / Washington, D.C.: Sheed and Ward / Georgetown University Press, 1990.

Tillard, J.-M. R., OP. *Church of Churches: The Ecclesiology of Communion.* Translated by R. C. De Peaux, O. Praem. Collegeville, Minn.: Liturgical Press, 1992.

———. *Flesh of the Church, Flesh of Christ: At the Source of the Ecclesiology of Communion.* Translated by Madeleine Beaumont. Collegeville, Minn.: Liturgical Press, 2001.

Torrell, J.-P., OP. "La causalité salvifique de la resurrection du Christ selon saint Thomas." *Revue Thomiste* 96, no. 2 (1996): 179–208.

Trenner, Veronika. "Braut." In *Marienlexicon* 1:561b–571b. Edited by Remigius Bäumer and Leo Scheffczyk. St. Ottilien: EOS Verlag, 1988.

Tschipke, Theophil. *L'humanité du Christ comme instrument de salut de la divinité.* Translated by Philibert Secrétan. Studia Friburgensia 94. Fribourg: Academic Press Fribourg, 2003.

Vansina, Jan. *Oral Tradition as History.* Madison: University of Wisconsin Press, 1985.

Vollert, Cyril. *A Theology of Mary.* New York: Herder and Herder, 1965.

———. "Mary, Blessed Virgin, II: Mary and the Church." *The New Catholic Encyclopedia,* 9:354a–358a. Second edition. Farmington Hills, Mich.: Thomas Gale, 2002.

Vonier, Anscar. *The Spirit and the Bride.* London: Burns, Oates and Washbourne, 1935.

———. *The People of God.* London: Burns, Oates and Washbourne, 1937.

Wahlberg, Mats. *Revelation as Testimony: A Philosophical-Theological Study*. Grand Rapids, Mich.: Eerdmans, 2014.

Walgrave, Jan. *Unfolding Revelation: The Nature of Doctrinal Development*. Philadelphia: Westminster, 1972.

White, Kevin. "Aquinas on Oral Teaching." *The Thomist* 71, no. 4 (2007): 205–28.

White, Thomas Joseph, OP. *Exodus*. Brazos Theological Commentary on the Bible. Grand Rapids, Mich.: Brazos Press, 2016.

———. "The Universal Mediation of Christ and Non-Christian Religions." *Nova et Vetera* (English edition) 14, no. 1 (2016): 177–98.

———. "Gaudium et Spes." In *The Reception of Vatican II*, edited by Matthew L. Lamb and Matthew Levering, 113–43. Oxford: Oxford University Press, 2017.

———. *The Light of Christ: An Introduction to Catholicism*. Washington, D.C.: The Catholic University of America Press, 2017.

———. "Catholicism and Its Discontents: Revelation in an Ecumenical and Interreligious Context." *Nova et Vetera* (English edition) 16, no. 2 (2018): 387–99.

Wicks, Jared, SJ. *Investigating Vatican II: Its Theologians, Ecumenical Turn, and Biblical Commitment*. Washington, D.C.: The Catholic University of America Press, 2018.

Wright, N. T. *The Challenge of Jesus*. Downers Grove, Ill.: InterVarsity Press, 1999.

———. *The Resurrection of the Son of God*. Minneapolis, Minn.: Fortress Press, 2003.

Zhang Zhan Wu, Ignace. *Qui est l'Église? Quaestio disputata sur la personnalité de l'Église à la lumière de quelques auteurs du vengtième siècle*. Rome: Pontificia Università Lateranense, 2003.

INDEX

Aaron, 67, 77
Abel, 98n13
Abimelech, 96
Abraham: and calling of people, 70; and
Christ, 160; church and, 80; circumcision
and, 76; and failure of Israel, 75; fulfillment of promise to, 74, 78; and Judaism,
273; and knowledge of God, 96; and
messianic hope, 66; as nation, 156; offspring of, 161–62; and presence of God,
101–2; prophesy and, 85; and restoration
of man, 97; and sacrifice, 103; sacrifice
and, 108; and salvation, 299; sealing and,
76; and temple, 108, 113; and women,
130–31
Acts of the Apostles, 29, 45, 67, 80–82, 90,
115, 120–21, 147, 160, 212, 215, 245–47,
267, 278
Adam, 23, 71n10, 95–96, 98–99, 107, 120,
136–38, 140
Afanasiev, Nicholas, 177
affective access, 52–53
Amos, Book of, 135
anthropology, 23–24
antinomianism, 116
apologetic theology, 4–5
Apologia pro Vita Sua (Newman), 18
apology, public, 236–237
apostles: bishops and, 166; call and charge
of, 42–45; Christ as foundation and, 59;
as church foundation, 118, 122; grace and,
251; Holy Spirit and, 45, 114; Holy Week
and, 205–7; Israel and, 67; magisterium
and, 274; office, 247; prophecy and, 263;
in Revelation, 122; revelation and, 59;

sacrament and, 123, 199; sanctification of,
123–24; successors to, 247–48; temple
and, 122
Apostles' Creed, 60
apostolicity, of church, 242–44, 246–47
Aquinas. See Thomas Aquinas
Aristotle, 1, 11–12, 20, 192
Ark of the Covenant, 106, 125, 138
Athanasius, 62, 142
Augustine, 63, 159n23, 162, 171–72, 176,
280; Christ in, 159–62; as Church Father,
62; Israel and, 68–69; Mary in, 140n23,
143–44; natural law in, 297; sacrament
in, 200; sacrifice in, 123

baptism, 58, 77, 83, 135, 147, 150–51, 154, 199,
203–4, 251, 253
barrenness, 139
Bellarmine, Robert, 47, 172, 174–75, 198
Benedict XVI, Pope, 39, 142–43, 178,
260n64, 270. See also Ratzinger, Joseph
Benoît, Pierre, 150
Berengarius of Tours, 200
Bernard of Clairvaux, 172
Bethel, 103–5, 107, 111
Boniface VIII, Pope, 174
Bouyer, Louis, 102n31
Buddhism, 280

Cain, 98n13
Calvary, 46, 64, 86, 121
Calvin, John, 197, 197n37
Catherine of Siena, 233
Catholic Modernism, 57, 228
causality, 142, 165, 190–92, 249–53

321

Luke, Gospel of, 30–33, 39–43, 86, 110, 123, 138–39, 141, 144, 205, 245, 263, 266, 270, 300

Lumen Gentium (Second Vatican Council), 42, 48, 62, 165–67, 180–81, 181n5, 182, 188, 199, 210–11, 216–21, 226–27, 232, 244n7, 265, 275–76, 285, 303

Luther, Martin, 197

magisterium, 166–68, 215–16, 274–76
Manoah, 139
Mark, 31
Mark, Gospel of, 32–33, 41–43, 88, 111–14, 182–85, 205, 244, 246, 266–67, 300
marriage, 227–28, 241
Martin, Ralph, 285
Mary, 138–44, 205, 238
Matthew, 31
Matthew, Gospel of, 30–33, 39–41, 43–44, 46, 59, 81–85, 90, 101, 110–14, 122–23, 130, 144, 181, 199, 209, 219, 238, 244–46, 248n12, 266, 269–71
mediation of revealed truth, 254–64
membership, 226–29, 281–94
messianic people of God, 66–92
Metaphysics (Aristotle), 1
ministers, 190, 192–93
Modernism, Catholic, 57, 222, 228
Möhler, Johann Adam, 176–77
monism, 16–17
moral conscience, 15–17
Moses, 66, 69, 71–76, 96, 105, 133, 150, 156, 273, 299
Mystici Corporis (Pius XII), 116, 166–67, 177, 199, 211, 218–19, 298–99
mysticism, 16–17

Napoleon, 235n8
Nathan, 77–78, 104
naturalism, 34–35
natural law, 12n3, 18n17, 23, 73, 102, 124, 224, 257, 272, 276, 296–98
Nehemiah, 110
Nehemiah, Book of, 89
Neo-Platonism, 249
New Jerusalem, 100
Newman, John Henry, 18, 27n4, 261, 301–2
New Testament: and church as Jesus' bride, 133–36; church in, 68–69; communion

in, 188–90; dogmatic theology and, 54–56; historical trustworthiness of, 25–36; *mystêrion* in, 182–188; Old Testament and, 56; *sacramentum* in, 182–88
Nicene Creed, 2, 60
Nicolas, Jean-Hervé, 154, 204–5, 235–36
Nicomachean Ethics (Aristotle), 20
Nostra Aetate (Second Vatican Council), 236, 273
Numbers, Book of, 75, 114

objective holiness, 231–32
Oholah, 131
Oholibah, 131
Old Testament: and church as body of Christ, 156–58; and church as Jesus' bride, 129–32; historical credibility of, 26n1; New Testament and, 56; sacrifice in, 102–3
On the Papacy of Rome (Luther), 197
Orientalium Eccesiarum (Second Vatican Council), 219
original sin, 18, 95–96, 283

Pagé, Jean-Guy, 202n45
Passaglia, Carlo, 177
Passover, 111
Paul, 54, 84, 88, 115–18, 130, 135–36, 146–47, 245, 247
Paul VI, Pope, 275–76
Pentecost, 83, 120–21, 206, 246
Perrone, Giovanni, 177
Peter, 33, 44, 59, 118–19, 121–22, 245, 266–70
Phaedrus (Plato), 258
Philemon, Epistle to, 211
Philippians, Epistle to, 189, 219, 238
Philip the Fair, 174
Pius IX, Pope, 281, 285
Pius VII, Pope, 235n8
Pius XII, Pope, 12n3, 116, 166–67, 177, 199, 298–99
Plato, 258, 260
Plotinus, 292
Politics (Aristotle), 20
positivism, 15–16, 47, 287
practical access, 53
Presence of God, The (Daniélou), 100n28
presentness, of God, 93–94
Protestantism, 180, 195, 225, 228

Psalms, Book of, 67, 72n11, 74, 78, 80, 83, 94, 98, 112–13, 119, 159–62
public apology, 236–237

qahal, 89
quotation, human, 256–59

Rachel, 130, 139
Radhakrishnan, 16n12, 17
Rahner, Karl, 177, 281–82, 284–85, 288, 290–92
Ratzinger, Joseph, 16n12, 44–45, 178, 220, 238, 248, 248n13, 299, 302. See also Benedict XVI, Pope
reality: of church, 53; of representation, 67–68; truth vs., 58; words and, 54
Rebecca, 130, 139
reconciliation, 237–39
Redemptor Hominis (John Paul II), 275–76
Reformation, 173–75, 196–97, 236
representation, 67–68
resurrection, 34–35, 113, 150
revelation: abstractness of, 12; antecedent probability of, 13–19; in Aquinas, 12n4, 18n17; in deeds, 64; God and, 20–21; grace and, 21–22; history and, 27–29; reason and, 13–14
Revelation, Book of, 67, 81, 88, 100, 129
Romans, Epistle to, 18, 54–56, 83–85, 87, 93, 96, 138, 146–51, 161, 211–12, 251, 273, 291, 300
Roman School, 177
Romanticism, 176
Rule of Athanasius, 142

sacrament(s). See also baptism; Communion; Eucharist: apostolic authority and, 122–123; in Aquinas, 251; in Augustine, 162–63, 200; covenant and, 86–87; and death of Christ, 29; in dogmatic theology, 2; grace and, 85; of holy orders, 247–48; Holy Spirit and, 246; Holy Week and, 204–7; in John of Torquemada, 174; and kingdom of God, 42; law and, 122, 125; as *mystêrion,* 182–88; in Ratzinger, 44–45; sacrifice and, 108, 121
sacrifice, 101–105, 108, 123–124, 165–166, 181, 192, 203, 206, 253
Salaverri, Ioachim, 4, 244n7

salvation: in Acts ff the Apostles, 80–81; apostles and, 43; in Benoît, 150; and Christ as bridegroom, 134; Eucharist and, 165; faith and, 198; historical credibility of Gospels and, 29; in Isaiah, 40, 132; Israel and, 39; in John Paul II, 165; Mary and, 138; membership and, 226; mystery and, 186–88, 203, 242; of non-Catholics, 175–76; non-Christian religions and, 277–80; of non-Christians, 272–81, 298–302; religions in, 274–76; revelation and, 68, 129; sin and, 20; truth and, 57; women and, 130–31
Sarah, 130, 139
Saul, 77
Scheeben, Matthias, 177
Schillebeeckx, Edward, 177
Schleiermacher, F., 176
Schmemann, Alexander, 177
Schnackenburg, R., 89
Schrader, Clemens, 177
scientism, 15
2 Corinthians, 81, 84, 89–90, 116, 135, 212, 240, 246–47, 300
2 Peter, 251
2 Samuel, 78
2 Thessalonians, 212
2 Timothy, 219, 246–248
Second Vatican Council, 42, 48, 56, 60–64, 165–67, 180, 181n5, 188, 210–11, 216–20, 226–27, 244n7, 265, 273–75, 298
Semmelroth, Otto, 177
sin, 20–22, 95–96, 101n30, 196–97, 233–36, 283, 289
Sirach, Book of, 154
Solomon, 74, 78, 108
Song of Songs, 135
Spirit and the Bride, The (Vonier), 295
sports, 14–15
Stephen, 121, 245
Suarez, Francisco, 176
subjective holiness, 231–32
Suffering Servant, 80, 133, 157–58
Summa Contra Gentiles (Aquinas), 12n4
Summa Sententiarum Septem Tractatibus Distincta (attrib. Hugh of St. Victor), 200, 200n43
Summa Theologiae (Aquinas): ecclesiology in, 172–73; revelation in, 18n17; sacramental rites and, 190

Ecclesiology was designed in Garamond, with Scala Sans and Garda Titling display type, and composed by Kachergis Book Design of Pittsboro, North Carolina. It was printed on 60-pound Natural Eggshell and bound by McNaughton & Gunn of Saline, Michigan.